The John Harvard Library

The John Harvard Library, founded in 1959, publishes
essential American writings, including novels, poetry,
memoirs, criticism, and works of social and political history,
representing all periods, from the beginning of settlement in
America to the twenty-first century. The purpose of The John
Harvard Library is to make these works available to scholars
and general readers in affordable, authoritative editions.

JOHN
HARVARD
LIBRARY

Harriet Jacobs in 1894.

HARRIET A. JACOBS

INCIDENTS IN THE LIFE
OF A SLAVE GIRL

WRITTEN BY HERSELF

EDITED BY L. MARIA CHILD

ENLARGED EDITION

Now with "A True Tale of Slavery" by John S. Jacobs
Edited and with an Introduction by Jean Fagan Yellin

JOHN
HARVARD
LIBRARY

THE BELKNAP PRESS OF HARVARD UNIVERSITY PRESS
Cambridge, Massachusetts, and London, England   2009

Library of Congress Cataloging-in-Publication Data

Jacobs, Harriet A. (Harriet Ann), 1813–1897.
Incidents in the life of a slave girl : written by herself / by Harriet A. Jacobs ;
edited by L. Maria Child. Now with A True tale of slavery / by John S. Jacobs ;
edited and with an introduction by Jean Fagan Yellin.—Enlarged ed.
p.   cm.—(The John Harvard Library)
Includes bibliographical references and index.
ISBN 978-0-674-03583-6 (alk. paper)
1. Jacobs, Harriet A. (Harriet Ann), 1813–1897.   2. Slaves—United States—Biography.
3. Women Slaves—United States—Biography.   4. Slaves—United States—Social
conditions.   I. Jacobs, John S., 1815–1875. True tale of slavery.   II. Title.

E444.J17A3 2009
973.7′115092—dc22
[B]   2009016471

For Michael, Amelia, Mosé, and Blaze,
carrying it on

Preface

I FIRST READ *Incidents in the Life of a Slave Girl* more than a decade ago and, accepting received opinion, dismissed it as a false slave narrative. But I didn't forget it. Later, researching the black and white antislavery feminists in an effort to make amends for ignoring women in my earlier writing, I read through the works of Lydia Maria Child and again encountered *Incidents*. This time, schooled by the women's movement, I was struck by its radical feminist content. And this time, knowing more about Child, I took her seriously when she said she was the book's editor, not its author. I now knew that long before *Incidents* appeared, the abolitionists had withdrawn a slave narrative from circulation after the southern press publicized its inaccuracies, and I was sure that Child would not have published a fictional slave narrative for fear of harming the cause.

The editors of the Child Papers put me in touch with archivists at the University of Rochester who had recently acquired Harriet

Jacobs's letters to the abolitionist-feminist Amy Post. Reading these letters, I became convinced that Jacobs had written *Incidents* "by herself"—as her subtitle asserts.

The letters identify Nathaniel Parker Willis as Jacobs's New York employer, so I started looking through Willis's books for corroboration. I found it. Then, searching for more correspondence, I discovered at the Sophia Smith Collection at Smith College the letter identifying Edenton, North Carolina, as Jacobs's home town.

After locating Edenton on a map, I reread *Incidents,* this time as a historical record. Writing to state and local historical societies about the identity of the narrator's family and of the white family that owned them, I learned about the tavern keeper John Horniblow, his slave Molly Horniblow, and his son-in-law, Dr. James Norcom. Norcom's papers are in the State Archives, and when the North Carolina archivists recognized *Incidents* as a first-person account of antebellum life in Edenton, they used their considerable resources to help document Jacobs's text.

Readers of this edition will perhaps be dismayed (as I am) by parts of the book that are not yet documented—for example, the story of Jacobs's uncle Joseph, whom she calls Benjamin. But I think they will also be amazed (as I am) by how much has been established—including the identity of Jacobs's father, whose only monument is in the narratives his daughter and son wrote.

Since I first published an edition of *Incidents,* I have been thinking about—and annotating—the narrative Jacobs's brother serialized in London in 1861. John S. Jacobs's "A True Tale of Slavery" certainly provides testimony corroborating *Incidents.* But it does more. It presents the perspective of a male narrator on the people, places, and events in Jacobs's female-centered narrative. With the inclusion of "A True Tale of Slavery," this expanded edition of *Incidents* offers multiple layers: the text Jacobs published, her private correspondence discussing its creation and publication, and her brother's retelling of her story. This triple view is unique among slave narratives.

Incidents continues to fascinate me. Trying to place it within its multiple historical and literary contexts has engaged me and enmeshed me in a supportive scholarly network. And I am enthralled by Jacobs herself. She was, in Emerson's sense, "representative"; expressing the idea of the struggle for freedom, her life empowers others. On my desk her portrait, smiling, urges me onward.

J. F. Y.

Contents

INCIDENTS IN THE LIFE OF A SLAVE GIRL

Illustrations

Introduction

I have My dear friend—Striven faithfully to give a true and just account of my own life in Slavery—God knows I have tried to do it in a Christian spirit . . . I ask nothing—I have placed myself before you to be judged as a woman whether I deserve your pity or contempt—I have another object in view it is to come to you just as I am a poor Slave Mother—not to tell you what I have heard but what I have seen—and what I have suffered—and if their is any sympathy to give—let it be given to the thousands—of Slave Mothers that are still in bondage . . . let it plead for their helpless Children . . .[1]

These words were written in 1857 by Harriet Ann Jacobs, a recently freed fugitive slave and an activist in the abolitionist movement. Addressed to her white Quaker friend Amy Post, they describe the manuscript Jacobs was completing, an account of her life in slavery and her victorious struggle for freedom for herself and her children. After repeated efforts to find a publisher, Jacobs brought out the book on her own; it appeared in 1861 as *Incidents in the Life of a Slave Girl, Written by Herself.* Its title page credited the well-known abolitionist L. Maria Child as editor, but omitted the name of the author. The first-person narrator, who claimed to be relating her own autobiography, called herself Linda Brent.[2]

Like all slave narratives, *Incidents* was shaped by the empowering impulse that created the American Renaissance. Jacobs's book expressed democratic ideals and embodied a dual critique of nineteenth-century America: it challenged the institution of chattel slavery with its supporting ideology of white racism, as well as traditional patriarchal institutions and ideologies. Jacobs's achievement was the transformation of herself into a literary subject in and through the creation of her narrator, Linda Brent. This narrator tells a double tale, dramatizing the triumph of her efforts to prevent her master from raping her, to arrange for her children's rescue from him, to hide, to escape, and finally to achieve freedom; and simultaneously presenting her failure to adhere to sexual standards in which she believed. Unmarried, she entered into a sexual liaison, became pregnant, was condemned by her grandmother, and suffered terrible guilt. She writes that still, in middle age, she feels her youthful distress. But she also questions the condemnation of her behavior; reaching toward an alternative judgment, she suggests that the sexual standards mandated for free women were not relevant to women held in slavery. Further, by balancing her grandmother's rejection with her daughter's acceptance, she shows black women overcoming the divisive sexual ideology of the white patriarchy and establishing unity across the generations.

Contrasting literary styles express the contradictory thrusts of the story. Presenting herself as a heroic slave mother, Jacobs's narrator includes clear detail, uses straightforward language, and, when addressing the reader directly, utilizes standard abolitionist rhetoric to lament the inadequacy of her descriptions of slavery and to urge her audience to involve themselves in antislavery efforts. But she treats her sexual experiences obliquely and, when addressing the reader concerning her sexual behavior, pleads for forgiveness in the overwrought style of popular fiction. These melodramatic confessions are, however, subsumed within the text. What finally dominates is a new voice. It is the voice of a woman who, although she cannot discuss her sexual past without expressing deep conflict, nevertheless addresses this painful personal subject in order to politicize it, to insist that the forbidden topic of the sexual abuse of slave women be included in public discussions of the slavery question. By creating a narrator who presents her private sexual history as a subject of public political concern, Jacobs moves her book out of the world of conventional nineteenth-century polite discourse. In and through her creation of Linda Brent, who yokes her success story as a heroic slave mother to her confession as a woman who mourns that she is not a storybook heroine, Jacobs articulates her struggle to assert her womanhood and projects a new kind of female hero.[3]

> God . . . gave me a soul that burned for freedom and a heart nerved
> with determination to suffer even unto death in pursuit of . . . liberty.[4]

Newly found documents make it possible to trace Harriet Jacobs's life, to establish her authorship of *Incidents*, and to identify the people and places she presented pseudonymously in her book.[5] She was born a slave in Edenton, North Carolina, around 1813. Her maternal grandmother, Molly Horniblow (called Aunt Martha in the book), who had been freed in middle age, owned a house on West King Street in Edenton and earned her living there as a baker. Jacobs's father was apparently the skilled carpenter Elijah, a slave of Dr. Andrew Knox and perhaps the son of Henry Jacobs, who lived near the old Knox plantation. Her mother, Delilah, was owned by Elizabeth Pritchard Horniblow, widow of Edenton tavernkeeper John Horniblow.

Harriet Jacobs and her younger brother John S. (William) were orphaned as children. Her first mistress, Margaret Horniblow, who taught her to read and sew, died when Jacobs was eleven and willed her to Mary Matilda Norcom (Miss Emily Flint), whose family lived a block away from Jacobs's grandmother. The father of her three-year-old mistress, Dr. James Norcom (Dr. Flint), had earlier bought her brother John S. Jacobs. Norcom proved to be a licentious master. As Jacobs matured he subjected her to unrelenting sexual harassment. In her teens she became sexually involved with a neighbor, the young white lawyer Samuel Tredwell Sawyer (Mr. Sands), and gave birth to two children, Joseph (Benjamin) and Louisa Matilda (Ellen).

In 1835 Norcom threatened that if Jacobs refused to become his concubine she would have to work on one of his plantations. She would not yield and was sent to Auburn, a plantation several miles from town. Then, learning that he planned to move her son and daughter from her grandmother's home to Auburn, she resolved to rescue them from plantation slavery. Believing that if she were gone her master might find the children troublesome and sell them, she ran away. She was temporarily sheltered by sympathetic black and white neighbors, then for years was hidden in a tiny crawlspace above a storeroom in her grandmother's house. She succeeded in protecting her children. Shortly after she went into hiding, their father, Sawyer, bought them and her brother. Sawyer allowed the children to continue to live with her grandmother, and later he took Louisa Matilda to a free state, but he failed to keep his promise to Jacobs to emancipate the children.

In hiding Jacobs sewed, practiced writing, and read to fill her days. The easy use of biblical quotations and references throughout her narrative testifies to her familiarity with the Scriptures, particularly the books of Isaiah and Job. In 1842, after nearly seven years in hiding, she escaped to the North. She went to Brooklyn to make contact with her daughter and arranged for her son to be sent to her brother, who had escaped from Sawyer and was living in Boston. (Joseph had been left in the care of her grandmother, who evidently believed that Sawyer planned to free him and would not object to his going north.) Jacobs found work as a nursemaid in New York City, caring for Imogen, the baby daughter of Mary Stace Willis (Mrs. Bruce) and the magazine writer and editor Nathaniel Parker Willis (Mr. Bruce).[6]

Dr. Norcom repeatedly traveled to New York to catch his runaway slave. Forewarned, Jacobs explained to Mrs. Willis that she was a fugitive and that both she and her children were in danger. Aided by her brother and Mrs. Willis, she fled to Boston with Louisa Matilda in October 1844. The following spring Mrs. Willis died. Willis prevailed upon Jacobs to accompany him and little Imogen on a visit to his late wife's parents in England. When Jacobs returned to America after ten months, she learned that in her absence her son, whom she had apprenticed to a printer, had been subjected to racist abuse in the print shop and had shipped out to sea. Enrolling her daughter in a boarding school run by abolitionists in Clinton, New York, Jacobs moved to Rochester to join her brother, who was now lecturing for the abolitionist movement.

A decade earlier, when John S. Jacobs had walked away from Sawyer in New York, he had gone to New Bedford, Massachusetts, then shipped out on a whaling vessel. After three and a half years at sea, he returned to port able to read and write. He quickly involved himself in Boston's vibrant black community, joining the Adelphic Union Library Association and the Young Men's Literary Society and using his new literacy skills in serving as Corresponding Secretary of the New-England Freedom Association.[7] By 1846 he was an abolitionist activist. He spoke from the platform "in the name of three millions of American Slaves" at a meeting honoring the *Liberator*'s editor William Lloyd Garrison, demonstrated his commitment by spending all night on the docks in a futile attempt to aid the escape of a fugitive who was being hunted in Boston, and, acting as liaison between the black community and the Garrisonian movement, kept his abolitionist colleagues aware of his sister's danger of being kidnapped.[8]

Late in 1847 John S. undertook a four-and-a-half-month lecture tour with Captain Jonathan Walker, "the man with the branded hand"—who, tried for the crime of helping slaves escape, had been convicted, fined, imprisoned, pilloried, and branded with the letters "SS" (for "Slave Stealer"). John S. then began lecturing on his own and was hired by the abolitionists to speak at their highly publicized 100 Conventions, whose audiences numbered from 25 to 125 on weekdays and more on Sundays.[9] Moving west to Rochester, early in 1849 he began a sixteen-day tour with the militant Frederick Douglass that took them to fourteen hamlets, villages, and towns, where they delivered twenty speeches and sold twenty subscriptions to Douglass's newspaper *The North Star*.[10]

In Rochester Harriet Jacobs met her brother's circle of antislavery activists, and early in March 1849 she began working in the antislavery reading room, office, and bookstore they had established above the offices of *The North Star*. The breadth of the references to literature and current events in *Incidents* suggests that during her eighteen months in Rochester she read her way through the abolitionists' library of books and papers. "The latest and best work on slavery and other moral questions" they advertised for sale included polemics, personal accounts of the violence of slavery, and antislavery fiction.

Jacobs also had the opportunity to join the circle of abolitionist women who met each Thursday in the reading room "to sew, knit, read, and talk for the cause."[11]

With her brother often on the road lecturing, Jacobs lived for nine months in the home of the Quaker reformers Isaac and Amy Post. A participant in the first Woman's Rights Convention at Seneca Falls in July 1848, Amy Post had helped organize the follow-up Rochester Convention. Jacobs later admitted, "when I first came North I avoided the Antislavery people as much as possible because I felt that I could not be honest and tell the whole truth." In Rochester, however, with slavery seven years behind her, she made Post her confidante. Post urged her to make her personal history public to aid abolitionism.[12]

Jacobs's letters to Post spell out the close friendship between the two women and detail Jacobs's personal and political relationships with other black and white members of the circle of Rochester reformers. They also demonstrate the sophistication of Jacobs's vocabulary and syntax and trace the growth of her writing skills. Jacobs apologized for her "unconnected scrawl," but she felt comfortable enough with Post to maintain a regular correspondence from this period forward.[13]

In 1850 Congress passed a Fugitive Slave Law ruling that all citizens, including those in northern states where slavery had been abolished, were subject to punishment if they aided fugitives. Jacobs's brother, joining the protestors denouncing the law, urged armed defiance. He then headed west to pan for gold in California, where he was joined by Jacobs's son Joseph, back from the sea. By 1852 both men had gone on to try their luck in the Australian gold rush.[14]

Meanwhile, in 1850 Jacobs returned to New York City. Visiting Imogen, she met Nathaniel Parker Willis's new wife, Cornelia Grinnell Willis, and was employed to care for her newborn baby.

Mary Matilda Norcom, who had inherited Jacobs, was an adult by midcentury. Asserting that her father had had no right to sell Jacobs's children, she traveled to New York after his death with her husband, Daniel Messmore (Mr. Dodge), to seize Jacobs and her daughter under the provisions of the new Fugitive Slave Law. It seems likely that Jacobs was unaware that Dr. Norcom had legalized the sale of her children from his daughter's estate by substituting other slaves of equal value, but that Messmore knew of this substitution and, gambling on Jacobs's lack of information, threatened to seize Louisa Matilda if Jacobs did not surrender herself to him. Jacobs again went into hiding. To free her, and to reassure her about her children's freedom, Mrs. Willis arranged for the American Colonization Society to act as an intermediary and early in 1852 bought Jacobs from the Messmores for $300.00. Eager to use her freedom "to be useful in some way" to the abolitionist cause, Jacobs now seriously considered Post's suggestion that she tell her life story.[15]

> I have kept Louisa here this winter so that I might have my evenings to write. but poor Hatty [Harriet's] name is so much in demand that I cannot accomplish much. if I could steal away and have two quiet Months. to myself. I would work night and day though it should. all fall to the ground.[16]

In her letters to Post, Jacobs thrashed out the conflict she felt about making her life public. How could she tell all, when she had not been chaste? But how could she refuse, if telling her story would win converts to the movement? After finally deciding to make her sensational life public, she committed herself fully to the project. Her correspondence with Post provides a running account of her determined efforts to write and publish her autobiography, clarifies the role of her editor, Lydia Maria Child, and yields new information about an unlikely grouping of midcentury writers: litterateur Nathaniel Parker Willis and best-selling author Harriet Beecher Stowe, neither of whom Jacobs trusted, and black abolitionist William C. Nell and white abolitionist Child, whose aid she gratefully received.[17]

Jacobs was convinced that, unlike both his wives, Nathaniel Parker Willis was proslavery. Because of this, while she sought the time and privacy to write, she consistently refused to ask for Willis's help. She did not even want him to know she was writing. Although with her Rochester friends she openly discussed her efforts to complete her book, for years while living under Willis's roof she wrote secretly and at night.[18]

Jacobs also distrusted Harriet Beecher Stowe, not because of Stowe's attitudes toward slavery but because of her ideas about race. Jacobs's brief involvement with Stowe was decisive in the genesis of *Incidents*. When Jacobs first agreed to Post's urging that she produce a public account of her life, she thought the American Anti-Slavery Society could "propose" it. She did not intend to write it herself, but planned to enlist Stowe's aid in producing a dictated narrative, perhaps like the book Olive Gilbert had recently written for Sojourner Truth. To this end, Jacobs asked Post to approach Stowe with her story. Then, when the papers reported that the author of *Uncle Tom's Cabin* planned a trip to England, Jacobs persuaded Mrs. Willis to write suggesting that Jacobs's daughter accompany her. Jacobs thought that Louisa could interest Stowe in Jacobs's story, Stowe's patronage would benefit Louisa, and "Louisa would be a very good representative of a Southern Slave" for the English to meet.[19]

Stowe evidently responded by writing to Mrs. Willis that she would not take Jacobs's daughter because the British would spoil the girl with attention; that she was forwarding Amy Post's sketch of Jacobs's sensational life to Mrs. Willis for verification; and that, if Jacobs's story was true, she herself would use it in her forthcoming *Key to Uncle Tom's Cabin*. Jacobs was devastated. She had never revealed her sexual history to Mrs. Willis, and she felt Stowe had betrayed her as a woman, denigrated her as a mother, and threatened her as a writer. She later expressed her racial outrage to Post: "think dear Amy that a visit to Stafford House would spoil me as Mrs Stowe thinks petting is more than my race can bear well what a pity we poor blacks cant have the firmness and stability of character that you white people have."[20]

Jacobs decided to write her story herself and began sending apprentice pieces to the newspapers.[21] The first appeared anonymously in Horace Greeley's New York *Tribune* under the heading "Letter from a Fugitive Slave" with a note that the only editorial changes were "corrections in punctuation and spelling, and the omission of one or two passages." Jacobs's letter suggests both the content and the form of the narrative she would write. Here—as in *Incidents*—she discussed the sexual abuse of slave women. Here—as in *Incidents*—she used contrasting voices. Perhaps reacting to her rebuff from Stowe, she began with the straightforward announcement that she would tell her tale herself. "Poor as it may be, I had rather give [my story] from my own hand, than have it said that I employed others to do it for me." Then, as she would in her book, she adopted a dramatic style to express the pain she felt as she recalled and wrote about her life: "I was born a slave, raised in the Southern hotbed until I was the mother of two children, sold at the early age of two and four years old. I have been hunted through all of the Northern States—but no, I will not tell you of my own suffering—no, it would harrow up my soul."[22]

Revealing her authorship of this letter, Jacobs requested Post's help with the mechanics of writing:

> I cannot ask the favor of any one else without appearing very Ludicrous in their opinion I love you and can bear your severest criticism because you know what my advantages have been and what they have not been . . . the spelling I believe was evry word correct punctuation I did not attempt for I never studied Grammer there-

fore I know nothing about it but I have taken the hint and will
commence that one study with all my soul[23]

Jacobs secretly wrote more letters for publication. Her correspondence during this period reveals that she was determined to write,
apprehensive about her ability to do so, and fearful of being discovered: "No one here never suspected me [of writing to the *Tribune*] I
would not have Mrs W[illis] to know it before I had undertaken my
history for I must write just what I have lived and witnessed myself don't expect much of me dear Amy you shall have truth but not
talent."[24]

Her letters record other pressures. During the years in which Jacobs composed her narrative, the Willises built Idlewild, an eighteen-
room country estate at Cornwall in the Hudson highlands. Despite
her move to the country, Jacobs's comments about antislavery meetings, conventions, and speakers attest to her continuing participation in the organized abolitionist movement. Writing to Post, she expressed her longing for the political sisterhood of Rochester and her
desire for more current involvement: "I wish we were both at the Boston [antislavery] Bazar with busy hands doing much good."[25]

At Idlewild, with the addition of two more children to the Willis
family, Jacobs's workload increased. In letters to Post she voiced the
frustrations of a would-be writer who earned her living taking care of
other people's children. She went on to say, however, that she preferred the endless interruptions to revealing her project to her employers: "to get this time I should have to explain myself. and no one
here accept Louisa knows that I have ever written anything to be put
in print. I have not the Courage to meet the criticism and ridicule of
Educated people."[26]

Jacobs arranged for her daughter, who had been educated as a
teacher, to copy the manuscript, and doubtless Louisa Matilda stan-
dardized her mother's spelling and punctuation. But there is no evi-

dence to suggest that Louisa Matilda had any significant impact on either the subject matter or the style of the book. Some modern readers, responding to the tensions between its traditional forms and its untraditional content, have characterized the style of *Incidents* as genteel and, judging this an incongruous mode of expression for a former slave, have questioned the authenticity of the text. Both its style and its content, however, are completely consistent with Jacobs's private correspondence and with her pseudonymous public letters to the newspapers—which unquestionably she wrote by herself. However inappropriate these readers may find the form of Jacobs's narrative, the language and syntax of her letters make gratuitous the suggestion that *Incidents* was written by anyone else.[27]

Presenting her struggle for freedom, Jacobs's narrator characteristically writes in a straightforward fashion: "The war of my life had begun." When addressing the reader directly in connection with this subject, she uses the language of Garrisonian abolitionism to offer political instruction: "Talk to American slave-holders as you talk to savages in Africa. Tell *them* it is wrong to traffic in men." Passages presenting her sexual history, however, are full of omissions and circumlocutions. Addressing the reader on this issue, Linda Brent transforms herself into a penitent supplicant begging forgiveness: "Pity me and pardon me, O virtuous reader! You never knew what it is to be a slave."

Jacobs acknowledged the obscurity of her treatment of this subject—"There are somethings I might have made plainer, I know"—and explained to Post that it was much easier for a woman to "whisper" of sexual activities and abuses to a "dear friend" than to "record them for the world to read." Both determined and reluctant to address her sexual history, she consciously omitted "what I thought—the world might believe that a Slave Woman was too willing to pour out—that she might gain their sympathies." Lacking an appropriate form for her revelations, she used the style of the seduction novel.[28]

Then, troubled about her story's sensational elements, as the manuscript neared completion she asked Post to write a public endorsement that would lend it respectability.

> when I returned home from Europe I said that I would not mention my M. S. to my friends again until I had done something with it—little dreaming of the time that might elapse—but as time wore on difficulties seemed to thicken—and I became discouraged.[29]

Jacobs tried for several years to get her book into print. In 1858 she sailed to England with letters of introduction from Boston antislavery leaders to British abolitionists, but was unable to arrange for publication.[30] Back home, her persistence finally brought results. She reported to Post what the lack of an endorsement from Stowe or Willis had cost her, in a letter announcing that she had found a publisher willing to take the manuscript if she could provide an introduction by Lydia Maria Child: "I had never seen Mrs. Child past experience made me tremble at the thought of approaching another Sattellite of so great magnitude . . . but I . . . resolved to make my last effort through W C Nells ready kindness I meet Mrs Child—at the A.-S. [Anti-Slavery] Office Mrs C is like your self a whole souled Woman—we soon found the way to each others heart—I will send you some of her letters . . ."[31]

The character of Child's editorial help is revealed in these letters to Jacobs, where she describes her editorial procedures much as she later does in her Introduction to *Incidents*. In addition to routine changes, she made two substantive suggestions that Jacobs followed. She proposed that Jacobs expand the description of the antiblack violence after the Nat Turner rebellion; the result stands as Chapter 12. And she advised that a final chapter on John Brown—which Jacobs evidently had added to the end of her completed manuscript after the 1859 attack on Harpers Ferry—be dropped.[32]

Child wrote to a friend about her editorial work on Jacobs's book:

"I abridged, and struck out superfluous words sometimes; but I don't think I *altered* fifty words in the whole volume." She did note that she had drastically rearranged sections of the manuscript: "I put the savage cruelties into one chapter, entitled 'Neighboring Planters,' in order that those who shrink from 'supping upon horrors' might omit them, without interrupting the thread of the story." Child's characterization of her editorial role was later corroborated in a British review that quoted an anonymous source who read the text both before and after publication and attested "that the manuscript and the printed volume are substantially the same; whilst the narrative has been condensed and rendered more fluent and compact by the friendly assistance of Mrs. Child."[33] Child did significantly change the text when she dropped the final chapter and ended the book on a private, personal note with the death of the narrator's grandmother instead of on a public, political note with a discussion of the recent armed attack on slavery. But in doing so she restored Jacobs's manuscript to its original shape.

Twentieth-century scholars of Afro-American literature assign considerable significance not only to the role of the white editors of slave narratives but also to the authenticating documents that accompany these texts. Jacobs's narrative is not endorsed by prominent white males but by a white woman and a black man, both Jacobs's personal friends. Her correspondence reveals that she had arranged for Amy Post and George Lowther to write these documents before she met Child. Although she initially agreed to Child's proposal to use them instead to publicize *Incidents* in the press, when the book was published the letters appeared in it as Jacobs had originally planned.[34]

With Child committed to the project, arrangements for publication proceeded. In late September 1860 Child negotiated a contract for Jacobs with the Boston publishers Thayer and Eldridge. This apparently provided that Child would donate her services and that Jacobs would receive royalties of 10 percent on the list price. Initially Thayer and Eldridge had spoken to Jacobs in terms of an edition of only a thousand copies, but evidently Child, who had tried to convince the Anti-Slavery Society to get out Jacobs's book, persuaded the Hovey Committee—leading abolitionists in charge of a discretionary fund—to buy a number of copies for resale by antislavery agents. With this guaranteed sale, Thayer and Eldridge contracted to stereotype the book (an expensive printing process), and to publish a first edition of two thousand. Child committed herself to correcting proofsheets, Jacobs arranged to meet her in Massachusetts to make final decisions, and publication was set for November. Then on October 31 Cornelia Willis prematurely gave birth. In the absence of a doctor, Jacobs delivered the baby, who died the next day. Jacobs wrote Post that she was "very thankful" she had been able to care for Mrs. Willis, but disappointed she had missed the meeting with Child. Using discreet phrasing, she expressed a writer's determination not to relinquish control of her book, even to a famous editor. "I know that Mrs. Child will strive to do the best she can more than I can ever repay but I ought to have been there that we could have consulted together, and compared our views—although I know that hers are superior to mine yet we could have marked her great Ideas and my small ones together."[35]

November came and went. Thayer and Eldridge were in financial trouble; although early in December Wendell Phillips, acting for the Hovey Committee, apparently renegotiated the contract with them and guaranteed sales, they went bankrupt before they got the book out. Arrangements were somehow made enabling Jacobs to buy the plates from the Boston Stereotype Foundry and to have a Boston printer publish the book "for the author."[36]

Marketing *Incidents* proved no easier than writing or publishing it had been. The black and antislavery press publicized the book, although not as strenuously as Child urged, perhaps because in those weeks, as the nation moved toward civil war, yet another slave narrative seemed of minor importance. Jacobs, however, was eager to promote her work. She went to Philadelphia, made contact with local abolitionists, and by mid-January had sold fifty copies herself. Late that month her friend William C. Nell ran two items in the *Liberator:* an advertisement announcing *Incidents* for sale and a letter stressing its careful adherence to fact.

> It presents features more attractive than many of its predecessors purporting to be histories of slave life in America, because, in contrast with their mingling of fiction with fact, this record of complicated experience in the life of a young woman, a doomed victim to America's peculiar institution . . . surely need not the charms that any pen of fiction, however gifted and graceful, could lend. They shine by the lustre of their own truthfulness—a rhetoric which always commends itself to the wise head and honest heart.

In Ohio the Salem *Anti-Slavery Bugle* printed a review and urged western abolitionists to order the book, at a dollar a copy, from the Boston Anti-Slavery Office.[37]

The Hovey Committee paid Jacobs $100.00 for books, presumably to be distributed by antislavery agents, and in mid-February the *National Anti-Slavery Standard* ran a letter comparing *Incidents* to *Uncle Tom's Cabin*, approving its lack of sensationalism, and deploring its occasional moralizing:

> It is by no means an extreme picture of the delicate institution. The writer never suffers personal chastisement, and meets with white friends who comfort and assist. Her chief persecutor, a physician in good repute and practice, seems to have been subjected to all restraints that Southern public opinion can put upon a professional man . . . A few sentences in which the moral is rather oppressively

displayed, might have been omitted with advantage. These, it is to
be wished, Mrs. Child had felt herself authorized to expunge. They
are the strongest witnesses who leave the summing up to the Judge,
and the verdict to the jury.

The *Standard* formally reviewed the book the following week, noting
that it could be bought at the Anti-Slavery Office in New York.[38]

Jacobs quickly became known among abolitionists as the author
of *Incidents*. She used this limited celebrity to further a new project:
relief work with the "contraband"—slaves behind the lines of the
Union Army—and the freedmen. As an agent of the Philadelphia and
New York Quakers, she worked in Washington, D.C., in 1862, in Alexandria from 1863 to 1865, and in Savannah from 1865 to 1866, distributing clothing and supplies and organizing schools, nursing homes,
and orphanages. Throughout these years Jacobs used the public press
to raise money for her work and to report back to the reformers on
conditions in the South.[39]

Despite this publicity, by the twentieth century both Jacobs and
her book were forgotten. Those historians of the slave narrative who
did recall *Incidents* associated it only vaguely, if at all, with Jacobs's
name. Some thought it a narrative dictated by a fugitive slave, Jacobs,
to Child; others thought it an antislavery novel that Child had written
in the form of a slave narrative. In the 1960s the Civil Rights movement sparked republication of a number of slave narratives, including *Incidents*, and more recently the women's movement has created
interest in the book. But Jacobs's achievement remained in obscurity
until the accession of her letters in the Post Archive at the University of Rochester made it possible in 1981 to authenticate her authorship.[40]

It is the "oft-told tale" of American slavery, in another and more
revolting phase than that which is generally seen: More revolting

because it is of the spirit and not the flesh. In this volume, a woman tells. not how *she* was scourged and maimed, but that far more terrible sufferings endured by and inflicted upon women, by a system which legalized concubinage, and offers a premium to licentiousness.[41]

In 1861 this anonymous review in the *Weekly Anglo-African* focused on the unusual character of *Incidents*. Although the title of the book identifies its narrator in terms of gender and condition, this is not a female captivity narrative. (Still popular in Jacobs's time, captivity narratives presented a white female protagonist who "meekly submits before what she accepts as God's rightful chastening," her capture by Native Americans.)[42] In contrast, and like all slave narrators, Jacobs's Linda Brent presents herself as a black person struggling for freedom. In *Incidents* her characterization of Dr. Flint, and the incorporation of the letters and the wanted poster he composed to catch her, enact a sophisticated version of a power reversal in which the slave controls the master.[43]

Like the perspective of other slave narratives, the angle of vision in *Incidents* is revolutionary; and like other narrators, Jacobs asserts her authorship in the subtitle ("Written by Herself"), uses the first person, and addresses the subject of the oppression of chattel slavery and the struggle for freedom from the viewpoint of one who has been enslaved.[44] But this title is unusual in announcing that its narrator is female, and that her book is not the narrative of a life but of incidents in a life. The Preface, while claiming the truthfulness of her tale, reports that she has written pseudonymously and hidden the identities of people and places. The later assertion that "Slavery is terrible for men; but it is far more terrible for women" names the special subject of this narrative: a woman's struggle against her oppression in slavery as a sexual object and as a mother.

In important ways, *Incidents* diverges from received notions about

the slave narrative. This genre has been characterized as dramatizing "the quest for freedom and literacy."[45] But *Incidents*, perhaps the
most comprehensive slave narrative by an Afro-American woman,
presents a heroic slave mother struggling for freedom and a home.
She runs away to save her children—and particularly her daughter—
from slavery. Men and women were valued for contrasting qualities
in nineteenth-century America, and recent critics have pointed out
that Frederick Douglass's classic 1845 *Narrative* presents its protagonist in terms of physical bravery, an important "masculine" attribute.
It is not surprising that Jacobs presents Linda Brent in terms of moth-
erhood, the most valued "feminine" role.[46]

Much of Linda Brent's account of her triumphant battle for freedom as a "poor Slave Mother" does, however, follow patterns standard to the genre. As in other narratives, this struggle is seen as recurrent. Despite her escape from her master midway through the book
and her flight north a dozen chapters later, she does not achieve her
goal of freedom until the final pages. This pattern of repeated struggle
is underscored by her efforts to free her children. While their purchase by their white father apparently rescues them from their mother's hated master, its questionable legality keeps them vulnerable to
his demands. Because their father does not free them, although they
are later sent to the North, they are not out of danger from seizure by
their mother's young mistress until the end of the book.

The struggle for freedom is not only recurrent, it is ubiquitous. In
Incidents one group of interpolated chapters discusses the attempts of
Linda Brent's relatives—uncle, aunt, brother—to free themselves or
their families. Another establishes a larger framework for their rebel-
liousness by discussing aspects of slave life in America, such as ideo-
logical indoctrination and religious practices, and by commenting on
pertinent historical events such as the Nat Turner insurrection and
the 1850 Fugitive Slave Law.

The resulting text is densely patterned. Although the slave narrator has been likened to the "rootless alienated" picaro, Jacobs's Linda Brent locates herself firmly within a social matrix, prefiguring twentieth-century views of the South by commentators as diverse as the novelist William Faulkner and the sharecropper Nate Shaw.[47] Her recurrent efforts to free herself and her children are shown in the context of the attempts of successive generations of her family to free their children: her grandmother managed to emancipate one son; her father failed to free her or her brother.

Linda Brent presents herself in relation to both racial groups that make up the closed society of the town, and she suggests the complex interrelationships connecting four generations of her grandmother's family and four generations of their masters. Checked against what we know of Jacobs's own life, this recital is remarkably accurate; most discrepancies involve not the narrator or her family—whose experiences correspond quite precisely to those of Jacobs and her family—but whites. Linda Brent is inconsistent, for example, in citing the age of her young mistress, and confuses the death of a minister's wife with the death of his parishioner.[48]

Her grandmother's unusual status as a free woman with powerful white friends provides important protection for Linda Brent. It safe-guards the house from marauding white patrols after Nat Turner's rebellion; it gives Linda access to the female slaveholder who tries to stop Dr. Flint from harassing her and to the one who temporarily shelters her; and most important, it prevents Dr. Flint from raping her. Linda Brent positions herself as "grandmother's child" not only in relation to the white townspeople but also in relation to the community of slaves and free blacks. Writing of prayer meetings and folk medicine, recounting tales and snatches of songs, and describing festivities of the John Kuners—New World celebrants of a transplanted African ceremony—she records her involvement in black life.

In *Incidents* Linda Brent dramatizes her fight for freedom within the context of her family's active support. Despite terrible danger, grandmother, uncle, aunt, brother, even (she later learns) son and daughter—aid and abet her concealment and escape. Further, she presents her own efforts and those of her family within the larger configuration of an ongoing struggle for freedom by an entire black community. Charity's son James escapes, Luke runs from the speculator, Old Aggie is also hiding a runaway daughter. At crucial moments the narrator identifies members of this larger community—Sally, Betty, and Peter—who support the family conspiracy on her behalf. After escaping north to Philadelphia, she quickly locates herself within a circle of black activists and searches for black migrants from her home town; later she repeats this pattern in New York, Boston, and Rochester.

Linda Brent's story is also different from most slave narratives in that its protagonist does not escape and quickly run north; almost a quarter of the book chronicles her years in hiding in the South. During that time she is not solely occupied with reading and sewing. She uses her garret cell as a war room from which to spy on her enemy and to wage psychological warfare against him. From her cramped hiding place, she manipulates the sale of her children to their father, arranges for her daughter to be taken north, tricks her master into believing that she has left the South, and quite literally directs a performance in which Dr. Flint plays the fool while she watches, unseen.

Incidents is a major slave narrative. It is also a major work in the canon of writings by Afro-American women. Harriet E. Wilson's *Our Nig* (1859), which modified formal aspects of slave narratives and women's fiction, transforming the black woman as fictional object into fictional subject, was "ignored or overlooked" by Wilson's "colored brethren"; only when it was reprinted in 1983 was its importance recognized.[49] But *Incidents* was immediately acknowledged as a contribution to Afro-American letters.

Jacobs's book may well have influenced Frances Ellen Watkins Harper's novel *Iola Leroy; Or, Shadows Uplifted (1892)*, which in turn helped shape the writings of Zora Neale Hurston and other foremothers of black women writing today. Like Jacobs, Harper worked in the South during Reconstruction. She located her book in that setting, and in a note to her novel she asserted that she wove "from threads of fact and fiction" her story about three generations of female "white slaves."[50] *Iola Leroy* recalls *Incidents* not only in its focus on the struggle of a light-skinned woman who has been subjected to sexual abuse in slavery, but also in its choice of names and locations: Harper's characters representing the rich potential of black culture come from North Carolina, and their names are Harriet and Linda.

While Linda Brent's secondary goal—a home—remains elusive, *Incidents,* like all slave narratives, ends with the achievement of freedom, the narrator's primary goal. But even though her children, too, are free, Linda Brent's triumph is mixed. When her northern employer, Mrs. Bruce, offers to buy her in order to set her free, her relief is mingled with distress because her freedom is being achieved by purchase, a concession to slavery. Writing to Post, Jacobs likened her ordeal to the biblical models of Jacob and Job, expressing righteous outrage, then resignation: "I served for my liberty as faithfully as Jacob served for Rachel. At the end, he had large possessions; but I was robbed of my victory; I was obliged to resign my crown, to rid myself of a tyrant."[51] Literary critics would dispute this. By creating Linda Brent, by writing and publishing her life story, Jacobs gained her victory.

dear Amy if it was the life of a Heroine with no degradation associated with it . . . I have tried for the past two years to conquer [my stubborn pride] and I feel that God has helped me or I never would consent to give my past life to any one for I would not do it with out giving the whole truth if it could help save another from my fate it would be selfish and unchristian in me to keep it back[52]

It is no accident that many critics mistook Jacobs's narrative for fiction. Its confessional account of sexual error and guilt, like the passages in which Linda Brent presents herself to be judged by her reader, links *Incidents* to a popular genre, the seduction novel.

While it shares the subject of woman's sexual oppression with that genre, however, the responses of Jacobs's protagonist to this tyranny distinguish the ideology informing *Incidents* from that of fiction like Susannah Rowson's ever popular *Charlotte Temple* (1791), as well as from abolitionist versions of seduction tales, such as Child's "The Quadroons" (1842), that feature a victimized "tragic mulatto," a woman of mixed race betrayed by the white man she adores. Novels and tales of seduction present a helpless virtuous woman as man's prey; inevitably, she yields herself to him; inevitably, she dies. *Incidents* dramatizes something more complex. Linda Brent's incisive (although implicit) rejection of the tragic mulatto stereotype is embedded in her response to Miss Fanny, who "wished that I and all my grandmother's family were at rest in our graves, for not until then should she feel any peace about us. The good old soul did not dream that I was planning to bestow peace upon her, with regard to myself and my children; not by death, but by securing our freedom."[53]

Instead of coupling unsanctioned female sexual activity with self-destruction and death, *Incidents* presents it as a mistaken tactic in the struggle for freedom. Jacobs's narrator does not characterize herself conventionally as a passive female victim, but asserts that—even when young and a slave—she was an effective moral agent. She takes full responsibility for her actions: "I will not try to screen myself behind the plea of compulsion from a master; for it was not so. Neither can I plead ignorance or thoughtlessness . . . I knew what I did, and I did it with deliberate calculation."

Nor does this narrator mouth the standard notion that a woman's self-esteem is a simple function of her adherence to conventional sexual behavior. Although she discusses her efforts to preserve her virginity in connection with her struggle to maintain her self-esteem, she presents these as related, not identical, goals. Denied the protection of the laws, denied even an extralegal marriage to a man she loved, she writes that in a desperate attempt to prevent her hated master from forcing her into concubinage, she relinquished her "purity" in an effort to maintain her "self-respect"; she abandoned her attempt to avoid sexual involvements in an effort to assert her autonomy as a human being, to avoid being "entirely subject to the will of another." The narrator comments that at the time she saw her agreement to become Mr. Sands's mistress as a way to defy her master's demand that she be his concubine: "It was something to triumph over my tyrant even in that small way."

It is difficult to determine the extent to which Linda Brent's characterizations of her action as "a headlong plunge" and a "great sin" are merely conventional, and the extent to which these articulate a serious endorsement of a sexual standard that condemns her.[54] Like other slave narratives by women, *Incidents* consistently portrays a society in which female slaves are not only prevented from adhering to this standard but forced to conform to its opposite. In one of the most interesting sentences in the book, after recounting her youthful sexual history "with sorrow and shame," the middle-aged narrator shifts to the present tense and asserts a radical alternative to the sexual ideology that apparently informs her confession: "Still, in looking back, calmly, on the events of my life, I feel, that the slave woman ought not to be judged by the same standard as others." Does she here suggest, upon mature reflection, that women like herself should be judged (like men) on complex moral grounds—rather than (like women) on the single issue of their conformity to the sexual behavior mandated by the white patriarchy? Does Harriet Jacobs, the black fugitive slave author and creator of Linda Brent, the black fugitive slave narrator, here propose a new definition of female morality grounded in her own sexual experience in a brutal and corrupt patriarchal racist society? Located within the larger context of a narrative that affirms her value, this quiet comment resonates with the ringing interrogatives with which Sojourner Truth is said to have defined womanhood.[55]

At first reading, Jacobs's narrative of her seven-year self-incarceration suggests connections with the metaphor of "the madwoman in the attic," that aberrant alter-ego of "the angel in the house" who inhabits the parlor in popular nineteenth-century fiction.[56] Unlike this fiction, however, Jacobs's narrative focuses on the woman in the attic; and she is completely sane. Linda Brent chooses the space above her grandmother's storeroom in preference to her master's bed; and her grandmother, the apparently conforming woman in the kitchen below, supports her insurgency. The goals of Harriet Jacobs's woman in hiding are not destruction and self-destruction, but freedom and a home.

This endorsement of domestic values links *Incidents* to what has been called "woman's fiction." Written by women for a female audience, these works chronicle (in the words of Nina Baym) the "'trials and triumph' . . . of a heroine who, beset with hardships, finds within herself the qualities of intelligence, will, resourcefulness, and courage sufficient to overcome them." Ultimately, however, they identify an unhappy home as the source of evil and a happy home as the center of human bliss. Like such literature, Jacobs's book addresses a female audience. Instead of dramatizing the idea that the private sphere is women's appropriate area of concern, however, *Incidents* embodies a social analysis asserting that the denial of domestic and familial values by chattel slavery is a social issue that its female readers should address in the public arena. Jacobs's Linda Brent does not seek to inspire her audience to overcome individual character defects or to engage in reformist activity within the private sphere, but urges them to enter the public sphere and work to end chattel slavery and white racism. Informed not by "the cult of domesticity" or "domestic feminism" but by political feminism, *Incidents* is an attempt to move women to political action.[57]

In 1849, when Jacobs was in Rochester, the women in her circle were developing a critique of sexism patterned on the Garrisonian analysis of chattel slavery. Reflecting this model in their rhetoric, these abolitionist-feminists wrote of "the slavery of woman." The most committed, like Amy Post, did not confuse their own experience with the triple oppression of sex, condition, and race to which they knew slave women were subjected. It was nevertheless a sense of their own oppression that spurred freeborn white feminists to identify with a black fugitive slave woman like Jacobs.[58]

In shaping *Incidents,* Jacobs combined this feminist consciousness with the black feminist consciousness she had absorbed as "grandmother's child." Given its closed community split into two warring camps—blacks who oppose slavery and whites who support it—the narrative is surprising. We expect to encounter the supportive black women, both slave and free, as well as the fiendish neighboring female slaveholder and the jealous mistress. But how are we to explain the presence of the white women who defect from the slaveholders' ranks to help Linda Brent? How can we account for the lady who, at the request of the young slave's grandmother, tries to stop her master from molesting her? Even more strange, how can we account for the female slaveholder who hides the runaway female slave for a month?

Or the northern employer who entrusts her baby to Linda Brent so that she can flee slavecatchers by traveling as a nursemaid rather than as a fugitive? One explanation is that these women are responding to Linda Brent's oppression as a woman exploited sexually and as a mother trying to nurture her children. A central pattern in *Incidents* shows white women betraying allegiances of race and class to assert their stronger allegiance to the sisterhood of all women.

In her signed preface Jacobs's narrator invites this reading by the way in which she identifies her audience and announces her purpose: "I do earnestly desire to arouse the women of the North to a realizing sense of the condition of two millions of women at the South, still in bondage." Jacobs's book—reaching across the gulfs separating black women from white, slave from free, poor from rich, bridging the chasm separating "bad" women from "good"—represents an attempt to establish an American sisterhood and to activate that sisterhood in the public arena.

Further, between its covers a black American woman pseudonymously presents her shocking story in defiance of the rules of sexual propriety, and she is supported in this effort by a prominent white American woman writer. Almost thirty years earlier, Child had made an indelible mark on American letters by discussing the forbidden subject of slavery.[59] Presenting *Incidents,* a narrative by a pseudonymous "impure woman" on the "forbidden subject" of the sexual exploitation of women in slavery, she again broke taboos. In her Introduction Child announces that this defiance is deliberate: "I am well aware that many will accuse me of indecorum for presenting these pages to the public . . . This peculiar phase of Slavery has generally been kept veiled; but the public ought to be made acquainted with its monstrous features . . ." Both the writing and the publication of *Incidents* were significant events in the history of women's literature in America.

I am sorry to say, that with all the blood and guilt on the slave-holders' souls, there are Englishmen here that dare express sympathy for them. I hope it is their ignorance, and not the want of humanity.[60]

Unlike his sister, John S. Jacobs was a movement activist before he wrote his narrative. He had a history of political engagement in the United States, and in 1859 he renewed his commitment by joining the London Emancipation Committee. The committee's members included British Garrisonians and the expatriated African-American fugitive slaves William and Ellen Craft, and John S. was certainly aware of the Crafts' *Running a Thousand Miles for Freedom*—in 1860 the first major slave narrative published in England since the sensational appearance of Stowe's *Uncle Tom's Cabin* almost a decade earlier.[61] With the Crafts' book a success and his sister's book finally about to appear in Boston, John S. decided to write his own story.

His timing made good political sense. By the time the news reached England that on November 7, 1860, the palmetto flag had been raised to cheering crowds in Charleston, South Carolina, in defiance of Lincoln's election, it was clear to many that the States were breaking apart. In December a South Carolina convention, voting for secession, declared the Union dissolved, and one after another, states in the deep South were seizing Federal arsenals and forts. In January Mississippi, Florida, Alabama, Georgia, and Louisiana seceded. Then came Texas.[62]

The first of the four installments of John's serialized narrative appeared on February 4, 1861, the day representatives of the Confederate States met in convention. Before his final chapter was published on February 28, they had adopted a Constitution and inaugurated Jefferson Davis as the Provisional President of the Confederacy. (Lincoln would be sworn in the next week.) If John chose to write in line with the efforts of the London Emancipation Committee to persuade the British public not to support the secessionists—despite the ties binding the mills at Manchester to the southern cotton fields—he could not have chosen a better time. And if he chose his publisher for the same reason, he could not have picked a better vehicle than *The Leisure Hour: A Family Journal of Instruction and Recreation.*[63]

A product of the midcentury effort of Britain's Religious Tract Society to produce "a popular journal written from a decidedly Christian viewpoint," *The Leisure Hour* proposed to guide its almost 100,000 readers "to the attainment of every virtue which ought to elevate and gladden our English home." Each week its cover illustrated a work of fiction chosen to improve its "lower to middle class" audience, and its sixteen pages presented British history, popular science, and miscellaneous extracts, as well as poetry and advice to servants, workingmen, housewives, and the poor.[64] England had outlawed chattel slavery in 1837, and in keeping with British popular opinion and with its stated policy of avoiding controversy, the journal took a generally antislavery tone. When John S. submitted his manuscript, *The Leisure Hour* doubtless appeared a potential ally to members of the London Emancipation Society in their effort to win the hearts and minds of working-class Englishmen. A year later, mounting a concerted public campaign to counter the "Southern Clubs" organizing throughout Lancashire, Derbyshire, Cheshire, and Yorkshire, Emancipation Society members arranged for an English edition of *Incidents in the Life of a Slave Girl.*[65]

Like the stories *The Leisure Hour* was serializing in February 1861— "'Fast' and 'Steady': or the Career of Two Clerks" and "Cedar Creek: From the Shanty to the Settlement"—John S.'s "A True Tale of Slavery" is instructive. As a first-person account of a good man who is trying to behave morally in difficult circumstances, it conforms not only to popular uplift fiction but also to the model of the slave narrative epitomized by Frederick Douglass's 1845 *Narrative*.[66] In accord with this pattern, "True Tale" begins with a portrayal of the narrator's family and their life in slavery. The chapters following record their trials and struggles, and by the end of Chapter V he has described his escape. Chapter VI begins with the expected discussion of the narrator's life in freedom. But he then turns to his sister's story, and it is only after completing this extended digression that he presents the expected final chapter, in which he testifies to a series of atrocities and polemicizes against slavery and the new Fugitive Slave Law. The doubled shape of "A True Tale" reveals its deep connections with *Incidents in the Life of a Slave Girl*.

The careful attention John S. pays to his sister's history in Chapter VI is surprising because his earlier treatment of her situation is cursory. In less than a dozen sentences in Chapter II, which are strangely introduced with "But to return to my subject," he writes of his sister's children, her exile to the plantation, her fear of whipping, and her running away; and in Chapter IV he includes a description of her hiding place. Nowhere, however, does he mention her sexual history. He does not refer to her master's harassment and threats of concubinage, her desperate decision to become another man's mistress, her later commitment to save her infant daughter from sexual bondage in slavery, or her belief that if she runs away her master will sell the children to their father, who will free them. In "A True Tale," John S. erases his sister's sexual experiences and instead presents their consequences, noting the existence of her children, her exile to the plantation, her running away and the resulting punishment of the family, her years of hiding in Edenton, her escape to the North, and her master's efforts to catch her. Although he inserts his sister's story at length into Chapter VI, John S. leaves that story virtually untold. In his version she runs away because she fears whipping. This is no hero tale of a mother who liberates her children; nor is it the confession of an anguished "fallen woman." John S. suggests that his sister's story is very important by including the consequences of her sexual experiences in Chapter II and by distending the shape of his narrative to focus on her escape and manumission in Chapter VI. But without her sexual history—without the narrative of the tormented girl, the shamed woman, and the devoted mother, the unique center of the narrative is lost.

Its treatment of Harriet Jacobs's life is not all that distinguishes "A True Tale" from *Incidents in the Life of a Slave Girl*. Appropriate to its publication in a journal of Christian uplift, John S.'s text charts the developing integrity of its narrator. From his refusal to escape from jail (although handed the key) because he "would not have taken advantage of Mr. L——'s kindness," to his rejection of his uncle's offer to post his bond because he planned to escape; from his statement that "pride will not allow me to let a man feed and clothe me for nothing," to his assertion that when free, he "began to feel my responsibility, and the necessity of mental improvement"—John S. writes as a man recording his internalization of the ethics that *The Leisure Hour* is intent on instilling in its audience. At one point he even presents himself as an exemplar when, in a clever reference to the magazine's title, he comments on his successful quest for literacy by writing, "I had made the best possible use of my leisure hours."

His condemnation of lying and deception is interesting. Rather than reserving his outrage to denounce the immorality of chattel slavery, he voices moral disgust at the routine social practices of Washington ladies, who declare to visitors that they are "not at home." Underscoring his belief in the importance of truthfulness, he writes that when in Canada he abandoned his effort to obtain a seaman's protection when he learned that he could not get it "without swearing to a lie, which I did not feel disposed to do." Of the deceptions rooted in the false relationships between master and slave, he writes that in dealing with the doctor he decided he must "hide as much as possible my hatred of slavery, and affect a respect to my master," and that later, serving the lawyer, "I grew sick of myself in acting the deceitful part of a slave, and pretending love and friendship where I had none . . . yet, under the circumstances in which I was placed, I feel that I have done no wrong in so doing." Presenting himself as a model for his readers, John S.'s narrator contrasts sharply with his sister's conflicted Linda Brent.

John S. further contrasts with his sister's narrator by consistently including names and places when he testifies to the atrocities of slavery. In his final chapter we hear the practiced platform speaker challenging his audience as if addressing a jury: "I beg the reader to remember that I am not writing of what I have heard, but of what I have seen, and of what I defy the world to prove false." Here he testifies concerning the decapitation of George Cabarrus, the murder of Tom Hoskins, the shooting of Sirus, and the whipping of Agnes—although his London editors, while affirming his upright character and the truth of his assertions, gutted his testimony by publishing his narrative anonymously and routinely deleting all but initials except in the cases of Cabarrus and Hoskins.

Not only in its testimonials and moral posture but also in its tone, "A True Tale" is strikingly different from *Incidents*. Before she wrote, Jacobs could only "whisper her cruel wrongs in the ear of a dear friend," while John S. had developed his polished rhetorical style as he declaimed his story from platforms throughout New York and New England. Especially in its final pages, "A True Tale" echoes the hortatory style of these earlier speeches. Frederick Douglass had praised John S.'s "calm and feeling manner" on the platform, and news reports, commenting on his "witty allusions," had noted that audiences enjoyed the vivid language of this "sable man of noble brow" who spoke "with a fluency and depth of interest scarcely excelled by any of his predecessors—even by *Douglass* himself."[67] The fullest account of his oratory describes an 1850 speech denouncing the Fugitive Slave Law. Here, despite his color and fugitive status, he brashly identified himself as "an American citizen" and urged his New York City listeners to armed resistance: "They said that they cannot take us back to the South; but I say, under the present law they can; and now I say unto you, let them only take your dead bodies . . . I would, my friends, advise you to show a front to our tyrants, and arm yourselves; aye, and I would advise the women to have their knives too . . . Let us go on immediately, and act like men."[68]

John S.'s abrasive rhetorical style, which was characteristic of male Garrisonian abolitionists on both sides of the Atlantic, differed as much from his sister's manner as his British audience of men and women differed from her female American readers. While Linda explains that she is writing "to arouse the women of the North to a realizing sense of the conditions of two millions of women at the South," John S. announces that his purpose is to punish his oppressors: "If possible, let us make those whom we have left behind [in the United States] feel that the ground they till is cursed with slavery, the air they breathe poisoned with its venom breath, and that which made life dear to them is lost and gone." Where *Incidents* ends quietly with the claim that the author finds comfort in memories of her grandmother although it has been painful to recall her years in slavery, "A True Tale" ends as a jeremiad with an unspeakable vision of horror.

These differences are certainly consequences of the writers' personalities. But they are also expressive of the gender conventions of the period, which assigned an assertive public role to men and a retiring private role to women. Where *Incidents* dramatizes the struggle of a female slave who was excluded from the category of true womanhood because her status forbade her to practice the piety, purity, and domesticity required of women, "A True Tale" presents a male slave who was not permitted to assume the responsibility for his family that was required of men. Both in their literary styles and in the stories they tell—as well as in the stories they do not tell—brother and sister address nineteenth-century conventions of gender.

Among slave narratives, "A True Tale" has special importance because of its relationship to *Incidents*. Unlike any other known slave narrator, Harriet Jacobs left two interlocking texts: the book she wrote and published, and the private letters in which she discussed its inception, composition, and publication. "A True Tale" provides a third textual layer. To readers of *Incidents*, John S.'s narrative is valuable not only because it makes possible a series of identifications of people and places, and not only because it corroborates some of Linda Brent's most unlikely assertions. In retelling her story from a male perspective, "A True Tale" highlights the gendering of Harriet Jacobs's narrative and underscores her astonishing achievement.

By the time *Incidents* appeared, abolitionist literary critics like Thomas Wentworth Higginson were asserting that the lives of fugitive slaves constituted "the romance of American history." Most black women in Jacobs's generation, however, could not address an audience called "Reader." Because they lacked access to polite letters, their literary contributions were made within the oral tradition. Jacobs was one of a very small group of Afro-American women capable of creating a book that affords a new perspective on the American romance and on female characters like Hawthorne's Hester Prynne.[69] Even though its story lines conflict and at times its narrator appears trapped within traditional language and literary conventions inadequate to express her radically untraditional content, *Incidents*, like the great American romances, transforms the conventions of literature.

In Jacobs's hand, the passive woman of the captivity narrative acts to save herself; in her hand, the slave narrative is changed from the story of a hero who singlehandedly seeks freedom and literacy to the story of a hero tightly bound to family and community who seeks freedom and a home for her children. In her hand, the pathetic seduced "tragic mulatto" of white fiction is metamorphosed from a victim of white male deception and fickleness into an inexperienced girl making desperate choices in her struggle for autonomy; the "mammy" of white fiction becomes not the white babies' nurse but the nurturer and liberator of her own children. In her hand, the madwoman in the attic sanely plots for her freedom; instead of studying self-control within a domestic setting, the young woman learns to engage in political action. Harriet Jacobs tells a story new in black literature, in women's writings, and in American letters: a woman's "true and just account of my own life in slavery."

Note on the Text

The text of *Incidents* follows the first American edition (Boston, 1861). The text of "A True Tale of Slavery" is taken from its original publication in *The Leisure Hour: A Family Journal of Instruction and Recreation* (London, England), February 7, 14, 21, and 28, 1861. A few obvious typographical errors have been silently corrected. The Correspondence is reproduced as accurately as possible from the holographs. Jacobs capitalizes important words but omits capital letters at the beginnings of sentences. Because in the early letters she also omits most punctuation, even final periods, in this edition spaces marking full stops have been inserted to aid the reader. For photographs of two of Jacobs's letters, see pages 310 and 342.

Chronology

1813 Autumn: Harriet Ann Jacobs is born in Edenton, North Carolina, to Delilah, daughter of Molly Horniblow and slave of Margaret Horniblow, and the carpenter Elijah, slave of Dr. Andrew Knox.

1815 John S. Jacobs, Harriet's brother, is born.

1819 Harriet's mother dies; Harriet is taken into the Edenton home of her mistress Margaret Horniblow and taught to read, spell, and sew.

1825 Margaret Horniblow dies and wills Harriet to her three-year-old niece, Mary Matilda Norcom. Harriet is moved into the household of Dr. James Norcom with her brother John.

1826 Harriet's father dies.

1828 Harriet's brother John and grandmother Molly Horniblow are sold following the death of their mistress Elizabeth Horniblow. Dr. Norcom buys John. Through a series of maneuvers, Molly Horniblow is freed and buys her older son, Mark Ramsey. Her younger son, Joseph, knocks down his master and runs away. Although returned in chains, jailed for six months, and sold to New Orleans, he again escapes. After meeting briefly in New York with his brother, Joseph is lost to the family.

1829   Harriet Jacobs, forbidden to marry the man she loves and threatened
       with concubinage by her master Dr. Norcom, begins a sexual relation-
       ship with Samuel Tredwell Sawyer. After threats by Mrs. Norcom, she
       moves into her grandmother's house. Her son Joseph is born.

1831   Nat Turner's insurrection.

1833   Louisa Matilda, Jacobs's daughter by Sawyer, is born.

1835   Jacobs again rejects Dr. Norcom's sexual demands and is sent to a
       plantation several miles from Edenton. June: She runs away and hides
       with friends after learning that Norcom plans to send her children to
       the plantation to be "broken in." In retaliation, Norcom jails her Aunt
       Betty, her brother John, and her children—all of whom are his slaves.
       Through a trader, Sawyer buys John and the children, whom he per-
       mits to live with Jacobs's grandmother. August: Jacobs's family con-
       ceals her, first in a swamp and then in her grandmother's home. In
       hiding, she sews and reads the Bible.

1837   August: Sawyer is elected to Congress and, taking John S. with him,
       leaves Edenton for Washington without emancipating the children.

1838   August 11: With John S. accompanying him as his servant, Sawyer
       travels to Chicago, where he marries Lavinia Peyton. Late autumn: In
       New York, John S. runs away from Sawyer.

1839   August: John S. ships out of New Bedford, Mass., on a whaling voyage.

1840   Louisa Matilda goes to Washington, D.C., with Sawyer, his wife, and
       their baby; after five months there she is taken to his cousins in Brook-
       lyn, N.Y.

1842   Aunt Betty dies. June: Jacobs escapes to the North. In Philadelphia she
       is aided by the Vigilant Committee; in Brooklyn she sees her daugh-
       ter; in Boston she searches for her brother; in New York she finds em-
       ployment tending Mary Stace Willis's baby Imogen.

1843   February: John S., returned from three years at sea, meets Jacobs in
       New York. October: Fleeing slavecatchers, Jacobs goes to her brother,
       now an activist in Boston. She arranges for her son to be sent to her
       brother and returns to New York.

1844   Again threatened by slavecatchers, with John S.'s help Jacobs escapes
       with her daughter. She settles in Boston, supporting her children as a
       seamstress.

1845   March: Mary Stace Willis dies. Jacobs travels to England with the wid-
       owed Nathaniel Parker Willis as nurse for Imogen.

1846   Back home, Jacobs is harassed by Mary Matilda Norcom and her new husband, Daniel Messmore, who try to re-enslave her.

1849   With the help of John S., now an abolitionist lecturer, Jacobs arranges to send Louisa Matilda to school in Clinton, N.Y. March: Jacobs leaves Boston, moves to Rochester, and works with John S. in the Anti-Slavery Office and Reading Room, where she meets Amy Post and a circle of anti-slavery feminists.

1850   The new Fugitive Slave Law is passed as part of the Missouri Compromise. September: Jacobs returns to New York and resumes employment with the Willis family, caring for the baby of Willis's second wife, Cornelia Grinnell Willis. John S. goes to California to pan for gold; Jacobs's son follows him; by 1853 both are mining in Australia. November: Dr. Norcom dies in Edenton.

1851   Spring: Warned that Norcom has made plans for her capture, and unaware of his death, Jacobs flees New York and hides for a month in Massachusetts.

1852   February: Messmore travels to New York to catch Jacobs; she again escapes to Massachusetts. Cornelia Grinnell Willis arranges to purchase her. Jacobs is free.

1853   February: Jacobs considers Amy Post's suggestion that she tell her story. Rejecting Harriet Beecher Stowe's suggestion that her life be incorporated into *A Key to Uncle Tom's Cabin*, she decides to write her book herself and begins work. June and July: She publishes letters in the *New York Tribune*. July: She moves with the Willis family to Idlewild in Cornwall, New York, but maintains contact with organized abolitionism. September: Molly Horniblow dies in Edenton.

1858   Jacobs completes her manuscript. After traveling to Boston for letters of introduction to abolitionists abroad, she sails to England in May to sell her book. Unsuccessful, she returns in the autumn. Her uncle Mark Ramsey, who was freed in 1843, dies in Edenton.

1859   The Boston publishers Phillips and Sampson agree to publish Jacobs's narrative, then go bankrupt. John Brown raids the Federal Arsenal at Harpers Ferry.

1860   Jacobs sends her manuscript to the Boston publishers Thayer and Eldridge. They want a preface from Lydia Maria Child, and William C. Nell introduces Jacobs to Child. Child (acting for Jacobs) signs a contract to publish the book. Thayer and Eldridge then go bankrupt.

1861   Jacobs buys the stereotyped plates of her book; *Incidents* is published by a Boston printer "for the author." February: Jacobs goes to Philadelphia to sell *Incidents*. John S., now a member of the London Emancipation Committee, publishes his narrative, "A True Tale of Slavery," in *The Leisure Hour*. April 12: The Confederacy fires on Fort Sumter.

1862   *The Deeper Wrong*, the English edition of *Incidents*, is published with the help of John S.'s antislavery colleagues. September: Jacobs goes to Washington, D.C., to do relief work among the contrabands. The National Freedman's Relief Association is established.

1863   January 1: Emancipation Proclamation. January: Sponsored by Philadelphia and New York Quakers, Jacobs works distributing clothing, teaching, and providing health care in Alexandria, Va. November: Louisa Matilda joins Jacobs in Alexandria. Jacobs sends $400 to Australia in response to a letter asking for money for Joseph's passage home, but she never again hears from him.

1864   January 11: Jacobs and her daughter open the Jacobs School in Alexandria.

1865   March: Freedmen's Bureau is established. April: Lee surrenders; Lincoln is assassinated. October: Jacobs visits Edenton. November: Jacobs and Louisa Matilda go to Savannah, where Jacobs does relief work in the city and on rice plantations. Thirteenth Amendment.

1866   July: Jacobs and Louisa Matilda return north.

1867   May: Jacobs again visits Edenton, dispensing clothing and seeds. Reconstruction Act. Ku Klux Klan is organized.

1868   March: Jacobs and Louisa Matilda sail to London and raise £1,000 for an orphanage and a home for the aged in Savannah. Fourteenth Amendment.

1870   Fifteenth Amendment. Jacobs runs a boardinghouse in Cambridge, Mass.

1873   December: John S. Jacobs, who has returned to Massachusetts, dies and is buried in Mount Auburn Cemetery, Cambridge.

1877   Federal troops are withdrawn from the South. Harriet and Louisa Matilda Jacobs move to Washington, D.C.

1892   Jacobs sells her grandmother's Edenton house and lot for $425.

1896   Louisa Matilda Jacobs participates in organizing meetings of the National Association of Colored Women in Washington, D.C.

1897   March 7: Harriet Jacobs dies in Washington, D.C., and is buried next to her brother in Mount Auburn Cemetery, Cambridge.

INCIDENTS

IN THE

LIFE OF A SLAVE GIRL.

WRITTEN BY HERSELF.

"Northerners know nothing at all about Slavery. They think it is perpetual bondage only. They have no conception of the depth of *degradation* involved in that word, SLAVERY; if they had, they would never cease their efforts until so horrible a system was overthrown." A WOMAN OF NORTH CAROLINA.

"Rise up, ye women that are at ease! Hear my voice, ye careless daughters! Give ear unto my speech." ISAIAH xxxii. 9.

EDITED BY L. MARIA CHILD.

BOSTON:
PUBLISHED FOR THE AUTHOR.
1861.

The title page of the first edition.

Cast of Characters

LINDA BRENT	Harriet Ann Jacobs
AUNT MARTHA	Molly Horniblow, Jacobs's grandmother
UNCLE PHILLIP	Mark Ramsey, Molly Horniblow's older son
AUNT NANCY	Betty, Molly Horniblow's daughter
UNCLE BENJAMIN	Joseph, Molly Horniblow's younger son
WILLIAM	John S. Jacobs, Jacobs's brother
BENNY	Joseph Jacobs, Jacobs's son
ELLEN	Louisa Matilda Jacobs, Jacobs's daughter
MISS FANNY	Hannah Pritchard
DR. FLINT	Dr. James Norcom
MRS. FLINT	Mary Matilda Horniblow Norcom, Dr. Norcom's wife
YOUNG MR. FLINT	James Norcom, Jr.
MISS EMILY FLINT, later MRS. DODGE	Dr. Norcom's daughter Mary Matilda Norcom, later Mrs. Daniel Messmore
MR. SANDS	Samuel Tredwell Sawyer
MR. AND MRS. HOBBS	James Iredell Tredwell and Mary Bonner Blount Tredwell, Sawyer's cousins
MR. THORNE	Joseph Blount, Mrs. Tredwell's brother
MR. BRUCE	Nathaniel Parker Willis
MRS. BRUCE	Mary Stace Willis, Nathaniel Parker Willis's first wife
BABY MARY	Imogen Willis
THE SECOND MRS BRUCE	Cornelia Grinnell Willis, Nathaniel Parker Willis's second wife

Preface

BY THE AUTHOR

Reader, be assured this narrative is no fiction. I am aware that some of my adventures may seem incredible; but they are, nevertheless, strictly true. I have not exaggerated the wrongs inflicted by Slavery; on the contrary, my descriptions fall far short of the facts. I have concealed the names of places, and given persons fictitious names. I had no motive for secrecy on my own account, but I deemed it kind and considerate towards others to pursue this course.

I wish I were more competent to the task I have undertaken. But I trust my readers will excuse deficiencies in consideration of circumstances. I was born and reared in Slavery; and I remained in a Slave State twenty-seven years. Since I have been at the North, it has been necessary for me to work diligently for my own support, and the education of my children. This has not left me much leisure to make up for the loss of early opportunities to improve myself; and it has compelled me to write these pages at irregular intervals, whenever I could snatch an hour from household duties.[1]

When I first arrived in Philadelphia, Bishop Paine[2] advised me to publish a sketch of my life, but I told him I was altogether incompetent to such an undertaking. Though I have improved my mind somewhat since that time, I still remain of the same opinion; but I trust my motives will excuse what might otherwise seem presumptuous. I have not written my experiences in order to attract attention to myself; on the contrary, it would have been more pleasant to me to have been silent about my own history.[3] Neither do I care to excite sympathy for my own sufferings. But I do earnestly desire to arouse the women of the North to a realizing sense of the condition of two millions of women at the South, still in bondage, suffering what I suffered, and most of them far worse. I want to add my testimony to that of abler pens to convince the people of the Free States what Slavery really is. Only by experience can any one realize how deep, and dark, and foul is that pit of abominations.[4] May the blessing of God rest on this imperfect effort in behalf of my persecuted people!

Linda Brent

Introduction

BY THE EDITOR

T HE AUTHOR OF the following autobiography is personally known to me, and her conversation and manners inspire me with confidence.[1] During the last seventeen years, she has lived the greater part of the time with a distinguished family in New York, and has so deported herself as to be highly esteemed by them. This fact is sufficient, without further credentials of her character. I believe those who know her will not be disposed to doubt her veracity, though some incidents in her story are more romantic than fiction.

At her request, I have revised her manuscript; but such changes as I have made have been mainly for purposes of condensation and orderly arrangement. I have not added any thing to the incidents, or changed the import of her very pertinent remarks. With trifling exceptions, both the ideas and the language are her own. I pruned excrescences a little, but otherwise I had no reason for changing her lively and dramatic way of telling her own story.[2] The names of both persons and places are known to me; but for good reasons I suppress them.

It will naturally excite surprise that a woman reared in Slavery should be able to write so well. But circumstances will explain this. In the first place, nature endowed her with quick perceptions. Secondly, the mistress, with whom she lived till she was twelve years old, was a kind, considerate friend, who taught her to read and spell. Thirdly, she was placed in favorable circumstances after she came to the North; having frequent intercourse with intelligent persons, who felt a friendly interest in her welfare, and were disposed to give her opportunities for self-improvement.

I am well aware that many will accuse me of indecorum for presenting these pages to the public; for the experiences of this intelligent and much-injured woman belong to a class which some call delicate subjects, and others indelicate. This peculiar phase of Slavery has generally been kept veiled; but the public ought to be made acquainted with its monstrous features, and I willingly take the responsibility of presenting them with the veil withdrawn. I do this for the sake of my sisters in bondage, who are suffering wrongs so foul, that our ears are too delicate to listen to them. I do it with the hope of arousing conscientious and reflecting women at the North to a sense of their duty in the exertion of moral influence on the question of Slavery, on all possible occasions. I do it with the hope that every man who reads this narrative will swear solemnly before God that, so far as he has power to prevent it, no fugitive from Slavery shall ever be sent back to suffer in that loathsome den of corruption and cruelty.

L. Maria Child

I

Childhood

I WAS BORN A SLAVE; but I never knew it till six years of happy childhood had passed away. My father was a carpenter, and considered so intelligent and skilful in his trade, that, when buildings out of the common line were to be erected, he was sent for from long distances, to be head workman.[1] On condition of paying his mistress two hundred dollars a year, and supporting himself, he was allowed to work at his trade, and manage his own affairs. His strongest wish was to purchase his children; but, though he several times offered his hard earnings for that purpose, he never succeeded. In complexion my parents were a light shade of brownish yellow, and were termed mulattoes. They lived together in a comfortable home; and, though we were all slaves, I was so fondly shielded that I never dreamed I was a piece of merchandise, trusted to them for safe keeping, and liable to be demanded of them at any moment. I had one brother, William, who was two years younger than myself—a bright, affectionate child.[2]

I had also a great treasure in my maternal grandmother, who was a remarkable woman in many respects.[3] She was the daughter of a planter in South Carolina, who, at his death, left her mother and his three children free, with money to go to St. Augustine, where they had relatives. It was during the Revolutionary War; and they were captured on their passage, carried back, and sold to different purchasers.[4] Such was the story my grandmother used to tell me; but I do not remember all the particulars. She was a little girl when she was captured and sold to the keeper of a large hotel.[5] I have often heard her tell how hard she fared during childhood. But as she grew older she evinced so much intelligence, and was so faithful, that her master and mistress could not help seeing it was for their interest to take care of such a valuable piece of property. She became an indispensable personage in the household, officiating in all capacities, from cook and wet nurse to seamstress. She was much praised for her cooking; and her nice crackers became so famous in the neighborhood that many people were desirous of obtaining them. In consequence of numerous requests of this kind, she asked permission of her mistress to bake crackers at night, after all the household work was done; and she obtained leave to do it, provided she would clothe herself and her children from the profits. Upon these terms, after working hard all day for her mistress, she began her midnight bakings, assisted by her two oldest children.[6] The business proved profitable; and each year she laid by a little, which was saved for a fund to purchase her children. Her master died, and the property was divided among his heirs. The widow had her dower in the hotel, which she continued to keep open. My grandmother remained in her service as a slave; but her children were divided among her master's children. As she had five, Benjamin, the youngest one, was sold, in order that each heir might have an equal portion of dollars and cents.[7] There was so little difference in our ages that he seemed more like my brother than my uncle. He was a bright, handsome lad, nearly white; for he inherited the complexion my grandmother had derived from Anglo-Saxon ancestors. Though only ten years old, seven hundred and twenty dollars were paid for him. His sale was a terrible blow to my grandmother; but she was naturally hopeful, and she went to work with renewed energy, trusting in time to be able to purchase some of her children. She had laid up three hundred dollars, which her mistress one day begged as a loan, promising to pay her soon. The reader probably knows that no promise or writing given to a slave is legally binding; for, according to Southern laws, a slave, *being* property, can *hold* no property. When my grandmother lent her hard earnings to her mistress, she trusted solely to her honor. The honor of a slaveholder to a slave!

To this good grandmother I was indebted for many comforts. My brother Willie and I often received portions of the crackers, cakes, and preserves, she made to sell; and after we ceased to be children we were indebted to her for many more important services.

Such were the unusually fortunate circumstances of my early childhood. When I was six years old, my mother died;[8] and then, for the first time, I learned, by the talk around me, that I was a slave. My mother's mistress was the daughter of my grandmother's mistress. She was the foster sister of my mother; they were both nourished at my grandmother's breast. In fact, my mother had been weaned at three months old, that the babe of the mistress might obtain sufficient food. They played together as children; and, when they became women, my mother was a most faithful servant to her whiter foster sister. On her death-bed her mistress promised that her children should never suffer for any thing; and during her lifetime she kept her word. They all spoke kindly of my dead mother, who had been a slave merely in name, but in nature was noble and womanly. I grieved for her, and my young mind was troubled with the thought who would now take care of me and my little brother. I was told that my home

was now to be with her mistress; and I found it a happy one. No toil-
some or disagreeable duties were imposed upon me. My mistress was
so kind to me that I was always glad to do her bidding, and proud to
labor for her as much as my young years would permit. I would sit by
her side for hours, sewing diligently, with a heart as free from care as
that of any free-born white child. When she thought I was tired, she
would send me out to run and jump; and away I bounded, to gather
berries or flowers to decorate her room. Those were happy days—too
happy to last. The slave child had no thought for the morrow; but
there came that blight, which too surely waits on every human being
born to be a chattel.

When I was nearly twelve years old, my kind mistress sickened and
died.[9] As I saw the cheek grow paler, and the eye more glassy, how
earnestly I prayed in my heart that she might live! I loved her; for she
had been almost like a mother to me. My prayers were not answered.
She died, and they buried her in the little churchyard, where, day after
day, my tears fell upon her grave.

I was sent to spend a week with my grandmother.[10] I was now old
enough to begin to think of the future; and again and again I asked
myself what they would do with me. I felt sure I should never find
another mistress so kind as the one who was gone. She had promised
my dying mother that her children should never suffer for any thing;
and when I remembered that, and recalled her many proofs of attachment to me, I could not help having some hopes that she had left me
free. My friends were almost certain it would be so. They thought she
would be sure to do it, on account of my mother's love and faithful
service. But, alas! we all know that the memory of a faithful slave does
not avail much to save her children from the auction block.

After a brief period of suspense, the will of my mistress was read,
and we learned that she had bequeathed me to her sister's daughter,
a child of five years old.[11] So vanished our hopes. My mistress had

taught me the precepts of God's Word: "Thou shalt love thy neighbor as thyself."[12] "Whatsoever ye would that men should do unto you, do ye even so unto them."[13] But I was her slave, and I suppose she did not recognize me as her neighbor. I would give much to blot out from my memory that one great wrong. As a child, I loved my mistress; and, looking back on the happy days I spent with her, I try to think with less bitterness of this act of injustice. While I was with her, she taught me to read and spell; and for this privilege, which so rarely falls to the lot of a slave, I bless her memory.

She possessed but few slaves; and at her death those were all distributed among her relatives. Five of them were my grandmother's children, and had shared the same milk that nourished her mother's children.[14] Notwithstanding my grandmother's long and faithful service to her owners, not one of her children escaped the auction block. These God-breathing machines are no more, in the sight of their masters, than the cotton they plant, or the horses they tend.

II

The New Master and Mistress

D R. FLINT, a physician in the neighborhood, had married the sister of my mistress, and I was now the property of their little daughter.[1] It was not without murmuring that I prepared for my new home; and what added to my unhappiness, was the fact that my brother William was purchased by the same family.[2] My father, by his nature, as well as by the habit of transacting business as a skilful mechanic, had more of the feelings of a freeman than is common among slaves. My brother was a spirited boy; and being brought up under such influences, he early detested the name of master and mistress. One day, when his father and his mistress had happened to call him at the same time, he hesitated between the two; being perplexed to know which had the strongest claim upon his obedience. He finally concluded to go to his mistress. When my father reproved him for it, he said, "You both called me, and I didn't know which I ought to go to first."

"You are *my* child," replied our father, "and when I call you, you should come immediately, if you have to pass through fire and water."[3]

Poor Willie! He was now to learn his first lesson of obedience to a master. Grandmother tried to cheer us with hopeful words, and they found an echo in the credulous hearts of youth.

When we entered our new home we encountered cold looks, cold words, and cold treatment. We were glad when the night came. On my narrow bed I moaned and wept, I felt so desolate and alone.

I had been there nearly a year, when a dear little friend of mine was buried. I heard her mother sob, as the clods fell on the coffin of her only child, and I turned away from the grave, feeling thankful that I still had something left to love. I met my grandmother, who said, "Come with me, Linda"; and from her tone I knew that something sad had happened. She led me apart from the people, and then said, "My child, your father is dead."[4] Dead! How could I believe it? He had died so suddenly I had not even heard that he was sick. I went home with my grandmother. My heart rebelled against God, who had taken from me mother, father, mistress, and friend. The good grandmother tried to comfort me. "Who knows the ways of God?" said she. "Perhaps they have been kindly taken from the evil days to come." Years afterwards I often thought of this. She promised to be a mother to her grandchildren, so far as she might be permitted to do so; and strengthened by her love, I returned to my master's. I thought I should be allowed to go to my father's house the next morning; but I was ordered to go for flowers, that my mistress's house might be decorated for an evening party. I spent the day gathering flowers and weaving them into festoons, while the dead body of my father was lying within a mile of me. What cared my owners for that? he was merely a piece of property. Moreover, they thought he had spoiled his children, by teaching them to feel that they were human beings. This was blasphemous doctrine for a slave to teach; presumptuous in him, and dangerous to the masters.

The next day I followed his remains to a humble grave beside that of my dear mother. There were those who knew my father's worth, and respected his memory.

My home now seemed more dreary than ever. The laugh of the little slave-children sounded harsh and cruel. It was selfish to feel so about the joy of others. My brother moved about with a very grave face. I tried to comfort him, by saying, "Take courage, Willie; brighter days will come by and by."

"You don't know any thing about it, Linda," he replied. "We shall have to stay here all our days; we shall never be free."

I argued that we were growing older and stronger, and that perhaps we might, before long, be allowed to hire our own time, and then we could earn money to buy our freedom. William declared this was much easier to say than to do; moreover, he did not intend to *buy* his freedom. We held daily controversies upon this subject.

Little attention was paid to the slaves' meals in Dr. Flint's house. If they could catch a bit of food while it was going, well and good. I gave myself no trouble on that score, for on my various errands I passed my grandmother's house, where there was always something to spare for me. I was frequently threatened with punishment if I stopped there; and my grandmother, to avoid detaining me, often stood at the gate with something for my breakfast or dinner. I was indebted to *her* for all my comforts, spiritual or temporal. It was *her* labor that supplied my scanty wardrobe. I have a vivid recollection of the linsey-woolsey dress given me every winter by Mrs. Flint. How I hated it! It was one of the badges of slavery.

While my grandmother was thus helping to support me from her hard earnings, the three hundred dollars she had lent her mistress were never repaid. When her mistress died, her son-in-law, Dr. Flint, was appointed executor. When grandmother applied to him for payment, he said the estate was insolvent, and the law prohibited payment. It did not, however, prohibit him from retaining the silver candelabra, which had been purchased with that money. I presume they will be handed down in the family, from generation to generation.

My grandmother's mistress had always promised her that, at her death, she should be free; and it was said that in her will she made good the promise. But when the estate was settled, Dr. Flint told the faithful old servant that, under existing circumstances, it was necessary she should be sold.

On the appointed day, the customary advertisement was posted up, proclaiming that there would be a "public sale of negroes, horses, &c." Dr. Flint called to tell my grandmother that he was unwilling to wound her feelings by putting her up at auction, and that he would prefer to dispose of her at private sale.[5] My grandmother saw through his hypocrisy; she understood very well that he was ashamed of the job. She was a very spirited woman, and if he was base enough to sell her, when her mistress intended she should be free, she was determined the public should know it. She had for a long time supplied many families with crackers and preserves; consequently, "Aunt Marthy," as she was called, was generally known, and every body who knew her respected her intelligence and good character. Her long and faithful service in the family was also well known, and the intention of her mistress to leave her free. When the day of sale came, she took her place among the chattels, and at the first call she sprang upon the auction-block. Many voices called out, "Shame! Shame! Who is going to sell *you*, aunt Marthy? Don't stand there! That is no place for *you*." Without saying a word, she quietly awaited her fate. No one bid for her. At last, a feeble voice said, "Fifty dollars." It came from a maiden lady, seventy years old, the sister of my grandmother's deceased mistress. She had lived forty years under the same roof with my grandmother; she knew how faithfully she had served her owners, and how cruelly she had been defrauded of her rights; and she resolved to protect her. The auctioneer waited for a higher bid; but her wishes were respected; no one bid above her. She could neither read nor write; and when the bill of sale was made out, she signed it with a cross. But what consequence was that, when she had a big heart overflowing with human kindness? She gave the old servant her freedom.[6]

At that time, my grandmother was just fifty years old. Laborious years had passed since then; and now my brother and I were slaves to the man who had defrauded her of her money, and tried to defraud her of her freedom. One of my mother's sisters, called Aunt Nancy, was also a slave in his family.[7] She was a kind, good aunt to me; and supplied the place of both housekeeper and waiting maid to her mistress. She was, in fact, at the beginning and end of every thing.

Mrs. Flint, like many southern women, was totally deficient in energy. She had not strength to superintend her household affairs; but her nerves were so strong, that she could sit in her easy chair and see a woman whipped, till the blood trickled from every stroke of the lash. She was a member of the church; but partaking of the Lord's supper did not seem to put her in a Christian frame of mind. If dinner was not served at the exact time on that particular Sunday, she would station herself in the kitchen, and wait till it was dished, and then spit in all the kettles and pans that had been used for cooking. She did this to prevent the cook and her children from eking out their meagre fare with the remains of the gravy and other scrapings. The slaves could get nothing to eat except what she chose to give them. Provisions were weighed out by the pound and ounce, three times a day. I can assure you she gave them no chance to eat wheat bread from her flour barrel. She knew how many biscuits a quart of flour would make, and exactly what size they ought to be.[8]

Dr. Flint was an epicure. The cook never sent a dinner to his table without fear and trembling; for if there happened to be a dish not to his liking, he would either order her to be whipped, or compel her to eat every mouthful of it in his presence. The poor, hungry creature might not have objected to eating it; but she did object to having her master cram it down her throat till she choked.

They had a pet dog, that was a nuisance in the house. The cook was ordered to make some Indian mush for him. He refused to eat, and when his head was held over it, the froth flowed from his mouth into the basin. He died a few minutes after. When Dr. Flint came in, he said the mush had not been well cooked, and that was the reason the animal would not eat it. He sent for the cook, and compelled her to eat it. He thought that the woman's stomach was stronger than the dog's; but her sufferings afterwards proved that he was mistaken. This poor woman endured many cruelties from her master and mistress; sometimes she was locked up, away from her nursing baby, for a whole day and night.

When I had been in the family a few weeks, one of the plantation slaves was brought to town, by order of his master. It was near night when he arrived, and Dr. Flint ordered him to be taken to the work house, and tied up to the joist, so that his feet would just escape the ground. In that situation he was to wait till the doctor had taken his tea. I shall never forget that night. Never before, in my life, had I heard hundreds of blows fall, in succession, on a human being. His piteous groans, and his "O, pray don't, massa," rang in my ear for months afterwards. There were many conjectures as to the cause of this terrible punishment. Some said master accused him of stealing corn; others said the slave had quarrelled with his wife, in presence of the overseer, and had accused his master of being the father of her child. They were both black, and the child was very fair.

I went into the work house next morning, and saw the cowhide still wet with blood, and the boards all covered with gore. The poor man lived, and continued to quarrel with his wife. A few months afterwards Dr. Flint handed them both over to a slavetrader. The guilty man put their value into his pocket, and had the satisfaction of knowing that they were out of sight and hearing. When the mother was delivered into the trader's hands, she said, "You *promised* to treat me well." To which he replied, "You have let your tongue run too far; damn you!" She had forgotten that it was a crime for a slave to tell who was the father of her child.

From others than the master persecution also comes in such cases. I once saw a young slave girl dying soon after the birth of a child nearly white. In her agony she cried out, "O Lord, come and take me!" Her mistress stood by, and mocked at her like an incarnate fiend. "You suffer, do you?" she exclaimed. "I am glad of it. You deserve it all, and more too."

The girl's mother said, "The baby is dead, thank God; and I hope my poor child will soon be in heaven, too."

"Heaven!" retorted the mistress. "There is no such place for the like of her and her bastard."

The poor mother turned away, sobbing. Her dying daughter called her, feebly, and as she bent over her, I heard her say, "Don't grieve so, mother; God knows all about it; and HE will have mercy upon me."

Her sufferings, afterwards, became so intense, that her mistress felt unable to stay; but when she left the room, the scornful smile was still on her lips. Seven children called her mother. The poor black woman had but the one child, whose eyes she saw closing in death, while she thanked God for taking her away from the greater bitterness of life.

III

The Slaves' New Year's Day

D R. FLINT OWNED a fine residence in town, several farms, and about fifty slaves, besides hiring a number by the year.[1]

Hiring-day at the south takes place on the 1st of January.[2] On the 2d, the slaves are expected to go to their new masters. On a farm, they work until the corn and cotton are laid. They then have two holidays. Some masters give them a good dinner under the trees. This over, they work until Christmas eve. If no heavy charges are meantime brought against them, they are given four or five holidays, whichever the master or overseer may think proper. Then comes New Year's eve; and they gather together their little alls, or more properly speaking, their little nothings, and wait anxiously for the dawning of day. At the appointed hour the grounds are thronged with men, women, and children, waiting, like criminals, to hear their doom pronounced. The slave is sure to know who is the most humane, or cruel master, within forty miles of him.

It is easy to find out, on that day, who clothes and feeds his slaves well; for he is surrounded by a crowd, begging, "Please, massa, hire me this year. I will work *very* hard, massa."

If a slave is unwilling to go with his new master, he is whipped, or locked up in jail, until he consents to go, and promises not to run away during the year. Should he chance to change his mind, thinking it justifiable to violate an extorted promise, woe unto him if he is caught! The whip is used till the blood flows at his feet; and his stiffened limbs are put in chains, to be dragged in the field for days and days!

If he lives until the next year, perhaps the same man will hire him again, without even giving him an opportunity of going to the hiring-ground. After those for hire are disposed of, those for sale are called up.

O, you happy free women, contrast *your* New Year's day with that of the poor bond-woman! With you it is a pleasant season, and the light of the day is blessed. Friendly wishes meet you every where, and gifts are showered upon you. Even hearts that have been estranged from you soften at this season, and lips that have been silent echo back, "I wish you a happy New Year." Children bring their little offerings, and raise their rosy lips for a caress. They are your own, and no hand but that of death can take them from you.

But to the slave mother New Year's day comes laden with peculiar sorrows. She sits on her cold cabin floor, watching the children who may all be torn from her the next morning; and often does she wish that she and they might die before the day dawns. She may be an ignorant creature, degraded by the system that has brutalized her from childhood; but she has a mother's instincts, and is capable of feeling a mother's agonies.

On one of these sale days, I saw a mother lead seven children to the auction-block. She knew that *some* of them would be taken from her;

but they took *all*. The children were sold to a slave-trader, and their mother was bought by a man in her own town. Before night her children were all far away. She begged the trader to tell her where he intended to take them; this he refused to do. How *could* he, when he knew he would sell them, one by one, wherever he could command the highest price? I met that mother in the street, and her wild, haggard face lives today in my mind. She wrung her hands in anguish, and exclaimed, "Gone! All gone! Why *don't* God kill me?" I had no words wherewith to comfort her. Instances of this kind are of daily, yea, of hourly occurrence.

Slaveholders have a method, peculiar to their institution, of getting rid of *old* slaves, whose lives have been worn out in their service. I knew an old woman, who for seventy years faithfully served her master. She had become almost helpless, from hard labor and disease. Her owners moved to Alabama, and the old black woman was left to be sold to any body who would give twenty dollars for her.

IV

The Slave Who Dared to Feel like a Man

TWO YEARS HAD passed since I entered Dr. Flint's family, and those years had brought much of the knowledge that comes from experience, though they had afforded little opportunity for any other kinds of knowledge.

My grandmother had, as much as possible, been a mother to her orphan grandchildren. By perseverance and unwearied industry, she was now mistress of a snug little home, surrounded with the necessaries of life.[1] She would have been happy could her children have shared them with her. There remained but three children and two grandchildren, all slaves. Most earnestly did she strive to make us feel that it was the will of God: that He had seen fit to place us under such circumstances; and though it seemed hard, we ought to pray for contentment.

It was a beautiful faith, coming from a mother who could not call her children her own. But I, and Benjamin, her youngest boy, condemned it. We reasoned that it was much more the will of God that we should be situated as she was. We longed for a home like hers. There we always found sweet balsam for our troubles. She was so loving, so sympathizing! She always met us with a smile, and listened with patience to all our sorrows. She spoke so hopefully, that unconsciously the clouds gave place to sunshine. There was a grand big oven there, too, that baked bread and nice things for the town, and we knew there was always a choice bit in store for us.

But, alas! even the charms of the old oven failed to reconcile us to our hard lot. Benjamin was now a tall, handsome lad, strongly and gracefully made, and with a spirit too bold and daring for a slave. My brother William, now twelve years old, had the same aversion to the word master that he had when he was an urchin of seven years. I was his confidant. He came to me with all his troubles. I remember one instance in particular. It was on a lovely spring morning, and when I marked the sunlight dancing here and there, its beauty seemed to mock my sadness. For my master, whose restless, craving, vicious nature roved about day and night, seeking whom to devour, had just left me, with stinging, scorching words; words that scathed ear and brain like fire. O, how I despised him! I thought how glad I should be, if some day when he walked the earth, it would open and swallow him up, and disencumber the world of a plague.

When he told me that I was made for his use, made to obey his command in *every* thing; that I was nothing but a slave, whose will must and should surrender to his, never before had my puny arm felt half so strong.

So deeply was I absorbed in painful reflections afterwards, that I neither saw nor heard the entrance of any one, till the voice of William sounded close beside me. "Linda," he said, "what makes you look so sad? I love you. O, Linda, isn't this a bad world? Every body seems so cross and unhappy. I wish I had died when poor father did."

I told him that every body was *not* cross, or unhappy; that those who had pleasant homes, and kind friends, and who were not afraid to love them, were happy. But we, who were slave-children, without father or mother, could not expect to be happy. We must be good; perhaps that would bring us contentment.

"Yes," he said, "I try to be good; but what's the use? They are all the time troubling me." Then he proceeded to relate his afternoon's difficulty with young master Nicholas. It seemed that the brother of master Nicholas had pleased himself with making up stories about William. Master Nicholas said he should be flogged, and he would do it. Whereupon he went to work; but William fought bravely, and the young master, finding he was getting the better of him, undertook to tie his hands behind him. He failed in that likewise. By dint of kicking and fisting, William came out of the skirmish none the worse for a few scratches.[2]

He continued to discourse on his young master's *meanness;* how he whipped the *little* boys, but was a perfect coward when a tussle ensued between him and white boys of his own size. On such occasions he always took to his legs. William had other charges to make against him. One was his rubbing up pennies with quicksilver, and passing them off for quarters of a dollar on an old man who kept a fruit stall. William was often sent to buy fruit, and he earnestly inquired of me what he ought to do under such circumstances. I told him it was certainly wrong to deceive the old man, and that it was his duty to tell him of the impositions practised by his young master. I assured him the old man would not be slow to comprehend the whole, and there the matter would end. William thought it might with the old man, but not with *him.* He said he did not mind the smart of the whip, but he did not like the *idea* of being whipped.

While I advised him to be good and forgiving I was not unconscious of the beam in my own eye.[3] It was the very knowledge of my own shortcomings that urged me to retain, if possible, some sparks of my brother's God-given nature. I had not lived fourteen years in slavery for nothing. I had felt, seen, and heard enough, to read the characters, and question the motives, of those around me. The war of my life had begun; and though one of God's most powerless creatures, I resolved never to be conquered. Alas, for me!

If there was one pure, sunny spot for me, I believed it to be in Benjamin's heart, and in another's, whom I loved with all the ardor of a girl's first love. My owner knew of it, and sought in every way to render me miserable. He did not resort to corporal punishment, but to all the petty, tyrannical ways that human ingenuity could devise.

I remember the first time I was punished. It was in the month of February. My grandmother had taken my old shoes, and replaced them with a new pair. I needed them; for several inches of snow had fallen, and it still continued to fall. When I walked through Mrs. Flint's room, their creaking grated harshly on her refined nerves. She called me to her, and asked what I had about me that made such a horrid noise. I told her it was my new shoes. "Take them off," said she; "and if you put them on again, I'll throw them into the fire."

I took them off, and my stockings also. She then sent me a long distance, on an errand. As I went through the snow, my bare feet tingled. That night I was very hoarse; and I went to bed thinking the next day would find me sick, perhaps dead. What was my grief on waking to find myself quite well!

I had imagined if I died, or was laid up for some time, that my mistress would feel a twinge of remorse that she had so hated "the little imp," as she styled me. It was my ignorance of that mistress that gave rise to such extravagant imaginings.

Dr. Flint occasionally had high prices offered for me; but he always said, "She don't belong to me. She is my daughter's property, and I have no right to sell her." Good, honest man! My young mistress was still a child, and I could look for no protection from her. I loved her, and she returned my affection. I once heard her father allude to her attachment to me; and his wife promptly replied that it proceeded from fear. This put unpleasant doubts into my mind. Did the child feign what she did not feel? or was her mother jealous of the mite of love she bestowed on me? I concluded it must be the latter. I said to myself, "Surely, little children are true."

One afternoon I sat at my sewing, feeling unusual depression of spirits. My mistress had been accusing me of an offence, of which I assured her I was perfectly innocent; but I saw, by the contemptuous curl of her lip, that she believed I was telling a lie.

I wondered for what wise purpose God was leading me through such thorny paths, and whether still darker days were in store for me. As I sat musing thus, the door opened softly, and William came in. "Well, brother," said I, "what is the matter this time?"

"O Linda, Ben and his master have had a dreadful time!" said he.

My first thought was that Benjamin was killed. "Don't be frightened, Linda," said William; "I will tell you all about it."

It appeared that Benjamin's master had sent for him, and he did not immediately obey the summons. When he did, his master was angry, and began to whip him. He resisted. Master and slave fought, and finally the master was thrown.[4] Benjamin had cause to tremble; for he had thrown to the ground his master—one of the richest men in town. I anxiously awaited the result.

That night I stole to my grandmother's house, and Benjamin also stole thither from his master's. My grandmother had gone to spend a day or two with an old friend living in the country.

"I have come," said Benjamin, "to tell you good by. I am going away."

I inquired where.

"To the north," he replied.

I looked at him to see whether he was in earnest. I saw it all in his firm, set mouth. I implored him not to go, but he paid no heed to my words. He said he was no longer a boy, and every day made his yoke more galling. He had raised his hand against his master, and was to be publicly whipped for the offence.[5] I reminded him of the poverty and hardships he must encounter among strangers. I told him he might be caught and brought back; and that was terrible to think of.

He grew vexed, and asked if poverty and hardships with freedom, were not preferable to our treatment in slavery. "Linda," he continued, "we are dogs here; foot-balls, cattle, every thing that's mean. No, I will not stay. Let them bring me back. We don't die but once."

He was right; but it was hard to give him up. "Go," said I, "and break your mother's heart."

I repented of my words ere they were out.

"Linda," said he, speaking as I had not heard him speak that evening, "how *could* you say that? Poor mother! be kind to her, Linda; and you, too, cousin Fanny."

Cousin Fanny was a friend who had lived some years with us.[6]

Farewells were exchanged, and the bright, kind boy, endeared to us by so many acts of love, vanished from our sight.

It is not necessary to state how he made his escape. Suffice it to say, he was on his way to New York when a violent storm overtook the vessel. The captain said he must put into the nearest port. This alarmed Benjamin, who was aware that he would be advertised in every port near his own town. His embarrassment was noticed by the captain. To port they went. There the advertisement met the captain's eye. Benjamin so exactly answered its description, that the captain laid hold on him, and bound him in chains. The storm passed, and they proceeded to New York. Before reaching that port Benjamin managed to get off his chains and throw them overboard. He escaped from the vessel, but was pursued, captured, and carried back to his master.[7]

When my grandmother returned home and found her youngest

child had fled, great was her sorrow; but, with characteristic piety, she said, "God's will be done." Each morning, she inquired if any news had been heard from her boy. Yes, news *was* heard. The master was rejoicing over a letter, announcing the capture of his human chattel.

That day seems but as yesterday, so well do I remember it. I saw him led through the streets in chains, to jail. His face was ghastly pale, yet full of determination. He had begged one of the sailors to go to his mother's house and ask her not to meet him. He said the sight of her distress would take from him all self-control. She yearned to see him, and she went; but she screened herself in the crowd, that it might be as her child had said.

We were not allowed to visit him; but we had known the jailer for years, and he was a kind-hearted man.[8] At midnight he opened the jail door for my grandmother and myself to enter, in disguise. When we entered the cell not a sound broke the stillness. "Benjamin, Benjamin!" whispered my grandmother. No answer. "Benjamin!" she again faltered. There was a jingle of chains. The moon had just risen, and cast an uncertain light through the bars of the window. We knelt down and took Benjamin's cold hands in ours. We did not speak. Sobs were heard, and Benjamin's lips were unsealed; for his mother was weeping on his neck. How vividly does memory bring back that sad night! Mother and son talked together. He asked her pardon for the suffering he had caused her. She said she had nothing to forgive; she could not blame his desire for freedom. He told her that when he was captured, he broke away, and was about casting himself into the river, when thoughts of *her* came over him, and he desisted. She asked if he did not also think of God. I fancied I saw his face grow fierce in the moonlight. He answered, "No, I did not think of him. When a man is hunted like a wild beast he forgets there is a God, a heaven. He forgets every thing in his struggle to get beyond the reach of the bloodhounds."

"Don't talk so, Benjamin," said she. "Put your trust in God. Be humble, my child, and your master will forgive you."

"Forgive me for *what*, mother? For not letting him treat me like a dog? No! I will never humble myself to him. I have worked for him for nothing all my life, and I am repaid with stripes and imprisonment. Here I will stay till I die, or till he sells me."

The poor mother shuddered at his words. I think he felt it; for when he next spoke, his voice was calmer. "Don't fret about me, mother. I ain't worth it," said he. "I wish I had some of your goodness. You bear every thing patiently, just as though you thought it was all right. I wish I could."

She told him she had not always been so; once, she was like him; but when sore troubles came upon her, and she had no arm to lean upon, she learned to call on God, and he lightened her burdens. She besought him to do likewise.

We overstaid our time, and were obliged to hurry from the jail.

Benjamin had been imprisoned three weeks, when my grandmother went to intercede for him with his master. He was immovable. He said Benjamin should serve as an example to the rest of his slaves; he should be kept in jail till he was subdued, or be sold if he got but one dollar for him. However, he afterwards relented in some degree. The chains were taken off, and we were allowed to visit him.

As his food was of the coarsest kind, we carried him as often as possible a warm supper, accompanied with some little luxury for the jailer.

Three months elapsed, and there was no prospect of release or of a purchaser. One day he was heard to sing and laugh. This piece of indecorum was told to his master, and the overseer was ordered to re-chain him. He was now confined in an apartment with other prisoners, who were covered with filthy rags. Benjamin was chained near them, and was soon covered with vermin. He worked at his chains till he succeeded in getting out of them. He passed them through the bars of the window, with a request that they should be taken to his master, and he should be informed that he was covered with vermin.

This audacity was punished with heavier chains, and prohibition of our visits.

My grandmother continued to send him fresh changes of clothes. The old ones were burned up. The last night we saw him in jail his mother still begged him to send for his master, and beg his pardon. Neither persuasion nor argument could turn him from his purpose. He calmly answered, "I am waiting his time."

Those chains were mournful to hear.

Another three months passed, and Benjamin left his prison walls. We that loved him waited to bid him a long and last farewell. A slave trader had bought him.[9] You remember, I told you what price he brought when ten years of age. Now he was more than twenty years old, and sold for three hundred dollars. The master had been blind to his own interest. Long confinement had made his face too pale, his form too thin; moreover, the trader had heard something of his character, and it did not strike him as suitable for a slave. He said he would give any price if the handsome lad was a girl. We thanked God that he was not.

Could you have seen that mother clinging to her child, when they fastened the irons upon his wrists; could you have heard her heart-rending groans, and seen her bloodshot eyes wander wildly from face to face, vainly pleading for mercy; could you have witnessed that scene as I saw it, you would exclaim, *Slavery is damnable!*

Benjamin, her youngest, her pet, was forever gone! She could not realize it. She had had an interview with the trader for the purpose of ascertaining if Benjamin could be purchased. She was told it was impossible, as he had given bonds not to sell him till he was out of the state. He promised that he would not sell him till he reached New Orleans.

With a strong arm and unvaried trust, my grandmother began her work of love. Benjamin must be free. If she succeeded, she knew they would still be separated; but the sacrifice was not too great. Day and night she labored. The trader's price would treble that he gave; but she was not discouraged.

She employed a lawyer to write to a gentleman, whom she knew, in New Orleans. She begged him to interest himself for Benjamin, and he willingly favored her request. When he saw Benjamin, and stated his business, he thanked him; but said he preferred to wait a while before making the trader an offer. He knew he had tried to obtain a high price for him, and had invariably failed. This encouraged him to make another effort for freedom. So one morning, long before day, Benjamin was missing. He was riding over the blue billows, bound for Baltimore.

For once his white face did him a kindly service. They had no suspicion that it belonged to a slave; otherwise, the law would have been followed out to the letter, and the *thing* rendered back to slavery. The brightest skies are often overshadowed by the darkest clouds. Benjamin was taken sick, and compelled to remain in Baltimore three weeks. His strength was slow in returning; and his desire to continue his journey seemed to retard his recovery. How could he get strength without air and exercise? He resolved to venture on a short walk. A by-street was selected, where he thought himself secure of not being met by any one that knew him; but a voice called out, "Halloo, Ben, my boy! what are you doing *here?*"

His first impulse was to run; but his legs trembled so that he could not stir. He turned to confront his antagonist, and behold, there stood his old master's next door neighbor! He thought it was all over with him now; but it proved otherwise. That man was a miracle. He possessed a goodly number of slaves, and yet was not quite deaf to that mystic clock, whose ticking is rarely heard in the slaveholder's breast.[10]

"Ben, you are sick," said he. "Why, you look like a ghost. I guess I gave you something of a start. Never mind, Ben, I am not going to touch you. You had a pretty tough time of it, and you may go on your way rejoicing for all me. But I would advise you to get out of this place plaguy quick, for there are several gentlemen here from our town." He described the nearest and safest route to New York, and added, "I shall be glad to tell your mother I have seen you. Good by, Ben."

Benjamin turned away, filled with gratitude, and surprised that the town he hated contained such a gem—a gem worthy of a purer setting.

This gentleman was a Northerner by birth, and had married a southern lady. On his return, he told my grandmother that he had seen her son, and of the service he had rendered him.

Benjamin reached New York safely, and concluded to stop there until he had gained strength enough to proceed further. It happened that my grandmother's only remaining son had sailed for the same city on business for his mistress.[11] Through God's providence, the brothers met. You may be sure it was a happy meeting. "O Phil," exclaimed Benjamin, "I am here at last." Then he told him how near he came to dying, almost in sight of free land, and how he prayed that he might live to get one breath of free air. He said life was worth something now, and it would be hard to die. In the old jail he had not valued it; once, he was tempted to destroy it; but something, he did not know what, had prevented him; perhaps it was fear. He had heard those who profess to be religious declare there was no heaven for self-murderers; and as his life had been pretty hot here, he did not desire a continuation of the same in another world. "If I die now," he exclaimed, "thank God, I shall die a freeman!"

He begged my uncle Phillip not to return south; but stay and work with him, till they earned enough to buy those at home. His brother told him it would kill their mother if he deserted her in her trouble. She had pledged her house, and with difficulty had raised money to buy him.[12] Would he be bought?

"No, never!" he replied. "Do you suppose, Phil, when I have got so far out of their clutches, I will give them one red cent? No! And do you suppose I would turn mother out of her home in her old age? That I would let her pay all those hard-earned dollars for me, and never to see me? For you know she will stay south as long as her other children are slaves. What a good mother! Tell her to buy *you*, Phil. You have been a comfort to her, and I have been a trouble. And Linda, poor Linda; what'll become of her? Phil, you don't know what a life they lead her. She has told me something about it, and I wish old Flint was dead, or a better man. When I was in jail, he asked her if she didn't want *him* to ask my master to forgive me, and take me home again. She told him, No; that I didn't want to go back. He got mad, and said we were all alike. I never despised my own master half as much as I do that man. There is many a worse slaveholder than my master; but for all that I would not be his slave."

While Benjamin was sick, he had parted with nearly all his clothes to pay necessary expenses. But he did not part with a little pin I fastened in his bosom when we parted. It was the most valuable thing I owned, and I thought none more worthy to wear it. He had it still.

His brother furnished him with clothes, and gave him what money he had.

They parted with moistened eyes; and as Benjamin turned away, he said, "Phil, I part with all my kindred." And so it proved. We never heard from him again.

Uncle Phillip came home; and the first words he uttered when he entered the house were, "Mother, Ben is free! I have seen him in New York." She stood looking at him with a bewildered air. "Mother, don't you believe it?" he said, laying his hand softly upon her shoulder. She raised her hands, and exclaimed, "God be praised! Let us thank him." She dropped on her knees, and poured forth her heart in prayer. Then Phillip must sit down and repeat to her every word Benjamin had said. He told her all; only he forbore to mention how sick and pale her darling looked. Why should he distress her when she could do him no good?

The brave old woman still toiled on, hoping to rescue some of her other children. After a while she succeeded in buying Phillip. She paid eight hundred dollars, and came home with the precious document that secured his freedom.[13] The happy mother and son sat together by the old hearthstone that night, telling how proud they were of each other, and how they would prove to the world that they could take care of themselves, as they had long taken care of others.[14] We all concluded by saying, "He that is *willing* to be a slave, let him be a slave."

V

The Trials of Girlhood

D URING THE FIRST years of my service in Dr. Flint's family, I was accustomed to share some indulgences with the children of my mistress. Though this seemed to me no more than right, I was grateful for it, and tried to merit the kindness by the faithful discharge of my duties. But I now entered on my fifteenth year—a sad epoch in the life of a slave girl. My master began to whisper foul words in my ear. Young as I was, I could not remain ignorant of their import. I tried to treat them with indifference or contempt. The master's age, my extreme youth, and the fear that his conduct would be reported to my grandmother, made him bear this treatment for many months. He was a crafty man, and resorted to many means to accomplish his purposes. Sometimes he had stormy, terrific ways, that made his victims tremble; sometimes he assumed a gentleness that he thought must surely subdue. Of the two, I preferred his stormy moods, although they left me trembling. He tried his utmost to corrupt the pure principles my grandmother had instilled. He peopled my young mind with unclean images, such as only a vile monster could think of. I turned from him with disgust and hatred. But he was my master. I was compelled to live under the same roof with him—where I saw a man forty years my senior daily violating the most sacred commandments of nature.[1] He told me I was his property; that I must be subject to his will in all things. My soul revolted against the mean tyranny. But where could I turn for protection? No matter whether the slave girl be as black as ebony or as fair as her mistress. In either case, there is no shadow of law to protect her from insult, from violence, or even from death; all these are inflicted by fiends who bear the shape of men.[2] The mistress, who ought to protect the helpless victim, has no other feelings towards her but those of jealousy and rage. The degradation, the wrongs, the vices, that grow out of slavery, are more than I can describe. They are greater than you would willingly believe. Surely, if you credited one half the truths that are told you concerning the helpless millions suffering in this cruel bondage, you at the north would not help to tighten the yoke. You surely would refuse to do for the master, on your own soil, the mean and cruel work which trained bloodhounds and the lowest class of whites do for him at the south.[3]

Every where the years bring to all enough of sin and sorrow; but in slavery the very dawn of life is darkened by these shadows. Even the little child, who is accustomed to wait on her mistress and her children, will learn, before she is twelve years old, why it is that her mistress hates such and such a one among the slaves. Perhaps the child's own mother is among those hated ones. She listens to violent outbreaks of jealous passion, and cannot help understanding what is the cause. She will become prematurely knowing in evil things. Soon she will learn to tremble when she hears her master's footfall. She will be compelled to realize that she is no longer a child: If God has bestowed beauty upon her, it will prove her greatest curse. That which commands admiration in the white woman only hastens the degradation of the female slave. I know that some are too much brutalized by slavery to feel the humiliation of their position; but many slaves feel it most acutely, and shrink from the memory of it. I cannot tell how much I suffered in the presence of these wrongs, nor how I am still pained by the retrospect. My master met me at every turn, reminding me that I belonged to him, and swearing by heaven and earth that he would compel me to submit to him. If I went out for a breath of fresh air, after a day of unwearied toil, his footsteps dogged me. If I knelt by my mother's grave, his dark shadow fell on me even there. The light heart which nature had given me became heavy with sad forebodings. The other slaves in my master's house noticed the change. Many of them pitied me; but none dared to ask the cause. They had no need to inquire. They knew too well the guilty practices under that roof; and they were aware that to speak of them was an offence that never went unpunished.

I longed for some one to confide in. I would have given the world to have laid my head on my grandmother's faithful bosom, and told her all my troubles. But Dr. Flint swore he would kill me, if I was not as silent as the grave. Then, although my grandmother was all in all to me, I feared her as well as loved her. I had been accustomed to look up to her with a respect bordering upon awe. I was very young, and felt shamefaced about telling her such impure things, especially as I knew her to be very strict on such subjects. Moreover, she was a woman of a high spirit. She was usually very quiet in her demeanor; but if her indignation was once roused, it was not very easily quelled. I had been told that she once chased a white gentleman with a loaded pistol, because he insulted one of her daughters.[4] I dreaded the consequences of a violent outbreak; and both pride and fear kept me silent. But though I did not confide in my grandmother, and even evaded her vigilant watchfulness and inquiry, her presence in the neighborhood was some protection to me. Though she had been a slave, Dr. Flint was afraid of her. He dreaded her scorching rebukes. Moreover, she was known and patronized by many people; and he did not wish to have his villainy made public. It was lucky for me that I did not live on a distant plantation, but in a town not so large that the inhabitants were ignorant of each other's affairs. Bad as are the laws and customs in a slaveholding community, the doctor, as a professional man, deemed it prudent to keep up some outward show of decency.

O, what days and nights of fear and sorrow that man caused me! Reader, it is not to awaken sympathy for myself that I am telling you truthfully what I suffered in slavery. I do it to kindle a flame of compassion in your hearts for my sisters who are still in bondage, suffering as I once suffered.

I once saw two beautiful children playing together. One was a fair white child; the other was her slave, and also her sister. When I saw them embracing each other, and heard their joyous laughter, I turned sadly away from the lovely sight. I foresaw the inevitable blight that would fall on the little slave's heart. I knew how soon her laughter would be changed to sighs. The fair child grew up to be a still fairer woman. From childhood to womanhood her pathway was blooming with flowers, and overarched by a sunny sky. Scarcely one day of her life had been clouded when the sun rose on her happy bridal morning.

How had those years dealt with her slave sister, the little playmate of her childhood? She, also, was very beautiful; but the flowers and sunshine of love were not for her. She drank the cup of sin, and shame, and misery, whereof her persecuted race are compelled to drink.

In view of these things, why are ye silent, ye free men and women of the north? Why do your tongues falter in maintenance of the right?

Would that I had more ability! But my heart is so full, and my pen is so weak! There are noble men and women who plead for us, striving to help those who cannot help themselves. God bless them! God give them strength and courage to go on! God bless those, every where, who are laboring to advance the cause of humanity!

VI

The Jealous Mistress

I WOULD TEN THOUSAND times rather that my children should be the half-starved paupers of Ireland than to be the most pampered among the slaves of America.[1] I would rather drudge out my life on a cotton plantation, till the grave opened to give me rest, than to live with an unprincipled master and a jealous mistress. The felon's home in a penitentiary is preferable. He may repent, and turn from the error of his ways, and so find peace; but it is not so with a favorite slave. She is not allowed to have any pride of character. It is deemed a crime in her to wish to be virtuous.

Mrs. Flint possessed the key to her husband's character before I was born. She might have used this knowledge to counsel and to screen the young and the innocent among her slaves; but for them she had no sympathy. They were the objects of her constant suspicion and malevolence. She watched her husband with unceasing vigilance; but he was well practised in means to evade it. What he could not find opportunity to say in words he manifested in signs. He invented more than were ever thought of in a deaf and dumb asylum. I let them pass, as if I did not understand what he meant; and many were the curses and threats bestowed on me for my stupidity. One day he caught me teaching myself to write.[2] He frowned, as if he was not well pleased; but I suppose he came to the conclusion that such an accomplishment might help to advance his favorite scheme. Before long, notes were often slipped into my hand. I would return them, saying, "I can't read them, sir." "Can't you?" he replied; "then I must read them to you." He always finished the reading by asking, "Do you understand?" Sometimes he would complain of the heat of the tea room, and order his supper to be placed on a small table in the piazza. He would seat himself there with a well-satisfied smile, and tell me to stand by and brush away the flies. He would eat very slowly, pausing between the mouthfuls. These intervals were employed in describing the happiness I was so foolishly throwing away, and in threatening me with the penalty that finally awaited my stubborn disobedience. He boasted much of the forbearance he had exercised towards me, and reminded me that there was a limit to his patience. When I succeeded in avoiding opportunities for him to talk to me at home, I was ordered to come to his office, to do some errand. When there, I was obliged to stand and listen to such language as he saw fit to address to me. Sometimes I so openly expressed my contempt for him that he would become violently enraged, and I wondered why he did not strike me. Circumstanced as he was, he probably thought it was better policy to be forbearing. But the state of things grew worse and worse daily. In desperation I told him that I must and would apply to my grandmother for protection. He threatened me with death, and worse than death, if I made any complaint to her. Strange to say, I did not despair. I was naturally of a buoyant disposition, and always I had a hope of somehow getting out of his clutches. Like many a poor, simple slave before me, I trusted that some threads of joy would yet be woven into my dark destiny.

I had entered my sixteenth year, and every day it became more apparent that my presence was intolerable to Mrs. Flint. Angry words frequently passed between her and her husband. He had never punished me himself, and he would not allow any body else to punish me. In that respect, she was never satisfied; but, in her angry moods, no terms were too vile for her to bestow upon me. Yet I, whom she detested so bitterly, had far more pity for her than he had, whose duty it was to make her life happy. I never wronged her, or wished to wrong her; and one word of kindness from her would have brought me to her feet.

After repeated quarrels between the doctor and his wife, he announced his intention to take his youngest daughter, then four years old, to sleep in his apartment.[3] It was necessary that a servant should sleep in the same room, to be on hand if the child stirred. I was selected for that office, and informed for what purpose that arrangement had been made. By managing to keep within sight of people, as much as possible, during the day time, I had hitherto succeeded in eluding my master, though a razor was often held to my throat to force me to change this line of policy. At night I slept by the side of my great aunt, where I felt safe. He was too prudent to come into her room. She was an old woman, and had been in the family many years.[4] Moreover, as a married man, and a professional man, he deemed it necessary to save appearances in some degree. But he resolved to remove the obstacle in the way of his scheme; and he thought he had planned it so that he should evade suspicion. He was well aware how much I prized my refuge by the side of my old aunt, and he determined to dispossess me of it. The first night the doctor had the little child in his room alone. The next morning, I was ordered to take my station as nurse the following night. A kind Providence interposed in my favor. During the day Mrs. Flint heard of this new arrangement, and a storm followed. I rejoiced to hear it rage.

After a while my mistress sent for me to come to her room. Her first question was, "Did you know you were to sleep in the doctor's room?"

"Yes, ma'am."

"Who told you?"

"My master."

"Will you answer truly all the questions I ask?"

"Yes, ma'am."

"Tell me, then, as you hope to be forgiven, are you innocent of what I have accused you?"

"I am."

She handed me a Bible, and said, "Lay your hand on your heart, kiss this holy book, and swear before God that you tell me the truth."

I took the oath she required, and I did it with a clear conscience.

"You have taken God's holy word to testify your innocence," said she. "If you have deceived me, beware! Now take this stool, sit down, look me directly in the face, and tell me all that has passed between your master and you."

I did as she ordered. As I went on with my account her color changed frequently, she wept, and sometimes groaned. She spoke in tones so sad, that I was touched by her grief. The tears came to my eyes; but I was soon convinced that her emotions arose from anger and wounded pride. She felt that her marriage vows were desecrated, her dignity insulted; but she had no compassion for the poor victim of her husband's perfidy. She pitied herself as a martyr; but she was incapable of feeling for the condition of shame and misery in which her unfortunate, helpless slave was placed.

Yet perhaps she had some touch of feeling for me; for when the conference was ended, she spoke kindly, and promised to protect me.

I should have been much comforted by this assurance if I could have had confidence in it; but my experiences in slavery had filled me with distrust. She was not a very refined woman, and had not much control over her passions. I was an object of her jealousy, and, consequently, of her hatred; and I knew I could not expect kindness or confidence from her under the circumstances in which I was placed. I could not blame her. Slaveholders' wives feel as other women would under similar circumstances. The fire of her temper kindled from small sparks, and now the flame became so intense that the doctor was obliged to give up his intended arrangement.

I knew I had ignited the torch, and I expected to suffer for it afterwards; but I felt too thankful to my mistress for the timely aid she rendered me to care much about that. She now took me to sleep in a room adjoining her own. There I was an object of her especial care, though not of her especial comfort, for she spent many a sleepless night to watch over me. Sometimes I woke up, and found her bending over me. At other times she whispered in my ear, as though it was her husband who was speaking to me, and listened to hear what I would answer. If she startled me, on such occasions, she would glide stealthily away; and the next morning she would tell me I had been talking in my sleep, and ask who I was talking to. At last, I began to be fearful for my life. It had been often threatened; and you can imagine, better than I can describe, what an unpleasant sensation it must produce to wake up in the dead of night and find a jealous woman bending over you. Terrible as this experience was, I had fears that it would give place to one more terrible.

My mistress grew weary of her vigils; they did not prove satisfactory. She changed her tactics. She now tried the trick of accusing my master of crime, in my presence, and gave my name as the author of the accusation. To my utter astonishment, he replied, "I don't believe it: but if she did acknowledge it, you tortured her into exposing me."

Tortured into exposing him! Truly, Satan had no difficulty in distinguishing the color of his soul! I understood his object in making this false representation. It was to show me that I gained nothing by seeking the protection of my mistress; that the power was still all in his own hands. I pitied Mrs. Flint. She was a second wife, many years the junior of her husband; and the hoary-headed miscreant was enough to try the patience of a wiser and better woman. She was completely foiled, and knew not how to proceed. She would gladly have had me flogged for my supposed false oath; but, as I have already stated, the doctor never allowed any one to whip me. The old sinner was politic. The application of the lash might have led to remarks that would have exposed him in the eyes of his children and grandchildren.[5] How often did I rejoice that I lived in a town where all the inhabitants knew each other! If I had been on a remote plantation, or lost among the multitude of a crowded city, I should not be a living woman at this day.

The secrets of slavery are concealed like those of the Inquisition. My master was, to my knowledge, the father of eleven slaves. But did the mothers dare to tell who was the father of their children? Did the other slaves dare to allude to it, except in whispers among themselves? No, indeed! They knew too well the terrible consequences.

My grandmother could not avoid seeing things which excited her suspicions. She was uneasy about me, and tried various ways to buy me; but the neverchanging answer was always repeated: "Linda does not belong to *me*. She is my daughter's property, and I have no legal right to sell her." The conscientious man! He was too scrupulous to *sell* me; but he had no scruples whatever about committing a much greater wrong against the helpless young girl placed under his guardianship, as his daughter's property. Sometimes my persecutor would ask me whether I would like to be sold. I told him I would rather be sold to any body than to lead such a life as I did. On such occasions he would assume the air of a very injured individual, and reproach me for my ingratitude. "Did I not take you into the house, and make you the companion of my own children?" he would say. "Have I ever treated you like a negro? I have never allowed you to be punished, not even to please your mistress. And this is the recompense I get, you ungrateful girl!" I answered that he had reasons of his own for screening me from punishment, and that the course he pursued made my mistress hate me and persecute me. If I wept, he would say, "Poor child! Don't cry! don't cry! I will make peace for you with your mistress. Only let me arrange matters in my own way. Poor, foolish girl! you don't know what is for your own good. I would cherish you. I would make a lady of you. Now go, and think of all I have promised you."

I did think of it.

Reader, I draw no imaginary pictures of southern homes. I am telling you the plain truth. Yet when victims make their escape from this wild beast of Slavery, northerners consent to act the part of bloodhounds, and hunt the poor fugitive back into his den, "full of dead men's bones, and all uncleanness."[6] Nay, more, they are not only willing, but proud, to give their daughters in marriage to slaveholders. The poor girls have romantic notions of a sunny clime, and of the flowering vines that all the year round shade a happy home. To what disappointments are they destined! The young wife soon learns that the husband in whose hands she has placed her happiness pays no regard to his marriage vows. Children of every shade of complexion play with her own fair babies, and too well she knows that they are born unto him of his own household. Jealousy and hatred enter the flowery home, and it is ravaged of its loveliness.

Southern women often marry a man knowing that he is the father of many little slaves. They do not trouble themselves about it. They regard such children as property, as marketable as the pigs on the plantation; and it is seldom that they do not make them aware of this by passing them into the slavetrader's hands as soon as possible, and thus getting them out of their sight. I am glad to say there are some honorable exceptions.

I have myself known two southern wives who exhorted their husbands to free those slaves towards whom they stood in a "parental relation"; and their request was granted. These husbands blushed before the superior nobleness of their wives' natures. Though they had only counselled them to do that which it was their duty to do, it commanded their respect, and rendered their conduct more exemplary. Concealment was at an end, and confidence took the place of distrust.

Though this bad institution deadens the moral sense, even in white women, to a fearful extent, it is not altogether extinct. I have heard southern ladies say of Mr. Such a one, "He not only thinks it no disgrace to be the father of those little niggers, but he is not ashamed to call himself their master. I declare, such things ought not to be tolerated in any decent society!"

VII

The Lover

WHY DOES THE SLAVE ever love? Why allow the tendrils of the heart to twine around objects which may at any moment be wrenched away by the hand of violence? When separations come by the hand of death, the pious soul can bow in resignation, and say, "Not my will, but thine be done, O Lord!"[1] But when the ruthless hand of man strikes the blow, regardless of the misery he causes, it is hard to be submissive. I did not reason thus when I was a young girl. Youth will be youth. I loved, and I indulged the hope that the dark clouds around me would turn out a bright lining. I forgot that in the land of my birth the shadows are too dense for light to penetrate. A land

"Where laughter is not mirth; nor thought the mind;
Nor words a language; nor e'en men mankind.

Where cries reply to curses, shrieks to blows,
And each is tortured in his separate hell."[2]

There was in the neighborhood a young colored carpenter; a free
born man. We had been well acquainted in childhood, and frequently
met together afterwards. We became mutually attached, and he proposed to marry me. I loved him with all the ardor of a young girl's
first love. But when I reflected that I was a slave, and that the laws gave
no sanction to the marriage of such, my heart sank within me.[3] My
lover wanted to buy me; but I knew that Dr. Flint was too wilful and
arbitrary a man to consent to that arrangement. From him, I was sure
of experiencing all sorts of opposition, and I had nothing to hope
from my mistress. She would have been delighted to have got rid of
me, but not in that way. It would have relieved her mind of a burden
if she could have seen me sold to some distant state, but if I was married near home I should be just as much in her husband's power as
I had previously been,—for the husband of a slave has no power to
protect her. Moreover, my mistress, like many others, seemed to think
that slaves had no right to any family ties of their own; that they were
created merely to wait upon the family of the mistress. I once heard
her abuse a young slave girl, who told her that a colored man wanted
to make her his wife. "I will have you peeled and pickled, my lady,"
said she, "if I ever hear you mention that subject again.[4] Do you suppose that I will have you tending *my* children with the children of that
nigger?" The girl to whom she said this had a mulatto child, of course
not acknowledged by its father. The poor black man who loved her
would have been proud to acknowledge his helpless offspring.

Many and anxious were the thoughts I revolved in my mind. I was
at a loss what to do. Above all things, I was desirous to spare my lover
the insults that had cut so deeply into my own soul. I talked with my

grandmother about it, and partly told her my fears. I did not dare to tell her the worst. She had long suspected all was not right, and if I confirmed her suspicions I knew a storm would rise that would prove the overthrow of all my hopes.

This love-dream had been my support through many trials; and I could not bear to run the risk of having it suddenly dissipated. There was a lady in the neighborhood, a particular friend of Dr. Flint's, who often visited the house. I had a great respect for her, and she had always manifested a friendly interest in me. Grandmother thought she would have great influence with the doctor. I went to this lady, and told her my story. I told her I was aware that my lover's being a free-born man would prove a great objection; but he wanted to buy me; and if Dr. Flint would consent to that arrangement, I felt sure he would be willing to pay any reasonable price. She knew that Mrs. Flint disliked me; therefore, I ventured to suggest that perhaps my mistress would approve of my being sold, as that would rid her of me. The lady listened with kindly sympathy, and promised to do her utmost to promote my wishes. She had an interview with the doctor, and I believe she pleaded my cause earnestly; but it was all to no purpose.

How I dreaded my master now! Every minute I expected to be summoned to his presence; but the day passed, and I heard nothing from him. The next morning, a message was brought to me: "Master wants you in his study." I found the door ajar, and I stood a moment gazing at the hateful man who claimed a right to rule me, body and soul. I entered, and tried to appear calm. I did not want him to know how my heart was bleeding. He looked fixedly at me, with an expression which seemed to say, "I have half a mind to kill you on the spot." At last he broke the silence, and that was a relief to both of us.

"So you want to be married, do you?" said he, "and to a free nigger."

"Yes, sir."

"Well, I'll soon convince you whether I am your master, or the nig-ger fellow you honor so highly. If you *must* have a husband, you may take up with one of my slaves."

What a situation I should be in, as the wife of one of *his* slaves, even if my heart had been interested!

I replied, "Don't you suppose, sir, that a slave can have some pref-erence about marrying? Do you suppose that all men are alike to her?"

"Do you love this nigger?" said he, abruptly.

"Yes, sir."

"How dare you tell me so!" he exclaimed, in great wrath. After a slight pause, he added, "I supposed you thought more of yourself; that you felt above the insults of such puppies."

I replied, "If he is a puppy I am a puppy, for we are both of the ne-gro race. It is right and honorable for us to love each other. The man you call a puppy never insulted me, sir; and he would not love me if he did not believe me to be a virtuous woman."

He sprang upon me like a tiger, and gave me a stunning blow. It was the first time he had ever struck me; and fear did not enable me to control my anger. When I had recovered a little from the effects, I exclaimed, "You have struck me for answering you honestly. How I despise you!"

There was silence for some minutes. Perhaps he was deciding what should be my punishment; or, perhaps, he wanted to give me time to reflect on what I had said, and to whom I had said it. Finally, he asked, "Do you know what you have said?"

"Yes, sir; but your treatment drove me to it."

"Do you know that I have a right to do as I like with you,—that I can kill you, if I please?"

"You have tried to kill me, and I wish you had; but you have no right to do as you like with me."

"Silence!" he exclaimed, in a thundering voice. "By heavens, girl, you forget yourself too far! Are you mad? If you are, I will soon bring you to your senses. Do you think any other master would bear what I have borne from you this morning? Many masters would have killed you on the spot. How would you like to be sent to jail for your insolence?"

"I know I have been disrespectful, sir," I replied; "but you drove me to it; I couldn't help it. As for the jail, there would be more peace for me there than there is here."

"You deserve to go there," said he, "and to be under such treatment, that you would forget the meaning of the word *peace*. It would do you good. It would take some of your high notions out of you. But I am not ready to send you there yet, notwithstanding your ingratitude for all my kindness and forbearance. You have been the plague of my life. I have wanted to make you happy, and I have been repaid with the basest ingratitude; but though you have proved yourself incapable of appreciating my kindness, I will be lenient towards you, Linda. I will give you one more chance to redeem your character. If you behave yourself and do as I require, I will forgive you and treat you as I always have done; but if you disobey me, I will punish you as I would the meanest slave on my plantation. Never let me hear that fellow's name mentioned again. If I ever know of your speaking to him, I will cowhide you both; and if I catch him lurking about my premises, I will shoot him as soon as I would a dog. Do you hear what I say? I'll teach you a lesson about marriage and free niggers! Now go, and let this be the last time I have occasion to speak to you on this subject."

Reader, did you ever hate? I hope not. I never did but once; and I trust I never shall again. Somebody has called it "the atmosphere of hell"; and I believe it is so.

For a fortnight the doctor did not speak to me. He thought to mortify me; to make me feel that I had disgraced myself by receiving the honorable addresses of a respectable colored man, in preference to the base proposals of a white man. But though his lips disdained to address me, his eyes were very loquacious. No animal ever watched its prey more narrowly than he watched me. He knew that I could write, though he had failed to make me read his letters; and he was now troubled lest I should exchange letters with another man. After a while he became weary of silence; and I was sorry for it. One morning, as he passed through the hall, to leave the house, he contrived to thrust a note into my hand. I thought I had better read it, and spare myself the vexation of having him read it to me. It expressed regret for the blow he had given me, and reminded me that I myself was wholly to blame for it. He hoped I had become convinced of the injury I was doing myself by incurring his displeasure. He wrote that he had made up his mind to go to Louisiana; that he should take several slaves with him, and intended I should be one of the number. My mistress would remain where she was; therefore I should have nothing to fear from that quarter. If I merited kindness from him, he assured me that it would be lavishly bestowed. He begged me to think over the matter, and answer the following day.

The next morning I was called to carry a pair of scissors to his room. I laid them on the table, with the letter beside them. He thought it was my answer, and did not call me back. I went as usual to attend my young mistress to and from school. He met me in the street, and ordered me to stop at his office on my way back. When I entered, he showed me his letter, and asked me why I had not answered it. I replied, "I am your daughter's property, and it is in your power to send me, or take me, wherever you please." He said he was very glad to find me so willing to go, and that we should start early in the autumn. He had a large practice in the town, and I rather thought he had made up the story merely to frighten me. However that might be, I was determined that I would never go to Louisiana with him.

Summer passed away, and early in the autumn Dr. Flint's eldest son was sent to Louisiana to examine the country, with a view to emigrating. That news did not disturb me. I knew very well that I should not be sent with *him*. That I had not been taken to the plantation before this time, was owing to the fact that his son was there. He was jealous of his son; and jealousy of the overseer had kept him from punishing me by sending me into the fields to work. Is it strange that I was not proud of these protectors? As for the overseer, he was a man for whom I had less respect than I had for a bloodhound.

Young Mr. Flint did not bring back a favorable report of Louisiana, and I heard no more of that scheme. Soon after this, my lover met me at the corner of the street, and I stopped to speak to him. Looking up, I saw my master watching us from his window. I hurried home, trembling with fear. I was sent for, immediately, to go to his room. He met me with a blow. "When is mistress to be married?" said he, in a sneering tone. A shower of oaths and imprecations followed. How thankful I was that my lover was a free man! that my tyrant had no power to flog him for speaking to me in the street!

Again and again I revolved in my mind how all this would end. There was no hope that the doctor would consent to sell me on any terms. He had an iron will, and was determined to keep me, and to conquer me. My lover was an intelligent and religious man. Even if he could have obtained permission to marry me while I was a slave, the marriage would give him no power to protect me from my master. It would have made him miserable to witness the insults I should have been subjected to. And then, if we had children, I knew they must "follow the condition of the mother." What a terrible blight that would be on the heart of a free, intelligent father! For *his* sake, I felt that I ought not to link his fate with my own unhappy destiny. He was going to Savannah to see about a little property left him by an uncle; and hard as it was to bring my feelings to it, I earnestly entreated him not to come back. I advised him to go to the Free States, where his tongue would not be tied, and where his intelligence would be of more avail to him. He left me, still hoping the day would come when I could be bought. With me the lamp of hope had gone out. The dream of my girlhood was over. I felt lonely and desolate.

Still I was not stripped of all. I still had my good grandmother, and my affectionate brother. When he put his arms round my neck, and looked into my eyes, as if to read there the troubles I dared not tell, I felt that I still had something to love. But even that pleasant emotion was chilled by the reflection that he might be torn from me at any moment, by some sudden freak of my master. If he had known how we love each other, I think he would have exulted in separating us. We often planned together how we could get to the north. But, as William remarked, such things are easier said than done. My movements were very closely watched, and we had no means of getting any money to defray our expenses. As for grandmother, she was strongly opposed to her children's undertaking any such project. She had not forgotten poor Benjamin's sufferings, and she was afraid that if another child tried to escape, he would have a similar or a worse fate. To me, nothing seemed more dreadful than my present life. I said to myself, "William *must* be free. He shall go to the north, and I will follow him." Many a slave sister has formed the same plans.

VIII

What Slaves Are Taught to Think of the North

S LAVEHOLDERS PRIDE THEMSELVES upon being honorable men; but if you were to hear the enormous lies they tell their slaves, you would have small respect for their veracity. I have spoken plain English. Pardon me. I cannot use a milder term. When they visit the north, and return home, they tell their slaves of the runaways they have seen, and describe them to be in the most deplorable condition. A slaveholder once told me that he had seen a runaway friend of mine in New York, and that she besought him to take her back to her master, for she was literally dying of starvation; that many days she had only one cold potato to eat, and at other times could get nothing at all. He said he refused to take her, because he knew her master would not thank him for bringing such a miserable wretch to his house. He ended by saying to me, "This is the punishment she brought on herself for running away from a kind master."

This whole story was false. I afterwards staid with that friend in

New York, and found her in comfortable circumstances. She had never thought of such a thing as wishing to go back to slavery. Many of the slaves believe such stories, and think it is not worth while to exchange slavery for such a hard kind of freedom. It is difficult to persuade such that freedom could make them useful men, and enable them to protect their wives and children. If those heathens in our Christian land had as much teaching as some Hindoos, they would think otherwise. They would know that liberty is more valuable than life. They would begin to understand their own capabilities, and exert themselves to become men and women.

But while the Free States sustain a law which hurls fugitives back into slavery, how can the slaves resolve to become men? There are some who strive to protect wives and daughters from the insults of their masters; but those who have such sentiments have had advantages above the general mass of slaves. They have been partially civilized and Christianized by favorable circumstances. Some are bold enough to *utter* such sentiments to their masters. O, that there were more of them!

Some poor creatures have been so brutalized by the lash that they will sneak out of the way to give their masters free access to their wives and daughters. Do you think this proves the black man to belong to an inferior order of beings? What would *you* be, if you had been born and brought up a slave, with generations of slaves for ancestors? I admit that the black man *is* inferior. But what is it that makes him so? It is the ignorance in which white men compel him to live; it is the torturing whip that lashes manhood out of him; it is the fierce bloodhounds of the South, and the scarcely less cruel human bloodhounds of the north, who enforce the Fugitive Slave Law. *They* do the work.[1]

Southern gentlemen indulge in the most contemptuous expressions about the Yankees, while they, on their part, consent to do the vilest work for them, such as the ferocious bloodhounds and the despised negro-hunters are employed to do at home. When southerners go to the north, they are proud to do them honor; but the northern man is not welcome south of Mason and Dixon's line, unless he suppresses every thought and feeling at variance with their "peculiar institution."[2] Nor is it enough to be silent. The masters are not pleased, unless they obtain a greater degree of subservience than that; and they are generally accommodated. Do they respect the northerner for this? I trow not. Even the slaves despise "a northern man with southern principles"; and that is the class they generally see. When northerners go to the south to reside, they prove very apt scholars. They soon imbibe the sentiments and disposition of their neighbors, and generally go beyond their teachers. Of the two, they are proverbially the hardest masters.

They seem to satisfy their consciences with the doctrine that God created the Africans to be slaves. What a libel upon the heavenly Father, who "made of one blood all nations of men!"[3] And then who *are* Africans? Who can measure the amount of Anglo-Saxon blood coursing in the veins of American slaves?

I have spoken of the pains slaveholders take to give their slaves a bad opinion of the north; but, notwithstanding this, intelligent slaves are aware that they have many friends in the Free States. Even the most ignorant have some confused notions about it. They knew that I could read; and I was often asked if I had seen any thing in the newspapers about white folks over in the big north, who were trying to get their freedom for them. Some believe that the abolitionists have already made them free, and that it is established by law, but that their masters prevent the law from going into effect. One woman begged me to get a newspaper and read it over. She said her husband told her that the black people had sent word to the queen of 'Merica that they were all slaves; that she didn't believe it, and went to Washington city to see the president about it. They quarrelled; she drew her sword upon him, and swore that he should help her to make them all free.

That poor, ignorant woman thought that America was governed by a Queen, to whom the President was subordinate. I wish the President was subordinate to Queen Justice.[4]

IX

Sketches of Neighboring Slaveholders

T HERE WAS A PLANTER in the country, not far from us, whom I will call Mr. Litch.[1] He was an ill-bred, uneducated man, but very wealthy. He had six hundred slaves, many of whom he did not know by sight. His extensive plantation was managed by well-paid overseers. There was a jail and a whipping post on his grounds; and whatever cruelties were perpetrated there, they passed without comment. He was so effectually screened by his great wealth that he was called to no account for his crimes, not even for murder.

Various were the punishments resorted to. A favorite one was to tie a rope round a man's body, and suspend him from the ground. A fire was kindled over him, from which was suspended a piece of fat pork. As this cooked, the scalding drops of fat continually fell on the bare flesh. On his own plantation, he required very strict obedience to the eighth commandment.[2] But depredations on the neighbors were allowable, provided the culprit managed to evade detection or suspicion. If a neighbor brought a charge of theft against any of his slaves, he was browbeaten by the master, who assured him that his slaves had enough of every thing at home, and had no inducement to steal. No sooner was the neighbor's back turned, than the accused was sought out, and whipped for his lack of discretion. If a slave stole from him even a pound of meat or a peck of corn, if detection followed, he was put in chains and imprisoned, and so kept till his form was attenuated by hunger and suffering.

A freshet once bore his wine cellar and meat house miles away from the plantation. Some slaves followed, and secured bits of meat and bottles of wine. Two were detected; a ham and some liquor being found in their huts. They were summoned by their master. No words were used, but a club felled them to the ground. A rough box was their coffin, and their interment was a dog's burial. Nothing was said.[3]

Murder was so common on his plantation that he feared to be alone after nightfall. He might have believed in ghosts.

His brother, if not equal in wealth, was at least equal in cruelty. His bloodhounds were well trained. Their pen was spacious, and a terror to the slaves. They were let loose on a runaway, and, if they tracked him, they literally tore the flesh from his bones. When this slaveholder died, his shrieks and groans were so frightful that they appalled his own friends. His last words were, "I am going to hell; bury my money with me."

After death his eyes remained open. To press the lids down, silver dollars were laid on them. These were buried with him. From this circumstance, a rumor went abroad that his coffin was filled with money. Three times his grave was opened, and his coffin taken out. The last time, his body was found on the ground, and a flock of buzzards were pecking at it. He was again interred, and a sentinel set over his grave. The perpetrators were never discovered.[4]

Cruelty is contagious in uncivilized communities. Mr. Conant, a neighbor of Mr. Litch, returned from town one evening in a partial state of intoxication. His body servant gave him some offence. He was divested of his clothes, except his shirt, whipped, and tied to a large tree in front of the house. It was a stormy night in winter. The wind blew bitterly cold, and the boughs of the old tree crackled under falling sleet. A member of the family, fearing he would freeze to death, begged that he might be taken down; but the master would not relent. He remained there three hours; and, when he was cut down, he was more dead than alive. Another slave, who stole a pig from this master, to appease his hunger, was terribly flogged. In desperation, he tried to run away. But at the end of two miles, he was so faint with loss of blood, he thought he was dying. He had a wife, and he longed to see her once more. Too sick to walk, he crept back that long distance on his hands and knees. When he reached his master's, it was night. He had not strength to rise and open the gate. He moaned, and tried to call for help. I had a friend living in the same family. At last his cry reached her. She went out and found the prostrate man at the gate. She ran back to the house for assistance, and two men returned with her. They carried him in, and laid him on the floor. The back of his shirt was one clot of blood. By means of lard, my friend loosened it from the raw flesh. She bandaged him, gave him cool drink, and left him to rest. The master said he deserved a hundred more lashes. When his own labor was stolen from him, he had stolen food to appease his hunger. This was his crime.

Another neighbor was a Mrs. Wade. At no hour of the day was there cessation of the lash on her premises. Her labors began with the dawn, and did not cease till long after nightfall. The barn was her particular place of torture. There she lashed the slaves with the might of a man. An old slave of hers once said to me, "It is hell in missis's house. 'Pears I can never get out. Day and night I prays to die."

The mistress died before the old woman, and, when dying, entreated her husband not to permit any one of her slaves to look on her after death. A slave who had nursed her children, and had still a child in her care, watched her chance, and stole with it in her arms to the room where lay her dead mistress. She gazed a while on her, then raised her hand and dealt two blows on her face, saying, as she did so, "The devil is got you *now!*" She forgot that the child was looking on. She had just begun to talk; and she said to her father, "I did see ma, and mammy did strike ma, so," striking her own face with her little hand. The master was startled. He could not imagine how the nurse could obtain access to the room where the corpse lay; for he kept the door locked. He questioned her. She confessed that what the child had said was true, and told how she had procured the key. She was sold to Georgia.

In my childhood I knew a valuable slave, named Charity, and loved her, as all children did. Her young mistress married, and took her to Louisiana. Her little boy, James, was sold to a good sort of master. He became involved in debt, and James was sold again to a wealthy slaveholder, noted for his cruelty. With this man he grew up to manhood, receiving the treatment of a dog. After a severe whipping, to save himself from further infliction of the lash, with which he was threatened, he took to the woods. He was in a most miserable condition—cut by the cowskin, half naked, half starved, and without the means of procuring a crust of bread.

Some weeks after his escape, he was captured, tied, and carried back to his master's plantation. This man considered punishment in his jail, on bread and water, after receiving hundreds of lashes, too mild for the poor slave's offence. Therefore he decided, after the overseer should have whipped him to his satisfaction, to have him placed between the screws of the cotton gin, to stay as long as he had been in the woods. This wretched creature was cut with the whip from his head to his feet, then washed with strong brine, to prevent the flesh from mortifying, and make it heal sooner than it otherwise would. He was then put into the cotton gin, which was screwed down, only allowing him room to turn on his side when he could not lie on his back. Every morning a slave was sent with a piece of bread and bowl of water, which were placed within reach of the poor fellow. The slave was charged, under penalty of severe punishment, not to speak to him.

Four days passed, and the slave continued to carry the bread and water. On the second morning, he found the bread gone, but the water untouched. When he had been in the press four days and five nights, the slave informed his master that the water had not been used for four mornings, and that a horrible stench came from the gin house. The overseer was sent to examine into it. When the press was unscrewed, the dead body was found partly eaten by rats and vermin. Perhaps the rats that devoured his bread had gnawed him before life was extinct. Poor Charity! Grandmother and I often asked each other how her affectionate heart would bear the news, if she should ever hear of the murder of her son. We had known her husband, and knew that James was like him in manliness and intelligence. These were the qualities that made it so hard for him to be a plantation slave. They put him into a rough box, and buried him with less feeling than would have been manifested for an old house dog. Nobody asked any questions. He was a slave; and the feeling was that the master had a right to do what he pleased with his own property. And what did *he* care for the value of a slave? He had hundreds of them. When they had finished their daily toil, they must hurry to eat their little morsels, and be ready to extinguish their pine knots before nine o'clock, when the overseer went his patrol rounds. He entered every cabin, to see that men and their wives had gone to bed together, lest the men, from over-fatigue, should fall asleep in the chimney corner, and remain there till the morning horn called them to their daily task. Women are considered of no value, unless they continually increase their owner's stock. They are put on a par with animals. This same master shot a woman through the head, who had run away and been brought back to him. No one called him to account for it. If a slave resisted being whipped, the bloodhounds were unpacked, and set upon him, to tear his flesh from his bones. The master who did these things was highly educated, and styled a perfect gentleman. He also boasted the name and standing of a Christian, though Satan never had a truer follower.

I could tell of more slaveholders as cruel as those I have described. They are not exceptions to the general rule. I do not say there are no humane slaveholders. Such characters do exist, notwithstanding the hardening influences around them. But they are "like angels' visits—few and far between."[5]

I knew a young lady who was one of these rare specimens. She was an orphan, and inherited as slaves a woman and her six children. Their father was a free man. They had a comfortable home of their own, parents and children living together. The mother and eldest daughter served their mistress during the day, and at night returned to their dwelling, which was on the premises. The young lady was very pious, and there was some reality in her religion. She taught her slaves to lead pure lives, and wished them to enjoy the fruit of their own industry. *Her* religion was not a garb put on for Sunday, and laid aside till Sunday returned again. The eldest daughter of the slave mother was promised in marriage to a free man; and the day before the wedding this good mistress emancipated her, in order that her marriage might have the sanction of *law*.

Report said that this young lady cherished an unrequited affection for a man who had resolved to marry for wealth. In the course of time a rich uncle of hers died. He left six thousand dollars to his two sons by a colored woman, and the remainder of his property to his orphan niece. The metal soon attracted the magnet. The lady and her weighty purse became his. She offered to manumit her slaves—telling them that her marriage might make unexpected changes in their destiny, and she wished to insure their happiness. They refused to take their freedom, saying that she had always been their best friend, and they could not be so happy any where as with her. I was not surprised. I had often seen them in their comfortable home, and thought that the whole town did not contain a happier family. They had never felt slavery; and, when it was too late, they were convinced of its reality.

When the new master claimed this family as his property, the father became furious, and went to his mistress for protection. "I can do nothing for you now, Harry," said she. "I no longer have the power I had a week ago. I have succeeded in obtaining the freedom of your wife; but I cannot obtain it for your children." The unhappy father swore that nobody should take his children from him. He concealed them in the woods for some days; but they were discovered and taken. The father was put in jail, and the two oldest boys sold to Georgia. One little girl, too young to be of service to her master, was left with the wretched mother. The other three were carried to their master's plantation. The eldest soon became a mother; and, when the slaveholder's wife looked at the babe, she wept bitterly. She knew that her own husband had violated the purity she had so carefully inculcated. She had a second child by her master, and then he sold her and his offspring to his brother. She bore two children to the brother, and was sold again. The next sister went crazy. The life she was compelled to lead drove her mad. The third one became the mother of five daughters. Before the birth of the fourth the pious mistress died. To the last, she rendered every kindness to the slaves that her unfortunate circumstances permitted. She passed away peacefully, glad to close her eyes on a life which had been made so wretched by the man she loved.

This man squandered the fortune he had received, and sought to retrieve his affairs by a second marriage; but, having retired after a night of drunken debauch, he was found dead in the morning. He was called a good master; for he fed and clothed his slaves better than most masters, and the lash was not heard on his plantation so frequently as on many others. Had it not been for slavery, he would have been a better man, and his wife a happier woman.

No pen can give an adequate description of the all-pervading corruption produced by slavery. The slave girl is reared in an atmosphere of licentiousness and fear. The lash and the foul talk of her master and his sons are her teachers. When she is fourteen or fifteen, her owner, or his sons, or the overseer, or perhaps all of them, begin to bribe her with presents. If these fail to accomplish their purpose, she is whipped or starved into submission to their will. She may have had religious principles inculcated by some pious mother or grandmother, or some good mistress; she may have a lover, whose good opinion and peace of mind are dear to her heart; or the profligate men who have power over her may be exceedingly odious to her. But resistance is hopeless.

"The poor worm
Shall prove her contest vain. Life's little day
Shall pass, and she is gone!"[6]

The slaveholder's sons are, of course, vitiated, even while boys, by the unclean influences every where around them. Nor do the master's daughters always escape. Severe retributions sometimes come upon him for the wrongs he does to the daughters of the slaves. The white daughters early hear their parents quarreling about some female slave. Their curiosity is excited, and they soon learn the cause.

They are attended by the young slave girls whom their father has corrupted; and they hear such talk as should never meet youthful ears, or any other ears. They know that the women slaves are subject to their father's authority in all things; and in some cases they exercise the same authority over the men slaves. I have myself seen the master of such a household whose head was bowed down in shame; for it was known in the neighborhood that his daughter had selected one of the meanest slaves on his plantation to be the father of his first grandchild. She did not make her advances to her equals, nor even to her father's more intelligent servants. She selected the most brutalized, over whom her authority could be exercised with less fear of exposure. Her father, half frantic with rage, sought to revenge himself on the offending black man; but his daughter, foreseeing the storm that would arise, had given him free papers, and sent him out of the state.

In such cases the infant is smothered, or sent where it is never seen by any who know its history. But if the white parent is the *father*, instead of the mother, the offspring are unblushingly reared for the market. If they are girls, I have indicated plainly enough what will be their inevitable destiny.

You may believe what I say; for I write only that whereof I know. I was twenty-one years in that cage of obscene birds.[7] I can testify, from my own experience and observation, that slavery is a curse to the whites as well as to the blacks. It makes the white fathers cruel and sensual; the sons violent and licentious; it contaminates the daughters, and makes the wives wretched. And as for the colored race, it needs an abler pen than mine to describe the extremity of their sufferings, the depth of their degradation.

Yet few slaveholders seem to be aware of the widespread moral ruin occasioned by this wicked system. Their talk is of blighted cotton crops—not of the blight on their children's souls.

If you want to be fully convinced of the abominations of slavery, go on a southern plantation, and call yourself a negro trader. Then there will be no concealment; and you will see and hear things that will seem to you impossible among human beings with immortal souls.

X

A Perilous Passage in the Slave Girl's Life

AFTER MY LOVER WENT AWAY, Dr. Flint contrived a new plan. He seemed to have an idea that my fear of my mistress was his greatest obstacle. In the blandest tones, he told me that he was going to build a small house for me, in a secluded place, four miles away from the town. I shuddered; but I was constrained to listen, while he talked of his intention to give me a home of my own, and to make a lady of me. Hitherto, I had escaped my dreaded fate, by being in the midst of people. My grandmother had already had high words with my master about me. She had told him pretty plainly what she thought of his character, and there was considerable gossip in the neighborhood about our affairs, to which the open-mouthed jealousy of Mrs. Flint contributed not a little. When my master said he was going to build a house for me, and that he could do it with little trouble and expense, I was in hopes something would happen to frustrate his scheme; but I soon heard that the house was actually begun. I vowed before my Maker that I would never enter it. I had rather toil on the plantation from dawn till dark; I had rather live and die in jail, than drag on, from day to day, through such a living death. I was determined that the master, whom I so hated and loathed, who had blighted the prospects of my youth, and made my life a desert, should not, after my long struggle with him, succeed at last in trampling his victim under his feet. I would do any thing, every thing, for the sake of defeating him. What *could* I do? I thought and thought, till I became desperate, and made a plunge into the abyss.

And now, reader, I come to a period in my unhappy life, which I would gladly forget if I could. The remembrance fills me with sorrow and shame. It pains me to tell you of it; but I have promised to tell you the truth, and I will do it honestly, let it cost me what it may. I will not try to screen myself behind the plea of compulsion from a master; for it was not so. Neither can I plead ignorance or thoughtlessness. For years, my master had done his utmost to pollute my mind with foul images, and to destroy the pure principles inculcated by my grandmother, and the good mistress of my childhood. The influences of slavery had had the same effect on me that they had on other young girls; they had made me prematurely knowing, concerning the evil ways of the world. I knew what I did, and I did it with deliberate calculation.

But, O, ye happy women, whose purity has been sheltered from childhood, who have been free to choose the objects of your affection, whose homes are protected by law, do not judge the poor desolate slave girl too severely! If slavery had been abolished, I, also, could have married the man of my choice; I could have had a home shielded by the laws; and I should have been spared the painful task of confessing what I am now about to relate; but all my prospects had been blighted by slavery. I wanted to keep myself pure; and, under the most adverse circumstances, I tried hard to preserve my self-respect; but I was struggling alone in the powerful grasp of the demon Slavery; and the monster proved too strong for me. I felt as if I was forsaken by God and man; as if all my efforts must be frustrated; and I became reckless in my despair.

I have told you that Dr. Flint's persecutions and his wife's jealousy had given rise to some gossip in the neighborhood. Among others, it chanced that a white unmarried gentleman had obtained some knowledge of the circumstances in which I was placed.[1] He knew my grandmother, and often spoke to me in the street. He became interested for me, and asked questions about my master, which I answered in part. He expressed a great deal of sympathy, and a wish to aid me. He constantly sought opportunities to see me, and wrote to me frequently. I was a poor slave girl, only fifteen years old.

So much attention from a superior person was, of course, flattering; for human nature is the same in all. I also felt grateful for his sympathy, and encouraged by his kind words. It seemed to me a great thing to have such a friend. By degrees, a more tender feeling crept into my heart. He was an educated and eloquent gentleman; too eloquent, alas, for the poor slave girl who trusted in him. Of course I saw whither all this was tending. I knew the impassable gulf between us; but to be an object of interest to a man who is not married, and who is not her master, is agreeable to the pride and feelings of a slave, if her miserable situation has left her any pride or sentiment. It seems less degrading to give one's self, than to submit to compulsion. There is something akin to freedom in having a lover who has no control over you, except that which he gains by kindness and attachment. A master may treat you as rudely as he pleases, and you dare not speak; moreover, the wrong does not seem so great with an unmarried man, as with one who has a wife to be made unhappy. There may be sophistry in all this; but the condition of a slave confuses all principles of morality, and, in fact, renders the practice of them impossible.

When I found that my master had actually begun to build the lonely cottage, other feelings mixed with those I have described. Revenge, and calculations of interest, were added to flattered vanity and sincere gratitude for kindness. I knew nothing would enrage Dr. Flint so much as to know that I favored another; and it was something to triumph over my tyrant even in that small way. I thought he would revenge himself by selling me, and I was sure my friend, Mr. Sands, would buy me. He was a man of more generosity and feeling than my master, and I thought my freedom could be easily obtained from him. The crisis of my fate now came so near that I was desperate. I shuddered to think of being the mother of children that should be owned by my old tyrant. I knew that as soon as a new fancy took him, his victims were sold far off to get rid of them; especially if they had children. I had seen several women sold, with his babies at the breast. He never allowed his offspring by slaves to remain long in sight of himself and his wife. Of a man who was not my master I could ask to have my children well supported; and in this case, I felt confident I should obtain the boon. I also felt quite sure that they would be made free. With all these thoughts revolving in my mind, and seeing no other way of escaping the doom I so much dreaded, I made a headlong plunge. Pity me, and pardon me, O virtuous reader! You never knew what it is to be a slave; to be entirely unprotected by law or custom; to have the laws reduce you to the condition of a chattel, entirely subject to the will of another. You never exhausted your ingenuity in avoiding the snares, and eluding the power of a hated tyrant; you never shuddered at the sound of his footsteps, and trembled within hearing of his voice. I know I did wrong. No one can feel it more sensibly than I do. The painful and humiliating memory will haunt me to my dying day. Still, in looking back, calmly, on the events of my life, I feel that the slave woman ought not to be judged by the same standard as others.

The months passed on. I had many unhappy hours. I secretly mourned over the sorrow I was bringing on my grandmother, who had so tried to shield me from harm. I knew that I was the greatest comfort of her old age, and that it was a source of pride to her that I had not degraded myself, like most of the slaves. I wanted to confess to her that I was no longer worthy of her love; but I could not utter the dreaded words.

As for Dr. Flint, I had a feeling of satisfaction and triumph in the thought of telling *him*. From time to time he told me of his intended arrangements, and I was silent. At last, he came and told me the cottage was completed, and ordered me to go to it. I told him I would never enter it. He said, "I have heard enough of such talk as that. You shall go, if you are carried by force; and you shall remain there."

I replied, "I will never go there. In a few months I shall be a mother."

He stood and looked at me in dumb amazement, and left the house without a word. I thought I should be happy in my triumph over him. But now that the truth was out, and my relatives would hear of it, I felt wretched. Humble as were their circumstances, they had pride in my good character. Now, how could I look them in the face? My self-respect was gone! I had resolved that I would be virtuous, though I was a slave. I had said, "Let the storm beat! I will brave it till I die." And now, how humiliated I felt!

I went to my grandmother. My lips moved to make confession, but the words stuck in my throat. I sat down in the shade of a tree at her door and began to sew. I think she saw something unusual was the matter with me. The mother of slaves is very watchful. She knows there is no security for her children. After they have entered their teens she lives in daily expectation of trouble. This leads to many questions. If the girl is of a sensitive nature, timidity keeps her from answering truthfully, and this well-meant course has a tendency to drive her from maternal counsels. Presently, in came my mistress, like a mad woman, and accused me concerning her husband. My grandmother, whose suspicions had been previously awakened, believed what she said. She exclaimed, "O Linda! has it come to this? I had rather see you dead than to see you as you now are. You are a disgrace to your dead mother." She tore from my fingers my mother's wedding ring and her silver thimble. "Go away!" she exclaimed, "and never come to my house, again." Her reproaches fell so hot and heavy, that they left me no chance to answer. Bitter tears, such as the eyes never shed but once, were my only answer. I rose from my seat, but fell back again, sobbing. She did not speak to me; but the tears were running down her furrowed cheeks, and they scorched me like fire. She had always been so kind to me! So kind! How I longed to throw myself at her feet, and tell her all the truth! But she had ordered me to go, and never to come there again. After a few minutes, I mustered strength, and started to obey her. With what feelings did I now close that little gate, which I used to open with such an eager hand in my childhood! It closed upon me with a sound I never heard before.

Where could I go? I was afraid to return to my master's. I walked on recklessly, not caring where I went, or what would become of me. When I had gone four or five miles, fatigue compelled me to stop. I sat down on the stump of an old tree. The stars were shining through the boughs above me. How they mocked me, with their bright, calm light! The hours passed by, and as I sat there alone a chilliness and deadly sickness came over me. I sank on the ground. My mind was full of horrid thoughts. I prayed to die; but the prayer was not answered. At last, with great effort I roused myself, and walked some distance further, to the house of a woman who had been a friend of my mother. When I told her why I was there, she spoke soothingly to me; but I could not be comforted. I thought I could bear my shame if I could only be reconciled to my grandmother. I longed to open my heart to her. I thought if she could know the real state of the case, and all I had been bearing for years, she would perhaps judge me less harshly. My friend advised me to send for her. I did so; but days of agonizing suspense passed before she came. Had she utterly forsaken me? No. She came at last. I knelt before her, and told her the things that had poisoned my life; how long I had been persecuted; that I saw no way of escape; and in an hour of extremity I had become desperate. She listened in silence. I told her I would bear any thing and do any thing, if in time I had hopes of obtaining her forgiveness. I begged of her to pity me, for my dead mother's sake. And she did pity me. She did not say, "I forgive you"; but she looked at me lovingly, with her eyes full of tears. She laid her old hand gently on my head, and murmured, "Poor child! Poor child!"

XI

The New Tie to Life

I RETURNED TO MY good grandmother's house. She had an interview with Mr. Sands. When she asked him why he could not have left her one ewe lamb,—whether there were not plenty of slaves who did not care about character,—he made no answer; but he spoke kind and encouraging words. He promised to care for my child, and to buy me, be the conditions what they might.

I had not seen Dr. Flint for five days. I had never seen him since I made the avowal to him. He talked of the disgrace I had brought on myself; how I had sinned against my master, and mortified my old grandmother. He intimated that if I had accepted his proposals, he, as a physician, could have saved me from exposure. He even condescended to pity me. Could he have offered wormwood more bitter? He, whose persecutions had been the cause of my sin!

"Linda," said he, "though you have been criminal towards me, I feel for you, and I can pardon you if you obey my wishes. Tell me whether the fellow you wanted to marry is the father of your child. If you deceive me, you shall feel the fires of hell."

I did not feel as proud as I had done. My strongest weapon with him was gone. I was lowered in my own estimation, and had resolved to bear his abuse in silence. But when he spoke contemptuously of the lover who had always treated me honorably; when I remembered that but for *him* I might have been a virtuous, free, and happy wife, I lost my patience. "I have sinned against God and myself," I replied; "but not against you."

He clinched his teeth, and muttered, "Curse you!" He came towards me, with ill-suppressed rage, and exclaimed, "You obstinate girl! I could grind your bones to powder! You have thrown yourself away on some worthless rascal. You are weak-minded, and have been easily persuaded by those who don't care a straw for you. The future will settle accounts between us. You are blinded now; but hereafter you will be convinced that your master was your best friend. My lenity towards you is a proof of it. I might have punished you in many ways. I might have had you whipped till you fell dead under the lash. But I wanted you to live; I would have bettered your condition. Others cannot do it. You are my slave. Your mistress, disgusted by your conduct, forbids you to return to the house; therefore I leave you here for the present; but I shall see you often. I will call tomorrow."

He came with frowning brows, that showed a dissatisfied state of mind. After asking about my health, he inquired whether my board was paid, and who visited me. He then went on to say that he had neglected his duty; that as a physician there were certain things that he ought to have explained to me. Then followed talk such as would have made the most shameless blush. He ordered me to stand up before him. I obeyed. "I command you," said he, "to tell me whether the father of your child is white or black." I hesitated. "Answer me this instant!" he exclaimed. I did answer. He sprang upon me like a wolf, and grabbed my arm as if he would have broken it. "Do you love him?" said he, in a hissing tone.

"I am thankful that I do not despise him," I replied.

He raised his hand to strike me; but it fell again. I don't know what arrested the blow. He sat down, with lips tightly compressed. At last he spoke. "I came here," said he, "to make you a friendly proposition; but your ingratitude chafes me beyond endurance. You turn aside all my good intentions towards you. I don't know what it is that keeps me from killing you." Again he rose, as if he had a mind to strike me.

But he resumed. "On one condition I will forgive your insolence and crime. You must henceforth have no communication of any kind with the father of your child. You must not ask any thing from him, or receive any thing from him. I will take care of you and your child. You had better promise this at once, and not wait till you are deserted by him. This is the last act of mercy I shall show towards you."

I said something about being unwilling to have my child supported by a man who had cursed it and me also. He rejoined, that a woman who had sunk to my level had no right to expect any thing else. He asked, for the last time, would I accept his kindness? I answered that I would not.

"Very well," said he; "then take the consequences of your wayward course. Never look to me for help. You are my slave, and shall always be my slave. I will never sell you, that you may depend upon."

Hope died away in my heart as he closed the door after him. I had calculated that in his rage he would sell me to a slave-trader; and I knew the father of my child was on the watch to buy me.

About this time my uncle Phillip was expected to return from a voyage. The day before his departure I had officiated as bridesmaid to a young friend. My heart was then ill at ease, but my smiling countenance did not betray it. Only a year had passed; but what fearful changes it had wrought! My heart had grown gray in misery. Lives that flash in sunshine, and lives that are born in tears, receive their hue from circumstances. None of us know what a year may bring forth.

I felt no joy when they told me my uncle had come. He wanted to see me, though he knew what had happened. I shrank from him at first; but at last consented that he should come to my room. He received me as he always had done. O, how my heart smote me when I felt his tears on my burning cheeks! The words of my grandmother came to my mind,—"Perhaps your mother and father are taken from the evil days to come."[1] My disappointed heart could now praise God that it was so. But why, thought I, did my relatives ever cherish hopes for me? What was there to save me from the usual fate of slave girls? Many more beautiful and more intelligent than I had experienced a similar fate, or a far worse one. How could they hope that I should escape?

My uncle's stay was short, and I was not sorry for it. I was too ill in mind and body to enjoy my friends as I had done. For some weeks I was unable to leave my bed. I could not have any doctor but my master, and I would not have him sent for. At last, alarmed by my increasing illness, they sent for him. I was very weak and nervous; and as soon as he entered the room, I began to scream. They told him my state was very critical. He had no wish to hasten me out of the world, and he withdrew.

When my babe was born, they said it was premature. It weighed only four pounds; but God let it live.[2] I heard the doctor say I could not survive till morning. I had often prayed for death; but now I did not want to die, unless my child could die too. Many weeks passed before I was able to leave my bed. I was a mere wreck of my former self. For a year there was scarcely a day when I was free from chills and fever. My babe also was sickly. His little limbs were often racked with pain. Dr. Flint continued his visits, to look after my health; and he did not fail to remind me that my child was an addition to his stock of slaves.

I felt too feeble to dispute with him, and listened to his remarks in silence. His visits were less frequent; but his busy spirit could not remain quiet. He employed my brother in his office, and he was made the medium of frequent notes and messages to me. William was a bright lad, and of much use to the doctor. He had learned to put up medicines, to leech, cup, and bleed. He had taught himself to read and spell. I was proud of my brother; and the old doctor suspected as much. One day, when I had not seen him for several weeks, I heard his steps approaching the door. I dreaded the encounter, and hid myself. He inquired for me, of course; but I was nowhere to be found. He went to his office, and despatched William with a note. The color mounted to my brother's face when he gave it to me; and he said, "Don't you hate me, Linda, for bringing you these things?" I told him I could not blame him; he was a slave, and obliged to obey his master's will. The note ordered me to come to his office. I went. He demanded to know where I was when he called. I told him I was at home. He flew into a passion, and said he knew better. Then he launched out upon his usual themes,—my crimes against him, and my ingratitude for his forbearance. The laws were laid down to me anew, and I was dismissed. I felt humiliated that my brother should stand by, and listen to such language as would be addressed only to a slave. Poor boy! He was powerless to defend me; but I saw the tears, which he vainly strove to keep back. This manifestation of feeling irritated the doctor. William could do nothing to please him. One morning he did not arrive at the office so early as usual; and that circumstance afforded his master an opportunity to vent his spleen. He was put in jail. The next day my brother sent a trader to the doctor, with a request to be sold. His master was greatly incensed at what he called his insolence. He said he had put him there to reflect upon his bad conduct, and he certainly was not giving any evidence of repentance. For two days he harassed himself to find somebody to do his office work; but every thing went wrong without William. He was released, and ordered to take his old stand, with many threats, if he was not careful about his future behavior.

As the months passed on, my boy improved in health. When he was a year old, they called him beautiful. The little vine was taking deep root in my existence, though its clinging fondness excited a mixture of love and pain. When I was most sorely oppressed I found a solace in his smiles. I loved to watch his infant slumbers; but always there was a dark cloud over my enjoyment. I could never forget that he was a slave. Sometimes I wished that he might die in infancy. God tried me. My darling became very ill. The bright eyes grew dull, and the little feet and hands were so icy cold that I thought death had already touched them. I had prayed for his death, but never so earnestly as I now prayed for his life; and my prayer was heard. Alas, what mockery it is for a slave mother to try to pray back her dying child to life! Death is better than slavery. It was a sad thought that I had no name to give my child. His father caressed him and treated him kindly, whenever he had a chance to see him. He was not unwilling that he should bear his name; but he had no legal claim to it; and if I had bestowed it upon him, my master would have regarded it as a new crime, a new piece of insolence, and would, perhaps, revenge it on the boy. O, the serpent of Slavery has many and poisonous fangs![3]

XII

Fear of Insurrection

NOT FAR FROM this time Nat Turner's insurrection broke out; and the news threw our town into great commotion.[1] Strange that they should be alarmed, when their slaves were so "contented and happy"! But so it was.

It was always the custom to have a muster every year. On that occasion every white man shouldered his musket. The citizens and the so-called country gentlemen wore military uniforms. The poor whites took their places in the ranks in every-day dress, some without shoes, some without hats. This grand occasion had already passed; and when the slaves were told there was to be another muster, they were surprised and rejoiced. Poor creatures! They thought it was going to be a holiday. I was informed of the true state of affairs, and imparted it to the few I could trust. Most gladly would I have proclaimed it to every slave; but I dared not. All could not be relied on. Mighty is the power of the torturing lash.

By sunrise, people were pouring in from every quarter within twenty miles of the town. I knew the houses were to be searched; and I expected it would be done by country bullies and the poor whites. I knew nothing annoyed them so much as to see colored people living in comfort and respectability; so I made arrangements for them with especial care. I arranged every thing in my grandmother's house as neatly as possible. I put white quilts on the beds, and decorated some of the rooms with flowers. When all was arranged, I sat down at the window to watch. Far as my eye could reach, it rested on a motley crowd of soldiers. Drums and fifes were discoursing martial music. The men were divided into companies of sixteen, each headed by a captain. Orders were given, and the wild scouts rushed in every direction, wherever a colored face was to be found.

It was a grand opportunity for the low whites, who had no negroes of their own to scourge. They exulted in such a chance to exercise a little brief authority, and show their subserviency to the slaveholders; not reflecting that the power which trampled on the colored people also kept themselves in poverty, ignorance, and moral degradation. Those who never witnessed such scenes can hardly believe what I know was inflicted at this time on innocent men, women, and children, against whom there was not the slightest ground for suspicion. Colored people and slaves who lived in remote parts of the town suffered in an especial manner. In some cases the searchers scattered powder and shot among their clothes, and then sent other parties to find them, and bring them forward as proof that they were plotting insurrection. Every where men, women, and children were whipped till the blood stood in puddles at their feet. Some received five hundred lashes; others were tied hands and feet, and tortured with a bucking paddle, which blisters the skin terribly. The dwellings of the colored people, unless they happened to be protected by some influential white person, who was nigh at hand, were robbed of clothing and every thing else the marauders thought worth carrying away. All day long these unfeeling wretches went round, like a troop of demons, terrifying and tormenting the helpless. At night, they formed themselves into patrol bands, and went wherever they chose among the colored people, acting out their brutal will. Many women hid themselves in woods and swamps, to keep out of their way. If any of the husbands or fathers told of these outrages, they were tied up to the public whipping post, and cruelly scourged for telling lies about white men. The consternation was universal. No two people that had the slightest tinge of color in their faces dared to be seen talking together.[2]

I entertained no positive fears about our household, because we were in the midst of white families who would protect us. We were ready to receive the soldiers whenever they came. It was not long before we heard the tramp of feet and the sound of voices. The door was rudely pushed open; and in they tumbled, like a pack of hungry wolves. They snatched at every thing within their reach. Every box, trunk, closet, and corner underwent a thorough examination. A box in one of the drawers containing some silver change was eagerly pounced upon. When I stepped forward to take it from them, one of the soldiers turned and said angrily, "What d'ye foller us fur? D'ye s'pose white folks is come to steal?"

I replied, "You have come to search; but you have searched that box, and I will take it, if you please."

At that moment I saw a white gentleman who was friendly to us; and I called to him, and asked him to have the goodness to come in and stay till the search was over. He readily complied. His entrance into the house brought in the captain of the company, whose business it was to guard the outside of the house, and see that none of the inmates left it. This officer was Mr. Litch, the wealthy slaveholder whom I mentioned, in the account of neighboring planters, as being notorious for his cruelty.[3] He felt above soiling his hands with the search. He merely gave orders; and, if a bit of writing was discovered, it was carried to him by his ignorant followers, who were unable to read.

My grandmother had a large trunk of bedding and table cloths. When that was opened, there was a great shout of surprise; and one exclaimed, "Where'd the damned niggers git all dis sheet an' table clarf?"

My grandmother, emboldened by the presence of our white protector, said, "You may be sure we didn't pilfer 'em from *your* houses."

"Look here, mammy," said a grim-looking fellow without any coat, "you seem to feel mighty gran' 'cause you got all them 'ere fixens. White folks oughter have 'em all."

His remarks were interrupted by a chorus of voices shouting, "We's got 'em! We's got 'em! Dis 'ere yaller gal's got letters!"

There was a general rush for the supposed letter, which, upon examination, proved to be some verses written to me by a friend. In packing away my things, I had overlooked them. When their captain informed them of their contents, they seemed much disappointed. He inquired of me who wrote them. I told him it was one of my friends. "Can you read them?" he asked. When I told him I could, he swore, and raved, and tore the paper into bits. "Bring me all your letters!" said he, in a commanding tone. I told him I had none. "Don't be afraid," he continued, in an insinuating way. "Bring them all to me. Nobody shall do you any harm." Seeing I did not move to obey him, his pleasant tone changed to oaths and threats. "Who writes to you? half free niggers?" inquired he. I replied, "O, no; most of my letters are from white people. Some request me to burn them after they are read, and some I destroy without reading."

An exclamation of surprise from some of the company put a stop to our conversation. Some silver spoons which ornamented an old-fashioned buffet had just been discovered. My grandmother was in the habit of preserving fruit for many ladies in the town, and of preparing suppers for parties; consequently she had many jars of preserves. The closet that contained these was next invaded, and the contents tasted. One of them, who was helping himself freely, tapped his neighbor on the shoulder, and said, "Wal done! Don't wonder de niggers want to kill all de white folks, when dey live on 'sarves" [meaning preserves]. I stretched out my hand to take the jar, saying, "You were not sent here to search for sweetmeats."

"And what *were* we sent for?" said the captain, bristling up to me. I evaded the question.

The search of the house was completed, and nothing found to condemn us. They next proceeded to the garden, and knocked about every bush and vine, with no better success. The captain called his men together, and, after a short consultation, the order to march was given. As they passed out of the gate, the captain turned back, and pronounced a malediction on the house. He said it ought to be burned to the ground, and each of its inmates receive thirty-nine lashes. We came out of this affair very fortunately; not losing any thing except some wearing apparel.

Towards evening the turbulence increased. The soldiers, stimulated by drink, committed still greater cruelties. Shrieks and shouts continually rent the air. Not daring to go to the door, I peeped under the window curtain. I saw a mob dragging along a number of colored people, each white man, with his musket upraised, threatening instant death if they did not stop their shrieks. Among the prisoners was a respectable old colored minister. They had found a few parcels of shot in his house, which his wife had for years used to balance her scales. For this they were going to shoot him on Court House Green. What a spectacle was that for a civilized country! A rabble, staggering under intoxication, assuming to be the administrators of justice!

The better class of the community exerted their influence to save the innocent, persecuted people; and in several instances they succeeded, by keeping them shut up in jail till the excitement abated. At last the white citizens found that their own property was not safe from the lawless rabble they had summoned to protect them. They rallied the drunken swarm, drove them back into the country, and set a guard over the town.

The next day, the town patrols were commissioned to search colored people that lived out of the city; and the most shocking outrages were committed with perfect impunity. Every day for a fortnight, if I looked out, I saw horsemen with some poor panting negro tied to their saddles, and compelled by the lash to keep up with their speed, till they arrived at the jail yard. Those who had been whipped too unmercifully to walk were washed with brine, tossed into a cart, and carried to jail. One black man, who had not fortitude to endure scourging, promised to give information about the conspiracy. But it turned out that he knew nothing at all. He had not even heard the name of Nat Turner. The poor fellow had, however, made up a story, which augmented his own sufferings and those of the colored people.[4]

The day patrol continued for some weeks, and at sundown a night guard was substituted. Nothing at all was proved against the colored people, bond or free. The wrath of the slaveholders was somewhat appeased by the capture of Nat Turner. The imprisoned were released. The slaves were sent to their masters, and the free were permitted to return to their ravaged homes. Visiting was strictly forbidden on the plantations. The slaves begged the privilege of again meeting at their little church in the woods, with their burying ground around it. It was built by the colored people, and they had no higher happiness than to meet there and sing hymns together, and pour out their hearts in spontaneous prayer. Their request was denied, and the church was demolished.[5] They were permitted to attend the white churches, a certain portion of the galleries being appropriated to their use. There, when every body else had partaken of the communion, and the benediction had been pronounced, the minister said, "Come down, now, my colored friends." They obeyed the summons, and partook of the bread and wine, in commemoration of the meek and lowly Jesus, who said, "God is your Father, and all ye are brethren."[6]

XIII

The Church and Slavery

AFTER THE ALARM caused by Nat Turner's insurrection had subsided, the slaveholders came to the conclusion that it would be well to give the slaves enough of religious instruction to keep them from murdering their masters. The Episcopal clergyman offered to hold a separate service on Sundays for their benefit.[1] His colored members were very few, and also very respectable—a fact which I presume had some weight with him. The difficulty was to decide on a suitable place for them to worship. The Methodist and Baptist churches admitted them in the afternoon; but their carpets and cushions were not so costly as those at the Episcopal church. It was at last decided that they should meet at the house of a free colored man, who was a member.

I was invited to attend, because I could read. Sunday evening came, and, trusting to the cover of night, I ventured out. I rarely ventured out by daylight, for I always went with fear, expecting at every turn to encounter Dr. Flint, who was sure to turn me back, or order me to his office to inquire where I got my bonnet, or some other article of dress. When the Rev. Mr. Pike came, there were some twenty persons present. The reverend gentleman knelt in prayer, then seated himself, and requested all present, who could read, to open their books, while he gave out the portions he wished them to repeat or respond to.

His text was, "Servants, be obedient to them that are your masters according to the flesh, with fear and trembling, in singleness of your heart, as unto Christ."[2]

Pious Mr. Pike brushed up his hair till it stood upright, and, in deep, solemn tones, began: "Hearken, ye servants! Give strict heed unto my words. You are rebellious sinners. Your hearts are filled with all manner of evil. 'Tis the devil who tempts you. God is angry with you, and will surely punish you, if you don't forsake your wicked ways. You that live in town are eye-servants behind your master's back. Instead of serving your masters faithfully, which is pleasing in the sight of your heavenly Master, you are idle, and shirk your work. God sees you. You tell lies. God hears you. Instead of being engaged in worshipping him, you are hidden away somewhere, feasting on your master's substance; tossing coffee-grounds with some wicked fortuneteller, or cutting cards with another old hag. Your masters may not find you out, but God sees you, and will punish you. O, the depravity of your hearts! When your master's work is done, are you quietly together, thinking of the goodness of God to such sinful creatures? No; you are quarrelling, and tying up little bags of roots to bury under the door-steps to poison each other with.[3] God sees you. You men steal away to every grog shop to sell your master's corn, that you may buy rum to drink. God sees you. You sneak into the back streets, or among the bushes, to pitch coppers. Although your masters may not find you out, God sees you; and he will punish you. You must forsake your sinful ways, and be faithful servants. Obey your old master and your young master—your old mistress and your young mistress. If you disobey your earthly master, you offend your heavenly Master.

You must obey God's commandments. When you go from here, don't stop at the corners of the streets to talk, but go directly home, and let your master and mistress see that you have come."

The benediction was pronounced. We went home, highly amused at brother Pike's gospel teaching, and we determined to hear him again. I went the next Sabbath evening, and heard pretty much a repetition of the last discourse. At the close of the meeting, Mr. Pike informed us that he found it very inconvenient to meet at the friend's house, and he should be glad to see us, every Sunday evening, at his own kitchen.

I went home with the feeling that I had heard the Reverend Mr. Pike for the last time. Some of his members repaired to his house, and found that the kitchen sported two tallow candles; the first time, I am sure, since its present occupant owned it, for the servants never had any thing but pine knots. It was so long before the reverend gentleman descended from his comfortable parlor that the slaves left, and went to enjoy a Methodist shout. They never seem so happy as when shouting and singing at religious meetings. Many of them are sincere, and nearer to the gate of heaven than sanctimonious Mr. Pike, and other longfaced Christians, who see wounded Samaritans, and pass by on the other side.[4]

The slaves generally compose their own songs and hymns; and they do not trouble their heads much about the measure. They often sing the following verses:

"Old Satan is one busy ole man;
    He rolls dem blocks all in my way;
But Jesus is my bosom friend;
    He rolls dem blocks away.

"If I had died when I was young,
    Den how my stam'ring tongue would have sung;

But I am ole, and now I stand
   A narrow chance for to tread dat heavenly land."[5]

I well remember one occasion when I attended a Methodist class meeting. I went with a burdened spirit, and happened to sit next a poor, bereaved mother, whose heart was still heavier than mine. The class leader was the town constable—a man who bought and sold slaves, who whipped his brethren and sisters of the church at the public whipping post, in jail or out of jail. He was ready to perform that Christian office any where for fifty cents. This white-faced, black-hearted brother came near us, and said to the stricken woman, "Sister, can't you tell us how the Lord deals with your soul? Do you love him as you did formerly?"

She rose to her feet, and said, in piteous tones, "My Lord and Master, help me! My load is more than I can bear. God has hid himself from me, and I am left in darkness and misery." Then, striking her breast, she continued, "I can't tell you what is in here! They've got all my children. Last week they took the last one. God only knows where they've sold her. They let me have her sixteen years, and then——O! O! Pray for her brothers and sisters! I've got nothing to live for now. God make my time short!"

She sat down, quivering in every limb. I saw that constable class leader become crimson in the face with suppressed laughter, while he held up his handkerchief, that those who were weeping for the poor woman's calamity might not see his merriment. Then, with assumed gravity, he said to the bereaved mother, "Sister, pray to the Lord that every dispensation of his divine will may be sanctified to the good of your poor needy soul!"

The congregation struck up a hymn, and sung as though they were as free as the birds that warbled round us,—

"Ole Satan thought he had a mighty aim;
He missed my soul, and caught my sins.

Cry Amen, cry Amen, cry Amen to God!

"He took my sins upon his back;
Went muttering and grumbling down to hell.
Cry Amen, cry Amen, cry Amen to God!

"Ole Satan's church is here below.
Up to God's free church I hope to go.
Cry Amen, cry Amen, cry Amen to God!"[6]

Precious are such moments to the poor slaves. If you were to hear them at such times, you might think they were happy. But can that hour of singing and shouting sustain them through the dreary week, toiling without wages, under constant dread of the lash?

The Episcopal clergyman, who, ever since my earliest recollection, had been a sort of god among the slaveholders, concluded, as his family was large, that he must go where money was more abundant.[7] A very different clergyman took his place.[8] The change was very agreeable to the colored people, who said, "God has sent us a good man this time." They loved him, and their children followed him for a smile or a kind word. Even the slaveholders felt his influence. He brought to the rectory five slaves. His wife taught them to read and write, and to be useful to her and themselves. As soon as he was settled, he turned his attention to the needy slaves around him. He urged upon his parishioners the duty of having a meeting expressly for them every Sunday, with a sermon adapted to their comprehension. After much argument and importunity, it was finally agreed that they might occupy the gallery of the church on Sunday evenings. Many colored people, hitherto unaccustomed to attend church, now gladly went to hear the gospel preached. The sermons were simple, and they understood them. Moreover, it was the first time they had ever been addressed as human beings. It was not long before his white parishioners began to be dissatisfied. He was accused of preaching better sermons to the negroes than he did to them. He honestly confessed that he bestowed more pains upon those sermons than upon any others; for the slaves were reared in such ignorance that it was a difficult task to adapt himself to their comprehension. Dissensions arose in the parish. Some wanted he should preach to them in the evening, and to the slaves in the afternoon. In the midst of these disputings his wife died, after a very short illness. Her slaves gathered round her dying bed in great sorrow. She said, "I have tried to do you good and promote your happiness; and if I have failed, it has not been for want of interest in your welfare. Do not weep for me; but prepare for the new duties that lie before you. I leave you all free. May we meet in a better world." Her liberated slaves were sent away, with funds to establish them comfortably. The colored people will long bless the memory of that truly Christian woman. Soon after her death her husband preached his farewell sermon, and many tears were shed at his departure.[9]

Several years after, he passed through our town and preached to his former congregation. In his afternoon sermon he addressed the colored people. "My friends," said he, "it affords me great happiness to have an opportunity of speaking to you again. For two years I have been striving to do something for the colored people of my own parish; but nothing is yet accomplished. I have not even preached a sermon to them. Try to live according to the word of God, my friends. Your skin is darker than mine; but God judges men by their hearts, not by the color of their skins." This was strange doctrine from a southern pulpit. It was very offensive to slaveholders. They said he and his wife had made fools of their slaves, and that he preached like a fool to the negroes.

I knew an old black man, whose piety and childlike trust in God were beautiful to witness. At fifty-three years old he joined the Baptist church. He had a most earnest desire to learn to read. He thought he should know how to serve God better if he could only read the Bible. He came to me, and begged me to teach him. He said he could not pay me, for he had no money; but he would bring me nice fruit when the season for it came. I asked him if he didn't know it was contrary to law; and that slaves were whipped and imprisoned for teaching each other to read. This brought the tears into his eyes. "Don't be troubled, uncle Fred," said I. "I have no thoughts, of refusing to teach you. I only told you of the law, that you might know the danger, and be on your guard." He thought he could plan to come three times a week without its being suspected. I selected a quiet nook, where no intruder was likely to penetrate, and there I taught him his A, B, C. Considering his age, his progress was astonishing. As soon as he could spell in two syllables he wanted to spell out words in the Bible. The happy smile that illuminated his face put joy into my heart. After spelling out a few words, he paused, and said, "Honey, it 'pears when I can read dis good book I shall be nearer to God. White man is got all de sense. He can larn easy. It ain't easy for ole black man like me. I only wants to read dis book, dat I may know how to live; den I hab no fear 'bout dying."

I tried to encourage him by speaking of the rapid progress he had made. "Hab patience, child," he replied. "I larns slow."

I had no need of patience. His gratitude, and the happiness I imparted, were more than a recompense for all my trouble.

At the end of six months he had read through the New Testament, and could find any text in it. One day, when he had recited unusually well, I said, "Uncle Fred, how do you manage to get your lessons so well?"

"Lord bress you, chile," he replied. "You nebber gibs me a lesson dat I don't pray to God to help me to understan' what I spells and what I reads. And he *does* help me, chile. Bress his holy name!"

There are thousands, who, like good uncle Fred, are thirsting for the water of life; but the law forbids it, and the churches withhold it.[10] They send the Bible to heathen abroad, and neglect the heathen at home. I am glad that missionaries go out to the dark corners of the earth; but I ask them not to overlook the dark corners at home. Talk to American slaveholders as you talk to savages in Africa. Tell *them* it is wrong to traffic in men. Tell them it is sinful to sell their own children, and atrocious to violate their own daughters. Tell them that all men are brethren, and that man has no right to shut out the light of knowledge from his brother. Tell them they are answerable to God for sealing up the Fountain of Life from souls that are thirsting for it.[11]

There are men who would gladly undertake such missionary work as this; but, alas! their number is small. They are hated by the south, and would be driven from its soil, or dragged to prison to die, as others have been before them. The field is ripe for the harvest, and awaits the reapers.[12] Perhaps the great grandchildren of uncle Fred may have freely imparted to them the divine treasures, which he sought by stealth, at the risk of the prison and the scourge.

Are doctors of divinity blind, or are they hypocrites? I suppose some are the one, and some the other; but I think if they felt the interest in the poor and the lowly, that they ought to feel, they would not be so *easily* blinded. A clergyman who goes to the south, for the first time, has usually some feeling, however vague, that slavery is wrong. The slaveholder suspects this, and plays his game accordingly. He makes himself as agreeable as possible; talks on theology, and other kindred topics. The reverend gentleman is asked to invoke a blessing on a table loaded with luxuries. After dinner he walks round the premises, and sees the beautiful groves and flowering vines, and the comfortable huts of favored household slaves. The southerner invites him to talk with these slaves. He asks them if they want to be free, and they say, "O, no, massa." This is sufficient to satisfy him. He comes home to publish a "South-Side View of Slavery," and to complain of the exaggerations of abolitionists. He assures people that he has been to the south, and seen slavery for himself; that it is a beautiful "patriarchal institution"; that the slaves don't want their freedom; that they have hallelujah meetings, and other religious privileges.[13]

What does *he* know of the half-starved wretches toiling from dawn till dark on the plantations? of mothers shrieking for their children, torn from their arms by slave traders? of young girls dragged down into moral filth? of pools of blood around the whipping post? of hounds trained to tear human flesh? of men screwed into cotton gins to die? The slaveholder showed him none of these things, and the slaves dared not tell of them if he had asked them.

There is a great difference between Christianity and religion at the south.[14] If a man goes to the communion table, and pays money into the treasury of the church, no matter if it be the price of blood, he is called religious. If a pastor has offspring by a woman not his wife, the church dismiss him, if she is a white woman; but if she is colored, it does not hinder his continuing to be their good shepherd.

When I was told that Dr. Flint had joined the Episcopal church, I was much surprised.[15] I supposed that religion had a purifying effect on the character of men; but the worst persecutions I endured from him were after he was a communicant. The conversation of the doctor, the day after he had been confirmed, certainly gave *me* no indication that he had "renounced the devil and all his works." In answer to some of his usual talk, I reminded him that he had just joined the church. "Yes, Linda," said he. "It was proper for me to do so. I am getting in years, and my position in society requires it, and it puts an end to all the damned slang. You would do well to join the church, too, Linda."

"There are sinners enough in it already," rejoined I. "If I could be allowed to live like a Christian, I should be glad."

"You can do what I require; and if you are faithful to me, you will be as virtuous as my wife," he replied.

I answered that the Bible didn't say so.

His voice became hoarse with rage. "How dare you preach to me about your infernal Bible!" he exclaimed. "What right have you, who are my negro, to talk to me about what you would like, and what you wouldn't like? I am your master, and you shall obey me."

No wonder the slaves sing,—

"Ole Satan's church is here below;
Up to God's free church I hope to go."

XIV

Another Link to Life

I HAD NOT RETURNED to my master's house since the birth of my child. The old man raved to have me thus removed from his immediate power; but his wife vowed, by all that was good and great, she would kill me if I came back; and he did not doubt her word. Sometimes he would stay away for a season. Then he would come and renew the old threadbare discourse about his forbearance and my ingratitude. He labored, most unnecessarily, to convince me that I had lowered myself. The venomous old reprobate had no need of descanting on that theme. I felt humiliated enough. My unconscious babe was the ever-present witness of my shame. I listened with silent contempt when he talked about my having forfeited *his* good opinion; but I shed bitter tears that I was no longer worthy of being respected by the good and pure. Alas! slavery still held me in its poisonous grasp. There was no chance for me to be respectable. There was no prospect of being able to lead a better life.

Sometimes, when my master found that I still refused to accept what he called his kind offers, he would threaten to sell my child. "Perhaps that will humble you," said he.

Humble *me!* Was I not already in the dust?[1] But his threat lacerated my heart. I knew the law gave him power to fulfil it; for slaveholders have been cunning enough to enact that "the child shall follow the condition of the *mother*," not of the *father;* thus taking care that licentiousness shall not interfere with avarice. This reflection made me clasp my innocent babe all the more firmly to my heart. Horrid visions passed through my mind when I thought of his liability to fall into the slave trader's hands. I wept over him, and said, "O my child! perhaps they will leave you in some cold cabin to die, and then throw you into a hole, as if you were a dog."

When Dr. Flint learned that I was again to be a mother, he was exasperated beyond measure. He rushed from the house, and returned with a pair of shears. I had a fine head of hair; and he often railed about my pride of arranging it nicely. He cut every hair close to my head, storming and swearing all the time.[2] I replied to some of his abuse, and he struck me. Some months before, he had pitched me down stairs in a fit of passion; and the injury I received was so serious that I was unable to turn myself in bed for many days. He then said, "Linda, I swear by God I will never raise my hand against you again"; but I knew that he would forget his promise.

After he discovered my situation, he was like a restless spirit from the pit. He came every day; and I was subjected to such insults as no pen can describe. I would not describe them if I could; they were too low, too revolting. I tried to keep them from my grandmother's knowledge as much as I could. I knew she had enough to sadden her life, without having my troubles to bear. When she saw the doctor treat me with violence, and heard him utter oaths terrible enough to palsy a man's tongue, she could not always hold her peace. It was natural and motherlike that she should try to defend me; but it only made matters worse.

When they told me my new-born babe was a girl, my heart was heavier than it had ever been before.[3] Slavery is terrible for men; but it is far more terrible for women. Superadded to the burden common to all, *they* have wrongs, and sufferings, and mortifications peculiarly their own.

Dr. Flint had sworn that he would make me suffer, to my last day, for this new crime against *him,* as he called it; and as long as he had me in his power he kept his word. On the fourth day after the birth of my babe, he entered my room suddenly, and commanded me to rise and bring my baby to him. The nurse who took care of me had gone out of the room to prepare some nourishment, and I was alone. There was no alternative. I rose, took up my babe, and crossed the room to where he sat. "Now stand there," said he, "till I tell you to go back!" My child bore a strong resemblance to her father, and to the deceased Mrs. Sands, her grandmother.[4] He noticed this; and while I stood before him, trembling with weakness, he heaped upon me and my little one every vile epithet he could think of. Even the grandmother in her grave did not escape his curses. In the midst of his vituperations I fainted at his feet. This recalled him to his senses. He took the baby from my arms, laid it on the bed, dashed cold water in my face, took me up, and shook me violently, to restore my consciousness before any one entered the room. Just then my grandmother came in, and he hurried out of the house. I suffered in consequence of this treatment; but I begged my friends to let me die, rather than send for the doctor. There was nothing I dreaded so much as his presence. My life was spared; and I was glad for the sake of my little ones. Had it not been for these ties to life, I should have been glad to be released by death, though I had lived only nineteen years.

Always it gave me a pang that my children had no lawful claim to a name. Their father offered his; but, if I had wished to accept the offer, I dared not while my master lived. Moreover, I knew it would not be accepted at their baptism. A Christian name they were at least entitled to; and we resolved to call my boy for our dear good Benjamin, who had gone far away from us.[5]

My grandmother belonged to the church;[6] and she was very desirous of having the children christened. I knew Dr. Flint would forbid it, and I did not venture to attempt it. But chance favored me. He was called to visit a patient out of town, and was obliged to be absent during Sunday. "Now is the time," said my grandmother; "we will take the children to church, and have them christened."

When I entered the church, recollections of my mother came over me, and I felt subdued in spirit. There she had presented me for baptism, without any reason to feel ashamed. She had been married, and had such legal rights as slavery allows to a slave. The vows had at least been sacred to *her*, and she had never violated them. I was glad she was not alive, to know under what different circumstances her grandchildren were presented for baptism. Why had my lot been so different from my mother's? *Her* master had died when she was a child; and she remained with her mistress till she married. She was never in the power of any master; and thus she escaped one class of the evils that generally fall upon slaves.

When my baby was about to be christened, the former mistress of my father stepped up to me, and proposed to give it her Christian name.[7] To this I added the surname of my father, who had himself no legal right to it; for my grandfather on the paternal side was a white gentleman.[8] What tangled skeins are the genealogies of slavery! I loved my father; but it mortified me to be obliged to bestow his name on my children.

When we left the church, my father's old mistress invited me to go home with her. She clasped a gold chain around my baby's neck. I thanked her for this kindness; but I did not like the emblem. I wanted no chain to be fastened on my daughter, not even if its links were of gold. How earnestly I prayed that she might never feel the weight of slavery's chain, whose iron entereth into the soul![9]

XV

Continued Persecutions

M Y CHILDREN GREW FINELY; and Dr. Flint would often say to me, with an exulting smile, "These brats will bring me a handsome sum of money one of these days."

I thought to myself that, God being my helper, they should never pass into his hands. It seemed to me I would rather see them killed than have them given up to his power. The money for the freedom of myself and my children could be obtained; but I derived no advantage from that circumstance. Dr. Flint loved money, but he loved power more. After much discussion, my friends resolved on making another trial. There was a slaveholder about to leave for Texas, and he was commissioned to buy me. He was to begin with nine hundred dollars, and go up to twelve. My master refused his offers. "Sir," said he, "she don't belong to me. She is my daughter's property, and I have no right to sell her. I mistrust that you come from her paramour. If so, you may tell him that he cannot buy her for any money; neither can he buy her children."

The doctor came to see me the next day, and my heart beat quicker as he entered. I never had seen the old man tread with so majestic a step. He seated himself and looked at me with withering scorn. My children had learned to be afraid of him. The little one would shut her eyes and hide her face on my shoulder whenever she saw him; and Benny, who was now nearly five years old, often inquired, "What makes that bad man come here so many times? Does he want to hurt us?" I would clasp the dear boy in my arms, trusting that he would be free before he was old enough to solve the problem. And now, as the doctor sat there so grim and silent, the child left his play and came and nestled up by me. At last my tormentor spoke. "So you are left in disgust, are you?" said he. "It is no more than I expected. You remember I told you years ago that you would be treated so. So he is tired of you? Ha! ha! ha! The virtuous madam don't like to hear about it, does she? Ha! ha! ha!" There was a sting in his calling me virtuous madam. I no longer had the power of answering him as I had formerly done. He continued: "So it seems you are trying to get up another intrigue. Your new paramour came to me, and offered to buy you; but you may be assured you will not succeed. You are mine; and you shall be mine for life. There lives no human being that can take you out of slavery. I would have done it; but you rejected my kind offer."

I told him I did not wish to get up any intrigue; that I had never seen the man who offered to buy me.

"Do you tell me I lie?" exclaimed he, dragging me from my chair. "Will you say again that you never saw that man?"

I answered, "I do say so."

He clinched my arm with a volley of oaths. Ben began to scream, and I told him to go to his grandmother.

"Don't you stir a step, you little wretch!" said he. The child drew nearer to me, and put his arms round me, as if he wanted to protect me. This was too much for my enraged master. He caught him up and hurled him across the room. I thought he was dead, and rushed towards him to take him up.

"Not yet!" exclaimed the doctor. "Let him lie there till he comes to."

"Let me go! Let me go!" I screamed, "or I will raise the whole house." I struggled and got away; but he clinched me again. Somebody opened the door, and he released me. I picked up my insensible child, and when I turned my tormentor was gone. Anxiously I bent over the little form, so pale and still; and when the brown eyes at last opened, I don't know whether I was very happy.

All the doctor's former persecutions were renewed. He came morning, noon, and night. No jealous lover ever watched a rival more closely than he watched me and the unknown slaveholder, with whom he accused me of wishing to get up an intrigue. When my grandmother was out of the way he searched every room to find him.

In one of his visits, he happened to find a young girl, whom he had sold to a trader a few days previous. His statement was, that he sold her because she had been too familiar with the overseer. She had had a bitter life with him, and was glad to be sold. She had no mother, and no near ties. She had been torn from all her family years before. A few friends had entered into bonds for her safety, if the trader would allow her to spend with them the time that intervened between her sale and the gathering up of his human stock. Such a favor was rarely granted. It saved the trader the expense of board and jail fees, and though the amount was small, it was a weighty consideration in a slave-trader's mind.

Dr. Flint always had an aversion to meeting slaves after he had sold them. He ordered Rose out of the house; but he was no longer her master, and she took no notice of him. For once the crushed Rose was the conqueror. His gray eyes flashed angrily upon her; but that was the extent of his power. "How came this girl here?" he exclaimed. "What right had you to allow it, when you knew I had sold her?"

I answered "This is my grandmother's house, and Rose came to see her. I have no right to turn any body out of doors, that comes here for honest purposes."

He gave me the blow that would have fallen upon Rose if she had still been his slave. My grandmother's attention had been attracted by loud voices, and she entered in time to see a second blow dealt. She was not a woman to let such an outrage, in her own house, go unrebuked. The doctor undertook to explain that I had been insolent. Her indignant feelings rose higher and higher, and finally boiled over in words. "Get out of my house!" she exclaimed. "Go home, and take care of your wife and children, and you will have enough to do, without watching my family."

He threw the birth of my children in her face, and accused her of sanctioning the life I was leading. She told him I was living with her by compulsion of his wife; that he needn't accuse her, for he was the one to blame; he was the one who had caused all the trouble. She grew more and more excited as she went on. "I tell you what, Dr. Flint," said she, "you ain't got many more years to live, and you'd better be saying your prayers. It will take 'em all, and more too, to wash the dirt off your soul."[1]

"Do you know whom you are talking to?" he exclaimed.

She replied, "Yes, I know very well who I am talking to."

He left the house in a great rage. I looked at my grandmother. Our eyes met. Their angry expression had passed away, but she looked sorrowful and weary—weary of incessant strife. I wondered that it did not lessen her love for me; but if it did she never showed it. She was always kind, always ready to sympathize with my troubles. There might have been peace and contentment in that humble home if it had not been for the demon Slavery.

The winter passed undisturbed by the doctor. The beautiful spring came; and when Nature resumes her loveliness, the human soul is apt to revive also. My drooping hopes came to life again with the flowers. I was dreaming of freedom again; more for my children's sake than my own. I planned and I planned. Obstacles hit against plans. There seemed no way of overcoming them; and yet I hoped.

Back came the wily doctor. I was not at home when he called. A friend had invited me to a small party, and to gratify her I went. To my great consternation, a messenger came in haste to say that Dr. Flint was at my grandmother's, and insisted on seeing me. They did not tell him where I was, or he would have come and raised a disturbance in my friend's house. They sent me a dark wrapper; I threw it on and hurried home. My speed did not save me; the doctor had gone away in anger. I dreaded the morning, but I could not delay it; it came, warm and bright. At an early hour the doctor came and asked me where I had been last night. I told him. He did not believe me, and sent to my friend's house to ascertain the facts. He came in the afternoon to assure me he was satisfied that I had spoken the truth. He seemed to be in a facetious mood, and I expected some jeers were coming. "I suppose you need some recreation," said he, "but I am surprised at your being there, among those negroes. It was not the place for *you*. Are you *allowed* to visit such people?"

I understood this covert fling at the white gentleman who was my friend; but I merely replied, "I went to visit my friends, and any company they keep is good enough for me."

He went on to say, "I have seen very little of you of late, but my interest in you is unchanged. When I said I would have no more mercy on you I was rash. I recall my words. Linda, you desire freedom for yourself and your children, and you can obtain it only through me. If you agree to what I am about to propose, you and they shall be free. There must be no communication of any kind between you and their father. I will procure a cottage, where you and the children can live to-

gether. Your labor shall be light, such as sewing for my family. Think
what is offered you, Linda—a home and freedom! Let the past be forgotten. If I have been harsh with you at times, your wilfulness drove
me to it. You know I exact obedience from my own children, and I
consider you as yet a child."[2]

He paused for an answer, but I remained silent.

"Why don't you speak?" said he. "What more do you wait for?"

"Nothing, sir."

"Then you accept my offer?"

"No, sir."

His anger was ready to break loose; but he succeeded in curbing it,
and replied, "You have answered without thought. But I must let you
know there are two sides to my proposition; if you reject the bright
side, you will be obliged to take the dark one. You must either accept
my offer, or you and your children shall be sent to your young master's plantation, there to remain till your young mistress is married;
and your children shall fare like the rest of the negro children. I give
you a week to consider of it."[3]

He was shrewd; but I knew he was not to be trusted. I told him I
was ready to give my answer now.

"I will not receive it now," he replied. "You act too much from impulse. Remember that you and your children can be free a week from
to-day if you choose."

On what a monstrous chance hung the destiny of my children! I
knew that my master's offer was a snare, and that if I entered it escape
would be impossible. As for his promise, I knew him so well that I
was sure if he gave me free papers, they would be so managed as to
have no legal value. The alternative was inevitable. I resolved to go to
the plantation. But then I thought how completely I should be in his
power, and the prospect was appalling. Even if I should kneel before
him, and implore him to spare me, for the sake of my children, I knew

he would spurn me with his foot, and my weakness would be his triumph.

Before the week expired, I heard that young Mr. Flint was about to be married to a lady of his own stamp. I foresaw the position I should occupy in his establishment. I had once been sent to the plantation for punishment, and fear of the son had induced the father to recall me very soon. My mind was made up; I was resolved that I would foil my master and save my children, or I would perish in the attempt. I kept my plans to myself; I knew that friends would try to dissuade me from them, and I would not wound their feelings by rejecting their advice.

On the decisive day the doctor came, and said he hoped I had made a wise choice.

"I am ready to go to the plantation, sir," I replied.

"Have you thought how important your decision is to your children?" said he.

I told him I had.

"Very well. Go to the plantation, and my curse go with you," he replied. "Your boy shall be put to work, and he shall soon be sold; and your girl shall be raised for the purpose of selling well. Go your own ways!" He left the room with curses, not to be repeated.

As I stood rooted to the spot, my grandmother came and said, "Linda, child, what did you tell him?"

I answered that I was going to the plantation.

"*Must* you go?" said she. "Can't something be done to stop it?"

I told her it was useless to try; but she begged me not to give up. She said she would go to the doctor, and remind him how long and how faithfully she had served in the family, and how she had taken her own baby from her breast to nourish his wife. She would tell him I had been out of the family so long they would not miss me; that she would pay them for my time, and the money would procure a woman who had more strength for the situation than I had. I begged her not to go; but she persisted in saying, "He will listen to *me*, Linda." She went, and was treated as I expected. He coolly listened to what she said, but denied her request. He told her that what he did was for my good, that my feelings were entirely above my situation, and that on the plantation I would receive treatment that was suitable to my behavior.

My grandmother was much cast down. I had my secret hopes; but I must fight my battle alone. I had a woman's pride, and a mother's love for my children; and I resolved that out of the darkness of this hour a brighter dawn should rise for them. My master had power and law on his side; I had a determined will. There is might in each.

XVI

Scenes at the Plantation

EARLY THE NEXT morning I left my grandmother's with my youngest child. My boy was ill, and I left him behind. I had many sad thoughts as the old wagon jolted on. Hitherto, I had suffered alone; now, my little one was to be treated as a slave. As we drew near the great house, I thought of the time when I was formerly sent there out of revenge. I wondered for what purpose I was now sent. I could not tell. I resolved to obey orders so far as duty required; but within myself, I determined to make my stay as short as possible. Mr. Flint was waiting to receive us, and told me to follow him up stairs to receive orders for the day. My little Ellen was left below in the kitchen. It was a change for her, who had always been so carefully tended. My young master said she might amuse herself in the yard. This was kind of him, since the child was hateful to his sight. My task was to fit up the house for the reception of the bride. In the midst of sheets, table-cloths, towels, drapery, and carpeting, my head was as busy planning, as were my fingers with the needle. At noon I was allowed to go to Ellen. She had sobbed herself to sleep. I heard Mr. Flint say to a neighbor, "I've got her down here, and I'll soon take the town notions out of her head. My father is partly to blame for her nonsense. He ought to have broke her in long ago." The remark was made within my hearing, and it would have been quite as manly to have made it to my face. He *had* said things to my face which might, or might not, have surprised his neighbor if he had known of them. He was "a chip of the old block."

I resolved to give him no cause to accuse me of being too much of a lady, so far as work was concerned. I worked day and night, with wretchedness before me. When I lay down beside my child, I felt how much easier it would be to see her die than to see her master beat her about, as I daily saw him beat other little ones. The spirit of the mothers was so crushed by the lash, that they stood by, without courage to remonstrate. How much more must I suffer, before I should be "broke in" to that degree?

I wished to appear as contented as possible. Sometimes I had an opportunity to send a few lines home; and this brought up recollections that made it difficult, for a time, to seem calm and indifferent to my lot. Notwithstanding my efforts, I saw that Mr. Flint regarded me with a suspicious eye. Ellen broke down under the trials of her new life. Separated from me, with no one to look after her, she wandered about, and in a few days cried herself sick. One day, she sat under the window where I was at work, crying that weary cry which makes a mother's heart bleed. I was obliged to steel myself to bear it. After a while it ceased. I looked out, and she was gone. As it was near noon, I ventured to go down in search of her. The great house was raised two feet above the ground. I looked under it, and saw her about midway, fast asleep. I crept under and drew her out. As I held her in my arms, I thought how well it would be for her if she never waked up; and I uttered my thought aloud. I was startled to hear some one say, "Did you speak to me?" I looked up, and saw Mr. Flint standing beside me. He said nothing further, but turned, frowning, away. That night he sent Ellen a biscuit and a cup of sweetened milk. This generosity surprised me. I learned afterwards, that in the afternoon he had killed a large snake, which crept from under the house; and I supposed that incident had prompted his unusual kindness.

The next morning the old cart was loaded with shingles for town. I put Ellen into it, and sent her to her grandmother. Mr. Flint said I ought to have asked his permission. I told him the child was sick, and required attention which I had no time to give. He let it pass; for he was aware that I had accomplished much work in a little time.

I had been three weeks on the plantation, when I planned a visit home. It must be at night, after every body was in bed. I was six miles from town, and the road was very dreary. I was to go with a young man, who, I knew, often stole to town to see his mother. One night, when all was quiet, we started. Fear gave speed to our steps, and we were not long in performing the journey. I arrived at my grandmother's. Her bed room was on the first floor, and the window was open, the weather being warm. I spoke to her and she awoke. She let me in and closed the window, lest some late passer-by should see me. A light was brought, and the whole household gathered round me, some smiling and some crying. I went to look at my children, and thanked God for their happy sleep. The tears fell as I leaned over them. As I moved to leave, Benny stirred. I turned back, and whispered, "Mother is here." After digging at his eyes with his little fist, they opened, and he sat up in bed, looking at me curiously. Having satisfied himself that it was I, he exclaimed, "O mother! you ain't dead, are you? They didn't cut off your head at the plantation, did they?"

My time was up too soon, and my guide was waiting for me. I laid Benny back in his bed, and dried his tears by a promise to come again soon. Rapidly we retraced our steps back to the plantation. About halfway we were met by a company of four patrols.[1] Luckily we heard their horses' hoofs before they came in sight, and we had time to hide behind a large tree. They passed, hallooing and shouting in a manner that indicated a recent carousal. How thankful we were that they had not their dogs with them! We hastened our footsteps, and when we arrived on the plantation we heard the sound of the hand-mill. The slaves were grinding their corn. We were safely in the house before the horn summoned them to their labor. I divided my little parcel of food with my guide, knowing that he had lost the chance of grinding his corn, and must toil all day in the field.

Mr. Flint often took an inspection of the house, to see that no one was idle. The entire management of the work was trusted to me, because he knew nothing about it; and rather than hire a superintendent he contented himself with my arrangements. He had often urged upon his father the necessity of having me at the plantation to take charge of his affairs, and make clothes for the slaves; but the old man knew him too well to consent to that arrangement.

When I had been working a month at the plantation, the great aunt of Mr. Flint came to make him a visit.[2] This was the good old lady who paid fifty dollars for my grandmother, for the purpose of making her free, when she stood on the auction block. My grandmother loved this old lady, whom we all called Miss Fanny. She often came to take tea with us. On such occasions the table was spread with a snow-white cloth, and the china cups and silver spoons were taken from the old-fashioned buffet. There were hot muffins, tea rusks, and delicious sweetmeats. My grandmother kept two cows, and the fresh cream was Miss Fanny's delight. She invariably declared that it was the best in town. The old ladies had cosey times together. They would work and chat, and sometimes, while talking over old times, their spectacles would get dim with tears, and would have to be taken off

and wiped. When Miss Fanny bade us good by, her bag was
grandmother's best cakes, and she was urged to come agai

There had been a time when Dr. Flint's wife came to ta
us, and when her children were also sent to have a feast of "Aunt Marthy's" nice cooking. But after I became an object of her jealousy and
spite, she was angry with grandmother for giving a shelter to me and
my children. She would not even speak to her in the street. This
wounded my grandmother's feelings, for she could not retain ill will
against the woman whom she had nourished with her milk when a
babe. The doctor's wife would gladly have prevented our intercourse
with Miss Fanny if she could have done it, but fortunately she was not
dependent on the bounty of the Flints. She had enough to be independent; and that is more than can ever be gained from charity, however lavish it may be.

Miss Fanny was endeared to me by many recollections, and I was
rejoiced to see her at the plantation. The warmth of her large, loyal
heart made the house seem pleasanter while she was in it. She staid a
week, and I had many talks with her. She said her principal object in
coming was to see how I was treated, and whether any thing could be
done for me. She inquired whether she could help me in any way. I
told her I believed not. She condoled with me in her own peculiar
way; saying she wished that I and all my grandmother's family were at
rest in our graves, for not until then should she feel any peace about
us. The good old soul did not dream that I was planning to bestow
peace upon her, with regard to myself and my children; not by death,
but by securing our freedom.

Again and again I had traversed those dreary twelve miles, to and
from the town; and all the way, I was meditating upon some means of
escape for myself and my children. My friends had made every effort
that ingenuity could devise to effect our purchase, but all their plans
had proved abortive. Dr. Flint was suspicious, and determined not to

loosen his grasp upon us. I could have made my escape alone; but it was more for my helpless children than for myself that I longed for freedom. Though the boon would have been precious to me, above all price, I would not have taken it at the expense of leaving them in slavery. Every trial I endured, every sacrifice I made for their sakes, drew them closer to my heart, and gave me fresh courage to beat back the dark waves that rolled and rolled over me in a seemingly endless night of storms.

The six weeks were nearly completed, when Mr. Flint's bride was expected to take possession of her new home. The arrangements were all completed, and Mr. Flint said I had done well. He expected to leave home on Saturday, and return with his bride the following Wednesday. After receiving various orders from him, I ventured to ask permission to spend Sunday in town. It was granted; for which favor I was thankful. It was the first I had ever asked of him, and I intended it should be the last. It needed more than one night to accomplish the project I had in view; but the whole of Sunday would give me an opportunity. I spent the Sabbath with my grandmother. A calmer, more beautiful day never came down out of heaven. To me it was a day of conflicting emotions. Perhaps it was the last day I should ever spend under that dear, old sheltering roof! Perhaps these were the last talks I should ever have with the faithful old friend of my whole life! Perhaps it was the last time I and my children should be together! Well, better so, I thought, than that they should be slaves. I knew the doom that awaited my fair baby in slavery, and I determined to save her from it, or perish in the attempt. I went to make this vow at the graves of my poor parents, in the burying-ground of the slaves. "There the wicked cease from troubling, and there the weary be at rest. There the prisoners rest together; they hear not the voice of the oppressor; the servant is free from his master."[3] I knelt by the graves of my parents, and thanked God, as I had often done before, that they had not lived to witness my trials, or to mourn over my sins. I had received my mother's blessing when she died; and in many an hour of tribulation I had seemed to hear her voice, sometimes chiding me, sometimes whispering loving words into my wounded heart. I have shed many and bitter tears, to think that when I am gone from my children they cannot remember me with such entire satisfaction as I remembered my mother.

The graveyard was in the woods, and twilight was coming on. Nothing broke the death-like stillness except the occasional twitter of a bird. My spirit was overawed by the solemnity of the scene. For more than ten years I had frequented this spot, but never had it seemed to me so sacred as now. A black stump, at the head of my mother's grave, was all that remained of a tree my father had planted. His grave was marked by a small wooden board, bearing his name, the letters of which were nearly obliterated. I knelt down and kissed them, and poured forth a prayer to God for guidance and support in the perilous step I was about to take. As I passed the wreck of the old meeting house, where, before Nat Turner's time, the slaves had been allowed to meet for worship, I seemed to hear my father's voice come from it, bidding me not to tarry till I reached freedom or the grave. I rushed on with renovated hopes. My trust in God had been strengthened by that prayer among the graves.

My plan was to conceal myself at the house of a friend, and remain there a few weeks till the search was over. My hope was that the doctor would get discouraged, and, for fear of losing my value, and also of subsequently finding my children among the missing, he would consent to sell us; and I knew somebody would buy us. I had done all in my power to make my children comfortable during the time I expected to be separated from them. I was packing my things, when grandmother came into the room, and asked what I was doing. "I am putting my things in order," I replied. I tried to look and speak cheerfully; but her watchful eye detected something beneath the surface. She drew me towards her, and asked me to sit down. She looked earnestly at me, and said, "Linda, do you want to kill your old grandmother? Do you mean to leave your little, helpless children? I am old now, and cannot do for your babies as I once did for you."

I replied, that if I went away, perhaps their father would be able to secure their freedom.

"Ah, my child," said she, "don't trust too much to him. Stand by your own children, and suffer with them till death. Nobody respects a mother who forsakes her children; and if you leave them, you will never have a happy moment. If you go, you will make me miserable the short time I have to live. You would be taken and brought back, and your sufferings would be dreadful. Remember poor Benjamin. Do give it up, Linda. Try to bear a little longer. Things may turn out better than we expect."

My courage failed me, in view of the sorrow I should bring on that faithful, loving old heart. I promised that I would try longer, and that I would take nothing out of her house without her knowledge.

Whenever the children climbed on my knee, or laid their heads on my lap, she would say, "Poor little souls! what would you do without a mother? She don't love you as I do." And she would hug them to her own bosom, as if to reproach me for my want of affection; but she knew all the while that I loved them better than my life. I slept with her that night, and it was the last time. The memory of it haunted me for many a year.

On Monday I returned to the plantation, and busied myself with preparations for the important day. Wednesday came.[4] It was a beautiful day, and the faces of the slaves were as bright as the sunshine. The poor creatures were merry. They were expecting little presents from the bride, and hoping for better times under her administration. I had no such hopes for them. I knew that the young wives of slaveholders often thought their authority and importance would be best established and maintained by cruelty; and what I had heard of young Mrs. Flint gave me no reason to expect that her rule over them would be less severe than that of the master and overseer. Truly, the colored race are the most cheerful and forgiving people on the face of the earth. That their masters sleep in safety is owing to their super-abundance of heart; and yet they look upon their sufferings with less pity than they would bestow on those of a horse or a dog.

I stood at the door with others to receive the bridegroom and bride. She was a handsome, delicate-looking girl, and her face flushed with emotion at sight of her new home. I thought it likely that visions of a happy future were rising before her. It made me sad; for I knew how soon clouds would come over her sunshine. She examined every part of the house, and told me she was delighted with the arrange-ments I had made. I was afraid old Mrs. Flint had tried to prejudice her against me, and I did my best to please her.

All passed off smoothly for me until dinner time arrived. I did not mind the embarrassment of waiting on a dinner party, for the first time in my life, half so much as I did the meeting with Dr. Flint and his wife, who would be among the guests. It was a mystery to me why Mrs. Flint had not made her appearance at the plantation during all the time I was putting the house in order. I had not met her, face to face, for five years, and I had no wish to see her now. She was a pray-ing woman, and, doubtless, considered my present position a special answer to her prayers. Nothing could please her better than to see me humbled and trampled upon. I was just where she would have me—in the power of a hard, unprincipled master. She did not speak to me when she took her seat at table; but her satisfied, triumphant smile, when I handed her plate, was more eloquent than words. The old doctor was not so quiet in his demonstrations. He ordered me here and there, and spoke with peculiar emphasis when he said "your *mis-*

tress." I was drilled like a disgraced soldier. When all was over, and the last key turned, I sought my pillow, thankful that God had appointed a season of rest for the weary.

The next day my new mistress began her housekeeping. I was not exactly appointed maid of all work; but I was to do whatever I was told. Monday evening came. It was always a busy time. On that night the slaves received their weekly allowance of food. Three pounds of meat, a peck of corn, and perhaps a dozen herring were allowed to each man. Women received a pound and a half of meat, a peck of corn, and the same number of herring. Children over twelve years old had half the allowance of the women. The meat was cut and weighed by the foreman of the field hands, and piled on planks before the meat house. Then the second foreman went behind the building, and when the first foreman called out, "Who takes this piece of meat?" he answered by calling somebody's name. This method was resorted to as means of preventing partiality in distributing the meat. The young mistress came out to see how things were done on her plantation, and she soon gave a specimen of her character. Among those in waiting for their allowance was a very old slave, who had faithfully served the Flint family through three generations. When he hobbled up to get his bit of meat, the mistress said he was too old to have any allowance; that when niggers were too old to work, they ought to be fed on grass. Poor old man! He suffered much before he found rest in the grave.

My mistress and I got along very well together. At the end of a week, old Mrs. Flint made us another visit, and was closeted a long time with her daughter-in-law. I had my suspicions what was the subject of the conference. The old doctor's wife had been informed that I could leave the plantation on one condition, and she was very desirous to keep me there. If she had trusted me, as I deserved to be trusted by her, she would have had no fears of my accepting that condition. When she entered her carriage to return home, she said to young Mrs.

Flint, "Don't neglect to send for them as quick as possible." My heart was on the watch all the time, and I at once concluded that she spoke of my children. The doctor came the next day, and as I entered the room to spread the tea table, I heard him say, "Don't wait any longer. Send for them to-morrow." I saw through the plan. They thought my children's being there would fetter me to the spot, and that it was a good place to break us all in to abject submission to our lot as slaves. After the doctor left, a gentleman called, who had always manifested friendly feelings towards my grandmother and her family. Mr. Flint carried him over the plantation to show him the results of labor performed by men and women who were unpaid, miserably clothed, and half famished. The cotton crop was all they thought of. It was duly admired, and the gentleman returned with specimens to show his friends. I was ordered to carry water to wash his hands. As I did so, he said, "Linda, how do you like your new home?" I told him I liked it as well as I expected. He replied, "They don't think you are contented, and to-morrow they are going to bring your children to be with you. I am sorry for you, Linda. I hope they will treat you kindly." I hurried from the room, unable to thank him. My suspicions were correct. My children were to be brought to the plantation to be "broke in."

To this day I feel grateful to the gentleman who gave me this timely information. It nerved me to immediate action.

XVII

The Flight

M R. FLINT WAS hard pushed for house servants, and rather than lose me he had restrained his malice. I did my work faithfully, though not, of course, with a willing mind. They were evidently afraid I should leave them. Mr. Flint wished that I should sleep in the great house instead of the servants' quarters. His wife agreed to the proposition, but said I mustn't bring my bed into the house, because it would scatter feathers on her carpet. I knew when I went there that they would never think of such a thing as furnishing a bed of any kind for me and my little one. I therefore carried my own bed, and now I was forbidden to use it. I did as I was ordered. But now that I was certain my children were to be put in their power, in order to give them a stronger hold on me, I resolved to leave them that night. I remembered the grief this step would bring upon my dear old grandmother; and nothing less than the freedom of my children would have induced me to disregard her advice. I went about my evening work with trembling steps. Mr. Flint twice called from his chamber door to inquire why the house was not locked up. I replied that I had not done my work. "You have had time enough to do it," said he. "Take care how you answer me!"

I shut all the windows, locked all the doors, and went up to the third story, to wait till midnight. How long those hours seemed, and how fervently I prayed that God would not forsake me in this hour of utmost need! I was about to risk every thing on the throw of a die; and if I failed, O what would become of me and my poor children? They would be made to suffer for my fault.

At half past twelve I stole softly down stairs. I stopped on the second floor, thinking I heard a noise. I felt my way down into the parlor, and looked out of the window. The night was so intensely dark that I could see nothing. I raised the window very softly and jumped out. Large drops of rain were falling, and the darkness bewildered me. I dropped on my knees, and breathed a short prayer to God for guidance and protection. I groped my way to the road, and rushed towards the town with almost lightning speed. I arrived at my grandmother's house, but dared not see her. She would say, "Linda, you are killing me"; and I knew that would unnerve me. I tapped softly at the window of a room, occupied by a woman, who had lived in the house several years. I knew she was a faithful friend, and could be trusted with my secret. I tapped several times before she heard me. At last she raised the window, and I whispered, "Sally, I have run away. Let me in, quick." She opened the door softly, and said in low tones, "For God's sake, don't. Your grandmother is trying to buy you and de chillern. Mr. Sands was here last week. He tole her he was going away on business, but he wanted her to go ahead about buying you and de chillern, and he would help her all he could. Don't run away, Linda. Your grandmother is all bowed down wid trouble now."

I replied, "Sally, they are going to carry my children to the plantation to-morrow; and they will never sell them to any body so long as they have me in their power. Now, would you advise me to go back?"

"No, chile, no," answered she. "When dey finds you is gone, dey won't want de plague ob de chillern; but where is you going to hide? Dey knows ebery inch ob dis house."

I told her I had a hiding-place, and that was all it was best for her to know. I asked her to go into my room as soon as it was light, and take all my clothes out of my trunk, and pack them in hers; for I knew Mr. Flint and the constable would be there early to search my room. I feared the sight of my children would be too much for my full heart; but I could not go out into the uncertain future without one last look. I bent over the bed where lay my little Benny and baby Ellen. Poor little ones! fatherless and motherless! Memories of their father came over me. He wanted to be kind to them; but they were not all to him, as they were to my womanly heart. I knelt and prayed for the innocent little sleepers. I kissed them lightly, and turned away.

As I was about to open the street door, Sally laid her hand on my shoulder, and said, "Linda, is you gwine all alone? Let me call your uncle."

"No, Sally," I replied, "I want no one to be brought into trouble on my account."

I went forth into the darkness and rain. I ran on till I came to the house of the friend who was to conceal me.

Early the next morning Mr. Flint was at my grandmother's inquiring for me. She told him she had not seen me, and supposed I was at the plantation. He watched her face narrowly, and said, "Don't you know any thing about her running off?" She assured him that she did not. He went on to say, "Last night she ran off without the least provocation. We had treated her very kindly. My wife liked her. She will soon be found and brought back. Are her children with you?" When told that they were, he said, "I am very glad to hear that. If they are

here, she cannot be far off. If I find out that any of my niggers have
had any thing to do with this damned business, I'll give 'em five hundred lashes." As he started to go to his father's, he turned round and
added, persuasively, "Let her be brought back, and she shall have her
children to live with her."

The tidings made the old doctor rave and storm at a furious rate.
It was a busy day for them. My grandmother's house was searched
from top to bottom. As my trunk was empty, they concluded I had
taken my clothes with me. Before ten o'clock every vessel northward
bound was thoroughly examined, and the law against harboring fugitives was read to all on board. At night a watch was set over the town.
Knowing how distressed my grandmother would be, I wanted to send
her a message; but it could not be done. Every one who went in or
out of her house was closely watched. The doctor said he would take
my children, unless she became responsible for them; which of course
she willingly did. The next day was spent in searching. Before night,
the following advertisement was posted at every corner, and in every
public place for miles round:—

> "$300 REWARD! Ran away from the subscriber, an intelligent,
> bright, mulatto girl, named Linda, 21 years of age. Five feet four
> inches high. Dark eyes, and black hair inclined to curl; but it can be
> made straight. Has a decayed spot on a front tooth. She can read
> and write, and in all probability will try to get to the Free States. All
> persons are forbidden, under penalty of the law, to harbor or em-
> ploy said slave. $150 will be given to whoever takes her in the state,
> and $300 if taken out of the state and delivered to me, or lodged in
> jail.
>
>   DR. FLINT."[1]

XVIII

Months of Peril

THE SEARCH FOR ME was kept up with more perseverance than I had anticipated. I began to think that escape was impossible. I was in great anxiety lest I should implicate the friend who harbored me. I knew the consequences would be frightful; and much as I dreaded being caught, even that seemed better than causing an innocent person to suffer for kindness to me. A week had passed in terrible suspense, when my pursuers came into such close vicinity that I concluded they had tracked me to my hiding-place. I flew out of the house, and concealed myself in a thicket of bushes. There I remained in an agony of fear for two hours. Suddenly, a reptile of some kind seized my leg. In my fright, I struck a blow which loosened its hold, but I could not tell whether I had killed it; it was so dark, I could not see what it was; I only knew it was something cold and slimy. The pain I felt soon indicated that the bite was poisonous. I was compelled to leave my place of concealment, and I groped my way back into the house. The pain had become intense, and my friend was startled by my look of anguish. I asked her to prepare a poultice of warm ashes and vinegar, and I applied it to my leg, which was already much swollen. The application gave me some relief, but the swelling did not abate. The dread of being disabled was greater than the physical pain I endured. My friend asked an old woman, who doctored among the slaves, what was good for the bite of a snake or a lizard. She told her to steep a dozen coppers in vinegar, over night, and apply the cankered vinegar to the inflamed part.[*1]

I had succeeded in cautiously conveying some messages to my relatives. They were harshly threatened, and despairing of my having a chance to escape, they advised me to return to my master, ask his forgiveness, and let him make an example of me. But such counsel had no influence with me. When I started upon this hazardous undertaking, I had resolved that, come what would, there should be no turning back. "Give me liberty, or give me death," was my motto.[2] When my friend contrived to make known to my relatives the painful situation I had been in for twenty-four hours, they said no more about my going back to my master. Something must be done, and that speedily; but where to turn for help, they knew not. God in his mercy raised up "a friend in need."

Among the ladies who were acquainted with my grandmother, was one who had known her from childhood, and always been very friendly to her. She had also known my mother and her children, and felt interested for them. At this crisis of affairs she called to see my grandmother, as she not unfrequently did. She observed the sad and troubled expression of her face, and asked if she knew where Linda

---

*The poison of a snake is a powerful acid, and is counteracted by powerful alkalies, such as potash, ammonia, &c. The Indians are accustomed to apply wet ashes, or plunge the limb into strong lye. White men, employed to lay out railroads in snaky places, often carry ammonia with them as an antidote.—EDITOR.

was, and whether she was safe. My grandmother shook her head, without answering. "Come, Aunt Martha," said the kind lady, "tell me all about it. Perhaps I can do something to help you." The husband of this lady held many slaves, and bought and sold slaves. She also held a number in her own name; but she treated them kindly, and would never allow any of them to be sold. She was unlike the majority of slaveholders' wives. My grandmother looked earnestly at her. Something in the expression of her face said "Trust me!" and she did trust her. She listened attentively to the details of my story, and sat thinking for a while. At last she said, "Aunt Martha, I pity you both. If you think there is any chance of Linda's getting to the Free States, I will conceal her for a time. But first you must solemnly promise that my name shall never be mentioned. If such a thing should become known, it would ruin me and my family. No one in my house must know of it, except the cook. She is so faithful that I would trust my own life with her; and I know she likes Linda. It is a great risk; but I trust no harm will come of it. Get word to Linda to be ready as soon as it is dark, before the patrols are out. I will send the housemaids on errands, and Betty shall go to meet Linda." The place where we were to meet was designated and agreed upon. My grandmother was unable to thank the lady for this noble deed; overcome by her emotions, she sank on her knees and sobbed like a child.[3]

I received a message to leave my friend's house at such an hour, and go to a certain place where a friend would be waiting for me. As a matter of prudence no names were mentioned. I had no means of conjecturing who I was to meet, or where I was going. I did not like to move thus blindfolded, but I had no choice. It would not do for me to remain where I was. I disguised myself, summoned up courage to meet the worst, and went to the appointed place. My friend Betty was there; she was the last person I expected to see. We hurried along in silence. The pain in my leg was so intense that it seemed as if I should drop; but fear gave me strength. We reached the house and entered unobserved. Her first words were: "Honey, now you is safe. Dem devils ain't coming to search *dis* house. When I get you into missis' safe place, I will bring some nice hot supper. I specs you need it after all dis skeering." Betty's vocation led her to think eating the most important thing in life. She did not realize that my heart was too full for me to care much about supper.

The mistress came to meet us, and led me up stairs to a small room over her own sleeping apartment. "You will be safe here, Linda," said she; "I keep this room to store away things that are out of use. The girls are not accustomed to be sent to it, and they will not suspect any thing unless they hear some noise. I always keep it locked, and Betty shall take care of the key. But you must be very careful, for my sake as well as your own; and you must never tell my secret; for it would ruin me and my family. I will keep the girls busy in the morning, that Betty may have a chance to bring your breakfast; but it will not do for her to come to you again till night. I will come to see you sometimes. Keep up your courage. I hope this state of things will not last long." Betty came with the "nice hot supper," and the mistress hastened down stairs to keep things straight till she returned. How my heart overflowed with gratitude! Words choked in my throat; but I could have kissed the feet of my benefactress. For that deed of Christian womanhood, may God forever bless her!

I went to sleep that night with the feeling that I was for the present the most fortunate slave in town. Morning came and filled my little cell with light. I thanked the heavenly Father for this safe retreat. Opposite my window was a pile of feather beds. On the top of these I could lie perfectly concealed, and command a view of the street through which Dr. Flint passed to his office. Anxious as I was, I felt a gleam of satisfaction when I saw him. Thus far I had outwitted him, and I triumphed over it. Who can blame slaves for being cunning?

They are constantly compelled to resort to it. It is the only weapon of the weak and oppressed against the strength of their tyrants.

I was daily hoping to hear that my master had sold my children; for I knew who was on the watch to buy them. But Dr. Flint cared even more for revenge than he did for money. My brother William, and the good aunt who had served in his family twenty years, and my little Benny, and Ellen, who was a little over two years old, were thrust into jail, as a means of compelling my relatives to give some information about me.[4] He swore my grandmother should never see one of them again till I was brought back. They kept these facts from me for several days. When I heard that my little ones were in a loathsome jail, my first impulse was to go to them. I was encountering dangers for the sake of freeing them, and must I be the cause of their death? The thought was agonizing. My benefactress tried to soothe me by telling me that my aunt would take good care of the children while they remained in jail. But it added to my pain to think that the good old aunt, who had always been so kind to her sister's orphan children, should be shut up in prison for no other crime than loving them. I suppose my friends feared a reckless movement on my part, knowing, as they did, that my life was bound up in my children. I received a note from my brother William. It was scarcely legible, and ran thus: "Wherever you are, dear sister, I beg of you not to come here. We are all much better off than you are. If you come, you will ruin us all. They would force you to tell where you had been, or they would kill you. Take the advice of your friends; if not for the sake of me and your children, at least for the sake of those you would ruin."

Poor William! He also must suffer for being my brother. I took his advice and kept quiet. My aunt was taken out of jail at the end of a month, because Mrs. Flint could not spare her any longer. She was tired of being her own housekeeper. It was quite too fatiguing to order her dinner and eat it too. My children remained in jail, where brother William did all he could for their comfort. Betty went to see them sometimes, and brought me tidings. She was not permitted to enter the jail; but William would hold them up to the grated window while she chatted with them. When she repeated their prattle, and told me how they wanted to see their ma, my tears would flow. Old Betty would exclaim, "Lors, chile! what's you crying 'bout? Dem young uns vil kill you dead. Don't be so chick'n hearted! If you does, you vil nebber git thro' dis world."

Good old soul! She had gone through the world childless. She had never had little ones to clasp their arms round her neck; she had never seen their soft eyes looking into hers; no sweet little voices had called her mother; she had never pressed her own infants to her heart, with the feeling that even in fetters there was something to live for. How could she realize my feelings? Betty's husband loved children dearly, and wondered why God had denied them to him. He expressed great sorrow when he came to Betty with the tidings that Ellen had been taken out of jail and carried to Dr. Flint's. She had the measles a short time before they carried her to jail, and the disease had left her eyes affected. The doctor had taken her home to attend to them. My children had always been afraid of the doctor and his wife. They had never been inside of their house. Poor little Ellen cried all day to be carried back to prison. The instincts of childhood are true. She knew she was loved in the jail. Her screams and sobs annoyed Mrs. Flint. Before night she called one of the slaves, and said, "Here, Bill, carry this brat back to the jail. I can't stand her noise. If she would be quiet I should like to keep the little minx. She would make a handy waiting-maid for my daughter by and by. But if she staid here, with her white face, I suppose I should either kill her or spoil her. I hope the doctor will sell them as far as wind and water can carry them. As for their mother, her ladyship will find out yet what she gets by running away. She hasn't so much feeling for her children as a cow has for its calf. If she had, she would have come back long ago, to get them out of jail, and save all this expense and trouble. The good-for-nothing hussy! When she is caught, she shall stay in jail, in irons, for one six months, and then be sold to a sugar plantation. I shall see her broke in yet. What do you stand there for, Bill? Why don't you go off with the brat? Mind, now, that you don't let any of the niggers speak to her in the street!"

When these remarks were reported to me, I smiled at Mrs. Flint's saying that she should either kill my child or spoil her. I thought to myself there was very little danger of the latter. I have always considered it as one of God's special providences that Ellen screamed till she was carried back to jail.

That same night Dr. Flint was called to a patient, and did not return till near morning. Passing my grandmother's, he saw a light in the house, and thought to himself, "Perhaps this has something to do with Linda." He knocked, and the door was opened. "What calls you up so early?" said he. "I saw your light, and I thought I would just stop and tell you that I have found out where Linda is. I know where to put my hands on her, and I shall have her before twelve o'clock." When he had turned away, my grandmother and my uncle looked anxiously at each other. They did not know whether or not it was merely one of the doctor's tricks to frighten them. In their uncertainty, they thought it was best to have a message conveyed to my friend Betty. Unwilling to alarm her mistress, Betty resolved to dispose of me herself. She came to me, and told me to rise and dress quickly. We hurried down stairs, and across the yard, into the kitchen. She locked the door, and lifted up a plank in the floor. A buffalo skin and a bit of carpet were spread for me to lie on, and a quilt thrown over me. "Stay dar," said she, "till I sees if dey know 'bout you. Dey say dey vil put thar hans on you afore twelve o'clock. If dey *did* know whar you are, dey won't know *now*. Dey'll be disapinted dis time. Dat's all I got to say. If dey comes rummagin 'mong *my* tings, dey'll get one bressed sarssin from dis 'ere nigger." In my shallow bed I had but just room enough to bring my hands to my face to keep the dust out of my eyes; for Betty walked over me twenty times in an hour, passing from the dresser to the fireplace. When she was alone, I could hear her pronouncing anathemas over Dr. Flint and all his tribe, every now and then saying, with a chuckling laugh, "Dis nigger's too cute for 'em dis time." When the housemaids were about, she had sly ways of drawing them out, that I might hear what they would say. She would repeat stories she had heard about my being in this, or that, or the other place. To which they would answer, that I was not fool enough to be staying round there; that I was in Philadelphia or New York before this time. When all were abed and asleep, Betty raised the plank, and said, "Come out, chile; come out. Dey don't know nottin 'bout you. 'Twas only white folks' lies, to skeer de niggers."

Some days after this adventure I had a much worse fright. As I sat very still in my retreat above stairs, cheerful visions floated through my mind. I thought Dr. Flint would soon get discouraged, and would be willing to sell my children, when he lost all hopes of making them the means of my discovery. I knew who was ready to buy them. Suddenly I heard a voice that chilled my blood. The sound was too familiar to me, it had been too dreadful, for me not to recognize at once my old master. He was in the house, and I at once concluded he had come to seize me. I looked round in terror. There was no way of escape. The voice receded. I supposed the constable was with him, and they were searching the house. In my alarm I did not forget the trouble I was bringing on my generous benefactress. It seemed as if I were born to bring sorrow on all who befriended me, and that was the bitterest drop in the bitter cup of my life. After a while I heard approaching footsteps; the key was turned in my door. I braced myself against the wall to keep from falling. I ventured to look up, and there stood my kind benefactress alone. I was too much overcome to speak, and sunk down upon the floor.

"I thought you would hear your master's voice," she said; "and knowing you would be terrified, I came to tell you there is nothing to fear. You may even indulge in a laugh at the old gentleman's expense. He is so sure you are in New York, that he came to borrow five hundred dollars to go in pursuit of you. My sister had some money to loan on interest. He has obtained it, and proposes to start for New York to-night. So, for the present, you see you are safe. The doctor will merely lighten his pocket hunting after the bird he has left behind."

XIX

The Children Sold

THE DOCTOR CAME back from New York, of course without accomplishing his purpose.[1] He had expended considerable money, and was rather disheartened. My brother and the children had now been in jail two months, and that also was some expense. My friends thought it was a favorable time to work on his discouraged feelings. Mr. Sands sent a speculator to offer him nine hundred dollars for my brother William, and eight hundred for the two children. These were high prices, as slaves were then selling; but the offer was rejected. If it had been merely a question of money, the doctor would have sold any boy of Benny's age for two hundred dollars; but he could not bear to give up the power of revenge. But he was hard pressed for money, and he revolved the matter in his mind. He knew that if he could keep Ellen till she was fifteen, he could sell her for a high price; but I presume he reflected that she might die, or might be stolen away. At all events, he came to the conclusion that he had better accept the slave-trader's offer. Meeting him in the street, he inquired when he would leave town. "To-day, at ten o'clock," he replied. "Ah, do you go so soon?" said the doctor; "I have been reflecting upon your proposition, and I have concluded to let you have the three negroes if you will say nineteen hundred dollars." After some parley, the trader agreed to his terms. He wanted the bill of sale drawn up and signed immediately, as he had a great deal to attend to during the short time he remained in town. The doctor went to the jail and told William he would take him back into his service if he would promise to behave himself; but he replied that he would rather be sold. "And you *shall* be sold, you ungrateful rascal!" exclaimed the doctor. In less than an hour the money was paid, the papers were signed, sealed, and delivered, and my brother and children were in the hands of the trader.[2]

It was a hurried transaction; and after it was over, the doctor's characteristic caution returned. He went back to the speculator, and said, "Sir, I have come to lay you under obligations of a thousand dollars not to sell any of those negroes in this state." "You come too late," replied the trader; "our bargain is closed." He had, in fact, already sold them to Mr. Sands, but he did not mention it. The doctor required him to put irons on "that rascal, Bill," and to pass through the back streets when he took his gang out of town. The trader was privately instructed to concede to his wishes. My good old aunt went to the jail to bid the children good by, supposing them to be the speculator's property, and that she should never see them again. As she held Benny in her lap, he said, "Aunt Nancy, I want to show you something." He led her to the door and showed her a long row of marks, saying, "Uncle Will taught me to count. I have made a mark for every day I have been here, and it is sixty days. It is a long time; and the speculator is going to take me and Ellen away. He's a bad man. It's wrong for him to take grandmother's children. I want to go to my mother."

My grandmother was told that the children would be restored to her, but she was requested to act as if they were really to be sent away. Accordingly, she made up a bundle of clothes and went to the jail. When she arrived, she found William handcuffed among the gang, and the children in the trader's cart. The scene seemed too much like reality. She was afraid there might have been some deception or mistake. She fainted, and was carried home.

When the wagon stopped at the hotel, several gentlemen came out and proposed to purchase William, but the trader refused their offers, without stating that he was already sold. And now came the trying hour for that drove of human beings, driven away like cattle, to be sold they knew not where. Husbands were torn from wives, parents from children, never to look upon each other again this side the grave. There was wringing of hands and cries of despair.

Dr. Flint had the supreme satisfaction of seeing the wagon leave town, and Mrs. Flint had the gratification of supposing that my children were going "as far as wind and water would carry them." According to agreement, my uncle followed the wagon some miles, until they came to an old farm house. There the trader took the irons from William,[3] and as he did so, he said, "You are a damned clever fellow. I should like to own you myself. Them gentlemen that wanted to buy you said you was a bright, honest chap, and I must git you a good home. I guess your old master will swear to-morrow, and call himself an old fool for selling the children. I reckon he'll never git their mammy back agin. I expect she's made tracks for the north. Good by, old boy. Remember, I have done you a good turn. You must thank me by coaxing all the pretty gals to go with me next fall. That's going to be my last trip. This trading in niggers is a bad business for a fellow that's got any heart. Move on, you fellows!" And the gang went on, God alone knows where.

Much as I despise and detest the class of slave-traders, whom I regard as the vilest wretches on earth, I must do this man the justice to say that he seemed to have some feeling. He took a fancy to William in the jail, and wanted to buy him. When he heard the story of my children, he was willing to aid them in getting out of Dr. Flint's power, even without charging the customary fee.

My uncle procured a wagon and carried William and the children back to town. Great was the joy in my grandmother's house! The curtains were closed, and the candles lighted. The happy grandmother cuddled the little ones to her bosom. They hugged her, and kissed her, and clapped their hands, and shouted. She knelt down and poured forth one of her heartfelt prayers of thanksgiving to God. The father was present for a while; and though such a "parental relation" as existed between him and my children takes slight hold of the hearts or consciences of slaveholders, it must be that he experienced some moments of pure joy in witnessing the happiness he had imparted.

I had no share in the rejoicings of that evening. The events of the day had not come to my knowledge. And now I will tell you something that happened to me; though you will, perhaps, think it illustrates the superstition of slaves. I sat in my usual place on the floor near the window, where I could hear much that was said in the street without being seen. The family had retired for the night, and all was still. I sat there thinking of my children, when I heard a low strain of music. A band of serenaders were under the window, playing "Home, sweet home."[4] I listened till the sounds did not seem like music, but like the moaning of children. It seemed as if my heart would burst. I rose from my sitting posture, and knelt. A streak of moonlight was on the floor before me, and in the midst of it appeared the forms of my two children. They vanished; but I had seen them distinctly. Some will call it a dream, others a vision. I know not how to account for it, but it made a strong impression on my mind, and I felt certain something had happened to my little ones.

I had not seen Betty since morning. Now I heard her softly turning the key. As soon as she entered, I clung to her, and begged her to let me know whether my children were dead, or whether they were sold; for I had seen their spirits in my room, and I was sure something had happened to them. "Lor, chile," said she, putting her arms round me, "you's got de highsterics. I'll sleep wid you to-night, 'cause you'll make a noise, and ruin missis. Something has stirred you up mightily. When you is done cryin, I'll talk wid you. De chillern is well, and mighty happy. I seed 'em myself. Does dat satisfy you? Dar, chile, be still! Somebody vill hear you." I tried to obey her. She lay down, and was soon sound asleep; but no sleep would come to my eyelids.

At dawn, Betty was up and off to the kitchen. The hours passed on, and the vision of the night kept constantly recurring to my thoughts. After a while I heard the voices of two women in the entry. In one of them I recognized the housemaid. The other said to her, "Did you know Linda Brent's children was sold to the speculator yesterday. They say ole massa Flint was mighty glad to see 'em drove out of town; but they say they've come back agin. I 'spect it's all their daddy's doings. They say he's bought William too. Lor! how it will take hold of ole massa Flint! I'm going roun' to aunt Marthy's to see 'bout it."

I bit my lips till the blood came to keep from crying out. Were my children with their grandmother, or had the speculator carried them off? The suspense was dreadful. Would Betty *never* come, and tell me the truth about it? At last she came, and I eagerly repeated what I had overheard. Her face was one broad, bright smile. "Lor, you foolish ting!" said she. "I'se gwine to tell you all 'bout it. De gals is eating thar breakfast, and missus tole me to let her tell you; but, poor creeter! t'aint right to keep you waitin', and I'se gwine to tell you. Brudder, chillern, all is bought by de daddy! I'se laugh more dan nuff, tinking 'bout ole massa Flint. Lor, how he *vill* swar! He's got ketched dis time, any how; but I must be getting out o' dis, or dem gals vill come and ketch *me*."

Betty went off laughing; and I said to myself, "Can it be true that my children are free? I have not suffered for them in vain. Thank God!"

Great surprise was expressed when it was known that my children had returned to their grandmother's. The news spread through the town, and many a kind word was bestowed on the little ones.

Dr. Flint went to my grandmother's to ascertain who was the owner of my children, and she informed him. "I expected as much," said he. "I am glad to hear it. I have had news from Linda lately, and I shall soon have her. You need never expect to see *her* free. She shall be my slave as long as I live, and when I am dead she shall be the slave of my children. If I ever find out that you or Phillip had any thing to do with her running off I'll kill him. And if I meet William in the street, and he presumes to look at me, I'll flog him within an inch of his life. Keep those brats out of my sight!"[5]

As he turned to leave, my grandmother said something to remind him of his own doings. He looked back upon her, as if he would have been glad to strike her to the ground.

I had my season of joy and thanksgiving. It was the first time since my childhood that I had experienced any real happiness. I heard of the old doctor's threats, but they no longer had the same power to trouble me. The darkest cloud that hung over my life had rolled away. Whatever slavery might do to me, it could not shackle my children. If I fell a sacrifice, my little ones were saved. It was well for me that my simple heart believed all that had been promised for their welfare. It is always better to trust than to doubt.

XX

New Perils

THE DOCTOR, more exasperated than ever, again tried to revenge himself on my relatives. He arrested uncle Phillip on the charge of having aided my flight. He was carried before a court, and swore truly that he knew nothing of my intention to escape, and that he had not seen me since I left my master's plantation. The doctor then demanded that he should give bail for five hundred dollars that he would have nothing to do with me. Several gentlemen offered to be security for him; but Mr. Sands told him he had better go back to jail, and he would see that he came out without giving bail.

The news of his arrest was carried to my grandmother, who conveyed it to Betty. In the kindness of her heart, she again stowed me away under the floor; and as she walked back and forth, in the performance of her culinary duties, she talked apparently to herself, but with the intention that I should hear what was going on. I hoped that my uncle's imprisonment would last but few days; still I was anxious.

I thought it likely Dr. Flint would do his utmost to taunt and insult him, and I was afraid my uncle might lose control of himself, and retort in some way that would be construed into a punishable offence; and I was well aware that in court his word would not be taken against any white man's. The search for me was renewed. Something had excited suspicions that I was in the vicinity. They searched the house I was in. I heard their steps and their voices. At night, when all were asleep, Betty came to release me from my place of confinement. The fright I had undergone, the constrained posture, and the dampness of the ground, made me ill for several days. My uncle was soon after taken out of prison; but the movements of all my relatives, and of all our friends, were very closely watched.

We all saw that I could not remain where I was much longer. I had already staid longer than was intended, and I knew my presence must be a source of perpetual anxiety to my kind benefactress. During this time, my friends had laid many plans for my escape, but the extreme vigilance of my persecutors made it impossible to carry them into effect.

One morning I was much startled by hearing somebody trying to get into my room. Several keys were tried, but none fitted. I instantly conjectured it was one of the housemaids; and I concluded she must either have heard some noise in the room, or have noticed the entrance of Betty. When my friend came, at her usual time, I told her what had happened. "I knows who it was," said she. "'Pend upon it, 'twas dat Jenny. Dat nigger allers got de debble in her."[1] I suggested that she might have seen or heard something that excited her curiosity.

"Tut! tut! chile!" exclaimed Betty, "she ain't seen notin', nor hearn notin'. She only 'spects something. Dat's all. She wants to fine out who hab cut and make my gownd. But she won't nebber know. Dat's sartin. I'll git missis to fix her."

I reflected a moment, and said, "Betty, I must leave here tonight."

"Do as you tink best, poor chile," she replied. "I'se mighty 'fraid dat 'ere nigger vill pop on you some time."

She reported the incident to her mistress, and received orders to keep Jenny busy in the kitchen till she could see my uncle Phillip. He told her he would send a friend for me that very evening. She told him she hoped I was going to the north, for it was very dangerous for me to remain any where in the vicinity. Alas, it was not an easy thing, for one in my situation, to go to the north. In order to leave the coast quite clear for me, she went into the country to spend the day with her brother, and took Jenny with her.[2] She was afraid to come and bid me good by, but she left a kind message with Betty. I heard her carriage roll from the door, and I never again saw her who had so generously befriended the poor, trembling fugitive! Though she was a slaveholder, to this day my heart blesses her!

I had not the slightest idea where I was going. Betty brought me a suit of sailor's clothes,—jacket, trowsers, and tarpaulin hat. She gave me a small bundle, saying I might need it where I was going. In cheery tones, she exclaimed, "I'se so glad you is gwine to free parts! Don't forget ole Betty. P'raps I'll come 'long by and by."

I tried to tell her how grateful I felt for all her kindness, but she interrupted me. "I don't want no tanks, honey. I'se glad I could help you, and I hope de good Lord vill open de path for you. I'se gwine wid you to de lower gate. Put your hands in your pockets, and walk rick-etty, like de sailors."

I performed to her satisfaction. At the gate I found Peter, a young colored man, waiting for me. I had known him for years. He had been an apprentice to my father, and had always borne a good character. I was not afraid to trust to him. Betty bade me a hurried good by, and we walked off. "Take courage, Linda," said my friend Peter. "I've got a dagger, and no man shall take you from me, unless he passes over my dead body."

It was a long time since I had taken a walk out of doors, and the fresh air revived me. It was also pleasant to hear a human voice speaking to me above a whisper. I passed several people whom I knew, but they did not recognize me in my disguise. I prayed internally that, for Peter's sake, as well as my own, nothing might occur to bring out his dagger. We walked on till we came to the wharf. My aunt Nancy's husband was a seafaring man, and it had been deemed necessary to let him into our secret.[3] He took me into his boat, rowed out to a vessel not far distant, and hoisted me on board. We three were the only occupants of the vessel. I now ventured to ask what they proposed to do with me. They said I was to remain on board till near dawn, and then they would hide me in Snaky Swamp, till my uncle Phillip had prepared a place of concealment for me.[4] If the vessel had been bound north, it would have been of no avail to me, for it would certainly have been searched. About four o'clock, we were again seated in the boat, and rowed three miles to the swamp. My fear of snakes had been increased by the venomous bite I had received, and I dreaded to enter this hiding-place. But I was in no situation to choose, and I gratefully accepted the best that my poor, persecuted friends could do for me.

Peter landed first, and with a large knife cut a path through bamboos and briers of all descriptions. He came back, took me in his arms, and carried me to a seat made among the bamboos. Before we reached it, we were covered with hundreds of mosquitos. In an hour's time they had so poisoned my flesh that I was a pitiful sight to behold. As the light increased, I saw snake after snake crawling round us. I had been accustomed to the sight of snakes all my life, but these were larger than any I had ever seen. To this day I shudder when I remember that morning. As evening approached, the number of snakes increased so much that we were continually obliged to thrash them with sticks to keep them from crawling over us. The bamboos were so high and so thick that it was impossible to see beyond a very short distance. Just before it became dark we procured a seat nearer to the entrance of the swamp, being fearful of losing our way back to the boat. It was not long before we heard the paddle of oars, and the low whistle, which had been agreed upon as a signal. We made haste to enter the boat, and were rowed back to the vessel. I passed a wretched night; for the heat of the swamp, the mosquitos, and the constant terror of snakes, had brought on a burning fever. I had just dropped asleep, when they came and told me it was time to go back to that horrid swamp. I could scarcely summon courage to rise. But even those large, venomous snakes were less dreadful to my imagination than the white men in that community called civilized. This time Peter took a quantity of tobacco to burn, to keep off the mosquitos. It produced the desired effect on them, but gave me nausea and severe headache. At dark we returned to the vessel. I had been so sick during the day, that Peter declared I should go home that night, if the devil himself was on patrol. They told me a place of concealment had been provided for me at my grandmother's. I could not imagine how it was possible to hide me in her house, every nook and corner of which was known to the Flint family. They told me to wait and see. We were rowed ashore, and went boldly through the streets, to my grandmother's. I wore my sailor's clothes, and had blackened my face with charcoal. I passed several people whom I knew. The father of my children came so near that I brushed against his arm; but he had no idea who it was.

"You must make the most of this walk," said my friend Peter, "for you may not have another very soon."

I thought his voice sounded sad. It was kind of him to conceal from me what a dismal hole was to be my home for a long, long time.

XXI

The Loophole of Retreat[1]

A SMALL SHED HAD been added to my grandmother's house years ago. Some boards were laid across the joists at the top, and between these boards and the roof was a very small garret, never occupied by any thing but rats and mice. It was a pent roof, covered with nothing but shingles, according to the southern custom for such buildings. The garret was only nine feet long and seven wide. The highest part was three feet high, and sloped down abruptly to the loose board floor. There was no admission for either light or air. My uncle Phillip, who was a carpenter, had very skilfully made a concealed trap-door, which communicated with the storeroom. He had been doing this while I was waiting in the swamp. The storeroom opened upon a piazza. To this hole I was conveyed as soon as I entered the house. The air was stifling; the darkness total. A bed had been spread on the floor. I could sleep quite comfortably on one side; but the slope was so sudden that I could not turn on the other without hitting the roof.[2] The rats and mice ran over my bed; but I was weary, and I slept such sleep as the wretched may, when a tempest has passed over them. Morning came. I knew it only by the noises I heard; for in my small den day and night were all the same. I suffered for air even more than for light. But I was not comfortless. I heard the voices of my children. There was joy and there was sadness in the sound. It made my tears flow. How I longed to speak to them! I was eager to look on their faces; but there was no hole, no crack, through which I could peep. This continued darkness was oppressive. It seemed horrible to sit or lie in a cramped position day after day, without one gleam of light. Yet I would have chosen this, rather than my lot as a slave, though white people considered it an easy one; and it was so compared with the fate of others. I was never cruelly over-worked; I was never lacerated with the whip from head to foot; I was never so beaten and bruised that I could not turn from one side to the other; I never had my heel-strings cut to prevent my running away; I was never chained to a log and forced to drag it about, while I toiled in the fields from morning till night; I was never branded with hot iron, or torn by bloodhounds. On the contrary, I had always been kindly treated, and tenderly cared for, until I came into the hands of Dr. Flint. I had never wished for freedom till then. But though my life in slavery was comparatively devoid of hardships, God pity the woman who is compelled to lead such a life!

My food was passed up to me through the trap-door my uncle had contrived; and my grandmother, my uncle Phillip, and aunt Nancy would seize such opportunities as they could, to mount up there and chat with me at the opening. But of course this was not safe in the daytime. It must all be done in darkness. It was impossible for me to move in an erect position, but I crawled about my den for exercise. One day I hit my head against something, and found it was a gimlet. My uncle had left it sticking there when he made the trap-door. I was as rejoiced as Robinson Crusoe could have been at finding such a treasure. It put a lucky thought into my head. I said to myself, "Now I will have some light. Now I will see my children." I did not dare to begin my work during the daytime, for fear of attracting attention. But I groped round; and having found the side next the street, where I could frequently see my children, I stuck the gimlet in and waited for evening. I bored three rows of holes, one above another; then I bored out the interstices between. I thus succeeded in making one hole about an inch long and an inch broad. I sat by it till late into the night, to enjoy the little whiff of air that floated in. In the morning I watched for my children. The first person I saw in the street was Dr. Flint.[3] I had a shuddering, superstitious feeling that it was a bad omen. Several familiar faces passed by. At last I heard the merry laugh of children, and presently two sweet little faces were looking up at me, as though they knew I was there, and were conscious of the joy they imparted. How I longed to *tell* them I was there!

My condition was now a little improved. But for weeks I was tormented by hundreds of little red insects, fine as a needle's point, that pierced through my skin, and produced an intolerable burning. The good grandmother gave me herb teas and cooling medicines, and finally I got rid of them. The heat of my den was intense, for nothing but thin shingles protected me from the scorching summer's sun. But I had my consolations. Through my peeping-hole I could watch the children, and when they were near enough, I could hear their talk. Aunt Nancy brought me all the news she could hear at Dr. Flint's. From her I learned that the doctor had written to New York to a colored woman, who had been born and raised in our neighborhood, and had breathed his contaminating atmosphere. He offered her a reward if she could find out any thing about me. I know not what was the nature of her reply; but he soon after started for New York in haste, saying to his family that he had business of importance to transact.[4] I peeped at him as he passed on his way to the steamboat. It was a satisfaction to have miles of land and water between us, even for a little while; and it was a still greater satisfaction to know that he believed me to be in the Free States. My little den seemed less dreary than it had done. He returned, as he did from his former journey to New York, without obtaining any satisfactory information. When he passed our house next morning, Benny was standing at the gate. He had heard them say that he had gone to find me, and he called out, "Dr. Flint, did you bring my mother home? I want to see her." The doctor stamped his foot at him in a rage, and exclaimed, "Get out of the way, you little damned rascal! If you don't, I'll cut off your head."

Benny ran terrified into the house, saying, "You can't put me in jail again. I don't belong to you now." It was well that the wind carried the words away from the doctor's ear. I told my grandmother of it, when we had our next conference at the trap-door; and begged of her not to allow the children to be impertinent to the irascible old man.

Autumn came, with a pleasant abatement of heat. My eyes had become accustomed to the dim light, and by holding my book or work in a certain position near the aperture I contrived to read and sew. That was a great relief to the tedious monotony of my life. But when winter came, the cold penetrated through the thin shingle roof, and I was dreadfully chilled. The winters there are not so long, or so severe, as in northern latitudes; but the houses are not built to shelter from cold, and my little den was peculiarly comfortless.[5] The kind grandmother brought me bed-clothes and warm drinks. Often I was obliged to lie in bed all day to keep comfortable; but with all my precautions, my shoulders and feet were frostbitten. O, those long, gloomy days, with no object for my eye to rest upon, and no thoughts to occupy my mind, except the dreary past and the uncertain future! I was thankful when there came a day sufficiently mild for me to wrap myself up and sit at the loophole to watch the passers by. Southerners have the habit of stopping and talking in the streets, and I heard many conversations not intended to meet my ears. I heard slave-hunters planning how to catch some poor fugitive. Several times I heard allusions to Dr. Flint, myself, and the history of my children, who, perhaps, were playing near the gate. One would say, "I wouldn't move my little finger to catch her, as old Flint's property." Another would say, "I'll catch *any* nigger for the reward. A man ought to have what belongs to him, if he *is* a damned brute." The opinion was often expressed that I was in the Free States. Very rarely did any one suggest that I might be in the vicinity. Had the least suspicion rested on my grandmother's house, it would have been burned to the ground. But it was the last place they thought of. Yet there was no place, where slavery existed, that could have afforded me so good a place of concealment.

Dr. Flint and his family repeatedly tried to coax and bribe my children to tell something they had heard said about me. One day the doctor took them into a shop, and offered them some bright little silver pieces and gay handkerchiefs if they would tell where their mother was. Ellen shrank away from him, and would not speak; but Benny spoke up, and said, "Dr. Flint, I don't know where my mother is. I guess she's in New York; and when you go there again, I wish you'd ask her to come home, for I want to see her; but if you put her in jail, or tell her you'll cut her head off, I'll tell her to go right back."

XXII

Christmas Festivities

CHRISTMAS WAS APPROACHING. Grandmother brought me materials, and I busied myself making some new garments and little playthings for my children. Were it not that hiring day is near at hand, and many families are fearfully looking forward to the probability of separation in a few days, Christmas might be a happy season for the poor slaves. Even slave mothers try to gladden the hearts of their little ones on that occasion. Benny and Ellen had their Christmas stockings filled. Their imprisoned mother could not have the privilege of witnessing their surprise and joy. But I had the pleasure of peeping at them as they went into the street with their new suits on. I heard Benny ask a little playmate whether Santa Claus brought him any thing. "Yes," replied the boy; "but Santa Claus ain't a real man. It's the children's mothers that put things into the stockings." "No, that can't be," replied Benny, "for Santa Claus brought Ellen and me these new clothes, and my mother has been gone this long time."

How I longed to tell him that his mother made those garments, and that many a tear fell on them while she worked!

Every child rises early on Christmas morning to see the Johnkannaus.[1] Without them, Christmas would be shorn of its greatest attraction. They consist of companies of slaves from the plantations, generally of the lower class. Two athletic men, in calico wrappers, have a net thrown over them, covered with all manner of bright-colored stripes. Cows' tails are fastened to their backs, and their heads are decorated with horns. A box, covered with sheepskin, is called the gumbo box. A dozen beat on this, while others strike triangles and jawbones, to which bands of dancers keep time. For a month previous they are composing songs, which are sung on this occasion. These companies, of a hundred each, turn out early in the morning, and are allowed to go round till twelve o'clock, begging for contributions. Not a door is left unvisited where there is the least chance of obtaining a penny or a glass of rum. They do not drink while they are out, but carry the rum home in jugs, to have a carousal. These Christmas donations frequently amount to twenty or thirty dollars. It is seldom that any white man or child refuses to give them a trifle. If he does, they regale his ears with the following song:—

"Poor massa, so dey say;
Down in de heel, so dey say;
Got no money, so dey say;
Not one shillin, so dey say;
God A'mighty bress you, so dey say."[2]

Christmas is a day of feasting, both with white and colored people. Slaves, who are lucky enough to have a few shillings, are sure to spend them for good eating; and many a turkey and pig is captured, without saying, "By your leave, sir." Those who cannot obtain these, cook a 'possum, or a raccoon, from which savory dishes can be made. My grandmother raised poultry and pigs for sale; and it was her established custom to have both a turkey and a pig roasted for Christmas dinner.

On this occasion, I was warned to keep extremely quiet, because two guests had been invited. One was the town constable, and the other was a free colored man, who tried to pass himself off for white, and who was always ready to do any mean work for the sake of currying favor with white people. My grandmother had a motive for inviting them. She managed to take them all over the house. All the rooms on the lower floor were thrown open for them to pass in and out; and after dinner, they were invited up stairs to look at a fine mocking bird my uncle had just brought home. There, too, the rooms were all thrown open, that they might look in. When I heard them talking on the piazza, my heart almost stood still. I knew this colored man had spent many nights hunting for me. Every body knew he had the blood of a slave father in his veins; but for the sake of passing himself off for white, he was ready to kiss the slaveholders' feet. How I despised him! As for the constable, he wore no false colors. The duties of his office were despicable, but he was superior to his companion, inasmuch as he did not pretend to be what he was not. Any white man, who could raise money enough to buy a slave, would have considered himself degraded by being a constable; but the office enabled its possessor to exercise authority. If he found any slave out after nine o'clock, he could whip him as much as he liked; and that was a privilege to be coveted. When the guests were ready to depart, my grandmother gave each of them some of her nice pudding, as a present for their wives. Through my peep-hole I saw them go out of the gate, and I was glad when it closed after them. So passed the first Christmas in my den.

XXIII

Still in Prison

W HEN SPRING RETURNED, and I took in the little patch of green the aperture commanded, I asked myself how many more summers and winters I must be condemned to spend thus. I longed to draw in a plentiful draught of fresh air, to stretch my cramped limbs, to have room to stand erect, to feel the earth under my feet again. My relatives were constantly on the lookout for a chance of escape; but none offered that seemed practicable, and even tolerably safe. The hot summer came again, and made the turpentine drop from the thin roof over my head.

During the long nights I was restless for want of air, and I had no room to toss and turn. There was but one compensation; the atmosphere was so stifled that even mosquitos would not condescend to buzz in it. With all my detestation of Dr. Flint, I could hardly wish him a worse punishment, either in this world or that which is to come, than to suffer what I suffered in one single summer. Yet the laws allowed *him* to be out in the free air, while I, guiltless of crime, was pent up here, as the only means of avoiding the cruelties the laws allowed him to inflict upon me! I don't know what kept life within me. Again and again, I thought I should die before long; but I saw the leaves of another autumn whirl through the air, and felt the touch of another winter. In summer the most terrible thunder storms were acceptable, for the rain came through the roof, and I rolled up my bed that it might cool the hot boards under it. Later in the season, storms sometimes wet my clothes through and through, and that was not comfortable when the air grew chilly. Moderate storms I could keep out by filling the chinks with oakum.

But uncomfortable as my situation was, I had glimpses of things out of doors, which made me thankful for my wretched hiding-place. One day I saw a slave pass our gate, muttering, "It's his own, and he can kill it if he will." My grandmother told me that woman's history. Her mistress had that day seen her baby for the first time, and in the lineaments of its fair face she saw a likeness to her husband. She turned the bondwoman and her child out of doors, and forbade her ever to return. The slave went to her master, and told him what had happened. He promised to talk with her mistress, and make it all right. The next day she and her baby were sold to a Georgia trader.

Another time I saw a woman rush wildly by, pursued by two men. She was a slave, the wet nurse of her mistress's children. For some trifling offence her mistress ordered her to be stripped and whipped. To escape the degradation and the torture, she rushed to the river, jumped in, and ended her wrongs in death.

Senator Brown, of Mississippi, could not be ignorant of many such facts as these, for they are of frequent occurrence in every Southern State. Yet he stood up in the Congress of the United States, and declared that slavery was "a great moral, social, and political blessing; a blessing to the master, and a blessing to the slave!"[1]

I suffered much more during the second winter than I did during the first. My limbs were benumbed by inaction, and the cold filled them with cramp. I had a very painful sensation of coldness in my head; even my face and tongue stiffened, and I lost the power of speech. Of course it was impossible, under the circumstances, to summon any physician. My brother William came and did all he could for me. Uncle Phillip also watched tenderly over me; and poor grandmother crept up and down to inquire whether there were any signs of returning life. I was restored to consciousness by the dashing of cold water in my face, and found myself leaning against my brother's arm, while he bent over me with streaming eyes. He afterwards told me he thought I was dying, for I had been in an unconscious state sixteen hours. I next became delirious, and was in great danger of betraying myself and my friends. To prevent this, they stupefied me with drugs. I remained in bed six weeks, weary in body and sick at heart. How to get medical advice was the question. William finally went to a Thompsonian doctor, and described himself as having all my pains and aches.[2] He returned with herbs, roots, and ointment. He was especially charged to rub on the ointment by a fire; but how could a fire be made in my little den? Charcoal in a furnace was tried, but there was no outlet for the gas, and it nearly cost me my life. Afterwards coals, already kindled, were brought up in an iron pan, and placed on bricks. I was so weak, and it was so long since I had enjoyed the warmth of a fire, that those few coals actually made me weep. I think the medicines did me some good; but my recovery was very slow. Dark thoughts passed through my mind as I lay there day after day. I tried to be thankful for my little cell, dismal as it was, and even to love it, as part of the price I had paid for the redemption of my children. Sometimes I thought God was a compassionate Father, who would forgive my sins for the sake of my sufferings. At other times, it seemed to me there was no justice or mercy in the divine government. I asked why the curse of slavery was permitted to exist, and why I had been so persecuted and wronged from youth upward. These things took the shape of mystery, which is to this day not so clear to my soul as I trust it will be hereafter.[3]

In the midst of my illness, grandmother broke down under the weight of anxiety and toil. The idea of losing her, who had always been my best friend and a mother to my children, was the sorest trial I had yet had. O, how earnestly I prayed that she might recover! How hard it seemed, that I could not tend upon her, who had so long and so tenderly watched over me!

One day the screams of a child nerved me with strength to crawl to my peeping-hole, and I saw my son covered with blood. A fierce dog, usually kept chained, had seized and bitten him. A doctor was sent for, and I heard the groans and screams of my child while the wounds were being sewed up. O, what torture to a mother's heart, to listen to this and be unable to go to him!

But childhood is like a day in spring, alternately shower and sunshine. Before night Benny was bright and lively, threatening the destruction of the dog; and great was his delight when the doctor told him the next day that the dog had bitten another boy and been shot. Benny recovered from his wounds; but it was long before he could walk.

When my grandmother's illness became known, many ladies, who were her customers, called to bring her some little comforts, and to inquire whether she had every thing she wanted. Aunt Nancy one night asked permission to watch with her sick mother, and Mrs. Flint replied, "I don't see any need of your going. I can't spare you." But when she found other ladies in the neighborhood were so attentive, not wishing to be outdone in Christian charity, she also sallied forth, in magnificent condescension, and stood by the bedside of her who had loved her in her infancy, and who had been repaid by such grievous wrongs. She seemed surprised to find her so ill, and scolded uncle Phillip for not sending for Dr. Flint. She herself sent for him immediately, and he came. Secure as I was in my retreat, I should have been terrified if I had known he was so near me. He pronounced my grandmother in a very critical situation, and said if her attending physician wished it, he would visit her. Nobody wished to have him coming to the house at all hours, and we were not disposed to give him a chance to make out a long bill.

As Mrs. Flint went out, Sally told her the reason Benny was lame was, that a dog had bitten him. "I'm glad of it," replied she. "I wish he had killed him. It would be good news to send to his mother. *Her* day will come. The dogs will grab *her* yet." With these Christian words she and her husband departed, and, to my great satisfaction, returned no more.

I heard from uncle Phillip, with feelings of unspeakable joy and gratitude, that the crisis was passed and grandmother would live. I could now say from my heart, "God is merciful. He has spared me the anguish of feeling that I caused her death."

XXIV

The Candidate for Congress

THE SUMMER HAD NEARLY ENDED, when Dr. Flint made a third visit to New York, in search of me. Two candidates were running for Congress, and he returned in season to vote. The father of my children was the Whig candidate. The doctor had hitherto been a stanch Whig; but now he exerted all his energies for the defeat of Mr. Sands. He invited large parties of men to dine in the shade of his trees, and supplied them with plenty of rum and brandy. If any poor fellow drowned his wits in the bowl, and, in the openness of his convivial heart, proclaimed that he did not mean to vote the Democratic ticket, he was shoved into the street without ceremony.

The doctor expended his liquor in vain. Mr. Sands was elected; an event which occasioned me some anxious thoughts.[1] He had not emancipated my children, and if he should die they would be at the mercy of his heirs. Two little voices, that frequently met my ear, seemed to plead with me not to let their father depart without striving to make their freedom secure. Years had passed since I had spoken to him. I had not even seen him since the night I passed him, unrecognized, in my disguise of a sailor. I supposed he would call before he left, to say something to my grandmother concerning the children, and I resolved what course to take.

The day before his departure for Washington[2] I made arrangements, towards evening, to get from my hiding-place into the storeroom below. I found myself so stiff and clumsy that it was with great difficulty I could hitch from one resting place to another. When I reached the storeroom my ankles gave way under me, and I sank exhausted on the floor. It seemed as if I could never use my limbs again. But the purpose I had in view roused all the strength I had. I crawled on my hands and knees to the window, and, screened behind a barrel, I waited for his coming. The clock struck nine, and I knew the steamboat would leave between ten and eleven. My hopes were failing. But presently I heard his voice, saying to some one, "Wait for me a moment. I wish to see aunt Martha." When he came out, as he passed the window, I said, "Stop one moment, and let me speak for my children." He started, hesitated, and then passed on, and went out of the gate. I closed the shutter I had partially opened, and sank down behind the barrel. I had suffered much; but seldom had I experienced a keener pang than I then felt. Had my children, then, become of so little consequence to him? And had he so little feeling for their wretched mother that he would not listen a moment while she pleaded for them? Painful memories were so busy within me, that I forgot I had not hooked the shutter, till I heard some one opening it. I looked up. He had come back. "Who called me?" said he, in a low tone. "I did," I replied. "Oh, Linda," said he, "I knew your voice; but I was afraid to answer, lest my friend should hear me. Why do you come here? Is it possible you risk yourself in this house? They are mad to allow it. I shall expect to hear that you are all ruined." I did not wish to impli-

cate him, by letting him know my place of concealment; so I merely
said, "I thought you would come to bid grandmother good by, and so
I came here to speak a few words to you about emancipating my children. Many changes may take place during the six months you are
gone to Washington, and it does not seem right for you to expose
them to the risk of such changes. I want nothing for myself; all I ask
is, that you will free my children, or authorize some friend to do it,
before you go."

He promised he would do it, and also expressed a readiness to
make any arrangements whereby I could be purchased.

I heard footsteps approaching, and closed the shutter hastily. I
wanted to crawl back to my den, without letting the family know what
I had done; for I knew they would deem it very imprudent. But he
stepped back into the house, to tell my grandmother that he had spoken with me at the storeroom window, and to beg of her not to allow
me to remain in the house over night. He said it was the height of
madness for me to be there; that we should certainly all be ruined.
Luckily, he was in too much of a hurry to wait for a reply, or the dear
old woman would surely have told him all.

I tried to go back to my den, but found it more difficult to go up
than I had to come down. Now that my mission was fulfilled, the little strength that had supported me through it was gone, and I sank
helpless on the floor. My grandmother, alarmed at the risk I had run,
came into the storeroom in the dark, and locked the door behind her.
"Linda," she whispered, "where are you?"

"I am here by the window," I replied. "I *couldn't* have him go away
without emancipating the children. Who knows what may happen?"

"Come, come, child," said she, "it won't do for you to stay here another minute. You've done wrong; but I can't blame you, poor thing!"

I told her I could not return without assistance, and she must call
my uncle. Uncle Phillip came, and pity prevented him from scolding

me. He carried me back to my dungeon, laid me tenderly on the bed, gave me some medicine, and asked me if there was any thing more he could do. Then he went away, and I was left with my own thoughts— starless as the midnight darkness around me.

My friends feared I should become a cripple for life; and I was so weary of my long imprisonment that, had it not been for the hope of serving my children, I should have been thankful to die; but, for their sakes, I was willing to bear on.

XXV

Competition in Cunning

D<small>R. FLINT HAD NOT</small> given me up. Every now and then he would say to my grandmother that I would yet come back, and voluntarily surrender myself; and that when I did, I could be purchased by my relatives, or any one who wished to buy me. I knew his cunning nature too well not to perceive that this was a trap laid for me; and so all my friends understood it. I resolved to match my cunning against his cunning. In order to make him believe that I was in New York, I resolved to write him a letter dated from that place. I sent for my friend Peter, and asked him if he knew any trustworthy seafaring person, who would carry such a letter to New York, and put it in the post office there.[1] He said he knew one that he would trust with his own life to the ends of the world. I reminded him that it was a hazardous thing for him to undertake. He said he knew it, but he was willing to do any thing to help me. I expressed a wish for a New York paper, to ascertain the names of some of the streets. He run his hand

into his pocket, and said, "Here is half a one, that was round a cap I
bought of a pedler yesterday." I told him the letter would be ready
the next evening. He bade me good by, adding, "Keep up your spirits,
Linda; brighter days will come by and by."

My uncle Phillip kept watch over the gate until our brief interview
was over. Early the next morning, I seated myself near the little aperture to examine the newspaper. It was a piece of the New York Herald;
and, for once, the paper that systematically abuses the colored people,
was made to render them a service.[2] Having obtained what information I wanted concerning streets and numbers, I wrote two letters,
one to my grandmother, the other to Dr. Flint. I reminded him how
he, a gray-headed man, had treated a helpless child, who had been
placed in his power, and what years of misery he had brought upon
her. To my grandmother, I expressed a wish to have my children sent
to me at the north, where I could teach them to respect themselves,
and set them a virtuous example; which a slave mother was not allowed to do at the south. I asked her to direct her answer to a certain
street in Boston, as I did not live in New York, though I went there
sometimes. I dated these letters ahead, to allow for the time it would
take to carry them, and sent a memorandum of the date to the messenger. When my friend came for the letters, I said, "God bless and
reward you, Peter, for this disinterested kindness. Pray be careful. If
you are detected, both you and I will have to suffer dreadfully. I have
not a relative who would dare to do it for me." He replied, "You may
trust to me, Linda. I don't forget that your father was my best friend,
and I will be a friend to his children so long as God lets me live."

It was necessary to tell my grandmother what I had done, in order
that she might be ready for the letter, and prepared to hear what Dr.
Flint might say about my being at the north. She was sadly troubled.
She felt sure mischief would come of it. I also told my plan to aunt
Nancy, in order that she might report to us what was said at Dr. Flint's

house. I whispered it to her through a crack, and she whispered back, "I hope it will succeed. I shan't mind being a slave all *my* life, if I can only see you and the children free."

I had directed that my letters should be put into the New York post office on the 20th of the month. On the evening of the 24th my aunt came to say that Dr. Flint and his wife had been talking in a low voice about a letter he had received, and that when he went to his office he promised to bring it when he came to tea. So I concluded I should hear my letter read the next morning. I told my grandmother Dr. Flint would be sure to come, and asked her to have him sit near a certain door, and leave it open, that I might hear what he said. The next morning I took my station within sound of that door, and remained motionless as a statue. It was not long before I heard the gate slam, and the well-known footsteps enter the house. He seated himself in the chair that was placed for him, and said, "Well, Martha, I've brought you a letter from Linda. She has sent me a letter, also. I know exactly where to find her; but I don't choose to go to Boston for her. I had rather she would come back of her own accord, in a respectable manner. Her uncle Phillip is the best person to go for her. With *him*, she would feel perfectly free to act. I am willing to pay his expenses going and returning. She shall be sold to her friends. Her children are free; at least I suppose they are; and when you obtain her freedom, you'll make a happy family. I suppose, Martha, you have no objection to my reading to you the letter Linda has written to you."

He broke the seal, and I heard him read it. The old villain! He had suppressed the letter I wrote to grandmother, and prepared a substitute of his own, the purport of which was as follows:—

"Dear Grandmother: I have long wanted to write to you; but the disgraceful manner in which I left you and my children made me ashamed to do it. If you knew how much I have suffered since I ran

away, you would pity and forgive me. I have purchased freedom at
a dear rate. If any arrangement could be made for me to return to
the south without being a slave, I would gladly come. If not, I beg
of you to send my children to the north. I cannot live any longer
without them. Let me know in time, and I will meet them in New
York or Philadelphia, whichever place best suits my uncle's conve-
nience. Write as soon as possible to your unhappy daughter.
      Linda."

"It is very much as I expected it would be," said the old hypocrite,
rising to go. "You see the foolish girl has repented of her rashness, and
wants to return. We must help her to do it, Martha. Talk with Phillip
about it. If he will go for her, she will trust to him, and come back. I
should like an answer tomorrow. Good morning, Martha."

As he stepped out on the piazza, he stumbled over my little girl.
"Ah, Ellen, is that you?" he said, in his most gracious manner. "I didn't
see you. How do you do?"

"Pretty well, sir," she replied. "I heard you tell grandmother that
my mother is coming home. I want to see her."

"Yes, Ellen, I am going to bring her home very soon," rejoined he;
"and you shall see her as much as you like, you little curly-headed
nigger."

This was as good as a comedy to me, who had heard it all;
but grandmother was frightened and distressed, because the doctor
wanted my uncle to go for me.

The next evening Dr. Flint called to talk the matter over. My uncle
told him that from what he had heard of Massachusetts, he judged he
should be mobbed if he went there after a runaway slave. "All stuff
and nonsense, Phillip!" replied the doctor. "Do you suppose I want
you to kick up a row in Boston? The business can all be done quietly.
Linda writes that she wants to come back. You are her relative, and
she would trust *you*. The case would be different if I went. She might

object to coming with *me;* and the damned abolitionists, if they knew I was her master, would not believe me, if I told them she had begged to go back. They would get up a row; and I should not like to see Linda dragged through the streets like a common negro.[3] She has been very ungrateful to me for all my kindness; but I forgive her, and want to act the part of a friend towards her. I have no wish to hold her as my slave. Her friends can buy her as soon as she arrives here."

Finding that his arguments failed to convince my uncle, the doctor "let the cat out of the bag," by saying that he had written to the mayor of Boston, to ascertain whether there was a person of my description at the street and number from which my letter was dated. He had omitted this date in the letter he had made up to read to my grandmother. If I had dated from New York, the old man would probably have made another journey to that city. But even in that dark region, where knowledge is so carefully excluded from the slave, I had heard enough about Massachusetts to come to the conclusion that slaveholders did not consider it a comfortable place to go to in search of a runaway. That was before the Fugitive Slave Law was passed; before Massachusetts had consented to become a "nigger hunter" for the south.

My grandmother, who had become skittish by seeing her family always in danger, came to me with a very distressed countenance, and said, "What will you do if the mayor of Boston sends him word that you haven't been there? Then he will suspect the letter was a trick; and maybe he'll find out something about it, and we shall all get into trouble. O Linda, I wish you had never sent the letters."

"Don't worry yourself, grandmother," said I. "The mayor of Boston won't trouble himself to hunt niggers for Dr. Flint. The letters will do good in the end. I shall get out of this dark hole some time or other."

"I hope you will, child," replied the good, patient old friend. "You have been here a long time; almost five years; but whenever you do go, it will break your old grandmother's heart. I should be expecting every day to hear that you were brought back in irons and put in jail. God help you, poor child! Let us be thankful that some time or other we shall go 'where the wicked cease from troubling, and the weary are at rest.'"[4] My heart responded, Amen.

The fact that Dr. Flint had written to the mayor of Boston convinced me that he believed my letter to be genuine, and of course that he had no suspicion of my being any where in the vicinity. It was a great object to keep up this delusion, for it made me and my friends feel less anxious, and it would be very convenient whenever there was a chance to escape. I resolved, therefore, to continue to write letters from the north from time to time.

Two or three weeks passed, and as no news came from the mayor of Boston, grandmother began to listen to my entreaty to be allowed to leave my cell, sometimes, and exercise my limbs to prevent my becoming a cripple. I was allowed to slip down into the small storeroom, early in the morning, and remain there a little while.[5] The room was all filled up with barrels, except a small open space under my trap-door. This faced the door, the upper part of which was of glass, and purposely left uncurtained, that the curious might look in. The air of this place was close; but it was so much better than the atmosphere of my cell, that I dreaded to return. I came down as soon as it was light, and remained till eight o'clock, when people began to be about, and there was danger that some one might come on the piazza. I had tried various applications to bring warmth and feeling into my limbs, but without avail. They were so numb and stiff that it was a painful effort to move; and had my enemies come upon me during the first mornings I tried to exercise them a little in the small unoccupied space of the storeroom, it would have been impossible for me to have escaped.

XXVI

Important Era in My Brother's Life

I MISSED THE COMPANY and kind attentions of my brother William, who had gone to Washington with his master, Mr. Sands. We received several letters from him, written without any allusion to me, but expressed in such a manner that I knew he did not forget me. I disguised my hand, and wrote to him in the same manner. It was a long session; and when it closed, William wrote to inform us that Mr. Sands was going to the north, to be gone some time, And that he was to accompany him. I knew that his master had promised to give him his freedom, but no time had been specified. Would William trust to a slave's chances? I remembered how we used to talk together, in our young days, about obtaining our freedom, and I thought it very doubtful whether he would come back to us.

Grandmother received a letter from Mr. Sands, saying that William had proved a most faithful servant, and he would also say a valued friend; that no mother had ever trained a better boy. He said he had travelled through the Northern States and Canada; and though the abolitionists had tried to decoy him away, they had never succeeded. He ended by saying they should be at home shortly.

We expected letters from William, describing the novelties of his journey, but none came. In time, it was reported that Mr. Sands would return late in the autumn, accompanied by a bride.[1] Still no letters from William. I felt almost sure I should never see him again on southern soil; but had he no word of comfort to send to his friends at home? to the poor captive in her dungeon? My thoughts wandered through the dark past, and over the uncertain future. Alone in my cell, where no eye but God's could see me, I wept bitter tears. How earnestly I prayed to him to restore me to my children, and enable me to be a useful woman and a good mother!

At last the day arrived for the return of the travellers. Grandmother had made loving preparations to welcome her absent boy back to the old hearthstone. When the dinner table was laid, William's plate occupied its old place. The stage coach went by empty. My grandmother waited dinner. She thought perhaps he was necessarily detained by his master. In my prison I listened anxiously, expecting every moment to hear my dear brother's voice and step. In the course of the afternoon a lad was sent by Mr. Sands to tell grandmother that William did not return with him; that the abolitionists had decoyed him away. But he begged her not to feel troubled about it, for he felt confident she would see William in a few days. As soon as he had time to reflect he would come back, for he could never expect to be so well off at the north as he had been with him.

If you had seen the tears, and heard the sobs, you would have thought the messenger had brought tidings of death instead of freedom. Poor old grandmother felt that she should never see her darling boy again. And I was selfish. I thought more of what I had lost, than of what my brother had gained. A new anxiety began to trouble me. Mr. Sands had expended a good deal of money, and would naturally feel irritated by the loss he had incurred. I greatly feared this might injure the prospects of my children, who were now becoming valuable property. I longed to have their emancipation made certain. The more so, because their master and father was now married. I was too familiar with slavery not to know that promises made to slaves, though with kind intentions, and sincere at the time, depend upon many contingencies for their fulfilment.

Much as I wished William to be free, the step he had taken made me sad and anxious. The following Sabbath was calm and clear; so beautiful that it seemed like a Sabbath in the eternal world. My grandmother brought the children out on the piazza, that I might hear their voices. She thought it would comfort me in my despondency; and it did. They chatted merrily, as only children can. Benny said, "Grandmother, do you think uncle Will has gone for good? Won't he ever come back again? May be he'll find mother. If he does, *won't* she be glad to see him! Why don't you and uncle Phillip, and all of us, go and live where mother is? I should like it; wouldn't you, Ellen?"

"Yes, I should like it," replied Ellen; "but how could we find her? Do you know the place, grandmother? I don't remember how mother looked—do you, Benny?"

Benny was just beginning to describe me when they were interrupted by an old slave woman, a near neighbor, named Aggie.[2] This poor creature had witnessed the sale of her children, and seen them carried off to parts unknown, without any hopes of ever hearing from them again. She saw that my grandmother had been weeping, and she said, in a sympathizing tone, "What's the matter, aunt Marthy?"

"O Aggie," she replied, "it seems as if I shouldn't have any of my children or grandchildren left to hand me a drink when I'm dying, and lay my old body in the ground. My boy didn't come back with Mr. Sands. He staid at the north."

Poor old Aggie clapped her hands for joy. "Is *dat* what you's crying fur?" she exclaimed. "Git down on your knees and bress de Lord! I don't know whar my poor chillern is, and I nebber 'spect to know. You don't know whar poor Linda's gone to; but you *do* know whar her brudder is. He's in free parts; and dat's de right place. Don't murmur at de Lord's doings, but git down on your knees and tank him for his goodness."

My selfishness was rebuked by what poor Aggie said. She rejoiced over the escape of one who was merely her fellow-bondman, while his own sister was only thinking what his good fortune might cost her children. I knelt and prayed God to forgive me; and I thanked him from my heart, that one of my family was saved from the grasp of slavery.

It was not long before we received a letter from William. He wrote that Mr. Sands had always treated him kindly, and that he had tried to do his duty to him faithfully. But ever since he was a boy, he had longed to be free; and he had already gone through enough to convince him he had better not lose the chance that offered. He concluded by saying, "Don't worry about me, dear grandmother. I shall think of you always; and it will spur me on to work hard and try to do right. When I have earned money enough to give you a home, perhaps you will come to the north, and we can all live happy together."

Mr. Sands told my uncle Phillip the particulars about William's leaving him. He said, "I trusted him as if he were my own brother, and treated him as kindly. The abolitionists talked to him in several places; but I had no idea they could tempt him. However, I don't blame William. He's young and inconsiderate, and those Northern rascals decoyed him. I must confess the scamp was very bold about it. I met him coming down the steps of the Astor House with his trunk on his shoulder, and I asked him where he was going. He said he was going to change his old trunk. I told him it was rather shabby, and asked if he didn't need some money. He said, No, thanked me, and went off. He did not return so soon as I expected; but I waited patiently. At last I went to see if our trunks were packed, ready for our journey. I found them locked, and a sealed note on the table informed me where I could find the keys. The fellow even tried to be religious. He wrote that he hoped God would always bless me, and reward me for my kindness; that he was not unwilling to serve me; but he wanted to be a free man; and that if I thought he did wrong, he hoped I would forgive him. I intended to give him his freedom in five years. He might have trusted me. He has shown himself ungrateful; but I shall not go for him, or send for him. I feel confident that he will soon return to me."

I afterwards heard an account of the affair from William himself.[3] He had not been urged away by abolitionists. He needed no information they could give him about slavery to stimulate his desire for freedom. He looked at his hands, and remembered that they were once in irons. What security had he that they would not be so again? Mr. Sands was kind to him; but he might indefinitely postpone the promise he had made to give him his freedom. He might come under pecuniary embarrassments, and his property be seized by creditors; or he might die, without making any arrangements in his favor. He had too often known such accidents to happen to slaves who had kind masters, and he wisely resolved to make sure of the present opportunity to own himself. He was scrupulous about taking any money from his master on false pretences; so he sold his best clothes to pay for his passage to Boston. The slaveholders pronounced him a base, ungrateful wretch, for thus requiting his master's indulgence. What would *they* have done under similar circumstances?

When Dr. Flint's family heard that William had deserted Mr. Sands, they chuckled greatly over the news. Mrs. Flint made her usual manifestations of Christian feeling, by saying, "I'm glad of it. I hope he'll never get him again. I like to see people paid back in their own coin. I reckon Linda's children will have to pay for it. I should be glad to see them in the speculator's hands again, for I'm tired of seeing those little niggers march about the streets."

XXVII

New Destination for the Children

M RS. FLINT PROCLAIMED her intention of informing Mrs. Sands who was the father of my children. She likewise proposed to tell her what an artful devil I was; that I had made a great deal of trouble in her family; that when Mr. Sands was at the north, she didn't doubt I had followed him in disguise, and persuaded William to run away. She had some reason to entertain such an idea; for I had written from the north, from time to time, and I dated my letters from various places. Many of them fell into Dr. Flint's hands, as I expected they would; and he must have come to the conclusion that I travelled about a good deal. He kept a close watch over my children, thinking they would eventually lead to my detection.

A new and unexpected trial was in store for me. One day, when Mr. Sands and his wife were walking in the street, they met Benny. The lady took a fancy to him, and exclaimed, "What a pretty little negro! Whom does he belong to?"

Benny did not hear the answer; but he came home very indignant with the stranger lady, because she had called him a negro. A few days afterwards, Mr. Sands called on my grandmother, and told her he wanted her to take the children to his house. He said he had informed his wife of his relation to them, and told her they were motherless; and she wanted to see them.

When he had gone, my grandmother came and asked what I would do. The question seemed a mockery. What *could* I do? They were Mr. Sands's slaves, and their mother was a slave, whom he had represented to be dead. Perhaps he thought I was. I was too much pained and puzzled to come to any decision; and the children were carried without my knowledge.

Mrs. Sands had a sister from Illinois staying with her.[1] This lady, who had no children of her own, was so much pleased with Ellen, that she offered to adopt her, and bring her up as she would a daughter. Mrs. Sands wanted to take Benjamin. When grandmother reported this to me, I was tried almost beyond endurance. Was this all I was to gain by what I had suffered for the sake of having my children free? True, the prospect *seemed* fair; but I knew too well how lightly slaveholders held such "parental relations." If pecuniary troubles should come, or if the new wife required more money than could conveniently be spared, my children might be thought of as a convenient means of raising funds. I had no trust in thee, O Slavery! Never should I know peace till my children were emancipated with all due formalities of law.

I was too proud to ask Mr. Sands to do any thing for my own benefit; but I could bring myself to become a supplicant for my children. I resolved to remind him of the promise he had made me, and to throw myself upon his honor for the performance of it. I persuaded my grandmother to go to him, and tell him I was not dead, and that I earnestly entreated him to keep the promise he had made me; that I had heard of the recent proposals concerning my children, and did not feel easy to accept them; that he had promised to emancipate them, and it was time for him to redeem his pledge. I knew there was some risk in thus betraying that I was in the vicinity; but what will not a mother do for her children? He received the message with surprise, and said, "The children are free. I have never intended to claim them as slaves. Linda may decide their fate. In my opinion, they had better be sent to the north. I don't think they are quite safe here. Dr. Flint boasts that they are still in his power. He says they were his daughter's property, and as she was not of age when they were sold, the contract is not legally binding."

So, then, after all I had endured for their sakes, my poor children were between two fires; between my old master and their new master! And I was powerless. There was no protecting arm of the law for me to invoke. Mr. Sands proposed that Ellen should go, for the present, to some of his relatives, who had removed to Brooklyn, Long Island.[2] It was promised that she should be well taken care of, and sent to school. I consented to it, as the best arrangement I could make for her. My grandmother, of course, negotiated it all; and Mrs. Sands knew of no other person in the transaction. She proposed that they should take Ellen with them to Washington, and keep her till they had a good chance of sending her, with friends, to Brooklyn. She had an infant daughter.[3] I had had a glimpse of it, as the nurse passed with it in her arms. It was not a pleasant thought to me, that the bondwoman's child should tend her free-born sister; but there was no alternative. Ellen was made ready for the journey. O, how it tried my heart to send her away, so young, alone, among strangers! Without a mother's love to shelter her from the storms of life; almost without memory of a mother! I doubted whether she and Benny would have for me the natural affection that children feel for a parent. I thought to myself that I might perhaps never see my daughter again, and I had a great desire that she should look upon me, before she went, that she might take my image with her in her memory. It seemed to me cruel to have her brought to my dungeon. It was sorrow enough for her young heart to know that her mother was a victim of slavery, without seeing the wretched hiding-place to which it had driven her. I begged permission to pass the last night in one of the open chambers, with my little girl. They thought I was crazy to think of trusting such a young child with my perilous secret. I told them I had watched her character, and I felt sure she would not betray me; that I was determined to have an interview, and if they would not facilitate it, I would take my own way to obtain it. They remonstrated against the rashness of such a proceeding; but finding they could not change my purpose, they yielded. I slipped through the trap-door into the storeroom, and my uncle kept watch at the gate, while I passed into the piazza and went up stairs, to the room I used to occupy. It was more than five years since I had seen it; and how the memories crowded on me! There I had taken shelter when my mistress drove me from her house; there came my old tyrant, to mock, insult, and curse me; there my children were first laid in my arms; there I had watched over them, each day with a deeper and sadder love; there I had knelt to God, in anguish of heart, to forgive the wrong I had done. How vividly it all came back! And after this long, gloomy interval, I stood there such a wreck!

In the midst of these meditations, I heard footsteps on the stairs. The door opened, and my uncle Phillip came in, leading Ellen by the hand. I put my arms round her, and said, "Ellen, my dear child, I am your mother." She drew back a little, and looked at me; then, with sweet confidence, she laid her cheek against mine, and I folded her to the heart that had been so long desolated. She was the first to speak. Raising her head, she said, inquiringly, "You really *are* my mother?" I told her I really was; that during all the long time she had not seen me, I had loved her most tenderly; and that now she was going away, I wanted to see her and talk with her, that she might remember me. With a sob in her voice, she said, "I'm glad you've come to see me; but why didn't you ever come before? Benny and I have wanted so much to see you! He remembers you, and sometimes he tells me about you. Why didn't you come home when Dr. Flint went to bring you?"

I answered, "I couldn't come before, dear. But now that I am with you, tell me whether you like to go away." "I don't know," said she, crying. "Grandmother says I ought not to cry; that I am going to a good place, where I can learn to read and write, and that by and by I can write her a letter. But I shan't have Benny, or grandmother, or uncle Phillip, or any body to love me. Can't you go with me? O, *do* go, dear mother!"

I told her I couldn't go now; but sometime I would come to her, and then she and Benny and I would live together, and have happy times. She wanted to run and bring Benny to see me now. I told her he was going to the north, before long, with uncle Phillip, and then I would come to see him before he went away. I asked if she would like to have me stay all night and sleep with her. "O, yes," she replied. Then, turning to her uncle, she said, pleadingly, "*May* I stay? Please, uncle! She is my own mother." He laid his hand on her head, and said, solemnly, "Ellen, this is the secret you have promised grandmother never to tell. If you ever speak of it to any body, they will never let you see your grandmother again, and your mother can never come to Brooklyn." "Uncle," she replied, "I will never tell." He told her she might stay with me; and when he had gone, I took her in my arms and told her I was a slave, and that was the reason she must never say she had seen me. I exhorted her to be a good child, to try to please the people where she was going, and that God would raise her up friends. I told her to say her prayers, and remember always to pray for her poor mother, and that God would permit us to meet again. She wept, and I did not check her tears. Perhaps she would never again have a chance to pour her tears into a mother's bosom. All night she nestled in my arms, and I had no inclination to slumber. The moments were too precious to lose any of them. Once, when I thought she was asleep, I kissed her forehead softly, and she said, "I am not asleep, dear mother."

Before dawn they came to take me back to my den. I drew aside the window curtain, to take a last look of my child. The moonlight shone on her face, and I bent over her, as I had done years before, that wretched night when I ran away. I hugged her close to my throbbing heart; and tears, too sad for such young eyes to shed, flowed down her cheeks, as she gave her last kiss, and whispered in my ear, "Mother, I will never tell." And she never did.

When I got back to my den, I threw myself on the bed and wept there alone in the darkness. It seemed as if my heart would burst. When the time for Ellen's departure grew nigh, I could hear neighbors and friends saying to her, "Good by, Ellen. I hope your poor mother will find you out. *Won't* you be glad to see her!" She replied, "Yes, ma'am"; and they little dreamed of the weighty secret that weighed down her young heart. She was an affectionate child, but naturally very reserved, except with those she loved, and I felt secure that my secret would be safe with her. I heard the gate close after her, with such feelings as only a slave mother can experience. During the day my meditations were very sad. Sometimes I feared I had been very selfish not to give up all claim to her, and let her go to Illinois, to be adopted by Mrs. Sands's sister. It was my experience of slavery that decided me against it. I feared that circumstances might arise that would cause her to be sent back. I felt confident that I should go to New York myself; and then I should be able to watch over her, and in some degree protect her.

Dr. Flint's family knew nothing of the proposed arrangement till after Ellen was gone, and the news displeased them greatly. Mrs. Flint called on Mrs. Sands's sister to inquire into the matter.[4] She expressed her opinion very freely as to the respect Mr. Sands showed for his wife, and for his own character, in acknowledging those "young niggers." And as for sending Ellen away, she pronounced it to be just as much stealing as it would be for him to come and take a piece of furniture out of her parlor. She said her daughter was not of age to sign the bill of sale, and the children were her property; and when she became of age, or was married, she could take them, wherever she could lay hands on them.

Miss Emily Flint, the little girl to whom I had been bequeathed, was now in her sixteenth year.[5] Her mother considered it all right and honorable for her, or her future husband, to steal my children; but she did not understand how any body could hold up their heads in respectable society, after they had purchased their own children, as Mr. Sands had done. Dr. Flint said very little. Perhaps he thought that Benny would be less likely to be sent away if he kept quiet. One of my letters, that fell into his hands, was dated from Canada; and he seldom spoke of me now. This state of things enabled me to slip down into the storeroom more frequently, where I could stand upright, and move my limbs more freely.

Days, weeks, and months passed, and there came no news of Ellen. I sent a letter to Brooklyn, written in my grandmother's name, to inquire whether she had arrived there. Answer was returned that she had not. I wrote to her in Washington; but no notice was taken of it. There was one person there, who ought to have had some sympathy with the anxiety of the child's friends at home; but the links of such relations as he had formed with me, are easily broken and cast away as rubbish. Yet how protectingly and persuasively he once talked to the poor, helpless slave girl! And how entirely I trusted him! But now suspicions darkened my mind. Was my child dead, or had they deceived me, and sold her?

If the secret memoirs of many members of Congress should be published, curious details would be unfolded. I once saw a letter from a member of Congress to a slave, who was the mother of six of his children. He wrote to request that she would send her children away from the great house before his return, as he expected to be accompanied by friends. The woman could not read, and was obliged to employ another to read the letter. The existence of the colored children did not trouble this gentleman, it was only the fear that friends might recognize in their features a resemblance to him.

At the end of six months, a letter came to my grandmother, from Brooklyn. It was written by a young lady in the family, and announced that Ellen had just arrived.[6] It contained the following message from her: "I do try to do just as you told me to, and I pray for you every night and morning." I understood that these words were meant for me; and they were a balsam to my heart. The writer closed her letter by saying, "Ellen is a nice little girl, and we shall like to have her with us. My cousin, Mr. Sands, has given her to me, to be my little waiting maid. I shall send her to school, and I hope some day she will write to you yourself." This letter perplexed and troubled me. Had my child's father merely placed her there till she was old enough to support herself? Or had he given her to his cousin, as a piece of property? If the last idea was correct, his cousin might return to the south at any time, and hold Ellen as a slave. I tried to put away from me the painful thought that such a foul wrong could have been done to us. I said to myself, "Surely there must be *some* justice in man"; then I remembered, with a sigh, how slavery perverted all the natural feelings of the human heart. It gave me a pang to look on my light-hearted boy. He believed himself free; and to have him brought under the yoke of slavery, would be more than I could bear. How I longed to have him safely out of the reach of its power!

XXVIII

Aunt Nancy

I HAVE MENTIONED MY great-aunt, who was a slave in Dr. Flint's family, and who had been my refuge during the shameful persecutions I suffered from him. This aunt had been married at twenty years of age; that is, as far as slaves *can* marry. She had the consent of her master and mistress, and a clergyman performed the ceremony. But it was a mere form, without any legal value. Her master or mistress could annul it any day they pleased. She had always slept on the floor in the entry, near Mrs. Flint's chamber door, that she might be within call. When she was married, she was told she might have the use of a small room in an outhouse. Her mother and her husband furnished it. He was a seafaring man, and was allowed to sleep there when he was at home. But on the wedding evening, the bride was ordered to her old post on the entry floor.

Mrs. Flint, at that time, had no children; but she was expecting to be a mother, and if she should want a drink of water in the night,

what could she do without her slave to bring it? So my aunt was compelled to lie at her door, until one midnight she was forced to leave,
to give premature birth to a child. In a fortnight she was required to
resume her place on the entry floor, because Mrs. Flint's babe needed
her attentions. She kept her station there through summer and winter, until she had given premature birth to six children; and all the
while she was employed as night-nurse to Mrs. Flint's children. Finally, toiling all day, and being deprived of rest at night, completely
broke down her constitution, and Dr. Flint declared it was impossible
she could ever become the mother of a living child. The fear of losing so valuable a servant by death, now induced them to allow her to
sleep in her little room in the out-house, except when there was sickness in the family. She afterwards had two feeble babes, one of whom
died in a few days, and the other in four weeks. I well remember her
patient sorrow as she held the last dead baby in her arms. "I wish it
could have lived," she said; "it is not the will of God that any of my
children should live. But I will try to be fit to meet their little spirits in
heaven."[1]

Aunt Nancy was housekeeper and waiting-maid in Dr. Flint's family. Indeed, she was the *factotum* of the household. Nothing went on
well without her. She was my mother's twin sister, and, as far as was in
her power, she supplied a mother's place to us orphans.[2] I slept with
her all the time I lived in my old master's house, and the bond between us was very strong. When my friends tried to discourage me
from running away, she always encouraged me. When they thought I
had better return and ask my master's pardon, because there was no
possibility of escape, she sent me word never to yield. She said if I
persevered I might, perhaps, gain the freedom of my children; and
even if I perished in doing it, that was better than to leave them to
groan under the same persecutions that had blighted my own life. After I was shut up in my dark cell, she stole away, whenever she could,

to bring me the news and say something cheering. How often did I
kneel down to listen to her words of consolation, whispered through
a crack! "I am old, and have not long to live," she used to say; "and
I could die happy if I could only see you and the children free. You
must pray to God, Linda, as I do for you, that he will lead you out of
this darkness." I would beg her not to worry herself on my account;
that there was an end of all suffering sooner or later, and that whether
I lived in chains or in freedom, I should always remember her as the
good friend who had been the comfort of my life. A word from her
always strengthened me; and not me only. The whole family relied
upon her judgment, and were guided by her advice.

I had been in my cell six years when my grandmother was summoned to the bedside of this, her last remaining daughter. She was
very ill, and they said she would die. Grandmother had not entered
Dr. Flint's house for several years. They had treated her cruelly, but
she thought nothing of that now. She was grateful for permission to
watch by the death-bed of her child. They had always been devoted
to each other; and now they sat looking into each other's eyes, longing to speak of the secret that had weighed so much on the hearts
of both. My aunt had been stricken with paralysis. She lived but two
days, and the last day she was speechless. Before she lost the power of
utterance, she told her mother not to grieve if she could not speak to
her; that she would try to hold up her hand, to let her know that all
was well with her. Even the hard-hearted doctor was a little softened
when he saw the dying woman try to smile on the aged mother, who
was kneeling by her side. His eyes moistened for a moment, as he said
she had always been a faithful servant, and they should never be able
to supply her place. Mrs. Flint took to her bed, quite overcome by the
shock. While my grandmother sat alone with the dead, the doctor
came in, leading his youngest son, who had always been a great pet
with aunt Nancy, and was much attached to her.[3] "Martha," said he,

"aunt Nancy loved this child, and when he comes where you are, I hope you will be kind to him, for her sake." She replied, "Your wife was my foster-child, Dr. Flint, the foster-sister of my poor Nancy, and you little know me if you think I can feel any thing but good will for her children."

"I wish the past could be forgotten, and that we might never think of it," said he; "and that Linda would come to supply her aunt's place. She would be worth more to us than all the money that could be paid for her. I wish it for your sake also, Martha. Now that Nancy is taken away from you, she would be a great comfort to your old age."

He knew he was touching a tender chord. Almost choking with grief, my grandmother replied, "It was not I that drove Linda away. My grandchildren are gone; and of my nine children only one is left.[4] God help me!"

To me, the death of this kind relative was an inexpressible sorrow. I knew that she had been slowly murdered; and I felt that my troubles had helped to finish the work. After I heard of her illness, I listened constantly to hear what news was bought from the great house; and the thought that I could not go to her made me utterly miserable. At last, as uncle Phillip came into the house, I heard some one inquire, "How is she?" and he answered, "She is dead." My little cell seemed whirling round, and I knew nothing more till I opened my eyes and found uncle Phillip bending over me. I had no need to ask any questions. He whispered, "Linda, she died happy." I could not weep. My fixed gaze troubled him. "Don't look *so*," he said. "Don't add to my poor mother's trouble. Remember how much she has to bear, and that we ought to do all we can to comfort her." Ah, yes, that blessed old grandmother, who for seventy-three years had borne the pelting storms of a slave-mother's life. She did indeed need consolation!

Mrs. Flint had rendered her poor foster-sister childless, apparently without any compunction; and with cruel selfishness had ruined her health by years of incessant, unrequited toil, and broken rest. But now she became very sentimental. I suppose she thought it would be a beautiful illustration of the attachment existing between slaveholder and slave, if the body of her old worn-out servant was buried at her feet. She sent for the clergyman and asked if he had any objection to burying aunt Nancy in the doctor's family burial-place. No colored person had ever been allowed interment in the white people's burying-ground, and the minister knew that all the deceased of our family reposed together in the old graveyard of the slaves. He therefore replied, "I have no objection to complying with your wish; but perhaps aunt Nancy's *mother* may have some choice as to where her remains shall be deposited."

It had never occurred to Mrs. Flint that slaves could have any feelings. When my grandmother was consulted, she at once said she wanted Nancy to lie with all the rest of her family, and where her own old body would be buried. Mrs. Flint graciously complied with her wish, though she said it was painful to her to have Nancy buried away from *her*. She might have added with touching pathos, "I was so long *used* to sleep with her lying near me, on the entry floor."

My uncle Phillip asked permission to bury his sister at his own expense; and slaveholders are always ready to grant *such* favors to slaves and their relatives. The arrangements were very plain, but perfectly respectable. She was buried on the Sabbath, and Mrs. Flint's minister read the funeral service. There was a large concourse of colored people, bond and free, and a few white persons who had always been friendly to our family. Dr. Flint's carriage was in the procession; and when the body was deposited in its humble resting place, the mistress dropped a tear, and returned to her carriage, probably thinking she had performed her duty nobly.

It was talked of by the slaves as a mighty grand funeral. Northern travellers, passing through the place, might have described this trib-

ute of respect to the humble dead as a beautiful feature in the "patriarchal institution"; a touching proof of the attachment between slaveholders and their servants; and tenderhearted Mrs. Flint would have
confirmed this impression, with handkerchief at her eyes. *We* could
have told them a different story. We could have given them a chapter of wrongs and sufferings, that would have touched their hearts,
if they *had* any hearts to feel for the colored people. We could have
told them how the poor old slave-mother had toiled, year after year,
to earn eight hundred dollars to buy her son Phillip's right to his own
earnings; and how that same Phillip paid the expenses of the funeral,
which they regarded as doing so much credit to the master. We could
also have told them of a poor, blighted young creature, shut up in a
living grave for years, to avoid the tortures that would be inflicted on
her, if she ventured to come out and look on the face of her departed
friend.

All this, and much more, I thought of, as I sat at my loophole,
waiting for the family to return from the grave; sometimes weeping,
sometimes falling asleep, dreaming strange dreams of the dead and
the living.

It was sad to witness the grief of my bereaved grandmother. She
had always been strong to bear, and now, as ever, religious faith supported her. But her dark life had become still darker, and age and
trouble were leaving deep traces on her withered face. She had four
places to knock for me to come to the trap-door, and each place had
a different meaning. She now came oftener than she had done, and
talked to me of her dead daughter, while tears trickled slowly down
her furrowed cheeks. I said all I could to comfort her; but it was a
sad reflection, that instead of being able to help her, I was a constant
source of anxiety and trouble. The poor old back was fitted to its burden. It bent under it, but did not break.

XXIX

Preparations for Escape

I HARDLY EXPECT THAT the reader will credit me, when I affirm that I lived in that little dismal hole, almost deprived of light and air, and with no space to move my limbs, for nearly seven years.[1] But it is a fact; and to me a sad one, even now; for my body still suffers from the effects of that long imprisonment, to say nothing of my soul. Members of my family, now living in New York and Boston, can testify to the truth of what I say.

Countless were the nights that I sat late at the little loophole scarcely large enough to give me a glimpse of one twinkling star. There, I heard the patrols and slave-hunters conferring together about the capture of runaways, well knowing how rejoiced they would be to catch me.

Season after season, year after year, I peeped at my children's faces, and heard their sweet voices, with a heart yearning all the while to say, "Your mother is here." Sometimes it appeared to me as if ages had rolled away since I entered upon that gloomy, monotonous existence. At times, I was stupefied and listless; at other times I became very impatient to know when these dark years would end, and I should again be allowed to feel the sunshine, and breathe the pure air.

After Ellen left us, this feeling increased. Mr. Sands had agreed that Benny might go to the north whenever his uncle Phillip could go with him; and I was anxious to be there also, to watch over my children, and protect them so far as I was able. Moreover, I was likely to be drowned out of my den, if I remained much longer; for the slight roof was getting badly out of repair, and uncle Phillip was afraid to remove the shingles, lest some one should get a glimpse of me. When storms occurred in the night, they spread mats and bits of carpet, which in the morning appeared to have been laid out to dry; but to cover the roof in the daytime might have attracted attention. Consequently, my clothes and bedding were often drenched; a process by which the pains and aches in my cramped and stiffened limbs were greatly increased. I revolved various plans of escape in my mind, which I sometimes imparted to my grandmother, when she came to whisper with me at the trap-door. The kind-hearted old woman had an intense sympathy for runaways. She had known too much of the cruelties inflicted on those who were captured. Her memory always flew back at once to the sufferings of her bright and handsome son, Benjamin, the youngest and dearest of her flock. So, whenever I alluded to the subject, she would groan out, "O, don't think of it, child. You'll break my heart." I had no good old aunt Nancy now to encourage me; but my brother William and my children were continually beckoning me to the north.

And now I must go back a few months in my story. I have stated that the first of January was the time for selling slaves, or leasing them out to new masters. If time were counted by heart-throbs, the poor slaves might reckon years of suffering during that festival so joyous to the free. On the New Year's day preceding my aunt's death, one of my friends, named Fanny, was to be sold at auction, to pay her master's debts. My thoughts were with her during all the day, and at night I anxiously inquired what had been her fate. I was told that she had been sold to one master, and her four little girls to another master, far distant; that she had escaped from her purchaser, and was not to be found. Her mother was the old Aggie I have spoken of. She lived in a small tenement belonging to my grandmother, and built on the same lot with her own house. Her dwelling was searched and watched, and that brought the patrols so near me that I was obliged to keep very close in my den. The hunters were somehow eluded; and not long afterwards Benny accidentally caught sight of Fanny in her mother's hut. He told his grandmother, who charged him never to speak of it, explaining to him the frightful consequences; and he never betrayed the trust. Aggie little dreamed that my grandmother knew where her daughter was concealed, and that the stooping form of her old neighbor was bending under a similar burden of anxiety and fear; but these dangerous secrets deepened the sympathy between the two old persecuted mothers.

My friend Fanny and I remained many weeks hidden within call of each other; but she was unconscious of the fact. I longed to have her share my den, which seemed a more secure retreat than her own; but I had brought so much trouble on my grandmother, that it seemed wrong to ask her to incur greater risks. My restlessness increased. I had lived too long in bodily pain and anguish of spirit. Always I was in dread that by some accident, or some contrivance, slavery would succeed in snatching my children from me. This thought drove me nearly frantic, and I determined to steer for the North Star at all hazards.[2] At this crisis, Providence opened an unexpected way for me to escape. My friend Peter came one evening, and asked to speak with me. "Your day has come, Linda," said he. "I have found a chance for you to go to the Free States. You have a fortnight to decide." The news seemed too good to be true; but Peter explained his arrangements, and told me all that was necessary was for me to say I would go. I was going to answer him with a joyful yes, when the thought of Benny came to my mind. I told him the temptation was exceedingly strong, but I was terribly afraid of Dr. Flint's alleged power over my child, and that I could not go and leave him behind. Peter remonstrated earnestly. He said such a good chance might never occur again; that Benny was free, and could be sent to me; and that for the sake of my children's welfare I ought not to hesitate a moment. I told him I would consult with uncle Phillip. My uncle rejoiced in the plan, and bade me go by all means. He promised, if his life was spared, that he would either bring or send my son to me as soon as I reached a place of safety. I resolved to go, but thought nothing had better be said to my grandmother till very near the time of departure. But my uncle thought she would feel it more keenly if I left her so suddenly. "I will reason with her," said he, "and convince her how necessary it is, not only for your sake, but for hers also. You cannot be blind to the fact that she is sinking under her burdens." I was not blind to it. I knew that my concealment was an ever-present source of anxiety, and that the older she grew the more nervously fearful she was of discovery. My uncle talked with her, and finally succeeded in persuading her that it was absolutely necessary for me to seize the chance so unexpectedly offered.

The anticipation of being a free woman proved almost too much for my weak frame. The excitement stimulated me, and at the same time bewildered me. I made busy preparations for my journey, and for my son to follow me. I resolved to have an interview with him before I went, that I might give him cautions and advice, and tell him how anxiously I should be waiting for him at the north. Grandmother stole up to me as often as possible to whisper words of counsel. She insisted upon my writing to Dr. Flint, as soon as I arrived in the Free States, and asking him to sell me to her. She said she would sacrifice her house, and all she had in the world, for the sake of having me safe with my children in any part of the world. If she could only live to know *that* she could die in peace. I promised the dear old faithful friend that I would write to her as soon as I arrived, and put the letter in a safe way to reach her; but in my own mind I resolved that not another cent of her hard earnings should be spent to pay rapacious slaveholders for what they called their property. And even if I had not been unwilling to buy what I had already a right to possess, common humanity would have prevented me from accepting the generous offer, at the expense of turning my aged relative out of house and home, when she was trembling on the brink of the grave.

I was to escape in a vessel; but I forbear to mention any further particulars. I was in readiness, but the vessel was unexpectedly detained several days. Meantime, news came to town of a most horrible murder committed on a fugitive slave, named James. Charity, the mother of this unfortunate young man, had been an old acquaintance of ours. I have told the shocking particulars of his death, in my description of some of the neighboring slaveholders. My grandmother, always nervously sensitive about runaways, was terribly frightened. She felt sure that a similar fate awaited me, if I did not desist from my enterprise. She sobbed, and groaned, and entreated me not to go. Her excessive fear was somewhat contagious, and my heart was not proof against her extreme agony. I was grievously disappointed, but I promised to relinquish my project.

When my friend Peter was apprised of this, he was both disappointed and vexed. He said, that judging from our past experience, it would be a long time before I had such another chance to throw away. I told him it need not be thrown away; that I had a friend concealed near by, who would be glad enough to take the place that had been provided for me. I told him about poor Fanny, and the kind-hearted, noble fellow, who never turned his back upon any body in distress, white or black, expressed his readiness to help her. Aggie was much surprised when she found that we knew her secret. She was rejoiced to hear of such a chance for Fanny, and arrangements were made for her to go on board the vessel the next night. They both supposed that I had long been at the north, therefore my name was not mentioned in the transaction. Fanny was carried on board at the appointed time, and stowed away in a very small cabin. This accommodation had been purchased at a price that would pay for a voyage to England. But when one proposes to go to fine old England, they stop to calculate whether they can afford the cost of the pleasure; while in making a bargain to escape from slavery, the trembling victim is ready to say, "Take all I have, only don't betray me!"

The next morning I peeped through my loophole, and saw that it was dark and cloudy. At night I received news that the wind was ahead, and the vessel had not sailed. I was exceedingly anxious about Fanny, and Peter too, who was running a tremendous risk at my instigation. Next day the wind and weather remained the same. Poor Fanny had been half dead with fright when they carried her on board, and I could readily imagine how she must be suffering now. Grandmother came often to my den, to say how thankful she was I did not go. On the third morning she rapped for me to come down to the storeroom. The poor old sufferer was breaking down under her weight of trouble. She was easily flurried now. I found her in a nervous, excited state, but I was not aware that she had forgotten to lock the door behind her, as usual. She was exceedingly worried about the detention of the vessel. She was afraid all would be discovered, and then Fanny, and Peter, and I, would all be tortured to death, and Phillip would be utterly ruined, and her house would be torn down. Poor Peter! If he should die such a horrible death as the poor slave James had lately done, and all for his kindness in trying to help me, how dreadful it would be for us all! Alas, the thought was familiar to me, and had sent many a sharp pang through my heart. I tried to suppress my own anxiety, and speak soothingly to her. She brought in some allusion to aunt Nancy, the dear daughter she had recently buried, and then she lost all control of herself. As she stood there, trembling and sobbing, a voice from the piazza called out, "Whar is you, aunt Marthy?" Grandmother was startled, and in her agitation opened the door, without thinking of me. In stepped Jenny, the mischievous housemaid, who had tried to enter my room, when I was concealed in the house of my white benefactress. "I's bin huntin ebery whar for you, aunt Marthy," said she. "My missis wants you to send her some crackers." I had slunk down behind a barrel, which entirely screened me, but I imagined that Jenny was looking directly at the spot, and my heart beat violently. My grandmother immediately thought what she had done, and went out quickly with Jenny to count the crackers locking the door after her. She returned to me, in a few minutes, the perfect picture of despair. "Poor child!" she exclaimed, "my careless-ness has ruined you. The boat ain't gone yet. Get ready immediately, and go with Fanny. I ain't got another word to say against it now; for there's no telling what may happen this day."

Uncle Phillip was sent for, and he agreed with his mother in think-ing that Jenny would inform Dr. Flint in less than twenty-four hours. He advised getting me on board the boat, if possible; if not, I had bet-ter keep very still in my den, where they could not find me without tearing the house down. He said it would not do for him to move in the matter, because suspicion would be immediately excited; but he promised to communicate with Peter. I felt reluctant to apply to him again, having implicated him too much already; but there seemed to be no alternative. Vexed as Peter had been by my indecision, he was true to his generous nature, and said at once that he would do his best to help me, trusting I should show myself a stronger woman this time.

He immediately proceeded to the wharf, and found that the wind had shifted, and the vessel was slowly beating down stream. On some pretext of urgent necessity, he offered two boatmen a dollar apiece to catch up with her. He was of lighter complexion than the boatmen he hired, and when the captain saw them coming so rapidly, he thought officers were pursuing his vessel in search of the runaway slave he had on board. They hoisted sails, but the boat gained upon them, and the indefatigable Peter sprang on board.

The captain at once recognized him. Peter asked him to go below, to speak about a bad bill he had given him. When he told his errand, the captain replied, "Why, the woman's here already; and I've put her where you or the devil would have a tough job to find her."

"But it is another woman I want to bring," said Peter. "*She* is in great distress, too, and you shall be paid any thing within reason, if you'll stop and take her."

"What's her name?" inquired the captain.

"Linda," he replied.

"That's the name of the woman already here," rejoined the captain. "By George! I believe you mean to betray me."

"O!" exclaimed Peter, "God knows I wouldn't harm a hair of your head. I am too grateful to you. But there really *is* another woman in great danger. Do have the humanity to stop and take her!"

After a while they came to an understanding. Fanny, not dreaming I was any where about in that region, had assumed my name, though she had called herself Johnson. "Linda is a common name," said Peter, "and the woman I want to bring is Linda Brent."

The captain agreed to wait at a certain place till evening, being handsomely paid for his detention.

Of course, the day was an anxious one for us all. But we concluded that if Jenny had seen me, she would be too wise to let her mistress know of it; and that she probably would not get a chance to see Dr. Flint's family till evening, for I knew very well what were the rules in that household. I afterwards believed that she did not see me; for nothing ever came of it, and she was one of those base characters that would have jumped to betray a suffering fellow being for the sake of thirty pieces of silver.[3]

I made all my arrangements to go on board as soon as it was dusk. The intervening time I resolved to spend with my son. I had not spoken to him for seven years, though I had been under the same roof, and seen him every day, when I was well enough to sit at the loophole. I did not dare to venture beyond the storeroom; so they brought him there, and locked *us* up together, in a place concealed from the piazza door. It was an agitating interview for both of us. After we had talked and wept together for a little while, he said, "Mother, I'm glad you're going away. I wish I could go with you. I knew you was here; and I have been *so* afraid they would come and catch you!"

I was greatly surprised, and asked him how he had found it out.

He replied, "I was standing under the eaves, one day, before Ellen went away, and I heard somebody cough up over the wood shed. I don't know what made me think it was you, but I did think so. I missed Ellen, the night before she went away; and grandmother brought her back into the room in the night; and I thought maybe she'd been to see *you*, before she went, for I heard grandmother whisper to her, 'Now go to sleep; and remember never to tell.'"

I asked him if he ever mentioned his suspicions to his sister. He said he never did; but after he heard the cough, if he saw her playing with other children on that side of the house, he always tried to coax her round to the other side, for fear they would hear me cough, too. He said he had kept a close lookout for Dr. Flint, and if he saw him speak to a constable, or a patrol, he always told grandmother. I now recollected that I had seen him manifest uneasiness, when people were on that side of the house, and I had at the time been puzzled to conjecture a motive for his actions. Such prudence may seem extraordinary in a boy of twelve years, but slaves, being surrounded by mysteries, deceptions, and dangers, early learn to be suspicious and watchful, and prematurely cautious and cunning. He had never asked a question of grandmother, or uncle Phillip, and I had often heard him chime in with other children, when they spoke of my being at the north.

I told him I was now really going to the Free States, and if he was a good, honest boy, and a loving child to his dear old grandmother, the Lord would bless him, and bring him to me, and we and Ellen would live together. He began to tell me that grandmother had not eaten any thing all day. While he was speaking, the door was unlocked, and she came in with a small bag of money, which she wanted me to take. I begged her to keep a part of it, at least, to pay for Benny's being sent to the north; but she insisted, while her tears were falling fast, that I should take the whole. "You may be sick among strangers," she said, "and they would send you to the poorhouse to die." Ah, that good grandmother!

For the last time I went up to my nook. Its desolate appearance no longer chilled me, for the light of hope had risen in my soul. Yet, even with the blessed prospect of freedom before me, I felt very sad at leaving forever that old homestead, where I had been sheltered so long by the dear old grandmother; where I had dreamed my first young dream of love; and where, after that had faded away, my children came to twine themselves so closely round my desolate heart. As the hour approached for me to leave, I again descended to the storeroom. My grandmother and Benny were there. She took me by the hand, and said, "Linda, let us pray." We knelt down together, with my child pressed to my heart, and my other arm round the faithful, loving old friend I was about to leave forever. On no other occasion has it ever been my lot to listen to so fervent a supplication for mercy and protection. It thrilled through my heart, and inspired me with trust in God.

Peter was waiting for me in the street. I was soon by his side, faint in body, but strong of purpose. I did not look back upon the old place, though I felt that I should never see it again.[4]

XXX

Northward Bound

I NEVER COULD TELL how we reached the wharf. My brain was all of a whirl, and my limbs tottered under me. At an appointed place we met my uncle Phillip, who had started before us on a different route, that he might reach the wharf first, and give us timely warning if there was any danger. A row-boat was in readiness. As I was about to step in, I felt something pull me gently, and turning round I saw Benny, looking pale and anxious. He whispered in my ear, "I've been peeping into the doctor's window, and he's at home. Good by, mother. Don't cry; I'll come." He hastened away. I clasped the hand of my good uncle, to whom I owed so much, and of Peter, the brave, generous friend who had volunteered to run such terrible risks to secure my safety. To this day I remember how his bright face beamed with joy, when he told me he had discovered a safe method for me to escape. Yet that intelligent, enterprising, noble-hearted man was a chattel! liable, by the laws of a country that calls itself civilized, to be sold with horses and pigs! We parted in silence. Our hearts were all too full for words!

Swiftly the boat glided over the water. After a while, one of the sailors said, "Don't be down-hearted, madam. We will take you safely to your husband, in —————." At first I could not imagine what he meant; but I had presence of mind to think that it probably referred to something the captain had told him; so I thanked him, and said I hoped we should have pleasant weather.

When I entered the vessel the captain came forward to meet me. He was an elderly man, with a pleasant countenance. He showed me to a little box of a cabin, where sat my friend Fanny. She started as if she had seen a spectre. She gazed on me in utter astonishment, and exclaimed, "Linda, can this be *you*? or is it your ghost?" When we were locked in each other's arms, my overwrought feelings could no longer be restrained. My sobs reached the ears of the captain, who came and very kindly reminded us, that for his safety, as well as our own, it would be prudent for us not to attract any attention. He said that when there was a sail in sight he wished us to keep below; but at other times, he had no objection to our being on deck. He assured us that he would keep a good lookout, and if we acted prudently, he thought we should be in no danger. He had represented us as women going to meet our husbands in —————. We thanked him, and promised to observe carefully all the directions he gave us.

Fanny and I now talked by ourselves, low and quietly, in our little cabin. She told me of the sufferings she had gone through in making her escape, and of her terrors while she was concealed in her mother's house. Above all, she dwelt on the agony of separation from all her children on that dreadful auction day. She could scarcely credit me, when I told her of the place where I had passed nearly seven years. "We have the same sorrows," said I. "No," replied she, "you are going to see your children soon, and there is no hope that I shall ever even hear from mine."

The vessel was soon under way, but we made slow progress. The wind was against us. I should not have cared for this, if we had been out of sight of the town; but until there were miles of water between us and our enemies, we were filled with constant apprehensions that the constables would come on board. Neither could I feel quite at ease with the captain and his men. I was an entire stranger to that class of people, and I had heard that sailors were rough, and sometimes cruel. We were so completely in their power, that if they were bad men, our situation would be dreadful. Now that the captain was paid for our passage, might he not be tempted to make more money by giving us up to those who claimed us as property? I was naturally of a confiding disposition, but slavery had made me suspicious of every body. Fanny did not share my distrust of the captain or his men. She said she was afraid at first, but she had been on board three days while the vessel lay in the dock, and nobody had betrayed her, or treated her otherwise than kindly.

The captain soon came to advise us to go on deck for fresh air. His friendly and respectful manner, combined with Fanny's testimony, reassured me, and we went with him. He placed us in a comfortable seat, and occasionally entered into conversation. He told us he was a Southerner by birth, and had spent the greater part of his life in the Slave States, and that he had recently lost a brother who traded in slaves. "But," said he, "it is a pitiable and degrading business, and I always felt ashamed to acknowledge my brother in connection with it." As we passed Snaky Swamp, he pointed to it, and said, "There is a slave territory that defies all the laws." I thought of the terrible days I had spent there, and though it was not called Dismal Swamp, it made me feel very dismal as I looked at it.[1]

I shall never forget that night. The balmy air of spring was so refreshing! And how shall I describe my sensations when we were fairly sailing on Chesapeake Bay? O, the beautiful sunshine! the exhilarating breeze! and I could enjoy them without fear or restraint. I had never realized what grand things air and sunlight are till I had been deprived of them.

Ten days after we left land we were approaching Philadelphia. The captain said we should arrive there in the night, but he thought we had better wait till morning, and go on shore in broad daylight, as the best way to avoid suspicion.

I replied, "You know best. But will you stay on board and protect us?"

He saw that I was suspicious, and he said he was sorry, now that he had brought us to the end of our voyage, to find I had so little confidence in him. Ah, if he had ever been a slave he would have known how difficult it was to trust a white man. He assured us that we might sleep through the night without fear; that he would take care we were not left unprotected. Be it said to the honor of this captain, Southerner as he was, that if Fanny and I had been white ladies, and our passage lawfully engaged, he could not have treated us more respectfully. My intelligent friend, Peter, had rightly estimated the character of the man to whose honor he had intrusted us.

The next morning I was on deck as soon as the day dawned. I called Fanny to see the sun rise, for the first time in our lives, on free soil; for such I *then* believed it to be. We watched the reddening sky, and saw the great orb come up slowly out of the water, as it seemed. Soon the waves began to sparkle, and every thing caught the beautiful glow. Before us lay the city of strangers. We looked at each other, and the eyes of both were moistened with tears. We had escaped from slavery, and we supposed ourselves to be safe from the hunters. But we were alone in the world, and we had left dear ties behind us; ties cruelly sundered by the demon Slavery.

XXXI

Incidents in Philadelphia

I HAD HEARD THAT the poor slave had many friends at the north. I trusted we should find some of them. Meantime, we would take it for granted that all were friends, till they proved to the contrary. I sought out the kind captain, thanked him for his attentions, and told him I should never cease to be grateful for the service he had rendered us. I gave him a message to the friends I had left at home, and he promised to deliver it. We were placed in a row-boat, and in about fifteen minutes were landed on a wood wharf in Philadelphia.[1] As I stood looking round, the friendly captain touched me on the shoulder, and said, "There is a respectable-looking colored man behind you. I will speak to him about the New York trains, and tell him you wish to go directly on." I thanked him, and asked him to direct me to some shops where I could buy gloves and veils. He did so, and said he would talk with the colored man till I returned. I made what haste I

could. Constant exercise on board the vessel, and frequent rubbing
with salt water, had nearly restored the use of my limbs. The noise of
the great city confused me, but I found the shops, and bought some
double veils and gloves for Fanny and myself. The shopman told me
they were so many levies. I had never heard the word before, but I did
not tell him so. I thought if he knew I was a stranger he might ask me
where I came from. I gave him a gold piece, and when he returned the
change, I counted it, and found out how much a levy was.[2] I made my
way back to the wharf, where the captain introduced me to the colored man, as the Rev. Jeremiah Durham, minister of Bethel church.[3]
He took me by the hand, as if I had been an old friend. He told us we
were too late for the morning cars to New York, and must wait until
the evening, or the next morning. He invited me to go home with
him, assuring me that his wife would give me a cordial welcome; and
for my friend he would provide a home with one of his neighbors.
I thanked him for so much kindness to strangers, and told him if I
must be detained, I should like to hunt up some people who formerly
went from our part of the country. Mr. Durham insisted that I should
dine with him, and then he would assist me in finding my friends.
The sailors came to bid us good by. I shook their hardy hands, with
tears in my eyes. They had all been kind to us, and they had rendered
us a greater service than they could possibly conceive of.

I had never seen so large a city, or been in contact with so many
people in the streets. It seemed as if those who passed looked at us
with an expression of curiosity. My face was so blistered and peeled,
by sitting on deck, in wind and sunshine, that I thought they could
not easily decide to what nation I belonged.

Mrs. Durham met me with a kindly welcome, without asking any
questions. I was tired, and her friendly manner was a sweet refresh-
ment. God bless her! I was sure that she had comforted other weary

hearts, before I received her sympathy. She was surrounded by her husband and children, in a home made sacred by protecting laws. I thought of my own children, and sighed.

After dinner Mr. Durham went with me in quest of the friends I had spoken of. They went from my native town, and I anticipated much pleasure in looking on familiar faces. They were not at home, and we retraced our steps through streets delightfully clean. On the way, Mr. Durham observed that I had spoken to him of a daughter I expected to meet; that he was surprised, for I looked so young he had taken me for a single woman. He was approaching a subject on which I was extremely sensitive. He would ask about my husband next, I thought, and if I answered him truly, what would he think of me? I told him I had two children, one in New York the other at the south. He asked some further questions, and I frankly told him some of the most important events of my life. It was painful for me to do it; but I would not deceive him. If he was desirous of being my friend, I thought he ought to know how far I was worthy of it. "Excuse me, if I have tried your feelings," said he. "I did not question you from idle curiosity. I wanted to understand your situation, in order to know whether I could be of any service to you, or your little girl. Your straight-forward answers do you credit; but don't answer every body so openly. It might give some heartless people a pretext for treating you with contempt."

That word *contempt* burned me like coals of fire. I replied, "God alone knows how I have suffered; and He, I trust, will forgive me. If I am permitted to have my children, I intend to be a good mother, and to live in such a manner that people cannot treat me with contempt."

"I respect your sentiments," said he. "Place your trust in God, and be governed by good principles, and you will not fail to find friends."

When we reached home, I went to my room, glad to shut out the world for a while. The words he had spoken made an indelible impression upon me. They brought up great shadows from the mournful past. In the midst of my meditations I was startled by a knock at the door. Mrs. Durham entered, her face all beaming with kindness, to say that there was an anti-slavery friend down stairs, who would like to see me. I overcame my dread of encountering strangers, and went with her. Many questions were asked concerning my experiences, and my escape from slavery; but I observed how careful they all were not to say any thing that might wound my feelings. How gratifying this was, can be fully understood only by those who have been accustomed to be treated as if they were not included within the pale of human beings. The anti-slavery friend had come to inquire into my plans, and to offer assistance, if needed. Fanny was comfortably established, for the present, with a friend of Mr. Durham. The Anti-Slavery Society agreed to pay her expenses to New York.[4] The same was offered to me, but I declined to accept it; telling them that my grandmother had given me sufficient to pay my expenses to the end of my journey. We were urged to remain in Philadelphia a few days, until some suitable escort could be found for us. I gladly accepted the proposition, for I had a dread of meeting slaveholders, and some dread also of railroads. I had never entered a railroad car in my life, and it seemed to me quite an important event.

That night I sought my pillow with feelings I had never carried to it before. I verily believed myself to be a free woman. I was wakeful for a long time, and I had no sooner fallen asleep, than I was roused by fire-bells.[5] I jumped up, and hurried on my clothes. Where I came from, every body hastened to dress themselves on such occasions. The white people thought a great fire might be used as a good opportunity for insurrection, and that it was best to be in readiness; and the colored people were ordered out to labor in extinguishing the flames. There was but one engine in our town, and colored women and children were often required to drag it to the river's edge and fill it. Mrs.

Durham's daughter slept in the same room with me, and seeing that she slept through all the din, I thought it was my duty to wake her. "What's the matter?" said she, rubbing her eyes.

"They're screaming fire in the streets, and the bells are ringing," I replied.

"What of that?" said she, drowsily. "We are used to it. We never get up, without the fire is very near. What good would it do?"

I was quite surprised that it was not necessary for us to go and help fill the engine. I was an ignorant child, just beginning to learn how things went on in great cities.

At daylight, I heard women crying fresh fish, berries, radishes, and various other things. All this was new to me. I dressed myself at an early hour, and sat at the window to watch that unknown tide of life. Philadelphia seemed to me a wonderfully great place. At the breakfast table, my idea of going out to drag the engine was laughed over, and I joined in the mirth.

I went to see Fanny, and found her so well contented among her new friends that she was in no haste to leave. I was also very happy with my kind hostess. She had had advantages for education, and was vastly my superior. Every day, almost every hour, I was adding to my little stock of knowledge. She took me out to see the city as much as she deemed prudent. One day she took me to an artist's room, and showed me the portraits of some of her children.[6] I had never seen any paintings of colored people before, and they seemed to me beautiful.

At the end of five days, one of Mrs. Durham's friends offered to accompany us to New York the following morning.[7] As I held the hand of my good hostess in a parting clasp, I longed to know whether her husband had repeated to her what I had told him. I supposed he had, but she never made any allusion to it. I presume it was the delicate silence of womanly sympathy.

When Mr. Durham handed us our tickets, he said, "I am afraid you will have a disagreeable ride; but I could not procure tickets for the first class cars."

Supposing I had not given him money enough, I offered more. "O, no," said he, "they could not be had for any money. They don't allow colored people to go in the first-class cars."

This was the first chill to my enthusiasm about the Free States. Colored people were allowed to ride in a filthy box, behind white people, at the south, but there they were not required to pay for the privilege. It made me sad to find how the north aped the customs of slavery.

We were stowed away in a large, rough car, with windows on each side, too high for us to look out without standing up. It was crowded with people, apparently of all nations. There were plenty of beds and cradles, containing screaming and kicking babies. Every other man had a cigar or pipe in his mouth, and jugs of whiskey were handed round freely. The fumes of the whiskey and the dense tobacco smoke were sickening to my senses, and my mind was equally nauseated by the coarse jokes and ribald songs around me. It was a very disagreeable ride. Since that time there has been some improvement in these matters.[8]

XXXII

The Meeting of Mother and Daughter

W HEN WE ARRIVED in New York, I was half crazed by the crowd of coachmen calling out, "Carriage, ma'am?" We bargained with one to take us to Sullivan Street for twelve shillings. A burly Irishman stepped up and said, "I'll tak' ye for sax shillings." The reduction of half the price was an object to us, and we asked if he could take us right away. "Troth an I will, ladies," he replied. I noticed that the hackmen smiled at each other, and I inquired whether his conveyance was decent. "Yes, it's dacent it is, marm. Devil a bit would I be after takin' ladies in a cab that was not dacent." We gave him our checks. He went for the baggage, and soon reappeared, saying, "This way, if you plase, ladies." We followed, and found our trunks on a truck, and we were invited to take our seats on them. We told him that was not what we bargained for, and he must take the trunks off. He swore they should not be touched till we had paid him six shillings. In our situation it was not prudent to attract attention, and I

was about to pay him what he required, when a man near by shook
his head for me not to do it. After a great ado we got rid of the Irishman, and had our trunks fastened on a hack. We had been recom-
mended to a boarding-house in Sullivan Street, and thither we drove.
There Fanny and I separated. The Anti-Slavery Society provided a
home for her, and I afterwards heard of her in prosperous circumstances. I sent for an old friend from my part of the country, who had
for some time been doing business in New York. He came immediately. I told him I wanted to go to my daughter, and asked him to aid
me in procuring an interview.[1]

I cautioned him not to let it be known to the family that I had just
arrived from the south, because they supposed I had been at the north
seven years. He told me there was a colored woman in Brooklyn who
came from the same town I did, and I had better go to her house, and
have my daughter meet me there. I accepted the proposition thank-
fully, and he agreed to escort me to Brooklyn. We crossed Fulton ferry,
went up Myrtle Avenue, and stopped at the house he designated.[2] I
was just about to enter, when two girls passed. My friend called my
attention to them. I turned, and recognized in the eldest, Sarah, the
daughter of a woman who used to live with my grandmother, but
who had left the south years ago. Surprised and rejoiced at this unexpected meeting, I threw my arms round her, and inquired concerning
her mother.

"You take no notice of the other girl," said my friend. I turned, and
there stood my Ellen! I pressed her to my heart, then held her away
from me to take a look at her. She had changed a good deal in the two
years since I parted from her. Signs of neglect could be discerned by
eyes less observing than a mother's. My friend invited us all to go into
the house; but Ellen said she had been sent on an errand, which she
would do as quickly as possible, and go home and ask Mrs. Hobbs to
let her come and see me. It was agreed that I should send for her the

next day. Her companion, Sarah, hastened to tell her mother of my arrival. When I entered the house, I found the mistress of it absent, and I waited for her return. Before I saw her, I heard her saying, "Where is Linda Brent? I used to know her father and mother." Soon Sarah came with her mother. So there was quite a company of us, all from my grandmother's neighborhood. These friends gathered round me and questioned me eagerly. They laughed, they cried, and they shouted. They thanked God that I had got away from my persecutors and was safe on Long Island. It was a day of great excitement. How different from the silent days I had passed in my dreary den!

The next morning was Sunday. My first waking thoughts were occupied with the note that I was to send to Mrs. Hobbs, the lady with whom Ellen lived. That I had recently come into that vicinity was evident; otherwise I should have sooner inquired for my daughter. It would not do to let them know I had just arrived from the south, for that would involve the suspicion of my having been harbored there, and might bring trouble, if not ruin, on several people.

I like a straightforward course, and am always reluctant to resort to subterfuges. So far as my ways have been crooked, I charge them all upon slavery. It was that system of violence and wrong which now left me no alternative but to enact a falsehood. I began my note by stating that I had recently arrived from Canada, and was very desirous to have my daughter come to see me. She came and brought a message from Mrs. Hobbs, inviting me to her house, and assuring me that I need not have any fears.[3] The conversation I had with my child did not leave my mind at ease. When I asked if she was well treated, she answered yes; but there was no heartiness in the tone, and it seemed to me that she said it from an unwillingness to have me troubled on her account. Before she left me, she asked very earnestly, "Mother, when will you take me to live with you?" It made me sad to think that I could not give her a home till I went to work and earned the means;

and that might take me a long time. When she was placed with Mrs. Hobbs, the agreement was that she should be sent to school. She had been there two years, and was now nine years old, and she scarcely knew her letters. There was no excuse for this, for there were good public schools in Brooklyn, to which she could have been sent without expense.[4]

She staid with me till dark, and I went home with her. I was received in a friendly manner by the family, and all agreed in saying that Ellen was a useful, good girl. Mrs. Hobbs looked me coolly in the face, and said, "I suppose you know that my cousin, Mr. Sands, has *given* her to my eldest daughter. She will make a nice waiting-maid for her when she grows up." I did not answer a word. How *could* she, who knew by experience the strength of a mother's love, and who was perfectly aware of the relation Mr. Sands bore to my children,—how *could* she look me in the face, while she thrust such a dagger into my heart?

I was no longer surprised that they had kept her in such a state of ignorance. Mr. Hobbs had formerly been wealthy, but he had failed, and afterwards obtained a subordinate situation in the Custom House.[5] Perhaps they expected to return to the south some day; and Ellen's knowledge was quite sufficient for a slave's condition. I was impatient to go to work and earn money, that I might change the uncertain position of my children. Mr. Sands had not kept his promise to emancipate them. I had also been deceived about Ellen. What security had I with regard to Benjamin? I felt that I had none.

I returned to my friend's house in an uneasy state of mind. In order to protect my children, it was necessary that I should own myself. I called myself free, and sometimes felt so; but I knew I was insecure. I sat down that night and wrote a civil letter to Dr. Flint, asking him to state the lowest terms on which he would sell me; and as I belonged by law to his daughter, I wrote to her also, making a similar request.

Since my arrival at the north I had not been unmindful of my dear brother William. I had made diligent inquiries for him, and having heard of him in Boston, I went thither. When I arrived there, I found he had gone to New Bedford. I wrote to that place, and was informed he had gone on a whaling voyage, and would not return for some months.[6] I went back to New York to get employment near Ellen. I received an answer from Dr. Flint, which gave me no encouragement. He advised me to return and submit myself to my rightful owners, and then any request I might make would be granted. I lent this letter to a friend, who lost it; otherwise I would present a copy to my readers.

XXXIII

A Home Found

M Y GREATEST ANXIETY now was to obtain employment. My health was greatly improved, though my limbs continued to trouble me with swelling whenever I walked much. The greatest difficulty in my way was, that those who employed strangers required a recommendation; and in my peculiar position, I could, of course, obtain no certificates from the families I had so faithfully served.

One day an acquaintance told me of a lady who wanted a nurse for her babe, and I immediately applied for the situation. The lady told me she preferred to have one who had been a mother, and accustomed to the care of infants. I told her I had nursed two babes of my own. She asked me many questions, but, to my great relief, did not require a recommendation from my former employers. She told me she was an English woman, and that was a pleasant circumstance to me, because I had heard they had less prejudice against color than Americans entertained. It was agreed that we should try each other for a week. The trial proved satisfactory to both parties, and I was engaged for a month.[1]

The heavenly Father had been most merciful to me in leading me to this place. Mrs. Bruce was a kind and gentle lady, and proved a true and sympathizing friend. Before the stipulated month expired, the necessity of passing up and down stairs frequently, caused my limbs to swell so painfully, that I became unable to perform my duties. Many ladies would have thoughtlessly discharged me; but Mrs. Bruce made arrangements to save me steps, and employed a physician to attend upon me. I had not yet told her that I was a fugitive slave. She noticed that I was often sad, and kindly inquired the cause. I spoke of being separated from my children, and from relatives who were dear to me; but I did not mention the constant feeling of insecurity which oppressed my spirits. I longed for some one to confide in; but I had been so deceived by white people, that I had lost all confidence in them. If they spoke kind words to me, I thought it was for some selfish purpose. I had entered this family with the distrustful feelings I had brought with me out of slavery; but ere six months had passed, I found that the gentle deportment of Mrs. Bruce and the smiles of her lovely babe were thawing my chilled heart. My narrow mind also began to expand under the influences of her intelligent conversation, and the opportunities for reading, which were gladly allowed me whenever I had leisure from my duties. I gradually became more energetic and more cheerful.

The old feeling of insecurity, especially with regard to my children, often threw its dark shadow across my sunshine. Mrs. Bruce offered me a home for Ellen; but pleasant as it would have been, I did not dare to accept it, for fear of offending the Hobbs family. Their knowledge of my precarious situation placed me in their power; and I felt that it was important for me to keep on the right side of them, till, by dint of labor and economy, I could make a home for my children.

I was far from feeling satisfied with Ellen's situation. She was not well cared for. She sometimes came to New York to visit me; but she generally brought a request from Mrs. Hobbs that I would buy her a pair of shoes, or some article of clothing. This was accompanied by a promise of payment when Mr. Hobbs's salary at the Custom House became due; but some how or other the pay-day never came. Thus many dollars of my earnings were expended to keep my child comfortably clothed. That, however, was a slight trouble, compared with the fear that their pecuniary embarrassments might induce them to sell my precious young daughter. I knew they were in constant communication with Southerners, and had frequent opportunities to do it. I have stated that when Dr. Flint put Ellen in jail, at two years old, she had an inflammation of the eyes, occasioned by measles. This disease still troubled her; and kind Mrs. Bruce proposed that she should come to New York for a while, to be under the care of Dr. Elliott, a well known oculist.[2] It did not occur to me that there was any thing improper in a mother's making such a request; but Mrs. Hobbs was very angry, and refused to let her go. Situated as I was, it was not politic to insist upon it. I made no complaint, but I longed to be entirely free to act a mother's part towards my children. The next time I went over to Brooklyn, Mrs. Hobbs, as if to apologize for her anger, told me she had employed her own physician to attend to Ellen's eyes, and that she had refused my request because she did not consider it safe to trust her in New York. I accepted the explanation in silence; but she had told me that my child *belonged* to her daughter, and I suspected that her real motive was a fear of my conveying her property away from her. Perhaps I did her injustice; but my knowledge of Southerners made it difficult for me to feel otherwise.

Sweet and bitter were mixed in the cup of my life, and I was thankful that it had ceased to be entirely bitter. I loved Mrs. Bruce's babe. When it laughed and crowed in my face, and twined its little tender

arms confidingly about my neck, it made me think of the time when
Benny and Ellen were babies, and my wounded heart was soothed.
One bright morning, as I stood at the window, tossing baby in my
arms, my attention was attracted by a young man in sailor's dress,
who was closely observing every house as he passed. I looked at him
earnestly. Could it be my brother William? It *must* be he—and yet,
how changed! I placed the baby safely, flew down stairs, opened the
front door, beckoned to the sailor, and in less than a minute I was
clasped in my brother's arms.[3] How much we had to tell each other!
How we laughed, and how we cried, over each other's adventures! I
took him to Brooklyn, and again saw him with Ellen, the dear child
whom he had loved and tended so carefully, while I was shut up in my
miserable den. He staid in New York a week. His old feelings of affection for me and Ellen were as lively as ever. There are no bonds so
strong as those which are formed by suffering together.

XXXIV

The Old Enemy Again

M Y YOUNG MISTRESS, Miss Emily Flint, did not return any answer to my letter requesting her to consent to my being sold. But after a while, I received a reply, which purported to be written by her younger brother. In order rightly to enjoy the contents of this letter, the reader must bear in mind that the Flint family supposed I had been at the north many years. They had no idea that I knew of the doctor's three excursions to New York in search of me; that I had heard his voice, when he came to borrow five hundred dollars for that purpose; and that I had seen him pass on his way to the steamboat. Neither were they aware that all the particulars of aunt Nancy's death and burial were conveyed to me at the time they occurred. I have kept the letter, of which I herewith subjoin a copy:—

"Your letter to sister was received a few days ago. I gather from it that you are desirous of returning to your native place, among your friends and relatives. We were all gratified with the contents of your letter; and let me assure you that if any members of the family have had any feeling of resentment towards you, they feel it no longer. We all sympathize with you in your unfortunate condition, and are ready to do all in our power to make you contented and happy. It is difficult for you to return home as a free person. If you were purchased by your grandmother, it is doubtful whether you would be permitted to remain, although it would be lawful for you to do so. If a servant should be allowed to purchase herself, after absenting herself so long from her owners, and return free, it would have an injurious effect. From your letter, I think your situation must be hard and uncomfortable. Come home. You have it in your power to be reinstated in our affections. We would receive you with open arms and tears of joy. You need not apprehend any unkind treatment, as we have not put ourselves to any trouble or expense to get you. Had we done so, perhaps we should feel otherwise. You know my sister was always attached to you, and that you were never treated as a slave. You were never put to hard work, nor exposed to field labor. On the contrary, you were taken into the house, and treated as one of us, and almost as free; and we, at least, felt that you were above disgracing yourself by running away. Believing you may be induced to come home voluntarily has induced me to write for my sister. The family will be rejoiced to see you; and your poor old grandmother expressed a great desire to have you come, when she heard your letter read. In her old age she needs the consolation of having her children round her. Doubtless you have heard of the death of your aunt. She was a faithful servant, and a faithful member of the Episcopal church. In her Christian life she taught us how to live—and, O, too high the price of knowledge, she taught us how to die![1] Could you have seen us round her death bed, with her mother, all mingling our tears in one common stream, you would have thought the same heartfelt tie existed between a master and his servant, as between a mother and her child.

But this subject is too painful to dwell upon. I must bring my letter to a close. If you are contented to stay away from your old grandmother, your child, and the friends who love you, stay where you are. We shall never trouble ourselves to apprehend you. But should you prefer to come home, we will do all that we can to make you happy. If you do not wish to remain in the family, I know that father, by our persuasion, will be induced to let you be purchased by any person you may choose in our community. You will please answer this as soon as possible, and let us know your decision. Sister sends much love to you. In the mean time believe me your sincere friend and well wisher."

This letter was signed by Emily's brother, who was as yet a mere lad.[2] I knew, by the style, that it was not written by a person of his age, and though the writing was disguised, I had been made too unhappy by it, in former years, not to recognize at once the hand of Dr. Flint. O, the hypocrisy of slaveholders! Did the old fox suppose I was goose enough to go into such a trap? Verily, he relied too much on "the stupidity of the African race." I did not return the family of Flints any thanks for their cordial invitation—a remissness for which I was, no doubt, charged with base ingratitude.

Not long afterwards I received a letter from one of my friends at the south, informing me that Dr. Flint was about to visit the north. The letter had been delayed, and I supposed he might be already on the way. Mrs. Bruce did not know I was a fugitive. I told her that important business called me to Boston, where my brother then was, and asked permission to bring a friend to supply my place as nurse, for a fortnight. I started on my journey immediately; and as soon as I arrived, I wrote to my grandmother that if Benny came, he must be sent to Boston. I knew she was only waiting for a good chance to send him north, and, fortunately, she had the legal power to do so, without asking leave of any body. She was a free woman; and when my children were purchased, Mr. Sands preferred to have the bill of sale drawn up in her name. It was conjectured that he advanced the money, but it was not known. At the south, a gentleman may have a shoal of colored children without any disgrace; but if he is known to purchase them, with the view of setting them free, the example is thought to be dangerous to their "peculiar institution," and he becomes unpopular.

There was a good opportunity to send Benny in a vessel coming directly to New York. He was put on board with a letter to a friend, who was requested to see him off to Boston. Early one morning, there was a loud rap at my door, and in rushed Benjamin, all out of breath. "O mother!" he exclaimed, "here I am! I run all the way; and I come all alone. How d'you do?"

O reader, can you imagine my joy? No, you cannot, unless you have been a slave mother. Benjamin rattled away as fast as his tongue could go. "Mother, why don't you bring Ellen here? I went over to Brooklyn to see her, and she felt very bad when I bid her good by. She said, 'O Ben, I wish I was going too.' I thought she'd know ever so much; but she don't know so much as I do; for I can read, and she can't. And, mother, I lost all my clothes coming. What can I do to get some more? I 'spose free boys can get along here at the north as well as white boys."

I did not like to tell the sanguine, happy little fellow how much he was mistaken. I took him to a tailor, and procured a change of clothes. The rest of the day was spent in mutual asking and answering of questions, with the wish constantly repeated that the good old grandmother was with us, and frequent injunctions from Benny to write to her immediately, and be sure to tell her every thing about his voyage, and his journey to Boston.

Dr. Flint made his visit to New York, and made every exertion to call upon me, and invite me to return with him; but not being able to ascertain where I was, his hospitable intentions were frustrated, and the affectionate family, who were waiting for me with "open arms," were doomed to disappointment.

As soon as I knew he was safely at home, I placed Benjamin in the care of my brother William, and returned to Mrs. Bruce. There I remained through the winter and spring, endeavoring to perform my duties faithfully, and finding a good degree of happiness in the attractions of baby Mary, the considerate kindness of her excellent mother, and occasional interviews with my darling daughter.

But when summer came, the old feeling of insecurity haunted me. It was necessary for me to take little Mary out daily, for exercise and fresh air, and the city was swarming with Southerners, some of whom might recognize me. Hot weather brings out snakes and slaveholders, and I like one class of the venomous creatures as little as I do the other. What a comfort it is, to be free to *say* so!

XXXV

Prejudice against Color

I T WAS A RELIEF TO my mind to see preparations for leaving the city. We went to Albany in the steamboat Knickerbocker.[1] When the gong sounded for tea, Mrs. Bruce said, "Linda, it is late, and you and baby had better come to the table with me." I replied, "I know it is time baby had her supper, but I had rather not go with you, if you please. I am afraid of being insulted." "O no, not if you are with *me*," she said. I saw several white nurses go with their ladies, and I ventured to do the same. We were at the extreme end of the table. I was no sooner seated, than a gruff voice said, "Get up! You know you are not allowed to sit here." I looked up, and, to my astonishment and indignation, saw that the speaker was a colored man. If his office required him to enforce the by-laws of the boat, he might, at least, have done it politely. I replied, "I shall not get up, unless the captain comes and takes me up." No cup of tea was offered me, but Mrs. Bruce handed me hers and called for another. I looked to see whether the other nurses were treated in a similar manner. They were all properly waited on.

Next morning, when we stopped at Troy for breakfast, every body was making a rush for the table. Mrs. Bruce said, "Take my arm, Linda, and we'll go in together." The landlord heard her, and said, "Madam, will you allow your nurse and baby to take breakfast with my family?" I knew this was to be attributed to my complexion; but he spoke courteously, and therefore I did not mind it.

At Saratoga we found the United States Hotel crowded, and Mr. Bruce took one of the cottages belonging to the hotel. I had thought, with gladness, of going to the quiet of the country, where I should meet few people, but here I found myself in the midst of a swarm of Southerners.[2] I looked round me with fear and trembling, dreading to see some one who would recognize me. I was rejoiced to find that we were to stay but a short time.

We soon returned to New York, to make arrangements for spending the remainder of the summer at Rockaway. While the laundress was putting the clothes in order, I took an opportunity to go over to Brooklyn to see Ellen. I met her going to a grocery store, and the first words she said, were, "O, mother, don't go to Mrs. Hobbs's. Her brother, Mr. Thorne, has come from the south, and may be he'll tell where you are." I accepted the warning. I told her I was going away with Mrs. Bruce the next day, and would try to see her when I came back.

Being in servitude to the Anglo-Saxon race, I was not put into a "Jim Crow car," on our way to Rockaway, neither was I invited to ride through the streets on the top of trunks in a truck; but every where I found the same manifestations of that cruel prejudice, which so discourages the feelings, and represses the energies of the colored people.[3] We reached Rockaway before dark, and put up at the Pavilion—a large hotel, beautifully situated by the sea-side—a great resort of the fashionable world.[4] Thirty or forty nurses were there, of a great variety of nations. Some of the ladies had colored waiting-maids and coachmen, but I was the only nurse tinged with the blood of Africa. When the tea bell rang, I took little Mary and followed the other nurses. Supper was served in a long hall. A young man, who had the ordering of things, took the circuit of the table two or three times, and finally pointed me to a seat at the lower end of it. As there was but one chair, I sat down and took the child in my lap. Whereupon the young man came to me and said, in the blandest manner possible, "Will you please to seat the little girl in the chair, and stand behind it and feed her? After they have done, you will be shown to the kitchen, where you will have a good supper."

This was the climax! I found it hard to preserve my self-control, when I looked round, and saw women who were nurses, as I was, and only one shade lighter in complexion, eyeing me with a defiant look, as if my presence were a contamination. However, I said nothing. I quietly took the child in my arms, went to our room, and refused to go to the table again. Mr. Bruce ordered meals to be sent to the room for little Mary and I. This answered for a few days; but the waiters of the establishment were white, and they soon began to complain, saying they were not hired to wait on negroes. The landlord requested Mr. Bruce to send me down to my meals, because his servants rebelled against bringing them up, and the colored servants of other boarders were dissatisfied because all were not treated alike.

My answer was that the colored servants ought to be dissatisfied with *themselves*, for not having too much self-respect to submit to such treatment; that there was no difference in the price of board for colored and white servants, and there was no justification for difference of treatment. I staid a month after this, and finding I was resolved to stand up for my rights, they concluded to treat me well. Let every colored man and woman do this, and eventually we shall cease to be trampled under foot by our oppressors.

XXXVI

The Hairbreadth Escape

A FTER WE RETURNED to New York, I took the earliest opportunity to go and see Ellen. I asked to have her called down stairs; for I supposed Mrs. Hobbs's southern brother might still be there, and I was desirous to avoid seeing him, if possible.[1] But Mrs. Hobbs came to the kitchen, and insisted on my going up stairs. "My brother wants to see you," said she, "and he is sorry you seem to shun him. He knows you are living in New York. He told me to say to you that he owes thanks to good old aunt Martha for too many little acts of kindness for him to be base enough to betray her grandchild."

This Mr. Thorne had become poor and reckless long before he left the south, and such persons had much rather go to one of the faithful old slaves to borrow a dollar, or get a good dinner, than to go to one whom they consider an equal. It was such acts of kindness as these for which he professed to feel grateful to my grandmother. I wished he had kept at a distance, but as he was here, and knew where I was, I concluded there was nothing to be gained by trying to avoid him; on the contrary, it might be the means of exciting his ill will. I followed his sister up stairs. He met me in a very friendly manner, congratulated me on my escape from slavery, and hoped I had a good place, where I felt happy.

I continued to visit Ellen as often as I could. She, good thoughtful child, never forgot my hazardous situation, but always kept a vigilant lookout for my safety. She never made any complaint about her own inconveniences and troubles; but a mother's observing eye easily perceived that she was not happy. On the occasion of one of my visits I found her unusually serious. When I asked her what was the matter, she said nothing was the matter. But I insisted upon knowing what made her look so very grave. Finally, I ascertained that she felt troubled about the dissipation that was continually going on in the house. She was sent to the store very often for rum and brandy, and she felt ashamed to ask for it so often; and Mr. Hobbs and Mr. Thorne drank a great deal, and their hands trembled so that they had to call her to pour out the liquor for them. "But for all that," said she, "Mr. Hobbs is good to me, and I can't help liking him. I feel sorry for him." I tried to comfort her, by telling her that I had laid up a hundred dollars, and that before long I hoped to be able to give her and Benjamin a home, and send them to school. She was always desirous not to add to my troubles more than she could help, and I did not discover till years afterwards that Mr. Thorne's intemperance was not the only annoyance she suffered from him. Though he professed too much gratitude to my grandmother to injure any of her descendants, he had poured vile language into the ears of her innocent great-grandchild.

I usually went to Brooklyn to spend Sunday afternoon. One Sunday, I found Ellen anxiously waiting for me near the house. "O, mother," said she, "I've been waiting for you this long time. I'm afraid Mr. Thorne has written to tell Dr. Flint where you are. Make haste and come in. Mrs. Hobbs will tell you all about it!"

The story was soon told. While the children were playing in the grape-vine arbor, the day before, Mr. Thorne came out with a letter in his hand, which he tore up and scattered about. Ellen was sweeping the yard at the time, and having her mind full of suspicions of him, she picked up the pieces and carried them to the children, saying, "I wonder who Mr. Thorne has been writing to."

"I'm sure I don't know, and don't care," replied the oldest of the children; "and I don't see how it concerns you."

"But it does concern me," replied Ellen; "for I'm afraid he's been writing to the south about my mother."

They laughed at her, and called her a silly thing, but good-naturedly put the fragments of writing together, in order to read them to her. They were no sooner arranged, than the little girl exclaimed, "I declare, Ellen, I believe you are right."

The contents of Mr. Thorne's letter, as nearly as I can remember, were as follows: "I have seen your slave, Linda, and conversed with her. She can be taken very easily, if you manage prudently. There are enough of us here to swear to her identity as your property. I am a patriot, a lover of my country, and I do this as an act of justice to the laws." He concluded by informing the doctor of the street and number where I lived. The children carried the pieces to Mrs. Hobbs, who immediately went to her brother's room for an explanation. He was not to be found. The servants said they saw him go out with a letter in his hand, and they supposed he had gone to the post office. The natural inference was, that he had sent to Dr. Flint a copy of those fragments. When he returned, his sister accused him of it, and he did not deny the charge. He went immediately to his room, and the next morning he was missing. He had gone over to New York, before any of the family were astir.

It was evident that I had no time to lose; and I hastened back to the city with a heavy heart. Again I was to be torn from a comfortable home, and all my plans for the welfare of my children were to be frustrated by that demon Slavery! I now regretted that I never told Mrs. Bruce my story. I had not concealed it merely on account of being a fugitive; that would have made her anxious, but it would have excited sympathy in her kind heart. I valued her good opinion, and I was afraid of losing it, if I told her all the particulars of my sad story. But now I felt that it was necessary for her to know how I was situated. I had once left her abruptly, without explaining the reason, and it would not be proper to do it again. I went home resolved to tell her in the morning. But the sadness of my face attracted her attention, and, in answer to her kind inquiries, I poured out my full heart to her, before bed time.[2] She listened with true womanly sympathy, and told me she would do all she could to protect me. How my heart blessed her!

Early the next morning, Judge Vanderpool and Lawyer Hopper were consulted.[3] They said I had better leave the city at once, as the risk would be great if the case came to trial. Mrs. Bruce took me in a carriage to the house of one of her friends, where she assured me I should be safe until my brother could arrive, which would be in a few days. In the interval my thoughts were much occupied with Ellen. She was mine by birth, and she was also mine by Southern law, since my grandmother held the bill of sale that made her so. I did not feel that she was safe unless I had her with me. Mrs. Hobbs, who felt badly about her brother's treachery, yielded to my entreaties, on condition that she should return in ten days. I avoided making any promise. She came to me clad in very thin garments, all outgrown, and with a school satchel on her arm, containing a few articles. It was late in October, and I knew the child must suffer; and not daring to go out in the streets to purchase any thing, I took off my own flannel skirt and converted it into one for her. Kind Mrs. Brace came to bid me good by, and when she saw that I had taken off my clothing for my child, the tears came to her eyes. She said, "Wait for me, Linda," and went out. She soon returned with a nice warm shawl and hood for Ellen. Truly, of such souls as hers are the kingdom of heaven.

My brother reached New York on Wednesday. Lawyer Hopper advised us to go to Boston by the Stonington route, as there was less Southern travel in that direction.[4] Mrs. Bruce directed her servants to tell all inquirers that I formerly lived there, but had gone from the city.

We reached the steamboat Rhode Island in safety.[5] That boat employed colored hands, but I knew that colored passengers were not admitted to the cabin. I was very desirous for the seclusion of the cabin, not only on account of exposure to the night air, but also to avoid observation. Lawyer Hopper was waiting on board for us. He spoke to the stewardess, and asked, as a particular favor, that she would treat us well. He said to me, "Go and speak to the captain yourself by and by. Take your little girl with you, and I am sure that he will not let her sleep on deck." With these kind words and a shake of the hand he departed.

The boat was soon on her way, bearing me rapidly from the friendly home where I had hoped to find security and rest. My brother had left me to purchase the tickets, thinking that I might have better success than he would. When the stewardess came to me, I paid what she asked, and she gave me three tickets with clipped corners. In the most unsophisticated manner I said, "You have made a mistake; I asked you for cabin tickets. I cannot possibly consent to sleep on deck with my little daughter." She assured me there was no mistake. She said on some of the routes colored people were allowed to sleep in the cabin, but not on this route, which was much travelled by the wealthy. I asked her to show me to the captain's office, and she said she would after tea. When the time came, I took Ellen by the hand and went to the captain, politely requesting him to change our tickets, as we should be very uncomfortable on deck. He said it was contrary to their custom, but he would see that we had berths below; he would also try to obtain comfortable seats for us in the cars; of that he was not certain, but he would speak to the conductor about it, when the boat arrived. I thanked him, and returned to the ladies' cabin. He came afterwards and told me that the conductor of the cars was on board, that he had spoken to him, and he had promised to take care of us. I was very much surprised at receiving so much kindness. I don't know whether the pleasing face of my little girl had won his heart, or whether the stewardess inferred from Lawyer Hopper's manner that I was a fugitive, and had pleaded with him in my behalf.

When the boat arrived at Stonington, the conductor kept his promise, and showed us to seats in the first car, nearest the engine. He asked us to take seats next the door, but as he passed through, we ventured to move on toward the other end of the car. No incivility was offered us, and we reached Boston in safety.

The day after my arrival was one of the happiest of my life. I felt as if I was beyond the reach of the bloodhounds; and, for the first time during many years, I had both my children together with me. They greatly enjoyed their reunion, and laughed and chatted merrily. I watched them with a swelling heart. Their every motion delighted me.

I could not feel safe in New York, and I accepted the offer of a friend, that we should share expenses and keep house together. I represented to Mrs. Hobbs that Ellen must have some schooling, and must remain with me for that purpose. She felt ashamed of being unable to read or spell at her age, so instead of sending her to school with Benny, I instructed her myself till she was fitted to enter an intermediate school.[6] The winter passed pleasantly, while I was busy with my needle, and my children with their books.

XXXVII

A Visit to England

IN THE SPRING, sad news came to me. Mrs. Bruce was dead.[1] Never again, in this world, should I see her gentle face, or hear her sympathizing voice. I had lost an excellent friend, and little Mary had lost a tender mother. Mr. Bruce wished the child to visit some of her mother's relatives in England, and he was desirous that I should take charge of her. The little motherless one was accustomed to me, and attached to me, and I thought she would be happier in my care than in that of a stranger. I could also earn more in this way than I could by my needle. So I put Benny to a trade, and left Ellen to remain in the house with my friend and go to school.[2]

We sailed from New York, and arrived in Liverpool after a pleasant voyage of twelve days.[3] We proceeded directly to London, and took lodgings at the Adelaide Hotel. The supper seemed to me less luxurious than those I had seen in American hotels; but my situation was indescribably more pleasant. For the first time in my life I was in a place where I was treated according to my deportment, without reference to my complexion. I felt as if a great millstone had been lifted from my breast. Ensconced in a pleasant room, with my dear little charge, I laid my head on my pillow, for the first time, with the delightful consciousness of pure, unadulterated freedom.

As I had constant care of the child, I had little opportunity to see the wonders of that great city; but I watched the tide of life that flowed through the streets, and found it a strange contrast to the stagnation in our Southern towns. Mr. Bruce took his little daughter to spend some days with friends in Oxford Crescent, and of course it was necessary for me to accompany her. I had heard much of the systematic method of English education, and I was very desirous that my dear Mary should steer straight in the midst of so much propriety. I closely observed her little playmates and their nurses, being ready to take any lessons in the science of good management. The children were more rosy than American children, but I did not see that they differed materially in other respects. They were like all children— sometimes docile and sometimes wayward.

We next went to Steventon, in Berkshire.⁴ It was a small town, said to be the poorest in the county. I saw men working in the fields for six shillings, and seven shillings, a week, and women for sixpence, and sevenpence, a day, out of which they boarded themselves. Of course they lived in the most primitive manner; it could not be otherwise, where a woman's wages for an entire day were not sufficient to buy a pound of meat. They paid very low rents, and their clothes were made of the cheapest fabrics, though much better than could have been procured in the United States for the same money. I had heard much about the oppression of the poor in Europe. The people I saw around me were, many of them, among the poorest poor. But when I visited them in their little thatched cottages, I felt that the condition of even the meanest and most ignorant among them was vastly superior to the condition of the most favored slaves in America. They labored hard; but they were not ordered out to toil while the stars were in the sky, and driven and slashed by an overseer, through heat and cold, till the stars shone out again. Their homes were very humble; but they were protected by law. No insolent patrols could come, in the dead of night, and flog them at their pleasure. The father, when he closed his cottage door, felt safe with his family around him. No master or overseer could come and take from him his wife, or his daughter. They must separate to earn their living; but the parents knew where their children were going, and could communicate with them by letters. The relations of husband and wife, parent and child, were too sacred for the richest noble in the land to violate with impunity. Much was being done to enlighten these poor people. Schools were established among them, and benevolent societies were active in efforts to ameliorate their condition. There was no law forbidding them to learn to read and write; and if they helped each other in spelling out the Bible, they were in no danger of thirty-nine lashes, as was the case with myself and poor, pious, old uncle Fred. I repeat that the most ignorant and the most destitute of these peasants was a thousand fold better off than the most pampered American slave.

I do not deny that the poor are oppressed in Europe. I am not disposed to paint their condition so rose-colored as the Hon. Miss Murray paints the condition of the slaves in the United States.[5] A small portion of *my* experience would enable her to read her own pages with anointed eyes. If she were to lay aside her title, and, instead of visiting among the fashionable, become domesticated, as a poor governess, on some plantation in Louisiana or Alabama, she would see and hear things that would make her tell quite a different story.

My visit to England is a memorable event in my life, from the fact of my having there received strong religious impressions. The contemptuous manner in which the communion had been administered to colored people, in my native place; the church membership of Dr. Flint, and others like him; and the buying and selling of slaves, by professed ministers of the gospel, had given me a prejudice against the Episcopal church. The whole service seemed to me a mockery and a sham. But my home in Steventon was in the family of a clergyman, who was a true disciple of Jesus. The beauty of his daily life inspired me with faith in the genuineness of Christian professions. Grace entered my heart, and I knelt at the communion table, I trust, in true humility of soul.

I remained abroad ten months, which was much longer than I had anticipated.[6] During all that time, I never saw the slightest symptom of prejudice against color. Indeed, I entirely forgot it, till the time came for us to return to America.

XXXVIII

Renewed Invitations to Go South

WE HAD A TEDIOUS winter passage, and from the distance spectres seemed to rise up on the shores of the United States. It is a sad feeling to be afraid of one's native country. We arrived in New York safely, and I hastened to Boston to look after my children. I found Ellen well, and improving at her school; but Benny was not there to welcome me. He had been left at a good place to learn a trade, and for several months every thing worked well. He was liked by the master, and was a favorite with his fellow-apprentices; but one day they accidentally discovered a fact they had never before suspected— that he was colored! This at once transformed him into a different being. Some of the apprentices were Americans, others American-born Irish; and it was offensive to their dignity to have a "nigger" among them, after they had been told that he *was* a "nigger." They began by treating him with silent scorn, and finding that he returned the same, they resorted to insults and abuse.[1] He was too spirited a boy to stand that, and he went off. Being desirous to do something to support himself, and having no one to advise him, he shipped for a whaling voyage. When I received these tidings I shed many tears, and bitterly reproached myself for having left him so long. But I had done it for the best, and now all I could do was to pray to the heavenly Father to guide and protect him.[2]

Not long after my return, I received the following letter from Miss Emily Flint, now Mrs. Dodge:[3]

"In this you will recognize the hand of your friend and mistress. Having heard that you had gone with a family to Europe, I have waited to hear of your return to write to you. I should have answered the letter you wrote to me long since, but as I could not then act independently of my father, I knew there could be nothing done satisfactory to you. There were persons here who were willing to buy you and run the risk of getting you. To this I would not consent. I have always been attached to you, and would not like to see you the slave of another, or have unkind treatment. I am married now, and can protect you. My husband expects to move to Virginia this spring, where we think of settling. I am very anxious that you should come and live with me. If you are not willing to come, you may purchase yourself; but I should prefer having you live with me. If you come, you may, if you like, spend a month with your grandmother and friends, then come to me in Norfolk, Virginia. Think this over, and write as soon as possible, and let me know the conclusion. Hoping that your children are well, I remain your friend and mistress."[4]

Of course I did not write to return thanks for this cordial invitation. I felt insulted to be thought stupid enough to be caught by such professions.

"'Come up into my parlor,' said the spider to the fly;
"'Tis the prettiest little parlor that ever you did spy.'"[5]

It was plain that Dr. Flint's family were apprised of my movements, since they knew of my voyage to Europe. I expected to have further trouble from them; but having eluded them thus far, I hoped to be as successful in future. The money I had earned, I was desirous to devote to the education of my children, and to secure a home for them. It seemed not only hard, but unjust, to pay for myself. I could not possibly regard myself as a piece of property. Moreover, I had worked many years without wages, and during that time had been obliged to depend on my grandmother for many comforts in food and clothing. My children certainly belonged to me; but though Dr. Flint had incurred no expense for their support, he had received a large sum of money for them. I knew the law would decide that I was his property, and would probably still give his daughter a claim to my children; but I regarded such laws as the regulations of robbers, who had no rights that I was bound to respect.

The Fugitive Slave Law had not then passed. The judges of Massachusetts had not then stooped under chains to enter her courts of justice, so called. I knew my old master was rather skittish of Massachusetts. I relied on her love of freedom, and felt safe on her soil. I am now aware that I honored the old Commonwealth beyond her deserts.[6]

XXXIX

The Confession

FOR TWO YEARS my daughter and I supported ourselves comfortably in Boston.[1] At the end of that time, my brother William offered to send Ellen to a boarding school. It required a great effort for me to consent to part with her, for I had few near ties, and it was her presence that made my two little rooms seem home-like. But my judgment prevailed over my selfish feelings. I made preparations for her departure. During the two years we had lived together I had often resolved to tell her something about her father; but I had never been able to muster sufficient courage. I had a shrinking dread of diminishing my child's love. I knew she must have curiosity on the subject, but she had never asked a question. She was always very careful not to say any thing to remind me of my troubles. Now that she was going from me, I thought if I should die before she returned, she might hear my story from some one who did not understand the palliating circumstances; and that if she were entirely ignorant on the subject, her sensitive nature might receive a rude shock.

When we retired for the night, she said, "Mother, it is very hard to leave you alone. I am almost sorry I am going, though I do want to improve myself. But you will write to me often; won't you, mother?"

I did not throw my arms round her. I did not answer her. But in a calm, solemn way, for it cost me great effort, I said, "Listen to me, Ellen; I have something to tell you!" I recounted my early sufferings in slavery, and told her how nearly they had crushed me. I began to tell her how they had driven me into a great sin, when she clasped me in her arms, and exclaimed, "O, don't, mother! Please don't tell me any more."

I said, "But, my child, I want you to know about your father."

"I know all about it, mother," she replied; "I am nothing to my father, and he is nothing to me. All my love is for you. I was with him five months in Washington, and he never cared for me. He never spoke to me as he did to his little Fanny. I knew all the time he was my father, for Fanny's nurse told me so; but she said I must never tell any body, and I never did. I used to wish he would take me in his arms and kiss me, as he did Fanny; or that he would sometimes smile at me, as he did at her. I thought if he was my own father, he ought to love me. I was a little girl then, and didn't know any better. But now I never think any thing about my father. All my love is for you." She hugged me closer as she spoke, and I thanked God that the knowledge I had so much dreaded to impart had not diminished the affection of my child. I had not the slightest idea she knew that portion of my history. If I had, I should have spoken to her long before; for my pent-up feelings had often longed to pour themselves out to some one I could trust. But I loved the dear girl better for the delicacy she had manifested towards her unfortunate mother.

The next morning, she and her uncle started on their journey to the village in New York, where she was to be placed at school.[2] It seemed as if all the sunshine had gone away. My little room was dreadfully lonely. I was thankful when a message came from a lady, accustomed to employ me, requesting me to come and sew in her family for several weeks. On my return, I found a letter from brother William. He thought of opening an anti-slavery reading room in Rochester, and combining with it the sale of some books and stationery; and he wanted me to unite with him. We tried it, but it was not successful.[3] We found warm anti-slavery friends there, but the feeling was not general enough to support such an establishment. I passed nearly a year in the family of Isaac and Amy Post, practical believers in the Christian doctrine of human brotherhood. They measured a man's worth by his character, not by his complexion. The memory of those beloved and honored friends will remain with me to my latest hour.[4]

XL

The Fugitive Slave Law

M Y BROTHER, being disappointed in his project, concluded to go to California; and it was agreed that Benjamin should go with him. Ellen liked her school, and was a great favorite there. They did not know her history, and she did not tell it, because she had no desire to make capital out of their sympathy. But when it was accidentally discovered that her mother was a fugitive slave, every method was used to increase her advantages and diminish her expenses.[1]

I was alone again. It was necessary for me to be earning money, and I preferred that it should be among those who knew me. On my return from Rochester, I called at the house of Mr. Bruce, to see Mary, the darling little babe that had thawed my heart, when it was freezing into a cheerless distrust of all my fellow-beings. She was growing a tall girl now, but I loved her always. Mr. Bruce had married again, and it was proposed that I should become nurse to a new infant.[2] I had but one hesitation, and that was my feeling of insecurity in New York, now greatly increased by the passage of the Fugitive Slave Law. However, I resolved to try the experiment. I was again fortunate in my employer. The new Mrs. Bruce was an American, brought up under aristocratic influences, and still living in the midst of them; but if she had any prejudice against color, I was never made aware of it; and as for the system of slavery, she had a most hearty dislike of it. No sophistry of Southerners could blind her to its enormity. She was a person of excellent principles and a noble heart. To me, from that hour to the present, she has been a true and sympathizing friend. Blessings be with her and hers!

About the time that I reëntered the Bruce family, an event occurred of disastrous import to the colored people. The slave Hamlin, the first fugitive that came under the new law, was given up by the bloodhounds of the north to the bloodhounds of the south. It was the beginning of a reign of terror to the colored population. The great city rushed on in its whirl of excitement, taking no note of the "short and simple annals of the poor."[3] But while fashionables were listening to the thrilling voice of Jenny Lind in Metropolitan Hall,[4] the thrilling voices of poor hunted colored people went up, in an agony of supplication, to the Lord, from Zion's church.[5] Many families, who had lived in the city for twenty years, fled from it now.[6] Many a poor washerwoman, who, by hard labor, had made herself a comfortable home, was obliged to sacrifice her furniture, bid a hurried farewell to friends, and seek her fortune among strangers in Canada. Many a wife discovered a secret she had never known before—that her husband was a fugitive, and must leave her to insure his own safety. Worse still, many a husband discovered that his wife had fled from slavery years ago, and as "the child follows the condition of its mother," the children of his love were liable to be seized and carried into slavery. Every where, in those humble homes, there was consternation and anguish. But what cared the legislators of the "dominant race" for the blood they were crushing out of trampled hearts?

When my brother William spent his last evening with me, before he went to California, we talked nearly all the time of the distress brought on our oppressed people by the passage of this iniquitous law; and never had I seen him manifest such bitterness of spirit, such stern hostility to our oppressors. He was himself free from the operation of the law; for he did not run from any Slaveholding State, being brought into the Free States by his master. But I was subject to it; and so were hundreds of intelligent and industrious people all around us. I seldom ventured into the streets; and when it was necessary to do an errand for Mrs. Bruce, or any of the family, I went as much as possible through back streets and by-ways.[7] What a disgrace to a city calling itself free, that inhabitants, guiltless of offence, and seeking to perform their duties conscientiously, should be condemned to live in such incessant fear, and have nowhere to turn for protection! This state of things, of course, gave rise to many impromptu vigilance committees. Every colored person, and every friend of their persecuted race, kept their eyes wide open. Every evening I examined the newspapers carefully, to see what Southerners had put up at the hotels. I did this for my own sake, thinking my young mistress and her husband might be among the list; I wished also to give information to others, if necessary; for if many were "running to and fro," I resolved that "knowledge should be increased."[8]

This brings up one of my Southern reminiscences, which I will here briefly relate. I was somewhat acquainted with a slave named Luke, who belonged to a wealthy man in our vicinity. His master died, leaving a son and daughter heirs to his large fortune. In the division of the slaves, Luke was included in the son's portion. This young man became a prey to the vices growing out of the "patriarchal institution," and when he went to the north, to complete his education, he carried his vices with him. He was brought home, deprived of the use of his limbs, by excessive dissipation. Luke was appointed to wait upon his bed-ridden master, whose despotic habits were greatly in creased by exasperation at his own helplessness. He kept a cowhide beside him, and, for the most trivial occurrence, he would order his attendant to bare his back, and kneel beside the couch, while he whipped him till his strength was exhausted. Some days he was not allowed to wear any thing but his shirt, in order to be in readiness to be flogged. A day seldom passed without his receiving more or less blows. If the slightest resistance was offered, the town constable was sent for to execute the punishment, and Luke learned from experience how much more the constable's strong arm was to be dreaded than the comparatively feeble one of his master. The arm of his tyrant grew weaker, and was finally palsied; and then the constable's services were in constant requisition. The fact that he was entirely dependent on Luke's care, and was obliged to be tended like an infant, instead of inspiring any gratitude or compassion towards his poor slave, seemed only to increase his irritability and cruelty. As he lay there on his bed, a mere degraded wreck of manhood, he took into his head the strangest freaks of despotism; and if Luke hesitated to submit to his orders, the constable was immediately sent for. Some of these freaks were of a nature too filthy to be repeated. When I fled from the house of bondage, I left poor Luke still chained to the bedside of this cruel and disgusting wretch.

One day, when I had been requested to do an errand for Mrs. Bruce, I was hurrying through back streets, as usual, when I saw a young man approaching, whose face was familiar to me. As he came nearer, I recognized Luke. I always rejoiced to see or hear of any one who had escaped from the black pit; but, remembering this poor fellow's extreme hardships, I was peculiarly glad to see him on Northern soil, though I no longer called it *free* soil. I well remembered what a desolate feeling it was to be alone among strangers, and I went up to him and greeted him cordially. At first, he did not know me; but when I mentioned my name, he remembered all about me. I told him of the

Fugitive Slave Law, and asked him if he did not know that New York was a city of kidnappers.

He replied, "De risk ain't so bad for me, as 'tis fur you. 'Cause I runned away from de speculator, and you runned away from de massa. Dem speculators vont spen dar money to come here fur a runaway, if dey ain't sartin sure to put dar hans right on him. An I tell you I's tuk good car 'bout dat. I had too hard times down dar, to let 'em ketch dis nigger."

He then told me of the advice he had received, and the plans he had laid. I asked if he had money enough to take him to Canada. "'Pend upon it, I hab," he replied. "I tuk car fur dat. I'd bin workin all my days fur dem cussed whites, an got no pay but kicks and cuffs. So I tought dis nigger had a right to money nuff to bring him to de Free States. Massa Henry he lib till ebery body vish him dead; an ven he did die, I knowed de debbil would hab him, an vouldn't vant him to bring his money 'long too. So I tuk some of his bills, and put 'em in de pocket of his ole trousers. An ven he was buried, dis nigger ask fur dem ole trousers, an dey gub 'em to me." With a low, chuckling laugh, he added, "You see I didn't *steal* it; dey *gub* it to me. I tell you, I had mighty hard time to keep de speculator from findin it; but he didn't git it."

This is a fair specimen of how the moral sense is educated by slavery. When a man has his wages stolen from him, year after year, and the laws sanction and enforce the theft, how can he be expected to have more regard to honesty than has the man who robs him? I have become somewhat enlightened, but I confess that I agree with poor, ignorant, much-abused Luke, in thinking he had a *right* to that money, as a portion of his unpaid wages. He went to Canada forthwith, and I have not since heard from him.

All that winter I lived in a state of anxiety. When I took the children out to breathe the air, I closely observed the countenances of all

I met. I dreaded the approach of summer, when snakes and slaveholders make their appearance. I was, in fact, a slave in New York, as subject to slave laws as I had been in a Slave State. Strange incongruity in a State called free!

Spring returned, and I received warning from the south that Dr. Flint knew of my return to my old place, and was making preparations to have me caught. I learned afterwards that my dress, and that of Mrs. Bruce's children, had been described to him by some of the Northern tools, which slaveholders employ for their base purposes, and then indulge in sneers at their cupidity and mean servility.

I immediately informed Mrs. Bruce of my danger, and she took prompt measures for my safety. My place as nurse could not be supplied immediately, and this generous, sympathizing lady proposed that I should carry her baby away.[9] It was a comfort to me to have the child with me; for the heart is reluctant to be torn away from every object it loves. But how few mothers would have consented to have one of their own babes become a fugitive, for the sake of a poor, hunted nurse, on whom the legislators of the country had let loose the bloodhounds! When I spoke of the sacrifice she was making, in depriving herself of her dear baby, she replied, "It is better for you to have baby with you, Linda; for if they get on your track, they will be obliged to bring the child to me; and then, if there is a possibility of saving you, you shall be saved."

This lady had a very wealthy relative, a benevolent gentleman in many respects, but aristocratic and pro-slavery. He remonstrated with her for harboring a fugitive slave; told her she was violating the laws of her country; and asked her if she was aware of the penalty. She replied, "I am very well aware of it. It is imprisonment and one thousand dollars fine. Shame on my country that it *is* so! I am ready to incur the penalty. I will go to the state's prison, rather than have any poor victim torn from *my* house, to be carried back to slavery."

The noble heart! The brave heart! The tears are in my eyes while I write of her. May the God of the helpless reward her for her sympathy with my persecuted people!

I was sent into New England, where I was sheltered by the wife of a senator, whom I shall always hold in grateful remembrance.[10] This honorable gentleman would not have voted for the Fugitive Slave Law, as did the senator in "Uncle Tom's Cabin"; on the contrary, he was strongly opposed to it; but he was enough under its influence to be afraid of having me remain in his house many hours. So I was sent into the country, where I remained a month with the baby. When it was supposed that Dr. Flint's emissaries had lost track of me, and given up the pursuit for the present, I returned to New York.

XLI

Free at Last[1]

MRS. BRUCE, and every member of her family, were exceedingly kind to me. I was thankful for the blessings of my lot, yet I could not always wear a cheerful countenance. I was doing harm to no one; on the contrary, I was doing all the good I could in my small way; yet I could never go out to breathe God's free air without trepidation at my heart. This seemed hard; and I could not think it was a right state of things in any civilized country.

From time to time I received news from my good old grandmother. She could not write; but she employed others to write for her. The following is an extract from one of her last letters:—

"Dear Daughter: I cannot hope to see you again on earth; but I pray to God to unite us above, where pain will no more rack this feeble body of mine; where sorrow and parting from my children will be no more.[2] God has promised these things if we are faithful unto the end. My age and feeble health deprive me of going to church now; but God is with me here at home. Thank your brother for his kindness. Give much love to him, and tell him to remember the Creator in the days of his youth, and strive to meet me in the Father's kingdom.[3] Love to Ellen and Benjamin. Don't neglect him. Tell him for me, to be a good boy. Strive, my child, to train them for God's children. May he protect and provide for you, is the prayer of your loving old mother."

These letters both cheered and saddened me. I was always glad to have tidings from the kind, faithful old friend of my unhappy youth; but her messages of love made my heart yearn to see her before she died, and I mourned over the fact that it was impossible. Some months after I returned from my flight to New England, I received a letter from her, in which she wrote, "Dr. Flint is dead. He has left a distressed family. Poor old man! I hope he made his peace with God."[4]

I remembered how he had defrauded my grandmother of the hard earnings she had loaned; how he had tried to cheat her out of the freedom her mistress had promised her, and how he had persecuted her children; and I thought to myself that she was a better Christian than I was, if she could entirely forgive him. I cannot say, with truth, that the news of my old master's death softened my feelings towards him. There are wrongs which even the grave does not bury. The man was odious to me while he lived, and his memory is odious now.

His departure from this world did not diminish my danger. He had threatened my grandmother that his heirs should hold me in slavery after he was gone; that I never should be free so long as a child of his survived. As for Mrs. Flint, I had seen her in deeper afflictions than I supposed the loss of her husband would be, for she had buried several children; yet I never saw any signs of softening in her heart. The doctor had died in embarrassed circumstances, and had little to will to his heirs, except such property as he was unable to grasp. I was well aware what I had to expect from the family of Flints; and my fears were confirmed by a letter from the south, warning me to be on my guard, because Mrs. Flint openly declared that her daughter could not afford to lose so valuable a slave as I was.

I kept close watch of the newspapers for arrivals; but one Saturday night, being much occupied, I forgot to examine the Evening Express as usual. I went down into the parlor for it, early in the morning, and found the boy about to kindle a fire with it. I took it from him and examined the list of arrivals. Reader, if you have never been a slave, you cannot imagine the acute sensation of suffering at my heart, when I read the names of Mr. and Mrs. Dodge, at a hotel in Courtland Street.[5] It was a third-rate hotel, and that circumstance convinced me of the truth of what I had heard, that they were short of funds and had need of my value, as *they* valued me; and that was by dollars and cents. I hastened with the paper to Mrs. Bruce. Her heart and hand were always open to every one in distress, and she always warmly sympathized with mine. It was impossible to tell how near the enemy was. He might have passed and repassed the house while we were sleeping. He might at that moment be waiting to pounce upon me if I ventured out of doors. I had never seen the husband of my young mistress, and therefore I could not distinguish him from any other stranger. A carriage was hastily ordered; and, closely veiled, I followed Mrs. Bruce, taking the baby again with me into exile. After various turnings and crossings, and returnings, the carriage stopped at the house of one of Mrs. Bruce's friends, where I was kindly received. Mrs. Bruce returned immediately, to instruct the domestics what to say if any one came to inquire for me.

It was lucky for me that the evening paper was not burned up before I had a chance to examine the list of arrivals. It was not long after Mrs. Bruce's return to her house, before several people came to inquire for me. One inquired for me, another asked for my daughter Ellen, and another said he had a letter from my grandmother, which he was requested to deliver in person.

They were told, "She *has* lived here, but she has left."

"How long ago?"

"I don't know, sir."

"Do you know where she went?"

"I do not, sir." And the door was closed.

This Mr. Dodge, who claimed me as his property, was originally a Yankee pedler in the south; then he became a merchant, and finally a slaveholder. He managed to get introduced into what was called the first society, and married Miss Emily Flint. A quarrel arose between him and her brother, and the brother cowhided him. This led to a family feud, and he proposed to remove to Virginia. Dr. Flint left him no property, and his own means had become circumscribed, while a wife and children depended upon him for support.[6] Under these circumstances, it was very natural that he should make an effort to put me into his pocket.

I had a colored friend, a man from my native place, in whom I had the most implicit confidence. I sent for him, and told him that Mr. and Mrs. Dodge had arrived in New York. I proposed that he should call upon them to make inquiries about his friends at the south, with whom Dr. Flint's family were well acquainted. He thought there was no impropriety in his doing so, and he consented. He went to the hotel, and knocked at the door of Mr. Dodge's room, which was opened by the gentleman himself, who gruffly inquired, "What brought you here? How came you to know I was in the city?"

"Your arrival was published in the evening papers, sir; and I called to ask Mrs. Dodge about my friends at home. I didn't suppose it would give any offence."

"Where's that negro girl, that belongs to my wife?"

"What girl, sir?"

"You know well enough. I mean Linda, that ran away from Dr. Flint's plantation, some years ago. I dare say you've seen her, and know where she is."

"Yes, sir, I've seen her, and know where she is. She is out of your reach, sir."

"Tell me where she is, or bring her to me, and I will give her a chance to buy her freedom."

"I don't think it would be of any use, sir. I have heard her say she would go to the ends of the earth, rather than pay any man or woman for her freedom, because she thinks she has a right to it. Besides, she couldn't do it, if she would, for she has spent her earnings to educate her children."

This made Mr. Dodge very angry, and some high words passed between them. My friend was afraid to come where I was; but in the course of the day I received a note from him. I supposed they had not come from the south, in the winter, for a pleasure excursion; and now the nature of their business was very plain.

Mrs. Bruce came to me and entreated me to leave the city the next morning. She said her house was watched, and it was possible that some clew to me might be obtained. I refused to take her advice. She pleaded with an earnest tenderness, that ought to have moved me; but I was in a bitter, disheartened mood. I was weary of flying from pillar to post. I had been chased during half my life, and it seemed as if the chase was never to end. There I sat, in that great city, guiltless of crime, yet not daring to worship God in any of the churches. I heard the bells ringing for afternoon service, and, with contemptuous sarcasm, I said, "Will the preachers take for their text, 'Proclaim liberty to the captive, and the opening of prison doors to them that are bound'? or will they preach from the text, 'Do unto others as ye would they should do unto you'?"[7] Oppressed Poles and Hungarians could find a safe refuge in that city; John Mitchell was free to proclaim in the City Hall his desire for "a plantation well stocked with slaves"; but there I sat, an oppressed American, not daring to show my face.[8] God forgive the black and bitter thoughts I indulged on that Sabbath day! The Scripture says, "Oppression makes even a wise man mad"; and I was not wise.[9]

I had been told that Mr. Dodge said his wife had never signed away her right to my children, and if he could not get me, he would take them.[10] This it was, more than any thing else, that roused such a tempest in my soul. Benjamin was with his uncle William in California, but my innocent young daughter had come to spend a vacation with me. I thought of what I had suffered in slavery at her age, and my heart was like a tiger's when a hunter tries to seize her young.

Dear Mrs. Bruce! I seem to see the expression of her face, as she turned away discouraged by my obstinate mood. Finding her expostulations unavailing, she sent Ellen to entreat me. When ten o'clock in the evening arrived and Ellen had not returned, this watchful and unwearied friend became anxious. She came to us in a carriage, bringing a well-filled trunk for my journey—trusting that by this time I would listen to reason. I yielded to her, as I ought to have done before.

The next day, baby and I set out in a heavy snow storm, bound for New England again. I received letters from the City of Iniquity, addressed to me under an assumed name. In a few days one came from Mrs. Bruce, informing me that my new master was still searching for me, and that she intended to put an end to this persecution by buying my freedom. I felt grateful for the kindness that prompted this offer, but the idea was not so pleasant to me as might have been expected. The more my mind had become enlightened, the more difficult it was for me to consider myself an article of property; and to pay money to those who had so grievously oppressed me seemed like taking from my sufferings the glory of triumph.[11] I wrote to Mrs. Bruce, thanking her, but saying that being sold from one owner to another seemed too much like slavery; that such a great obligation could not be easily cancelled; and that I preferred to go to my brother in California.

Without my knowledge, Mrs. Bruce employed a gentleman in New York to enter into negotiations with Mr. Dodge. He proposed to pay three hundred dollars down, if Mr. Dodge would sell me, and enter into obligations to relinquish all claim to me or my children forever after. He who called himself my master said he scorned so small an offer for such a valuable servant. The gentleman replied, "You can do as you choose, sir. If you reject this offer you will never get any thing; for the woman has friends who will convey her and her children out of the country."

Mr. Dodge concluded that "half a loaf was better than no bread," and he agreed to the proffered terms.[12] By the next mail I received this brief letter from Mrs. Bruce: "I am rejoiced to tell you that the money for your freedom has been paid to Mr. Dodge. Come home to-morrow. I long to see you and my sweet babe."

My brain reeled as I read these lines. A gentleman near me said, "It's true; I have seen the bill of sale." "The bill of sale!" Those words struck me like a blow. So I was *sold* at last! A human being *sold* in the free city of New York! The bill of sale is on record, and future generations will learn from it that women were articles of traffic in New York, late in the nineteenth century of the Christian religion. It may hereafter prove a useful document to antiquaries, who are seeking to measure the progress of civilization in the United States. I well know the value of that bit of paper; but much as I love freedom, I do not like to look upon it. I am deeply grateful to the generous friend who procured it, but I despise the miscreant who demanded payment for what never rightfully belonged to him or his.

I had objected to having my freedom bought, yet I must confess that when it was done I felt as if a heavy load had been lifted from my weary shoulders. When I rode home in the cars I was no longer afraid to unveil my face and look at people as they passed. I should have been glad to have met Daniel Dodge himself; to have had him seen me and known me, that he might have mourned over the untoward circumstances which compelled him to sell me for three hundred dollars.

When I reached home, the arms of my benefactress were thrown round me, and our tears mingled. As soon as she could speak, she said, "O Linda, I'm *so* glad it's all over! You wrote to me as if you thought you were going to be transferred from one owner to another. But I did not buy you for your services. I should have done just the same, if you had been going to sail for California tomorrow. I should, at least, have the satisfaction of knowing that you left me a free woman."

My heart was exceedingly full. I remembered how my poor father had tried to buy me, when I was a small child, and how he had been disappointed. I hoped his spirit was rejoicing over me now. I remembered how my good old grandmother had laid up her earnings to purchase me in later years, and how often her plans had been frustrated. How that faithful, loving old heart would leap for joy, if she could look on me and my children now that we were free! My relatives had been foiled in all their efforts, but God had raised me up a friend among strangers, who had bestowed on me the precious, long-desired boon. Friend! It is a common word, often lightly used. Like other good and beautiful things, it may be tarnished by careless handling; but when I speak of Mrs. Bruce as my friend, the word is sacred.

My grandmother lived to rejoice in my freedom; but not long after, a letter came with a black seal. She had gone "where the wicked cease from troubling, and the weary are at rest."[13]

Time passed on, and a paper came to me from the south, contain-

ing an obituary notice of my uncle Phillip.[14] It was the only case I ever
knew of such an honor conferred upon a colored person. It was written by one of his friends, and contained these words: "Now that death
has laid him low, they call him a good man and a useful citizen; but
what are eulogies to the black man, when the world has faded from
his vision? It does not require man's praise to obtain rest in God's
kingdom."[15] So they called a colored man a *citizen!* Strange words to
be uttered in that region![16]

Reader, my story ends with freedom; not in the usual way, with
marriage. I and my children are now free! We are as free from the
power of slaveholders as are the white people of the north; and though
that, according to my ideas, is not saying a great deal, it is a vast improvement in *my* condition. The dream of my life is not yet realized. I
do not sit with my children in a home of my own. I still long for a
hearthstone of my own, however humble. I wish it for my children's
sake far more than for my own. But God so orders circumstances as
to keep me with my friend Mrs. Bruce. Love, duty, gratitude, also bind
me to her side. It is a privilege to serve her who pities my oppressed
people, and who has bestowed the inestimable boon of freedom on
me and my children.

It has been painful to me, in many ways, to recall the dreary years I
passed in bondage. I would gladly forget them if I could. Yet the retro-
spection is not altogether without solace; for with those gloomy recollections come tender memories of my good old grandmother, like
light, fleecy clouds floating over a dark and troubled sea.

Appendix

The following statement is from Amy Post, a member of the Society of Friends in the State of New York, well known and highly respected by friends of the poor and the oppressed. As has been already stated, in the preceding pages, the author of this volume spent some time under her hospitable roof.[1]

L.M.C.

"The author of this book is my highly-esteemed friend. If its readers knew her as I know her, they could not fail to be deeply interested in her story. She was a beloved inmate of our family nearly the whole of the year 1849. She was introduced to us by her affectionate and conscientious brother, who had previously related to us some of the almost incredible events in his sister's life. I immediately became much interested in Linda; for her appearance was prepossessing, and her deportment indicated remarkable delicacy of feeling and purity of thought.

"As we became acquainted, she related to me, from time to time some of the incidents in her bitter experiences as a slave-woman. Though impelled by a natural craving for human sympathy, she passed through a baptism of suffering, even in recounting her trials to me, in private confidential conversations. The burden of these memories lay heavily upon her spirit—naturally virtuous and refined. I repeatedly urged her to consent to the publication of her narrative; for I felt that it would arouse people to a more earnest work for the disinthralment of millions still remaining in that soul-crushing condition, which was so unendurable to her. But her sensitive spirit shrank from publicity. She said, 'You know a woman can whisper her cruel wrongs in the ear of a dear friend much easier than she can record them for the world to read.' Even in talking with me, she wept so much, and seemed to suffer such mental agony, that I felt her story was too sacred to be drawn from her by inquisitive questions, and I left her free to tell as much, or as little, as she chose. Still, I urged upon her the duty of publishing her experience, for the sake of the good it might do; and, at last, she undertook the task.

"Having been a slave so large a portion of her life, she is unlearned; she is obliged to earn her living by her own labor, and she has worked untiringly to procure education for her children; several times she has been obliged to leave her employments, in order to fly from the man-hunters and woman-hunters of our land; but she pressed through all these obstacles and overcame them. After the labors of the day were over, she traced secretly and wearily, by the midnight lamp, a truthful record of her eventful life.

"This Empire State is a shabby place of refuge for the oppressed; but here, through anxiety, turmoil, and despair, the freedom of Linda and her children was finally secured, by the exertions of a generous friend. She was grateful for the boon; but the idea of having been *bought* was always galling to a spirit that could never acknowledge itself to be a chattel. She wrote to us thus, soon after the event: 'I thank you for your kind expressions in regard to my freedom; but the freedom I had before the money was paid was dearer to me. God gave me *that* freedom; but man put God's image in the scales with the paltry sum of three hundred dollars. I served for my liberty as faithfully as Jacob served for Rachel. At the end, he had large possessions; but I was robbed of my victory; I was obliged to resign my crown, to rid myself of a tyrant.'[2]

"Her story, as written by herself, cannot fail to interest the reader. It is a sad illustration of the condition of this country, which boasts of its civilization, while it sanctions laws and customs which make the experiences of the present more strange than any fictions of the past."

Amy Post

"Rochester, N.Y., Oct. 30th, 1859."

The following testimonial is from a man who is now a highly respectable colored citizen of Boston.[3]

L.M.C.

"This narrative contains some incidents so extraordinary, that, doubtless, many persons, under whose eyes it may chance to fall, will be ready to believe that it is colored highly, to serve a special purpose. But, however it may be regarded by the incredulous, I know that it is full of living truths. I have been well acquainted with the author from my boyhood. The circumstances recounted in her history are perfectly familiar to me. I knew of her treatment from her master; of the imprisonment of her children; of their sale and redemption; of her seven years' concealment; and of her subsequent escape to the North. I am now a resident of Boston, and am a living witness to the truth of this interesting narrative."

George W. Lowther

A True Tale of Slavery

JOHN S. JACOBS

Chapter I. Some Account of My Early Life*

I was born in Edenton, North Carolina, one of the oldest States in
the Union, and had four different owners in eighteen years. My first
owner was Miss Penelope H———, the invalid daughter of an inn-
keeper. After her death I became the property of her mother. My only
sister was given to a niece of hers, daughter of Dr. James R. N———,
also of Edenton.[1]

My father and mother were slaves. I have a slight recollection of
my mother, who died when I was young, though my father made impressions on my mind in childhood that can never be forgotten. I
should do my dear old grandmother injustice did I not mention her
too. There was a great difference between her meekness and my fa-

---

*The writer of these autobiographical sketches has, since his escape from slavery,
held positions of trust in free countries, and every statement may be relied on, although it is not thought advisable to publish names in full.

ther's violent temper, although, in justice to him, I must say that slavery was the cause of it.[2]

To be a man, and not to be a man—a father without authority—a husband and no protector—is the darkest of fates. Such was the condition of my father, and such is the condition of every slave throughout the United States: he owns nothing, he can claim nothing. His wife is not his: his children are not his; they can be taken from him, and sold at any minute, as far away from each other as the human fleshmonger may see fit to carry them. Slaves are recognised as property by the law, and can own nothing except by the consent of their masters. A slave's wife or daughter may be insulted before his eyes with impunity. He himself may be called on to torture them, and dare not refuse. To raise his hand in their defence is death by the law. He must bear all things and resist nothing. If he leaves his master's premises at any time without a written permit, he is liable to be flogged.[3] Yet, it is said by slaveholders and their apologists, that we are happy and contented. I will admit that slaves are sometimes cheerful; they sing and dance, as it is politic for them to do. I myself had changed owners three times before I could see the policy of this appearance of contentment. My father taught me to hate slavery, but forgot to teach me how to conceal my hatred. I could frequently perceive the pent-up agony of his soul, although he tried hard to conceal it in his own breast. The knowledge that he was a slave himself, and that his children were also slaves, embittered his life, but made him love us the more.

Up to this time our services had not been required, and the old lady to whom I belonged had paid little or no attention to how our time was spent. Our father, when working in or near the town, made our home his home.

I should state here that my father was owned by a Mrs. K———, a widow lady, who was, however, no relative of Mrs. H———, to whom I belonged.

Dr. N———, being related to the family of my owner, was permitted to take me from my father in my tenth year, and put me in his shop.[4] He too well knew the value of knowledge, and the danger of communicating it to human "property," to allow it to be disseminated among his slaves; and he therefore instructed his sons, who had charge of me, to see that I did not learn to write. Soon after this, my sister was taken into his house, but no interdict against the acquisition of knowledge, such as he had imposed upon me, could avail in her case. Our father had endeavoured to bestow upon both of us some rays of intellectual light, which the tyrant could not rob us of.

In the meanwhile, my father's young mistress married a rich planter, named C———, who lived in the neighbourhood of Edenton. Shortly afterwards the old lady died, and my father became Mr. James C———'s property. Being, as he was then considered, the best house-carpenter in or near the town, he was not put to field-work, although the privilege of working out, and paying his owner monthly, which he once enjoyed, was now denied him. This added another link to his galling chain—sent another arrow to his bleeding heart. My father, who had an intensely acute feeling of the wrongs of slavery, sank into a state of mental dejection, which, combined with bodily illness, occasioned his death when I was eleven years of age.[5] He left us the only legacy that a slave father can leave his child, his whips and chains. These he had taught us to hate, and we resolved to seek for liberty, though we travelled through the gates of death to find it.

Chapter II. A Further Account of My Family, and of My New Master

Time passed swiftly on, and in due season death smote down Mrs. H———, my mistress. The hungry heirs ordered us slaves to mount the auction-block; and all of us, old and young, male and female, married and single, were sold to the highest bidder. Even my grandmother's grey hairs and many years' hard service in the public-house did not save her from the auctioneer's hammer. But, fortunately for her, she possessed a tried and trusty friend, in whose hands she placed the savings of thirty years, that he might purchase her and her son Mark. She had two other children, a son and a daughter, but they were owned by other parties.[6]

They began to sell off the old slaves first, as rubbish. One very old man went for one dollar; the old cook sold for seventeen dollars. The prices varied from that to 1600 dollars, which was the price of a young man who was a carpenter. Dr. N—— bought me for a shop-boy.[7] It would be in vain for me to attempt to give a description of my feelings while standing under the auctioneer's hammer: I can safely say that I shall not realize such feelings again.

The man whom my grandmother trusted to do her business for her acted very honourably. As soon as it could be done, after the sale, he procured her free papers and the bill of sale of her son, to show that he was her property by right of purchase.[8] It may seem rather strange that my grandmother should hold her son a slave; but the law required it. She was obliged to give security that she would never be any expense to the town or state before she could come in possession of her freedom. Her property in him was sufficient to satisfy the law; he could be sold any minute to pay her debts, though it was not likely this would ever be the case. They had a snug home of their own, but their troubles were not yet at an end.

My uncle Joseph, who was owned by Mr. J. C——, ran away about this time, and got as far as New York, where he was seen by Mr. S—— of Edenton, who had him taken and sent back to his master. He was heavily manacled, and lodged in gaol, where he remained most of the winter, and was then sold to go to New Orleans.[9]

My uncle Mark, whom my grandmother had bought, was at that time steward on board of a packet or vessel of some kind, and some months after my uncle Joseph had been sold, my uncle Mark met him in New York. He had made his second escape. The vessel was about to sail, and they had but little time to spend with each other, though my uncle Joseph told him he had not come there to stop. His intention was to get beyond the reach of the stars and *stripes* of America. Unwilling to trust his liberty any longer in the hands of a professed Christian, he purposed seeking safety in another hemisphere.[10]

But to return to my subject. I left my sister in the doctor's family. Some six or eight years have passed since I was sold, and she has become the mother of two children. After the birth of her second child, she was sent to live on his plantation, where she remained for two or three months, and then ran away. As soon as she was gone, my aunt, the two children, and myself, were sent to gaol. My aunt was married, but happily her children were beyond the power of slavery. God had taken them to his rest.[11]

The old doctor no doubt thought that this would be the means of bringing my sister back; but you will by-and-by see that she did not leave with the intention of returning. She had not yet been called to make her back bare for the lash; but she had gone to live on the doctor's plantation, where she daily expected it. Her mental sufferings were more than she could longer bear. With her it was, in the language of one of our fathers, "liberty or death."[12]

The doctor offered 100 dollars reward for her, and threatened to punish to the extreme penalty of the law, any person or persons found harbouring, or assisting her in any way to make her escape.[13] He then wrote a letter to a gentleman by the name of T———, living in New York, who had formerly lived in North Carolina. I am not prepared to say that Mr. T——— took an interest in this letter. I rather believe he did not. But the news was soon circulated among the slave-catchers of the north, and they were sticking their unwanted faces in every coloured man's door, on account of my sister. The doctor pretended to sell me and the two children to a negro trader. In two or three weeks he received a letter from New York, stating (erroneously, as it turned out) that my sister was taken, and safely lodged in gaol. This called the old man from home.[14] He had got to prove property and pay expenses. Now that the old doctor was gone, I had a good time. Mr. L———, the gaoler, was an old acquaintance of mine. Though he was a white man, and I a slave, we had spent many hours together in Mr. J———'s family. We had taken tea there.[15]

To make my story short, and go back to the doctor—Mr. J——— had a very fine daughter, and we were very fond of each other.[16] Mr. L——had been a visitor of Mr. J———'s for many years. Now that he had me under lock and key, and knowing that it was not for any crime that I was there, he could not be otherwise than kind. He allowed me every indulgence. My friends, such as could come, could call and see me whenever they pleased, and stop as long as they liked; he would never turn the key on them. Sometimes he would give me the key on the inside. While the doctor had me here for safe keeping, I could have made my escape every day or night; but in the first place, if I had wanted to go, I would not have taken the advantage of Mr. L———'s kindness; in the second place, I saw no chance of bettering myself. I knew he would not get my sister, because she had not left town. My uncle-in-law, who was a seafaring man, had intended to take her to New York, but the doctor's threats frightened him so much, that he did not dare make the attempt.

While the old man was gone, I had a negro trader call with others to see me. His name was G———; he said he would buy me if the old doctor would sell me; I told him I thought he would—that he told me he intended to do so when he put me in gaol.[17]

After some two weeks the doctor returned home without my sister. The woman that had been taken up and put in gaol was a free woman; but what could she do with the wretch who put her there?

America is a free country, and a white man can do what he pleases with a coloured man or woman in most of the States. They may have a few friends now, who would not allow this if they knew it; but they are hated by the nation at large.

My aunt was taken out of gaol and sent home to the doctor's house; the children and myself were left in. The old man came to have a little talk with me about my sister.

"Well, John, I have not got Harriet, but I will have her yet. Don't you know where she is?"

"How can I know, sir? I have been in gaol ever since my sister left you. Mr. G——— was here while you were away, sir, and said that he wanted to buy me."

"Buy you! I don't want to sell you."

"You told me when you put me here that you did."

"Yes, but not if you will go back to the shop and behave yourself. Mr. G——— has not got money enough to buy you."

"I do not know how to behave differently from what I have done."

"Your behaviour will do; but I am afraid you are going to run away from me."

"I have not said anything about running away from you, sir."

"I know that; but your sister is gone, and you will be going next."

Up to this time I had heard nothing of my sister; but I felt sure that she was with her friends in Edenton.

Chapter III. My Uncle's Troubles———My Further Experience of the Doctor, and Our Parting

While the events described in the foregoing chapter were transpiring, my uncle-in-law Stephen returned from sea. His master, Mr. B———, was owner of the vessel in which he sailed; and, although he had had several chances to make his escape from slavery, yet he had returned on every voyage. The doctor, who owned my aunt, forbad his going to see her, although they had lived together for twenty years, and had never been known to quarrel. It was most cruel that they should be separated, not for their own, but for another's acts. The doctor was inexorable; they were strictly interdicted from seeing each other. The only tie that bound my uncle to slavery was his wife, to whom he was truly attached. When their sacred union—a union holy in the sight of God, however desecrated by wicked men—was broken, he would not longer submit to the yoke. He took advantage of his next voyage to release himself from it, and he returned no more. His wife was dead to him—ay, worse than dead. "That which God hath joined together, let no man put asunder," saith those Scriptures which the slaveholder professes to believe, but which he blasphemes day by day and hour by hour.[18]

At the doctor's last visit to the jail, he described to me the wretchedness of the free people of colour in New York, and stated that they had not the comforts of his slaves, and how much better off we were than they. To this I said nothing. My mind was fully made up, that I must, in order to effect an escape, hide as much as possible my hatred of slavery, and affect a respect to my master, who ever he might be. The doctor and myself knew each other too well for me to hope to get away from him. I must change owners in order to do that. Secondly, I had made up my mind that, let the condition of the coloured people of New York be what it might, I would rather die a free man than live a slave. The doctor evidently did not want to sell me, neither did he want to run the risk of losing me. Not that he had any particular regard for me, but he could not replace me for the same money that a slave-trader would give for me.

Before he left the jail, he told me that he did not want to keep me in jail any longer, and would let me out at any time when I would get my uncle Mark to be security that I would not run away from him.

When leaving, he told me to send for my uncle, and see if he would not do it for me. To all this I was dumb. I was in no particular hurry to get out of jail. I wanted a little time for serious reflection, and this was the only place where I could get an opportunity for it.

A few days passed, and he heard nothing from me. He saw my uncle, and told him that I wanted to see him at the jail. He accordingly came, and asked me if I wished him to become my security. I promptly told him no; that I wanted my liberty; that I would make good the first opportunity to secure it; that he might do as he pleased; but, God being my helper, I would die a free man. This satisfied my uncle at once, that he might as well take the money out of his pocket and pay for me as to become my security; and he thought, if I could get a chance to make my escape without bringing any expense on him, so much the better. Here we parted. The old doctor waited for an answer, but got none, which satisfied him that I no longer had a desire to make his shop my home.

There were two or three slaveholders in the town, that would give him more for me than he could get from a trader, but he would not sell me to any one in the town. Mr. S———, who afterwards bought me, came to the jail, and asked me if I would live with him if he bought me. I told him that I would; but the question was not asked how long.

I had been here just two months when Mr. S——— got a negro trader to buy the two children for my grandmother and me for himself.[19] The doctor at first tried to bind the trader not to sell me to any one in the State; but this he would not agree to, saying that he sold his slaves wherever he could get the most for them; he finally agreed to take me out of town in irons, but to sell me the first chance he could get. The old man did not think that he had bargained for me before I was sold. This important part of the business being settled, we were sold, the two children for 500 dollars, I believe, and I for 900 dollars.

The blacksmith's tools, handcuffs, and chain were all in readiness at the jail. The chain was thirty or forty feet long, with handcuffs every two or three feet. The slaves were handcuffed right and left on each side of the chain.[20] In the gang there was one who was free by birth. He was born not more than fifty miles from Edenton. He had been put in jail here for some trifling offence; not being able to pay the fine, he was sold for six months or a year to William R———, a planter, who was so cruel to him that he ran away from him. He was caught, and, after being flogged, was put in irons and set to work. He attempted to cut the irons off, and being caught in the act, was sent to jail, and finally sold to a trader. I saw the irons that he had been made to work in; they were fetters for the ankles, weighing from fifteen to twenty pounds in weight.[21]

Now we were all snugly chained up, the children in the cart, and the women walking behind; friends weeping, and taking a farewell shake of the hand—wives of their husbands, and parents of their children. I went with the gang as far as Mr. J. B. S———'s, the man that had my uncle taken in New York.[22] Here the cart was stopped and the blacksmith's tools taken out, and Mr. L——— began to hammer away at my irons. When they were off, he told me to take the children and go home to Mr. S———; the children went to my grandmother, and I to Mr. S———, who had purchased me for a body servant; but, knowing the temper of the doctor, who would be angry at being outwitted, he sent me to his plantation, where I stopped for three months.[23] During that time I was often in town of an evening to see my grandmother; and on two occasions he tried to trap me. What he would have done to me I know not; but up to the day that I left North Carolina, I never dared to trust myself in his power. Again and again he searched my grandmother's house for my sister, and at length he put my uncle Mark in jail. After a few days he was taken before the magistrate. The doctor could prove nothing against him, and yet the magistrate made my uncle pay the jail fees. Had my grandmother been destitute of friends, as many of the coloured people in the Slave States are, doubtless the doctor would have tried to extort from my uncle my sister's hiding-place. It was for this purpose he wanted to get hold of me, for, with oaths of the most dreadful kind, he told me he would butcher me. I had seen too much of his cruelty to doubt his purpose.

Chapter IV. My New Master's Plantation—My Medical Practice Among the Slaves—My Sister's Hiding-Place

During the three months that I was on the plantation, my master changed overseers. The last one was a member of a Christian church. He was particularly fond of two things, namely, singing hymns and flogging slaves; but he had been told to spare me from the lash. I could see that it went very much against his wishes to do so. Soon after this overseer came on the plantation, my master took me into town to live with him. He had one brother and a sister, who were both subject to fits, returning about every four weeks. When his brother Dr. M. E. S——— was sick with them, I stopped by him for a few days, until the illness was over. His sister died soon after I went to live with him.[24] My work had never been very hard, neither had I known, as many do, the want of food; and as for the lash, from a boy I had declared that I would never carry its stripes upon my back. It is true my condition was much bettered with my new master; but I was happier only as I could see my chance for escape clearer. At length I grew sick of myself in acting the deceitful part of a slave, and pretending love and friendship where I had none. Unpleasant as it was thus to act, yet, under the circumstances in which I was placed, I feel that I have done no wrong in so doing; I did everything that I could to please my master, who treated me with as much kindness as I could expect from any one to whom I was a slave.

Having been so long with Dr. N———, my master thought me

quite capable of visiting the sick slaves on the plantation. This part of my work caused the overseer much unpleasantness; he would sometimes want to give them oil, or something of the kind, saying they were not sick; at other times he would say they were well enough to go to work, and if they were too sick to work, they were too sick to eat.[25] Knowing that he would not strike me for having my own way in what I was sent there for—to see if they were sick and give them what they needed—I took great pleasure in differing with him on all occasions when I thought my patient dangerously ill. My judgment in regard to such diseases as are most common on a plantation was considered very good for one of my age; so much so, that a young planter who was studying medicine at the time, offered my master one thousand five hundred dollars for me. The way I came to know this was thus: he asked me one day if I wanted to be sold. This woke up a little of the old feeling, and I had almost forgotten myself for a minute. "No, sir," I said, "I am not anxious to be sold, but I know I have got to serve some one." Here he made me a promise which I shall never forget, though it was not consoling to me. He said, "You shall not serve any one after me: I have been offered a very handsome price for you; but I don't want to sell you." True, I was glad to hear him say that I should serve no one after him; this required a little consideration; he was but a few years older than me, and to wait for him to die looked to me too much like giving a man who was in want of his daily bread a cheque on the bank to be paid when he is dead. To have prayed for his death would have been wrong; to have killed him would have been worse; so, finally, I concluded to let him live as long as the Lord was willing he should, and I would get off as soon as possible. My pride would not allow me to let a man feed and clothe me for nothing; I would work the ends of my fingers off first.

I have said nothing about Mr. S———'s plantation slaves; I have only spoken of his treatment to me.[26] I am willing to acknowledge kindness, even in a slaveholder, wherever I have seen it; but had he treated all of his slaves as he treated me, the probability is that they would have been of as little value to him as I was. Some may try to make out of this a case of ingratitude; but I do not feel myself under the slightest obligation to any one who holds me against my will, though he starved himself to feast me. Doubtless he meant to do me a good turn; but he put it off too far. I appreciated his kindness, and endeavoured to be as useful as I could.

At this time my condition was so much better than my sister's, that I had almost ceased to speak of leaving in the presence of my grandmother; for there is an inexpressible feeling in the breast of a woman who has lost child after child, whether it has been taken by force or by the hand of death, that makes her cling with tighter grasp to the last one. No doubt many of my readers can picture to themselves the force of the prayers and tears of a pious mother under such trials. My uncle Joseph was gone, she knew not where, and my sister was so closely pursued that they were obliged to hide her in the house between the roof and the ceiling. They are now beyond the reach of the slave power, or I would not dare to tell how this was done.

My grandmother's house had seven rooms—two upper rooms, and five on the lower floor: on the west side there was a piazza. On the east side there were two rooms, with a lobby leading to the centre of the house. The room on the left on entering the lobby was used as a storeroom; the ceiling of this room was of boards, the roof was shingled; the space between the roof and ceiling was from three and a half to four feet in height, running off to a point. My uncle made a cupboard in one corner of this room, with the top attached to the ceiling. The part of the board that covered the top of the cupboard was cut and made into a trap-door; the whole of it was so small and neatly done that no one would have believed it to be what it was—the entrance to her hiding-place. Everything that she received was put in that little cupboard. One of the upper rooms was lathed and plastered; a hole was broken in the wall, through which she could speak to my uncle or grandmother; and, to prevent her losing the use of her limbs, the windows were sometimes closed that she might come down and walk about the room.[27] When she was sick, I visited her, and gave her such medicines as she needed. After my uncle-in-law left, Uncle Mark knew of no one in whom to confide; he was suspected by the doctor, and narrowly watched wherever he went; and although he could hear nothing of her, he somehow seemed to think that she had not made her escape. During the short time that my sister was on the plantation, she saw one of the women so cruelly whipped that she died in a few days: it was done by James N———, the doctor's son. These are called isolated cases; but we shall never know the wrongs that have been perpetrated in the slave states of America, until the oppressor and the oppressed shall stand before the Judge of all the world. The doctor's wife was as anxious as himself to get my sister again, and made promises of handsome presents to the slaves if they would try to find out where she was, but to no effect. She remained in that strange place of concealment six years and eleven months before she could get away!

Chapter V. My Master Goes to Washington as Member of Congress———He Is Engaged to Be Married———Wedding Trip to Chicago———Canada———New York———My Escape from Slavery

The latter end of the third year after I was sold, my master was elected Member of Congress.[28] I was ordered to get ready for Washington. We were not many days on the way to this place, which I so much wanted to see. It is a very lively place during the Session, and much enjoyed by the slaves, their privileges being greatly extended. They get up balls and parties, and seem to be as happy as their masters. I have had the pleasure of meeting some of these slaves in the Northern States, with whom I have danced, whose happiness, like mine, ended with the ball.

I could tell many things I observed of the life of members of Congress when at Washington, but I refrain from mentioning more than one or two customs of social life.

I will say it is twelve o'clock. The ladies have taken breakfast. A visitor comes and rings the door-bell, and you, on answering it, tell her that the mistress is not in; the reply most invariably is, "Go and tell her who it is, and she will be in." Just as well say, "Go and tell her she has lied, not knowing who has called to see her." The same is the case of the gentlemen. Here is a bill before the House, the merits and demerits of which they have spent weeks in discussing; it is now to be voted on at such an hour. The sergeant-at-arms is sent out in search of the absent members; some of them are having a little game of cards—could not think of waiting until after four o'clock; the pay is just the same for playing cards as though they were making laws, only you must lie a little when the sergeant-at-arms calls, and say that you are not in. I could not bear this system of lying. I avoided answering these calls whenever I could.

After my master had been there a short time, he went to board with Mrs. P———, who had two young nieces here, to one of whom he was soon engaged to be married.[29] As good luck would have it, this young lady had a sister living in Chicago, and no place would suit her like that to get married in.[30] I admired her taste much. I wanted to go there too. My master could not do otherwise than give his consent to go there with her. The next question to be settled was about taking me with him into a free state. Near the time for him to leave, he told me that he intended to marry. I was pleased at this, and anxious to know who the fortunate lady might be. He did not hesitate to tell me what he intended to do, stating at the same time that he would take me with him if I would not leave him. "Sir," said I, "I never thought that you suspected me of wanting to leave you."

"I do not suspect you, John. Some of the members of the House have tried to make me believe that you would run away if I took you with me. Well, get my things all ready; we are to leave on the first day of next week; I will try you, any how."

Everything was ready, and the hoped-for time came. He took his intended, and off we started for the West. When we were taking the boat at Baltimore for Philadelphia, he came up to me and said, "Call me Mr. Sawyer; and if anybody asks you who you are, and where you are going, tell them that you are a free man, and hired by me."

We stopped two or three days at the Niagara Falls; from thence we went to Buffalo, and took the boat for Chicago; Mr. Sawyer had been here but a few days before he was taken sick. In five weeks from the time of his arrival here, he was married and ready to leave for home.[31] On our return, we went into Canada. Here I wanted to leave him, but there was my sister and a friend of mine at home in slavery; I had succeeded in getting papers that might have been of great value to my friend. I had tried, but could not get anything to answer my purpose. I tried to get a seaman's protection from the English Custom-house, but could not without swearing to a lie, which I did not feel disposed to do.

We left here for New York, where we stopped three or four days. I went to see some of my old friends from home, who I knew were living there. I told them that I wanted their advice. They knew me, they knew my master, and they knew my friends also. "Now tell me my duty," said I. The answer was a very natural one, "Look out for yourself first." I weighed the matter in my mind, and found the balance in favour of stopping. If I returned along with my master, I could do my sister no good, and could see no further chance of my own escape. I then set myself to work to get my clothes out of the Astor House Hotel, where we were stopping; I brought them out in small parcels, as if to be washed. This job being done, the next thing was to get my trunk to put them in. I went to Mr. Johnson's shop, which was in sight of the Astor House Hotel, and told him that I wanted to get my trunk repaired.[32] The next morning I took my trunk in my hand with me: when I went down, whom should I see at the foot of the steps but Mr. Sawyer? I walked up to him, and showed him a rip in the top of the trunk, opening it at the same time that he might see that I was not running off. He told me that I could change it, or get a new one if I liked. I thanked him, and told him we were very near home now, and with a little repair the old one would do. At this we parted. I got a friend to call and get my trunk, and pack up my things for me, that I might be able to get them at any minute. Mr. Sawyer told me to get everything of his in, and be ready to leave for home the next day. I went to all the places where I had carried anything of his and where they were not done, I got their cards and left word for them to be ready by the next morning. What I had got were packed in his trunk; what I had not been able to get, there were the cards for them in his room. They dine at the Astor at three o'clock; they leave the room at four o'clock; at half-past four o'clock I was to be on board the boat for Providence.[33] Being unable to write myself at that time, and unwilling to leave him in suspense, I got a friend to write as follows:—

> "Sir—I have left you, not to return; when I have got settled, I will give you further satisfaction. No longer yours, John S. Jacobs."

This note was to be put into the post-office in time for him to get it the next morning. I waited on him and his wife at dinner. As the town clock struck four, I left the room. I then went through to New Bedford, where I stopped for a few months.

Thank God! I am now out of their reach; the old doctor is dead; I can forgive him for what he did do, and would have done if he could. The lawyer I have quite a friendly feeling for, and would be pleased to meet him as a countryman and a brother, but not as a master.[34]

Chapter VI. Sensations of Freedom———Self-Education——— a Whaling Voyage———I Meet My Sister, and Hear from Her about My Friends at Edenton———the Fugitive Slave Bill

On arriving at New Bedford, I was introduced to Mr. William P———, a very fatherly old man, who had been a slave in Alexandria.[35] For the first week or so I could not realize the great transformation from a chattel slave to a man; it seemed to me like a dream; but I soon began to feel my responsibility, and the necessity of mental improvement. The first thing, therefore, that I strove to do was to raise myself above the level of the beast, where slavery had left me, and fit myself for the society of man. I first tried this in New Bedford by working in the day and going to school at night. Sometimes my business would be such that I could not attend evening schools; so I thought the better plan would be to get such books as I should want, and go a voyage to sea. I accordingly shipped on board the "Frances Henrietta," of New Bedford. This was a whaling voyage; but I will not trouble you with any fishing stories. I will make it short. After being absent three years and a half, we returned home with a full ship, 1700 barrels of sperm oil and 1400 of whale oil.[36]

I had made the best possible use of my leisure hours on board, and kept the object that drove me from my friends and my home before me when on shore. I had promised myself, if what money I had coming to me would be an inducement to any one to bring my sister off from the south, that I would have her; but there was better news than that, in the bosom of an old friend, waiting to be delivered. The ship dropped her anchor, and the shore boats came off with friends of different persons on board, among whom was R. P———. He had scarcely spoken to me before he began to tell me about my sister; her coming to New Bedford in search of me, and her going back to New York, where, he told me, I should find her.[37] This news was to me quite unexpected. I said, if my sister was free from her oppressor, I was a happy man. I hurried on shore, drew some money of the owners, and made my way to New York. I found my sister living with a family as nurse at the Astor House. At first she did not look natural to me; but how should she look natural, after having been shut out from the light of heaven for six years and eleven months![38] I did not wish to know what her sufferings were, while living in her place of concealment. The change that it had made in her was enough to make one's soul cry out against this curse of curses, that has so long trampled humanity in the dust.

After she had recovered a little from the surprise of seeing me, I began to speak of home. "Oh, brother," she said, "grandmother was so disappointed in your stopping behind. Mr. S——— had written for them to make ready his house for his reception on such a day; grandmother got the news of it, and invited some of your old friends to come and spend the evening with you. Supper was all ready, and our ears were all intent to catch the first blast of the stage horn, when Uncle Mark left the room to go and meet you. The coach drove up to the tavern door, and the passengers had all got out, when Dr. W——— asked Mr. S——— what had become of you. He said the abolitionists had got you away from him in New York. When Uncle Mark returned, grandmother looked for awhile, and then asked, 'Where is my child?' 'He is gone, mother; he left Mr. S——— in New York.'

"When she heard that you were gone, she wept like a child. Aunt Sue Bent was there, and on seeing grandmother's tears, said to her: 'Molly, my child, this is no time for crying. Dry up those tears, fall upon your knees, and thank God that one more has made his escape from the house of bondage. I came here to see him, but I am glad he is not here. God bless the boy, and keep him from all harm.'[39]

"This (continued my sister) increased my anxiety, and caused me to adopt new plans for my escape. I wrote a letter to the doctor, asking him if he would sell me to my grandmother. It was sent to New York, and there mailed for Edenton. The letter was received by the doctor, and answered by his son Caspar. He could now no longer doubt that I was gone, and resorted to a cunningly-devised artifice to bring me back. Part of his son's letter ran as follows:—'Harriet, we are all glad to hear from you; and let me assure you, if our family ever did entertain anything different from the most friendly feelings for you, they exist no longer. We want to see you once more, with your old friends around you, made happy in your own home. We cannot sell you to your grandmother; the community would object to your returning to live in a state of freedom. Harriet, doubtless before this you have heard of the death of your aunt Betty. In her life she taught us how to live, and in her death she taught us how to die.'[40]

"From that letter, my uncle saw that escape was my only hope, and that there was no time like the present for action. While everybody believed that I was in New York was the best time to get there. He accordingly made arrangements with the captain of a vessel running between New York and Edenton, for my passage to the former port.[41]

"I had been here but a short time, when some of my friends sent for me to acquaint me of my danger. Mrs. T——— gave me a letter that Mr. T——— had received from Dr. N———. In that letter he said he wanted to catch me, to make an example of, for the good of the institution of slavery. But, brother, I have now fallen into new hands. Mary Matilda N——— is married to a northern man. He, too, is trying to find out where I am stopping in New York.[42] I know not where to go, nor what to do."

I could see my sister's danger, and well imagine her feelings. We selected Boston, Massachusetts, for our home, and remained there quietly for a few years. Massachusetts had so far precluded the slaveholders from her borders, as to make the hunted fugitive feel himself somewhat secure under the shadow of her laws. Her great men had not sold themselves to the slave power, and her little men had not learnt that they were slaves until after the passing of the Fugitive Slave Bill.[43] From that hour I resolved to seek a home in some foreign clime.

Mrs. ———, on hearing my intention to leave the north, sent for me. I called on her and was shown to her room by my sister, when the following conversation took place.

"John, I understand you intend to leave for some years."

"I do, madam."

"Then my business with you is with respect to your sister. She has spent many years in our family, and we are still desirous to have her remain with us. John, I know that the law is an absolute one, and that the prosecutors are deaf to the claims of justice and humanity; but I have resolved that Harriet shall not be taken out of my house. This I will promise you as a lady."[44]

A few months after the passing of the Fugitive Slave Bill, my sister was looking over the list of arrivals in one of the daily papers, when she saw the names of Mr. and Mrs. M——— of Edenton. She immediately made it known to Mrs. ———, who sent her out of the house without a moment's delay. As the little girl that she had charge of at the time would not be separated from her, they were both sent off together. In due time Mr. M——— came rapping at the door, not as an honest man, but as a slave-catcher. The door being opened, he said to the woman, "Go and tell Harriet that I have got a letter for her; it is from her grandmother, and I have promised to deliver it to her myself." The message was taken to Mrs. ———, who informed him that my sister had left town, and that he could not see her. M——— saw that all of his plans were frustrated, and sold my sister for 300 dollars. She was paid for by her mistress and her friends, and is now living in safety.[45]

Chapter VII. Cruel Treatment of Slaves——the Fugitive Slave Law——Slavery Opposed to Natural Rights and to Christianity

In concluding this short statement of my experience of slavery, I beg the reader to remember that I am not writing of what I have heard, but of what I have seen, and of what I defy the world to prove false. There lived about two miles up a river emptying itself into the Albemarle Sound, a planter, whose name was Carabas. His plantation was called Pembroke. At his death his slaves were sold. I mention this because slaves seldom or ever have more than one name; their surname is most generally that of their first master. The person I am now about to allude to was known by the name of George Carabas. After the death of his own master, he was owned by Mr. Popelston: after that by young John Horton, who sold him to a negro trader.[46]

George was chained in the gang with other slaves, and dragged from his wife and his friends. After a few days' travel on the road, by some means or other he made his escape, and returned back to the spot where he knew he could find one heart to feel for him, and in whom he could confide; but he had not been there long before the bloodthirsty negro-hunters got on his trail, one beautiful Sunday morning, about midsummer, while the church-bells were ringing. Four of the pursuers overtook poor George, and shot him dead.

"If he is outlawed," they doubtless argued, "we only need show his head, and the reward is ours; but if he is not outlawed, what then? Why, they may try to make us pay for him; but we will not be fools enough to say that we shot him, unless we are to be paid for shooting him." His body is put into a canoe, his head thrown in, which lies on his breast. These four southern gentlemen now return to the town, leaving the canoe to inquire how the advertisement reads. On finding that the reward was to be given to any one who would apprehend and confine him in any jail in the State, they saw that they could not publicly boast of their fiendish work.[47]

Now, the question is, what had this man done that he should be so inhumanly butchered and beheaded? The crime that he had committed, and the only crime, was to leave the unnatural trader in slaves and the souls of men, to return to his natural and affectionate wife. Nothing is done to the murderers. They only made a blunder. Slaves are outlawed and shot with impunity, and the tyrant who shoots them is paid for it; but in this case George was not outlawed, so their trouble was all for nothing, and the glory only known to themselves.

Tom Hoskins was a slave belonging to James N——— the son of Dr. N———. This slave was found just out of the town, in the scrub. He was shot in the back, and must have been killed instantly. There was no pay for this—only a feast of blood. Tom's crime was running away from one whom I know to be an unmerciful tyrant.[48] Another was shot, but not killed. There were three brothers, William, James, and Josiah N———. I know not which of the three this slave belonged to. They had been out that day with their bloodhounds hunting slaves. They shot Sirus a little before dark. By some means or other he made his escape from them, and reached Dr. S———'s shop soon after dark. He was taken in, and as many of the shots taken out of him as they could get at, and his wounds dressed. This being done, Dr. S——— sent a despatch to Mr. C———, to let him know that the slave that they had shot had come in to him, and got his wounds dressed. As soon as they received this intelligence, they mounted their horses, and rode off in fiendish glee for town. They came up to the shop, hooting and yelling as if all Bedlam was coming. When they had reached the door, the first cry from them was, "Bring him out—finish him." The doctor came out and said to them, "Gentlemen, the negro has given himself up to me, and I will be responsible for his safe delivery to you as soon as he is able to be moved from hence; but at present he is not." Seeing that the doctor would not let them have him, they returned home.[49]

The C———s were very rich; they owned a great many slaves, and shooting with them was common. They did not feel the loss of a slave or two; it was a common thing for them to offer fifty or a hundred dollars reward for a slave, dead or alive, so that there was satisfactory proof of his being killed.

Just at the back of the court-house and in front of the jail, is a whipping post, where I have seen men and women stripped, and struck from fifteen to one hundred times and more. Some whose backs were cut to pieces were washed down with strong brine or brandy; this is done to increase pain. But the most cruel torture is backing; the hands are crossed and tied, then taken over the knee and pinned by running a stick between the arms and the legs, which tightens the skin and renders the slave as helpless as a child. The backing paddle is made of oak, about an inch and a quarter thick, and five by eight inches in the blade, with about twelve inches of a handle. The blade is full of small holes, which makes the punishment severer. I have seen the flesh like a steak. Slaves flogged in this way are unable to sit down for months.

I will give you but one case of flogging in detail; that will be of Agnes, the slave of Augustus M———. She was hired to John B———; she was some six months advanced in pregnancy at the time. Being in an unfit state for field labour, she could not do as much as other slaves. For this cause, B——— tied her up and commenced whipping her. With my own hands have I dressed her back, and I solemnly declare that she had not a piece of skin left on it as wide as my finger.

She was a hired slave. Had B——— killed her at a single blow, her master could have punished B———, if he could have got white witnesses to certify to that effect, which is not likely; but she might have died in an hour after being cut down, and there was no law to harm him. It would have been death caused by moderate correction, which North Carolina does not punish a slaveholder for.[50]

I know that the picture I have drawn of slavery is a black one, and looks most unnatural; but here you have the State, the town, and the names of all the parties. One who has never felt the sting of slavery would naturally suppose that it was to the slaveholder's advantage to treat his slaves with kindness; but the more indulgent the master the more intelligent the slave; the more intelligent the slave the nearer he approximates to a man; the nearer he approximates to a man, the more determined he is to be a free man; and to argue that the slaves are happy, or can be happy while in slavery, is to argue that they have been brutalized to that degree that they cannot be considered men. What better proof do you want in favour of universal freedom than can be given? You can find thousands of ignorant men who will lay down their lives for their liberty; can you find one intelligent man who would prefer slavery?

The last thing that remained to be done to complete this hell on earth was done in 1850, in passing the Fugitive Slave Law. There is not a State, a city, nor a town left as a refuge for the hunted slave; there is not a United States officer but what has sworn to act the part of the bloodhound in hunting me down, if I dare visit the land of Stars and Stripes, the home of the brave, and land of the free. Yet, according to the American declaration of independence, it is a self-evident truth that all men are created by their Maker free and equal, and endowed with certain inalienable rights—life, liberty, and the pursuit of happiness.[51] Where are the coloured man's rights to-day in America? They once had rights allowed them. Yes, in the days that tried men's souls they had a right to bleed and die for the country; but their deeds are forgotten, their swords and bayonets have been beaten into chains and fetters to bind the limbs of their children. The first man that was seen to fall in the revolutionary struggle for liberty, was a coloured man; and I have seen one of his brethren, who had fled from his whips and chains, within sight of that monument erected to liberty, dragged from it into slavery, not by the slave-owners of the south, for they knew not of his being there, but by northern men.[52]

I cannot agree with that statesman who said, "What the law makes property, is property." What is law, but the will of the people—a mirror to reflect a nation's character? Robbery is robbery; it matters not whether it is done by one man or a million, whether they were organized or disorganized; the principle is the same. No law, unless there be one that can change my nature, can make property of me. Freedom is as natural for man as the air he breathes, and he who robs him of his freedom is also guilty of murder; for he has robbed him of his natural existence. On this subject the Church and the State are alike. One will tell a lie, and the other will swear to it. The State says, "That which the law makes property is property." The Church says that "organic sin is no sin at all"; both parties having reference to slavery. With a few exceptions, their politics and religion are alike oppressive, and rotten, and false. None but political tyrants would ever establish slavery, and none but religious hypocrites would ever support it. What says Matthew, 15th chapter, 8th and 9th verses: "This people draweth nigh unto me with their mouth, and honoureth me with their lips; but their heart is far from me. But in vain they worship me, teaching for doctrines the commandments of men."[53]

What is to be hoped of a people like this? They are full of lies and hypocrisy. Give me liberty amidst savages, rather than slavery with such professed Christians. No man should hold unlimited power over his fellow-man. From the repeated abuses of this power, he becomes the most brutal of the human species; and the more he himself has been abused, the more eager he is to abuse others. But slavery is unnatural, and it requires unnatural means to support it. Everything droops that feels its sting. Hope grows dimmer and dimmer, until life becomes bitter and burdensome. At last death frees the slave from his chains, but his wrongs are forgotten. He was oppressed, robbed, and murdered. Better would it be for the slaves, if they must submit to slavery, if the immortal part of them were blotted out. But, since God has breathed undying life into the soul of man, rather let us blot that out of existence which stands between man and his rights, God and his laws, the world and its progress. The Christian religion, that binds heart to heart and hand to hand, and makes each and every man a brother, is at war with it; and shall we, whose very souls it has wrung out, be longer at peace.[54] If possible, let us make those whom we have left behind feel that the ground they till is cursed with slavery, the air they breathe poisoned with its venom breath, and that which made life dear to them lost and gone.

In conclusion, let me say that the experience of the past, the present feeling, and above all this, the promise of God, assure me that the oppressor's rod shall be broken. But how it is to be done has been the question among our friends for years. After the prayers of twenty-five years, the slaves' chains are tighter than they were before, their escape more dangerous, and their cup of misery filled nearer its brim. Since I cannot forget that I was a slave, I will not forget those that are slaves. What I would have done for my liberty I am willing to do for theirs, whenever I can see them ready to fill a freeman's grave, rather than wear a tyrant's chain. The day must come; it will come. Human nature will be human nature; crush it as you may, it changes not; but woe to that country where the sun of liberty has to rise up out of the sea of blood. When I have thought of all that would pain the eye, sicken the heart, and make us turn our backs to the scene and weep, I then think of the oppressed struggling with their oppressors, and have a scene more horrible still. But I must drop this subject; I do not like to think of the past, nor look to the future, of wrongs like these.

Illustrations

Thought to be a photo of Dr. James Norcom.

Amy Post in the early 1860s.

Lydia Maria Child in the 1860s.

Cornelia Grinnell Willis at the Old Mansion, New Bedford, Massachusetts, in 1884.

Deathbed codicil of Margaret Horniblow, Jacobs's first mistress, willing "my negro girl Harriet" and "my bureau & work table & their contents" to her three-year-old niece Mary Matilda Norcom, July 3, 1825.

Petition for the emancipation of Jacobs's grandmother, Molly Horniblow, signed with an X by Hannah Pritchard, April 10, 1828.

$100 REWARD

WILL be given for the apprehension and delivery of my Servant Girl HARRIET. She is a light mulatto, 21 years of age, about 5 feet 4 inches high, of a thick and corpulent habit, having on her head a thick covering of black hair that curls naturally, but which can be easily combed straight. She speaks easily and fluently, and has an agreeable carriage and address. Being a good seamstress, she has been accustomed to dress well, has a variety of very fine clothes, made in the prevailing fashion, and will probably appear, if abroad, tricked out in gay and fashionable finery. As this girl absconded from the plantation of my son without any known cause or provocation, it is probable she designs to transport herself to the North.

The above reward, with all reasonable charges, will be given for apprehending her, or securing her in any prison or jail within the U. States.

All persons are hereby forewarned against harboring or entertaining her, or being in any way instrumental in her escape, under the most rigorous penalties of the law.

JAMES NORCOM.

Edenton, N. C. June 30

Advertisement for the capture of Harriet Jacobs, *American Beacon* (daily), Norfolk, Virginia, July 4, 1835. Dr. Norcom's newspaper ad, which ran on Tuesdays, Thursdays, and Saturdays for two weeks beginning June 30, was worded somewhat differently from the poster quoted in the text.

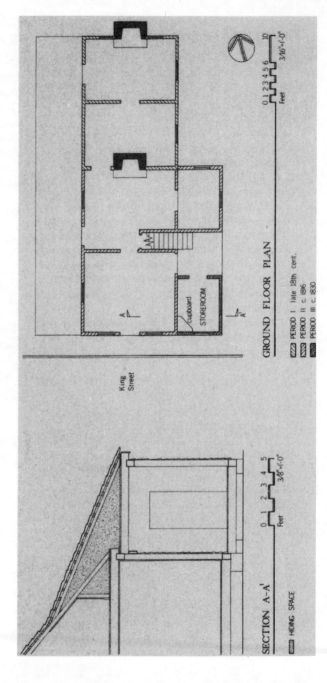

Molly Horniblow's house: reconstruction to scale of elevation and floor plan showing Jacobs's hiding place.

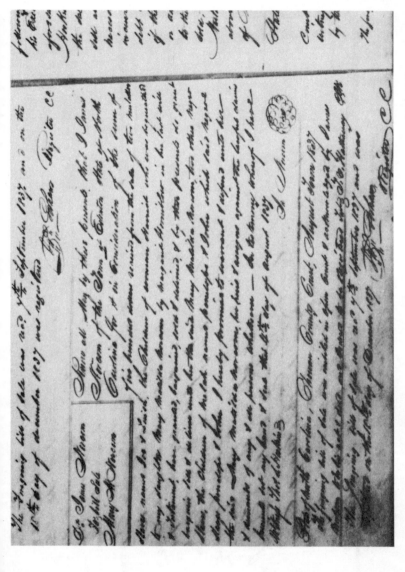

Dr. Norcom's note repaying his daughter for having sold her "two mulattoe Slaves named Joe & Louisa, the Children of woman Harriet," by substituting two other children, August 4, 1837.

Harriet Jacobs's receipt acknowledging a payment of $100 "to the purchase of cops. of 'Linda'" by the abolitionists' Hovey Fund, February 1, 1861.

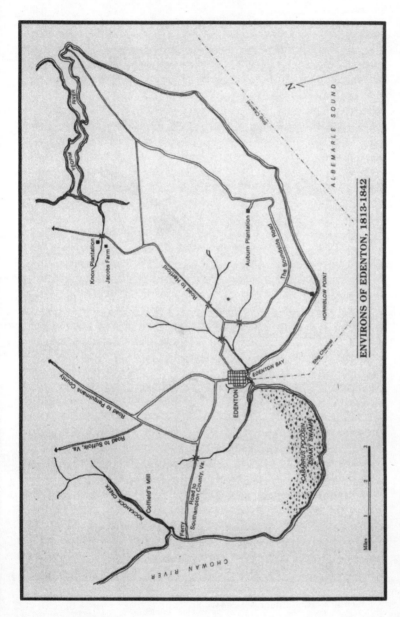

Map 1. Environs of Edenton, North Carolina, 1813–1842.

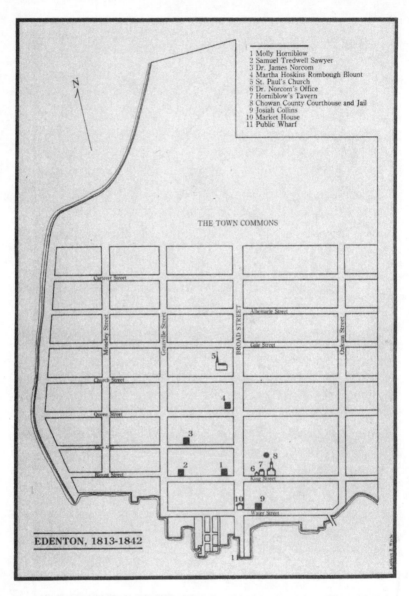

1 Molly Horniblow
2 Samuel Tredwell Sawyer
3 Dr. James Norcom
4 Martha Hoskins Rombough Blount
5 St. Paul's Church
6 Dr. Norcom's Office
7 Horniblow's Tavern
8 Chowan County Courthouse and Jail
9 Josiah Collins
10 Market House
11 Public Wharf

THE TOWN COMMONS

EDENTON, 1813-1842

Map 2. Edenton, North Carolina, 1813–1842.

Abbreviations

AL   Autograph letter, signature omitted or cut off.

ALS   Autograph letter, signed.

BAP   Black Abolitionist Papers. Seventeen reels with a published guide and index. New York: Microfilming Corporation of America, 1981–83: Ann Arbor: University Microfilms International, 1984–.

BPL   Boston Public Library. Boston, Mass.

IAPFP   Isaac and Amy Post Family Papers. Department of Rare Books, Manuscripts, and Archives, University of Rochester Library, Rochester, N.Y.

LMCP   Lydia Maria Child Papers. *The Collected Correspondence of Lydia Maria Child, 1817–1880*, ed. Patricia G. Holland and Milton Meltzer. Millwood, N.Y.: Kraus Microform, 1980.

NCSA   North Carolina State Archives. Raleigh, N.C.

NFP   Norcom Family Papers. North Carolina State Archives.

First page of Harriet Jacobs's letter to Amy Post [May 1849] (Letter 3).

Correspondence

1. Joshua Coffin to Lydia Maria Child[1]

Phila. 25 June 1842
Esteemed Friend,

 . . . I hope you will call & see, if she is now in the city, one of the most interesting cases of escape from slavery that you have ever seen. She was sent from this city yesterday morning & consigned to Mr. Johnston.[2] She is from N.C. was brought away by a sea captain. She was sold by her master to the speculators & to avoid being sent away she was hidden for 7 years! in a small upper room of a house occupied by colored people & within a hundred yards of her master's house, who did not know she was there. She had not seen her boy, for 7 years till within 3 days of her coming away. She has been shut up so long that she can hardly walk. Another woman was brought away from Delaware, who was found tied to a tree. If Mr. Johnston was the man he ought to be, he would invite you occasionally to see some of these remarkable cases, which are continually passing from Phil, to N.Y. The Vagrant [crossed out] what a queer mistake. The Vigilance Committee of this city are doing a fine business in weakening & de-lapidating the edifice of slavery. Success to them . . .

Joshua Coffin

ALS; Anti-Slavery Collection, BPL; LMCP 14:389–4.

1 I am grateful to Carolyn Karcher for calling this letter to my atten-tion. In 1842 Child was working in New York as editor of the Garrisonian newspaper, the *National Anti-Slavery Standard* (1840–1872) . Joshua Coffin (1792–1864), teacher, historian, and antiquarian, was a founder of the New England Anti-Slavery Society and the American Anti-Slavery Society; he wrote *An Account of Some of the Principal Slave Insurrections* (New York, 1860).

2 Lymis Johnson, porter, is named in minutes of the Philadelphia Vigilant Committee for 1840, 1843, and 1844; records for 1842 are sparse. Joseph A. Borome, "The Vigilant Committee of Philadelphia," *Pennsylvania Magazine of History and Biography* 92 (July 1968): 320–351; personal communication to Jean Fagan Yellin from Phil Lapsansky, Library Company of Philadelphia, 11 Oct. 1985.

2. John S. Jacobs to Sydney Howard Gay[1]

Chelsea Mass June 4th 1846
Friend Gay

They have let the cat out of the bag and I thort that I would tell you that it proved to be a devel in disguise my sister received a very affec-tionate letter lass week from her young mistress Mrs Mesmore[2] she writes of her having married and also of having heared that my sister had gone to England she has been waiting the arrival of Mr. W[illis] and now reminds my sister of her former love and in that affectionat manner so peculiar to this no soul Nation she want to know if she wont COME HOME that she had never consented for her Father to sell her becaus she did not wish her to be the slave of anyone but hirself who had always loved her and been kind to her—in deed it seems to me that the old Dr letter to the New York blood hounds and the young Dr letter to my sister with one received lass week would pusel [puzzle] all of the pïl makers in the city to get them into a shape sutable to our taste[3] let me give you an extract from all of them the old Dr writes his to New York to be put in to the hands of the smartest polease officer in the city offering $100 reward for her and after having discribed her as minutely as posable he sais that he dont wish to sell he at any price he wants to get her to make ensample [an example] of her for the good of the institution[4]

The young Dr writes as if he had Just come from A camp meeting his hole head is full of love the purest of the Delilah kind[5] he is afraid that she is not happy and comfortable away from all of her friends and relatives and after assuring her that the family still entertain the most friendly feelings towards her he then begs her to write him where she is that he might restore her to her former happiness (hell)

The letter that was written by Mesmore as you know was a compleat forgery and in addition to that it was as black er falsehood as every escaped the bottomless pit he said that a northern gentleman wished to buy her and that the Norcom family would have nothing to do with her when in fait he then intended and since has married in the Norcom family the newly made Mrs Mesmore wants her to return home or buy her self but as my sister has not the means of buy her self and finds these cold regons more healthy than the suny South they will have to love each other at a distance the sweetest love that can exist betweene master and Slave I dont know this Mr—Mesmore the New York men ketchers has run him in to Edenton since the baby stealers run me out but to Judge him by his letters I should say that he

was equil 15 grains of epecuaner [ipecacuanha][6] mixed in a like warm
water but poor fellow he has paid dear for his wife he has been shot
mobed and imprisoned[7] but for the want of time I must leave his interesting family may the Lord have mursey upon them

   Yours in behalf of the oppressed the world over

                                                        John S Jacobs

ALS; Sydney Howard Gay Collection, Columbia University Libraries.

   1 Sydney Howard Gay (1814–1888), abolitionist, author, and journalist,
lectured for the American Anti-Slavery Society and served for thirteen years
as chief editor of the *Standard*. *The Letters of William Lloyd Garrison*, ed.
Walter M. Merrill and Louis Ruchames, 6 vols. (Cambridge: Harvard
University Press, 1971–1981), III, p. 269.

   2 Mary Matilda Norcom, now married to Daniel Messmore. For her
letter, see Chapter XXXVIII.

   3 The old doctor is Dr. James Norcom. The young doctor is probably
his son Dr. John Norcom (1802–1856), a born-again Christian. NFP.

   4 The institution: chattel slavery.

   5 Delilah feigned love for Samson and betrayed him to his enemies.
Judges 16:4–21.

   6 Ipecacuanha is an emetic and expectorant.

   7 See Chapter XLI, note 6.

3. Harriet Jacobs to Amy Post

[Rochester, May 1849]

   Dear friend I send you those few lines to let you know that we are
getting along Dear little Willie[1] made us a visit last Sunday he seemed
much pleased and was a very good boy he loved Joanna and Jacob
more than any one else things seem to go on smoothly at home and
I feel so happy daily expecting to see my Son[2] I have not heard from
my Brother since he left went to hear Mr. Louis[3] Lecture last night and
I can assure you that he did not forget to hold up the name of Isac
and Ammy Post as the Coloured Man & Womans friend as much as

I love you I am glad that your nane is not too sacred to be held up by a coloured Man I suppose you know that Louis is out of prisan and his accuser in for the same bail[4] I hope Yourself and sister is having a pleasant time I know that if you are at Long Island you are happy for it is a great blessing to have parents to Visit you must certainly bring your sister Sarah[5] back with [you] every body will want to see her the Office go on as usual[6] had a few here to meeting on Sunday was entertained with a part of your letter I suppose we shall have Frederick[7] and the Miss Griffiths[8] here on Sunday to draw a full house Rochester is looking very pretty the trees are in full Bloom and the earth seems covered with a green mantle Miss Owen[9] & Miss Marse left yesterday Abby Thayer[10] left last week The Miss Griffiths has been here this afternoon Frederick went with them to the falls they seemed much pleased with the reading room I must stop hoping you will soon be at home

Yours
Harriet

ALS; IAPFP #787; BAP 16:0678–79.

1 Willett Post (1847–1917), Amy Post's youngest child.

2 Joseph Jacobs had returned from his whaling voyage. Isaac Post to Amy Post, May 7, 1849, and May 22, 1849, IAPFP.

3 On June 1, 1849, the *North Star* commented on lectures that H. G. R. Lewis had recently delivered "urging [the colored people] to aim at mental and moral superiority."

4 In the same article, the *North Star* noted that (unnamed) "slanders which have got abroad respecting Mr. Lewis are entirely unfounded."

5 Amy Post's youngest sister, Sarah Kirby Hallowell Willis (1818–1914), an abolitionist, feminist, and temperance advocate, was a member of the Committee of Arrangements of the Rochester Women's Rights Convention. IAPFP; Nancy Hewitt, *Women's Activism and Social Change, Rochester, New York, 1822–1872* (Ithaca: Cornell University Press, 1984), p. 231.

6 The Anti-Slavery Office and Reading Room on Buffalo Street, above Frederick Douglass's newspaper. See Chapter XXXIX. *Daily American Directory of the City of Rochester for 1849–50*, p. 155.

7 Frederick Douglass (c. 1819–1895), Afro-American reformer, speaker,

writer, and editor, escaped from slavery in 1838 and became prominent after his 1841 speech before the Massachusetts Anti-Slavery Society. In 1845 Douglass published his *Narrative of the Life of Frederick Douglass, an American Slave: Written by Himself.* He spent the next two years in England and Ireland, returned to the United States in April 1847, and published the first issue of his newspaper the *North Star* in Rochester that December. Benjamin Quarles, *Frederick Douglass* (1948; New York: Atheneum, 1969).

8 The English sisters Julia and Eliza Griffiths, whom Douglass had met in Britain, arrived in Rochester in mid-May 1849; Julia Griffiths stayed for six years. She became permanent secretary of the Rochester Ladies' Anti-Slavery Society, and her work to finance Douglass's paper helped ensure its success. To raise funds for the *North Star* in 1852 and 1853 she edited two gift books, both entitled *Autographs for Freedom.* Quarles, *Frederick Douglass,* pp. 91–95; Hewitt, *Women's Activism,* pp. 150–151.

9 Sarah Owen (?–1879), abolitionist and member of the Committee of Arrangements for the Rochester Women's Rights Convention in 1848, organized the Working Women's Protective Union with Amy Post. Hewitt, *Women's Activism,* pp. 231–232, 236; personal communication to Jean Fagan Yellin from Karl Kabelac, University of Rochester Library, 3 Feb. 1986.

10 Abby G. Thayer (1827–1853) was a Garrisonian abolitionist; her sister Phoebe was governess of the Douglass children. *Letters of William Lloyd Garrison,* III, 571, 572.

4. Harriet Jacobs to Amy Post

Cornwall, Orange County [New York] [1852?]
My Dear Friend

Yours of the 24 was received on the 27th and my pen will fail to describe my greatful feelings on reading it although you could never be forgotten yet you do not know how much itt cheers my sad heart and how much I appreciate a word of sympathy and friendship from those I love for you little know how much I have had to pass through since we last meet but it is a blessing that we can say a word in this way to each other many far more deserving than myself has been debared from this privilege

I answered Mrs. Hallowell[1] kind letter which I hope she recieved I wrote Mrs. Bush[2] also but I but I received a letter yesterday by the way of New York from her will you please say that I had written I am sorry to have given her so much trouble but I have been unfortunate twice and I thought this would be more sure to come to hand my best love to her I am glad her hopes were realised in a sweet little Daughter and hope she may be blessed in having her health and strength restored before she leaves our shores I am sorry to hear Dear little Willie looks so delicate I should dearly love to see him and oh my dear friend how much I would prise a few hours with you at this present time but we poor mortals must always strive to teach our hearts submission to our circumstances it is a hard lesson but it is a blessing to those who truly practice it

your proposal to me has been thought over and over again but not with out some most painful rememberances dear Amy if it was the life of a Heroine with no degradation associated with it far better to have been one of the starving poor of Ireland whose bones had to bleach on the highways than to have been a slave with the curse of slavery stamped upon yourself and Children your purity of heart and kindly sympathies won me at one time to speak of my children it is the only words that has passed my lips since I left my Mothers door I had determined to let others think as they pleased but my lips should be sealed and no one had a right to question me for this reason when I first came North I avoided the Antislavery people as much as possible because I felt that I could not be honest and tell the whole truth often have I gone to my poor Brother with my gurived and mortified spirits he would mingle his tears with mine while he would advise me to do what was right my conscience approved it but my stubborn pride would not yeild I have tried for the past two years to conquer it and I feel that God has helped me or I never would consent to give my past life to any one for I would not do it with out giving the whole truth if it could help save another from my fate it would be selfish and unchristian in me to keep it back situated as I am I do not see any way that I could put it forward Mrs. Willis[3] thinks it would do much good in Mrs. Stowe[4] hand but I could not ask her to take any step Mr. W[illis] is too proslavery he would tell me that it was very wrong and that I was trying to do harm or perhaps he was sorry for me to undertake it while I was in his family Mrs Willis thinks if [it] is not done in my day it will [be] a good legacy for my children to do it after my death but now is the time when their is so much excitement everywhere Mrs Hallowell said in her letter that you thought of going to New York in the course of a few weeks if you will let me know when I will meet you there I can give you my Ideas much better than write them

If the Antislavery society could propose [?] this I would be willing to exert myself in any way that they thought best for the welfare of the cause they do not know me they have heard of me as John Jacobs sister

my dear friend would you be willing to make this proposal I would rather have you do it than any one else you could do it better I should be happier in remembering it was you if Mrs. Stowe would undertake it I should like to be with her a Month I should want the History of my childhood and the first five years in one volume and the next three and my home in the northern states in the second besides I could give her some fine sketches for her pen on slavery give my love to your dear Husband and sons kiss Willie for me love to all God bless Yours

                                                              Harriet

ALS; IAPFP #84; BAP 16:0700–02.

    1 Sarah Kirby Hallowell, later Sarah Kirby Hallowell Willis.
    2 Abigail Norton Bush (1809 or 1810–1898?), feminist and abolitionist, presided over the 1848 Rochester Women's Rights Convention. In the spring of 1852 she served on the Business Committee at the annual meeting of the American Anti-Slavery Society, held in Rochester. Hewitt, *Women's Activism,*

pp. 313, 144, 168; personal communication to Jean Fagan Yellin from Karl Kabelac, University of Rochester Library, 3 Feb. 1986.

3 Cornelia Grinnell Willis.

4 Harriet Beecher Stowe.

5. Harriet Jacobs to Amy Post

Feby 14th [1853]

My Dear Friend

I recieved your kind letter yesterday if silence is expressive of ones deep feeling then in this way I must ask you to recieve the emotions of what my heart and pen cannot express hoping the time is not far distant when we may see each other but I must tell you what I am try-ing to accomplish having seen the notice in the paper of Mrs Stowe intention to visit England[1] I felt there would not be much hope of coming before her for some time and I thought if I could get her to take Louisa with her she might get interested enough[2] if she could do nothing herself she might help Louisa to do something besides I thought Louisa would be a very good representative of a Southern Slave she has improved much in her studies and I think that she has energy enough to do something for the cause, she only needs to be put in the field I told my Ideas to Mrs Willis she thought they were good and offered to write Mrs Stowe she wrote last Tuesday asking her protection [for Louisa] and if she would place her in some Anti-slavery family unless her services could be useful to her which I would prefer myself intending to pay her expenses there the letter was di-rected as yours when it is answered you shall know dear Amy since I have no fear of my name coming before those whom I have lived in dread of I cannot be happy without trying to be useful in some way I had a kind note from dear Sarah[3] saying that she would be in New York on the 20th and wished to know our street and number I am going down to see her and Mrs Bush and if Mrs B do not sail on the 20th will you drop me a line to let me know I send an answer to Sarah to day also as she will not be there unless Mrs B sails I shall be more than glad to see you all[4]

AL; IAPFP #785; BAP 16:0710–11.

    1 Stowe was invited to England on December 10, 1852; she sailed on March 30, 1853. Forrest Wilson, *Crusader in Crinoline* (1941; rpt. Westport, Conn.: Greenwood, 1972), pp. 328, 334–335.

    2 Jacobs was hoping that Louisa could interest Stowe in writing Jacobs's life story.

    3 The Post circle of anti-slavery feminists included Sarah Fish, Sarah Owen, and Sarah Thayer as well as Post's sister Sarah Kirby Hallowell Willis; it is not clear which Sarah this is. Hewitt, *Women's Activism*.

    4 The letter breaks off here.

6. Harriet Jacobs to Amy Post

March [crossed out] April 4th [1853]

    My Dear friend I steal this moment to scratch you a few lines I should have written you before but I have been waiting with the hope of having something to tell you from our friend Mrs Stowe but as it is I hardly know where to begin for my thoughts come rushing down with such a spirit of rivalry each wishing to be told you first so that they fill my heart and make my eyes dim therefore my silence must express to you what my poor pen is not capable of doing but you know dear Amy that I have a heart towards you filled with love and gratitude for all the interest you have so kindly shown in my behalf I wish that I could sit by you and talk insted of writing but that pleasure is denied and I am thankful for this Mrs Stowe recieved your letter and Mrs Willis she said it would be much care to her to take Louisa as she went by invitation it would not be right and she was afraid that if her [Louisa's] situation as a Slave should be known it would subject her to much petting and patronizing which would be more pleasing to a young Girl than useful and the English was very apt to do it and she was very much opposed to it with this class of people I will leave the rest for you to solve but remem[ber] I mene to pay Louisa expenses your letter she sent to Mrs. Willis asking might she trouble her so far as to ask if this most extraordinary event was true in all its bearings and if she might use it in her key[1] I had never opend my lips to Mrs Willis concerning my Children—in the Charitableness of her own heart she sympathised with me and never asked their origin my suffering she knew it embarrassed me at first but I told her the truth but we both thought it was wrong in Mrs Stowe to have sent you letter she might have written to enquire if she liked Mrs. Willis wrote her a very kind letter beging that she would not use any of the facts in her key saying that I wished it to be a history of my life entirely by itself which would do more good and it needed no romance but if she wanted some facts for her book that I would be most happy to give her some she never answered the letter she [Mrs. Willis] wrote again and I wrote twice with no better success it was not Lady like to treat Mrs Willis so she would not have done it to any one. I think she [Mrs. Stowe] did not like my objection I cant help it[2]

AL; IAPFP #788; BAP 16:0681–83.
    1 The extraordinary event was Jacobs's seven-year incarceration. Harriet Beecher Stowe was working on *A Key to Uncle Tom's Cabin, Presenting the Original Facts and Documents upon Which the Story is Founded . . .* (Boston, Cleveland, and London, 1853).
    2 The letter breaks off here.

7. Harriet Jacobs to Amy Post

Oct 9th [1853]
My Dear Friend

I was more than glad to recieve your welcome letter for must acknowledge that your long silence had troubled me much I should have written before this but we have had a little member added to the family[1] and I have had little time for any thing besides the extras it makes my heart sad to tell you that I have not heard from my Brother and Joseph and dear Amy I have lost that Dear old Grandmother that I so dearly loved oh her life has been one of sorrow and trial but he in whom she trusted has never forsaken her her Death was beautiful may my last end be like hers Louisa is with me I dont know how long she will remain I shall try and keep her all winter as I want to try and make arrangements to have some of my time

Mrs Stowe never answered any of my letters after I refused to have my history in her key perhaps its for the best at least I will try and think so have you seen any more of my scribling they were marked fugitive[2] William Nell told Louisa about the piece and sent her a Copy I was careful to keep it from her and no one here never suspected me I would not have Mrs W[illis] to know it before I had undertaken my history for I must write just what I have lived and witnessed myself dont expect much of me dear Amy you shall have truth but not talent God did not give me that gift but he gave me a soul that burned for freedom and a heart nerved with determination to suffer even unto death in pursuit of that liberty which without makes life an intolerable burden but dear A I fear that I am burdening you the request in your letter I told you it was true in all its statement accept to being my Mother and sister but we grew up together[3] the answer to the Slaves being outlawed in North Carolina I was at home when the poor outlawed was brung in town with his head severed from his body[4] the piece on Colonisation was just what my poor little indignart heart felt towards the society[5] and now my dear friend don't flatter me I am aware of my many mistakes and willing to be told of them only let me come before the world as I have been an uneducated oppressed Slave but I must stop love to all God bless you excuse the Hasty scrawl.

Yours

Harriet

1 O Clock

ALS; IAPFP #85; BAP 16:0713–14.

1 Edith Willis was born on September 28, 1853. Henry A. Beers, *Nathaniel Parker Willis*, American Men of Letters Series (Boston and New York: Houghton Mifflin, 1885, 1913).

2 Jacobs is referring to three letters she had written to newspapers: "Letter from a Fugitive Slave. Slaves Sold under Peculiar Circumstances," *New York Tribune*, June 21, 1853, p. 6; "Cruelty to Slaves," *New York Tribune*, July 25, 1853, p. 3; I have not located the piece on the Colonization Society.

3 The sexual abuse of slave sisters and their mothers' fruitless attempts to shield them were discussed in Jacobs's letter to the *Tribune* of June 21, 1853.

4 Jacobs's letter to the *Tribune* of July 25, 1853, described the decapitation of a fugitive slave in North Carolina. John S. Jacobs identifies the victim as George Carabus (actually spelled Cabarrus) in "A True Tale of Slavery." For court records concerning this atrocity, see Chowan County Miscellaneous Records (Inquests), Sept. 16, 1833, NCSA.

5 Organized in 1817, the American Colonization Society—attacked by abolitionists—proposed sending blacks back to Africa, and attempted to establish Liberia as "a Negro colony in Africa." John Hope Franklin, *From Slavery to Freedom: A History of American Negroes*, 2nd ed. (New York: Knopf, 1967), pp. 234–237.

8. Harriet Jacobs to Amy Post

Cornwall [New York], March [1854]
My Dear Friend

I recieved your kind and welcome letter and should have replied to it much earlier but various hindrances have prevented me and when I would have written I was in Bed with a severe attack of Rheumatism so that I could not raise my hands to my head I am still suffering with it in my shoulders and we have had much sickness in the family this winter I know my plea for want of time will find its way to your heart

my dear friend let me thank you for your kind and generous offer of the hospitality of your pleasant home which would afford me much pleasure to accept but as yet I cannot decide my friends Mr & Mrs Brackett[1] is very anxious that I should go to their home and write they live very quietly and retired they were here and spent a day and night with me and saw from my daily duties that it was hard for me to find much time to write as yet I have not written a single page by daylight Mrs W[illis] dont know from my lips that I am writing for a Book and has never seen a line of what I have written I told her in the Autumn that I would give her Louisa services through the winter if she would allow me my winter evenings to myself but with the care of the little baby the big Babies and at the household calls I have but a little time to think or write but I have tried in my poor way to do my best and that is not much

And you my dear friend must not expect much where there has been so little given[2] Yes dear Amy there has been more than a bountiful share of suffering given enough to crush the finer feelings of stouter hearts than this poor timid one of mine but I will try and not send you a portraiture of feelings just now the poor Book is in its Chrysalis state and though I can never make it a butterfly I am satisfied to have it creep meekly among some of the humbler bugs I some-

times wish that I could fall into a Rip Van Winkle[3] sleep and awake
with the blest belief of that little Witch Topsy[4] that I never was born
but you will say it is too late in the day I have outgrown the belief oh
yes and outlived it too but you know that my bump of hope is large[5]
how is my dear old friend Mr Post I have no doubt but that he is at
his Post perhaps heading a mighty Phalanx to put the Nebraska Bill
through[6] well he shall have my vote 1856 when *Arnold*[7] and *Belshassar*[8]
nocks down the avalanche[9] remember me with much kindness to all
the family tell Willie I want to see him very much when you write tell
me if I know the friend that you spoke of in your letter as soon as my
plans are more matured I will write you again it will be very difficult
for to get some one in my place yet it will be left for me to do I know
of but one person she is a Ladys nurse and her wages would be high
but I think that [I] can get her she is a nice person I must stop this
rambling letter let no one see it Lou sends much love to you I am
sorry you dont know her better you would love her God bless you.
write as soon as you can

Yours

H Jacobs

ALS; IAPFP #783; BAP 16:0679–80.

    1 The family of Zenas Brockett (1806–1883) of Manheim, New York,
were Jacobs's friends; see Louisa Matilda Jacobs to [John S. Jacobs], Nov. 5,
1849. In a letter to Amy Post, July 21, 1853, William C. Nell wrote, "At
Waterloo a good time with the McClintocks—spent one night at Zenas
Brockett's and was made happy in his family augmented of course by the
society of Louisa Jacobs." IAPFP. Little Falls (New York) *Journal and Courier,*
June 5, 1883.

    2 "For unto whomsoever much is given, of him shall be much required
. . ." Luke 12:48.

    3 Rip Van Winkle, a character in Washington Irving's *The Sketch Book*
(1819–1820), slept through the American Revolution.

4 Topsy is the black child in Stowe's *Uncle Tom's Cabin* who announced that she "just grow'd."

5 The pseudoscience of phrenology charted personality by studying the "bumps" or configurations of the skull.

6 The Nebraska Bill, introduced in January 1854 and supported by Senator Stephen A. Douglas and President Franklin Pierce, in effect repealed the Missouri Compromise by mandating that residents of Kansas and Nebraska could decide by popular vote whether these states would enter the Union as slave or free. Supporters of the Missouri Compromise and the Compromise of 1850 saw the Nebraska Bill as a betrayal of these measures and joined with the abolitionists to oppose it. Jacobs's suggestion that Isaac Post support the measure perhaps reflects the radical position of abolitionist Thomas Wentworth Higginson, published in *The Liberator,* Feb. 17, 1854: "Speaking as an agitator, I have . . . a feeling of profound gratitude to the movers of this measure. Every such proposition only shows more clearly that there is no such thing as peace for us, on the present terms."

7 "An effigy was found . . . suspended to the top of the flag-staff on Boston Common" inscribed, "Stephen A. Douglas, author of the Nebraska Bill—the Benedict Arnold of 1854." *The Liberator,* March 10, 1854, p. 38.

8 Belshazzar—in the Book of Daniel, a dissipated leader who ruled blindly, ignoring the needs of his people, and whose empire was destroyed—was often referred to in the political rhetoric of the day. Here, he may signify Pierce; *The Liberator,* March 17, 1854, p. 48, published a sermon on the Nebraska Bill citing Daniel 11:11 and 11:27.

9 *The Liberater,* Feb. 27, 1854, p. 28, printed a poem on the Nebraska Bill that ended:

> Just then, an avalanche of indignation fell
> From an insulted nation on their heads,
> And buried them in everlasting shame.
> It was an avalanche of freemen's votes,
> Which rolled from granite hills and mountains green.

9. Harriet Jacobs to Amy Post

Idlewild [New York], March [1857]
My Dear Friend

It has been a long time since you have seen the scratch of my pen —but it is much longer since I have recieved a letter from you—my

poor scrawls are nothing—while yours are a great deal to me—it
assures me that I am sometimes remembered by the friends that I
value and love—and I pray that your former kindness and Friendship
are not to be dwindled down—into a mere—Yearly—recognition of
each other—and then only for a few fleeting moments—you cannot
know—how disappointed I was at not seeing you again—when you
were in the City—I was at the Convention[1] the next morning after I
left you—but I felt so ill that I had to leave—before I had the opportunity to see you—having a severe Cough the stormy Weather kept
me in doors—and although I remained in the City for ten days I felt
that I had been deprived of all that had carried me to the City—I shall
endeavor to leave home this time—if nothing happens—to prevent—
a day or two before the Convention[2]—to attend to some of my affairs—that must be looked after—so that I may have nothing to do
but see you when it is convenient—I cannot remain more than two or
three days at farthest—as we are in expectation of a little Stranger
near that time—and those little important ones—make much ado in
household affairs[3]—when you write tell me all about Willie—if he
goes to School—if he is fond of reading—and if he has the little Pilgrim Grace Greenwood paper for Children[4]—I should love to see
him—with so many Years I think that I should scarcely recognise
the dear little fellow that used to call me Dah—But I forget you are
Grandma now I hope the honor [?] were delightfully—both to dear
Grandpa—and Grandma—please extend my kindest rememberance
to that dear good Man—also to Mr and Mrs Hallowell[5]—Mr and Mrs
Willis[6]—and all of my Rochester friends—

I have followed you all as well as I could through the Liberator—
and Standard[7]—I am glad to see there is some new Pioneers in the
field—may God bless their Labors—and I am so glad to see the stand
that W C Nell has taken[8]—the good and the sincere are needed—
when I see the evil that is spreading throughout the land my whole
soul sickens—oh my dear friend this poor heart that has bleed in

Slavery—is often wrung most bitterly to behold the injustice the wrongs—the oppression—the cruel outrages inflicted on on my race —sometimes I am almost ready to exclaim—where dwells that just Father—whom I love—and in whom whom I believe—is his arm Shortened[9]—Is his power Weakened—that all these high handed outrages reign supreme law throughout the land—God does not permit it—Man is following the evil devices of his own heart—for he is not willing even to acknowledge us made in Gods own Image[10]—have not the decision of the last few days—in Washington—decided this for us[11]—I see nothing for the Black Man—to look forward to—but to forget his old Motto—and learn a new one his long patient hope— must be might—and Strength—Liberty—or Death—

Lulu[12] would send her love if she was here—but she has been living on Long Island for the last ten Months—as Governess to a little Girl twelve years old—she likes her Situation—but I miss her very much indeed—I have not heard from my Brother since last Autumn—I had a letter from my Son—in January—he is still in Australia[13]—I must stop ere I weary your patience hoping to hear from you

Yours Tr

Harriet

[upside down across top of first page] that Book wait until I see you

ALS; IAPFP #86; BAP 16:0704–07.

1 The American Anti-Slavery Society had held its annual Convention in New York City in May 1856. *Letters of William Lloyd Garrison*, III, 336.

2 The 1857 Convention was held in New York City on May 11. Ibid., 477–480.

3 Bailey Willis was born on May 31, 1857. Henry A. Beers, *Nathaniel Parker Willis*, American Men of Letters Series (Boston and New York: Houghton Mifflin, 1885).

4 *The Little Pilgrim* (Philadelphia, 1853–1875).

5 Mary Post Hallowell (1823–1913) and William R. Hallowell (1816–1882); like Amy Post, her aunt and stepmother, Mary Hallowell was an active feminist. IAPFP; Hewitt, *Women's Activism*.

6 Amy Post's sister Sarah Kirby Hallowell had married Edmund P. Willis (?–1882) in 1853. IAPFP.

7 The American Anti-Slavery Society had held a convention in Rochester in February 1857. *The Liberator*, Feb. 27, 1857, p. 34; March 6, 1857, p. 38.

8 This may refer to Nell's letter from Boston, 16 Feb. 1857, "Equal School Rights for Colored Children," which appeared in *The Liberator*, Feb. 20, 1857, p. 31. His attack on the Dred Scott decision did not appear in *The Liberator* until May 8, 1857, p. 76.

9 "Behold, the Lord's hand is not shortened, that it cannot save; neither his ear heavy, that it cannot hear." Isaiah 59:1.

10 "So God created man in his own image, in the image of God created he him; male and female created he them." Genesis 1:27. For the idea that the races were of separate origin, see William Stanton, *The Leopard's Spots: Scientific Attitudes toward Race in America*, 1815–1839 (Chicago: University of Chicago Press, 1960).

11 In the Dred Scott decision of March 6, 1857, Chief Justice Roger B. Taney wrote the opinion of the United States Supreme Court ruling that Scott, a slave, was not a citizen and could not bring suit in the courts; and, declaring the Missouri Compromise unconstitutional, that masters could take their slaves anywhere in the territories and retain title in them. Franklin, *From Slavery to Freedom*, pp. 163–164.

12 Louisa Matilda Jacobs.

13 In a letter to Amy Post dated July 21, 1853, Nell wrote that Jacobs's brother and son had left California to mine in Australia. IAPFP.

10. Harriet Jacobs to Amy Post

June 21st [1857]
My Dear Friend

A heart full of thanks for your kind and welcome—letter which would have been answered immediately—but for want of time to think a moment. I would dearly love to talk with you as it would be more satisfactory—but as I cannot I will try to explain myself on paper as well as I can—

I have My dear friend—Striven faithfully to give a true and just account of my own life in Slavery—God knows I have tried to do it in a Christian spirit—there are somethings that I might have made plainer I know—Woman can whisper—her cruel wrongs into the ear of a very dear friend—much easier than she can record them for the world to read—I have left nothing out but what I thought—the world might believe that a Slave Woman was too willing to pour out—that she might gain their sympathies I ask nothing—I have placed myself before you to be judged as a woman whether I deserve your pity or contempt—I have another object in view—it is to come to you just as I am a poor Slave Mother—not to tell you what I have heard but what I have seen—and what I have suffered—and if their is any sympathy to give—let it be given to the thousands—of of Slave Mothers that are still in bondage—suffering far more than I have—let it plead for their helpless Children that they may enjoy the same liberties that my Children now enjoy—Say anything of me that you have had from a truthful source that you think best—ask me any question you like—in regard to the father of my Children I think I have stated all perhaps I did not tell you that he was a member of Congress at that time all of this I have written—I think it would be best for you to begin with our acquaintance and the length of time that I was in your family your advice about giving the history of my life in Slavery mention that I lived at service all the while that I was striving to get the Book out but do not say with whom I lived as I would not use the Willis name neither would I like to have people think that I was living an Idle life—and had got this book out merely to make money—my kind friend I do not restrict you in anything for you know far better than I do what to say I am only too happy to think that I am going to have it from you[1]—

I hope you will be able to read my unconnected scrawl—I have been interrupted and called away so often—that I hardly know what I have written—but I must send it for fear the opportunity will not come tomorrow—to do better—Proffessor Botta and Lady[2] with Ole Bull eldest son[3] is here—on a visit from the City—beside three other persons that we have had in to spend the day—and Baby[4] is just 4 weeks old this morning—housekeeping and looking after the Children occupy every moment of my time we have in all five Children—three Girls—and two boys. Imogen is at home for the Summer Louisa came up and spent a week—with me she desired much love to you—she is not well but looking miserably thin—

I have been thinking that I would so like to go away and sell my Book—I could then secure a copywright—to sell it both here and in England—and by identifying myself with—it I might do something for the Antislavery Cause—to do this I would have to get letters of introduction—from some of the leading Abolitionists of this Country to those of the Old—when you write tell me what you think of it[5] I must stop for I am in the only spot where I can have a light—and the mosquitoes have taken possession of me—much love to all my friends—and Willie—and believe me ever yours

Harriet

ALS; IAPFP #90; BAP 16:0676–78 (incomplete).

1 The final result was Post's testimonial, which appears in the Appendix dated 1859.

2 Vincenzo Botta (1818–?), later a professor of Italian at the University of the City of New York, had in 1855 married Anne Charlotte Lynch (1815–1891), a literary hostess and occasional contributor to Willis's *Home Journal. Notable American Women 1607–1950: A Biographical Dictionary,* ed. Edward T. James, et al., 3 vols. (Cambridge: Harvard University Press, 1971), I, 212–214. Beers, *Willis,* p. 193.

3 Ole Bull (1810–1880), a Norwegian violinist who toured the United States repeatedly, founded Oleana Colony for Norwegian immigrants. *Lydia Maria Child: Selected Letters, 1817–1880,* ed. Milton Meltzer and Patricia G. Holland (Amherst: University of Massachusetts Press, 1982), p. 213.

4 Bailey Willis.

5 For Jacobs's effort, see the letter she wrote while in England to

Ann Warren Weston, June 28 [1858?], Weston Papers, BPL; BAP 16:0717, 13:0605–06.

11. Lydia Maria Child to Harriet Jacobs

Wayland [Massachusetts], Aug. 13th 1860
Dear Mrs. Jacobs,

I have been busy with your M. S. ever since I saw you; and have only done one third of it. I have very little occasion to alter the language, which is wonderfully good, for one whose opportunities for education have been so limited. The events are interesting, and well told; the remarks are also good, and to the purpose. But I am copying a great deal of it, for the purpose of transposing sentences and pages, so as to bring the story into continuous *order,* and the remarks into *appropriate* places. I think you will see that this renders the story much more clear and entertaining.

I should not take so much pains, if I did not consider the book unusually interesting, and likely to do much service to the Anti-Slavery cause. So you need not feel under great personal obligations. You know I would go through fire and water to help give a blow to Slavery. I suppose you will want to see the M. S. after I have exercised my bump of mental order upon it; and I will send it wherever you direct, a fortnight hence.

My object in writing at this time is to ask you to write what you can recollect of the outrages committed on the colored people, in Nat Turner's time.[1] You say the reader would not believe what you saw "inflicted on men, women, and children, without the slightest ground of suspicion against them." What *were* those inflictions? Were any tortured to make them confess? And how? Where any killed? Please write down some of the most striking particulars, and let me have them to insert.

I think the last Chapter, about John Brown,[2] had better be omitted. It does not naturally come into your story, and the M. S. is already too long. Nothing can be so appropriate to end with, as the death of your grandmother.

Mr. Child[3] desires to be respectfully remembered to you.

Very cordially your friend,

L. Maria Child

ALS; IAPFP #1330; LMCP 46:1243.

1 See Chapter XII.

2 At the United States Arsenal at Harpers Ferry, Virginia, in October 1859, John Brown (1800–1859), had led an attack which he envisioned as the first blow in a struggle that would end chattel slavery; he was hanged on December 2, 1859. Child's letters to Brown were published in the *Correspondence between Lydia Maria Child and Gov. Wise and Mrs. Mason, of Virginia* (Boston, 1860), one of the best-selling pamphlets the abolitionists issued.

3 David Lee Child (1794–1874), abolitionist, teacher, politician, writer, and editor, assisted his wife in editing the *Standard* between 1843 and 1844.

12. Lydia Maria Child to Harriet Jacobs

Wayland [Massachusetts], Sep 27th, 1860

Dear Mrs. Jacobs,

I have signed and sealed the contract with Thayer & Eldridge, in my name, and told them to take out the copyright in my name. Under the circumstances *your* name could not be used, you know. I inquired of other booksellers, and could find none that were willing to undertake it, except Thayer & Eldridge.[1] I have never heard a word to the disparagement of either of them, and I do not think you could do better than to let them have it. They *ought* to have the monopoly of it for some time, if they *stereotype* it, because that process involves considerable expense, and if you changed publishers, their plates would be worth nothing to them.[2] When I spoke of limiting them to an edition of 2000, I did not suppose they intended to stereotype it. They have agreed to pay you ten per cent on the retail price of all sold, and to let you have as many as you want, at the lowest wholesale price. On your part, I have agreed that they may publish it for five years on those terms, and that you will not print any abridgement, or altered copy, meanwhile.

I have no reason whatever to think that Thayer & Eldridge are likely to fail. I merely made the suggestion because they were *beginners*. However, several of the *oldest* bookselling firms have failed within the last three years; mine among the rest. We must run for luck in these matters.

I have promised to correct the proof-sheets, and I don't think it would be of any use to the book to have you here at this time. They say they shall get it out by the 1'st of Nov. You had better let me know beforehand if you want to come to Wayland; because when I leave home, I generally stay over night, and in that case you would lose your time and your money. I saw your daughter a few minutes, and found her very prepossessing.

Write to me whenever you want to; and when I have time, I will answer.

I want you to sign the following paper, and send it back to me. It will make Thayer & Eldridge safe about the contract in *my* name, and in case of my death, will prove that the book is *your* property, not *mine*.

Cordially your friend,
L. Maria Child

ALS; IAPFP #1338; LMCP 46:1255.

1 Publishers Thayer and Eldridge were listed in the *Boston City Directory* for 1860, p. 468. They evidently went bankrupt, and were not listed the following year.

2 Stereotyping is a printing process whereby a plate is molded of the printing surface; this is then cast in type metal.

13. Harriet Jacobs to Amy Post

Oct 8th [1860]

My dear Friend—

I might begin this letter with a long preface—filled with apologies for my long silence—but for the present I shall dispense with it all—by simply telling you the truth—in the first place I am truly ashamed of it—and but too glad to write you again—when I returned home from Europe I said that I would not mention my M. S to my friends again until I had done something with it—little dreaming of the time that might elapse—but as time wore on difficulties seemed to thicken —and I became discouraged. I felt that I had cut myself of from my friends and I had no right to ask their Sympathy—my numerous undertakings must be left until we meet—my M. S. was read at Phillips and Sampson[1] they agreed to take it if I could get Mrs Stowe or Mr Willis[2] to write a preface for it—the former I had the second clinch from & the latter I would not ask—and before anything was done this Establishment failed. so I gave up the effort until this Autumn I sent it to Thayer and Eldridge of Boston—they were willing to publish it if I could obtain a Preface from Mrs. Child. they had no objection to the one I had—but that it must be by some one known to the public—to effect the sale of the Book. I had never seen Mrs. Child past experience made me tremble at the thought of approaching another Sattellite of so great magnitude. for I have learned that the courage of old age is not equal to youths but I tried to fan the flickering spark that was left and resolved to make my last effort through W C Nells[3] ready kindness I meet Mrs Child—at the A.-S. [Anti-Slavery] Office Mrs C is like your self a whole souled Woman—we soon found the way to each others heart—I will send you some of her letters which which will better describe her than my poor pen—I gave her my MS. to read your introduction. I told her of the feeling that had existed between us—that your advice and word of encouragement—had been my strongest promter in writting the Book she recognized Mrs Post and kept the introduction to have published in the standard with a criticism of the Book[4] I wanted to have it brought in as a letter but Mrs Child said it would do more good in the Standard and it will be in the Liberator.[5] a letter that I had for the Book written by a friend from home to substantiate facts, Mrs C will send to the Anglo Affrican.[6] Mr. Wendel Phillips[7] has agreed to take one thousand coppies. I take four hundred at the wholesale price to dispose of myself—the Book will be out 1st November I have ten percent. I hope my dear Friend that you will like my arrangments it was the only alternative I long to see you I went to the City with the hope of meeting you the first Convention after my return home and was so disappointed—I must beg a line of you although I know that I do not deserve it tell me about yourself and family lots of love to all my friends I shall try very hard to get to Rochester this winter and I have a hope of seeing my Brother this winter—Louisa is still in Boston I am going to the city this week to see how much Antislavery I can find there I will write you again after my return remember me most kindly to my dear old friend Mr Post and believe me the same always

HJ

[Upside down in margin of page one] Will you please send me G W Clarks address

ALS; IAPFP #1259; BAP 16:086–88.

   1 The Boston *City Directory* for 1859 lists (Moses D.) Phillips and (George R.) Sampson & Co., c/o S. C. Perkins, at A. K. Loring, booksellers, 13 Winter. The firm is not listed for 1860.

   2 Nathaniel Parker Willis.

   3 On June 13, 1854, W. C. Nell had written to Amy Post, "This reminds me of Harriet Jacobs' narrative which I have urged her putting to press, pledging any service in my power for its promotion." IAPFP.

   4 See "New Publications," *National Anti-Slavery Standard*, Feb. 23, 1861.

   5 For the treatment of *Incidents* in *The Liberator*, see "Linda, the Slave Girl," Jan. 25, 1861.

6 For the treatment of *Incidents* in the *Weekly Anglo-African* (New York), see "Linda," April 13, 1861.

7 Wendell Phillips was a member of the abolitionists' Hovey Committee.

14. Harriet Jacobs to Amy Post and Isaac Post

New York June 18th [1861]
My Dear Friends

I have just recieved a letter from my Brother[1] and one enclosed to his friend Mr Post. as it was not under cover I read it myself I then read mine which was only a few scolding lines—because I had not sent my Book to different people in England. in the first place it cost too much to send them while in debt, and in the next I did not care to give it a circulation then before I tried to turn it to some account so I have taken it very patiently—but I dont give up as I used to,[2]—the trouble is I begin to find out we poor Women has always been too meek,—when I hear a Man call a woman an Angel when she is out of sight—I begin to think about poor Leah of the Bible, not Leah of the spirits[3] I told our spirit friend it was better to be born lucky than rich—

but to my letter I read mine and a part of yours to Oliver Johnson[4] he wanted me to take some notes from it. with your permission, may I give them for the Liberator and the Standard,[5] what my Brother says about me is true, in his letter—I am going to Statten Island tomorrow for the first time, I shall register my Brother letter there is fifteen pounds enclosed in it—I meant to write you a long letter but they are waiting for me I am so tired. I long to see you. kindest rememberance to my friends

with much love
Harriet

ALS; IAPFP #1261; BAP 16:0694–0695.

1 John S. Jacobs had married an Englishwoman and was living primarily in London, where he was active in abolitionist circles and had published his slave narrative in the *Leisure Hour* in February 1861. He returned to the United States after the Civil War.

2 The London firm of William Tweedie published Jacobs's book on April 1, 1862, as *The Deeper Wrong; Or, Incidents in the Life of a Slave Girl.* It was advertised in the *Athenaeum* April 12, 1862, and received favorable notice in the *Londonderry Standard, Newcastle Daily Chronicle, Western Morning News, Caledonian Mercury, Morning Star,* and *Daily News,* according to an ad at the end of Harper Twelvetrees, *The Story of the Life of John Anderson, the Fugitive Slave* (London: Tweedie, 1863). I am grateful to Phil Lapsansky for calling my attention to this ad.

3 The biblical Leah was the unloved first wife of the patriarch Jacob. The Posts, who were Spiritualists, apparently were involved in seances with a Leah. As part of their circle, Jacobs had evidently experimented with Spiritualism. Nancy Hewitt, "Amy Kirby Post," *University of Rochester Library Bulletin* 37 (1984): 13.

4 Reformer Oliver Johnson (1809–1889) frequently served as substitute editor of *The Liberator* during Garrison's absences.

5 John S. Jacobs's letter to Isaac Post from London, June 5, 1861, appeared in the *National Anti-Slavery Standard,* June 29, 1861; BAP 15:0309.

15. Harriet Jacobs to Ednah Dow Cheney[1]

Edenton [North Carolina] April 25th [1867]

Dear Mrs Cheney

I felt I would like to write you a line from my old home. I am sitting under the old roof twelve feet from the spot where I suffered all the crushing weight of slavery. thank God the bitter cup is drained of its last dreg.[2] there is no more need of hiding places to conceal slave Mothers. yet it was little to purchase the blessings of freedom. I could have worn this poor life out there to save my Children from the misery and degradation of Slavery.

I had long thought I had no attachment to my old home. as I often sit here and think of those I loved of their hard struggle in life—their unfaltering love and devotion toward myself and Children. I love to sit here and think of them. they have made the few sunny spots in that dark sacred to me.

I cannot tell you how I feel in this place. the change is so great I can hardly take it all in I was born here, and amid all these new born blessings, the old dark cloud comes over me, and I find it hard to have faith in rebels. the past winter was very severe for this region of Country it caused much suffering, and the freedmen with but few exceptions were cheated out of their crop of cotton. their contract masters shiped it for them, and when they ask for a settlement, they are answered I am daily expecting the returns. these men have gone to work cheerfully, planted another crop without the returns to live on until their present crop is made. many of the large plantations of the once wealthy Planter, is worked under the control of Colored Men. the Owners let their Plantations to the freedmen in prefference to the poor Whites. they believe the Negro determined to make money, and they will get the largest portion of it. last years experience I think will be a profitable lesson many will learn to act for themselves. Negro suffrage is making a stir in this place. the rebels are striving to make these people feel they are their true friends, and they must not be led astray by the Yankees. the freedmen ask if Abraham Lincoln led them astray, that his friends is their friends his enemies their enemies.

I have spent much of my time on the Plantations distributing seed and trying to teach the women to make Yankee gardens.[3] they plant everything to mature in the summer, like their corn and cotton fields. I have hunted up all the old people, done what I could for them. I love to work for these old people. many of them I have known from Childhood

there is one School in Edenton well attended.[4] on some of the

Plantations there is from 15 to 25 Children that cannot attend School, the distance is so far. some of the freedmen are very anxious to establish Plantation schools, as soon as the more advanced Schools, can send out teachers. many of the freedmen are willing and will sustain their teachers. at present there is a great revival in the colored Churches. the Whites say the Niggers sung and prayed until they got their freedom, and they are not satisfied. now they are singing and praying for judgment. the white members of the Baptist Church invited the colored members to their Church, to help them sing and pray. I assure you they have done it with a will. I never saw such a state of excitement the Churches have been open night and day. these people have time to think of their souls, now they are not compelled to think for the Negro.

my love to Miss Daisy.⁵ I send her some Jassmine blossoms tell her they bear the fragrance of freedom.

Yours Truly
H Jacobs

ALS; Sophia Smith Collection.

1 Ednah Dow Littlehale Cheney (1824–1904), Boston philanthropist, writer, and abolitionist, served as secretary of the New England Freedmen's Aid Society from 1867 until 1875. She evidently became acquainted with Jacobs in connection with Jacobs's relief work in Alexandria and Savannah. *Notable American Women.*

2 "Awake, awake, stand up, O Jerusalem, which hast drunk at the hand of the Lord, the cup of his fury; thou has drunken the dregs of the cup of trembling, and wrung them out." Isaiah 51:17.

3 Jacobs made a practice of this. Child noted, "I found eleven letters awaiting me ... One of them was from Mrs. Jacobs, asking for garden seeds for some freedmen in Georgia, where she is at present." Child to [Lucy Osgood], April 1, 1866, LMCP 64:1715.

4 On October 23, 1866, it was "ordered that the freedmen of the Town

of Edenton be allowed to build a Schoolhouse in the Town Commons east of Oakum Street." In 1868, "The Sewing Society of colored persons" was granted use of the Town Hall for a fair to raise money to pay for the schoolhouse lot. Edenton, N.C., Town Minutes, 1865–1887, Oct. 13, 1866, p. 19; July 2, 1868, p. 32, NCSA.

    5 Cheney's daughter Margaret Swan Cheney (b. 1855).

Edenton, April 25th

Dear Mrs Cheney.

I felt I would like to write you a line from my old home. I am sitting under the old roof. twelve feet from the spot where I suffered all the crushing weight of Slavery. Thank God the bitter cup is drained of its last dreg. There is no more need of hiding places to conceal slave Mothers. yet it was little to purchase the blessings of freedom. I could have made this poor life out there to save my Children from the misery and degradation of Slavery.

I had long thought I had no attachment to my old home. As I often sit here and think of those I loved. of their hard struggle in life — Their unfaltering love and devotion toward myself

First page of Harriet Jacobs's letter to Ednah Dow Cheney, April 25 [1867] (Letter 15).

Notes

Introduction

1 Jacobs to Post, June 21 [1857], IAPFP #90, BAP 16:0676, 0677 (see Correspondence, Letter 10; hereafter, letter numbers in parentheses refer to the Correspondence section in this volume). This is one of thirty letters from Jacobs to Post in the Isaac and Amy Post Family Papers (IAPFP) in the Department of Rare Books and Special Collections, Rush Rhees Library, University of Rochester. All of the letters cited from Jacobs to Post, from Lydia Maria Child to Jacobs, and from William C. Nell to Post are in this collection and are reprinted by permission.

2 See illustration, page lxi. An English edition appeared the following year: *The Deeper Wrong; Or, Incidents in the Life of a Stave Girl. Written by Herself,* ed. L. Maria Child (London: W. Tweedie, 1862). Excerpts were included in Harriet Jacobs, "The Good Grandmother," *The Freedmen's Book,* ed. L. Maria Child (Boston: Ticknor and Fields, 1867), 206–218.

3 See Stephen T. Butterfield, "The Use of Language in the Slave Narratives," *Black American Literature Forum* (Fall 1972): 72–78; Lee R.

Edwards, *Psyche as Hero: Female Heroism and Fictional Form* (Middletown, Conn.: Wesleyan University Press, 1984).

4 Jacobs to Post, Oct. 9 [1853], IAPFP #85, BAP 16:0713–14 (Letter 7).

5 For the discovery of Jacobs's letters, see Jean Fagan Yellin, *"Written by Herself:* Harriet Jacobs's Slave Narrative," *American Literature* 53 (Nov. 1981): 479–486. Biographical information and identifications of people, places, and events mentioned in Jacobs's text appear in the notes to that text. For the contexts of Jacobs's experiences, see for example John Hope Franklin, *From Slavery to Freedom: A History of American Negroes* (New York: Knopf, 1967), and *The Free Negro in North Carolina, 1790–1860* (Chapel Hill: University of North Carolina Press, 1943); and Herbert G. Gutman, *The Black Family in Slavery and Freedom, 1750–1925* (New York: Random House, 1976).

6 Willis's records corroborate Jacobs's narrative. He refers to Jacobs directly—although not by name—in a *House and Home* column reprinted in *Outdoors at Idlewild* (New York, 1855), 275–276. Jacobs is named in Henry C. Beers, *Nathaniel Parker Willis,* American Men of Letters Series (Boston and New York: Houghton Mifflin, 1885), 284–286.

7 *Liberator,* Oct. 31, Dec. 12, 1845.

8 "Crowded Meeting of the Colored Population of Boston," *Liberator,* July 24, 1846; "Jonathan Walker and John S. Jacobs," *The North Star,* March 31, 1848; John S. Jacobs to Sydney Howard Gay, June 4, 1846 (Letter 2).

9 Jonathan Walker to Esteemed Friend, *Liberator,* May 26, 1848; "Jonathan Walker and John S. Jacobs," *Liberator,* March 31, 1848; *Liberator,* Aug. 18, 1848.

10 "Editorial Correspondence," *North Star,* March 9, 1849.

11 Literature available in the Antislavery Reading Room was advertised over John S. Jacobs's name in the *North Star* (Rochester, 1847–1863) from March 23 to July 27, 1849; see BAP os: 1067. "The Bazaar," *North Star,* Sept. 1, 1848.

12 Jacobs to Post, [1852?], IAPFP #84, BAP 16:0700–02 (Letter 4).

13 Jacobs to Post, June 21 [1857], IAPFP #90, BAP #676–78 (Letter 10).

14 Jacobs never saw her son again. Years later she sent $400 in response to a letter from Australia requesting money for his passage home, but this appeal was apparently fraudulent. Lydia Maria Child to John Fraser, Nov. 20, 1866, LMCP 66:1746.

15 Jacobs to Post, Feb. 14 [1853], IAPFP #785, BAP 16:0710–11 (Letter 5).

16 Jacobs to Post, Jan. 11 [1854?], IAPFP #786, BAP 16:0674–675.

17 Harriet Beecher Stowe (1811–1896) had serialized *Uncle Tom's Cabin*

NOTES TO PAGES xxvii-xxx

in the *National Era* (Washington, D.C.), June 3, 1851–April 2, 1852; it was published in book form in Boston in 1852. See Forrest Wilson, *Crusader in Crinoline: The Life of Harriet Beecher Stowe* (1941; rpt. Westport, Conn.: Greenwood, 1972). For William C. Nell (1816–1874), Douglass's assistant on the *North Star* and author of *Colored Patriots of the American Revolution* (1855), see Robert W. Smith, "William C. Nell: Crusading Black Abolitionist," *Journal of Negro History* 55 (1970): 182–197.

18 Jacobs to Post, [1852?], IAPFP #84, BAP 16:0700–02 (Letter 4); and March [1854], IAPFP #783, BAP 16:0679–80 (Letter 8); W. C. Nell to Post, June 13–July 21, 1854, IAPFP #1028, BAP 08:0870.

19 [Olive Gilbert], *Narrative of Sojourner Truth, a Northern Slave . . .* (Boston, 1850). This discussion of Jacobs and Stowe is based on five letters from Jacobs to Post: [1852?], IAPFP #84, BAP 16:0700–02 (Letter 4); Feb. 14 [1853], IAPFP #785, BAP 16:0710–11 (Letter 5); April 4 [1853], IAPFP #788, BAP 16:0681–83 (Letter 6); [Spring 1853?], IAPFP #80, BAP 16:0707–08; July 31 [1854?], IAPFP #88, BAP 16:0667. The quotation is from the letter of Feb. 14, 1853 (Letter 5). I have not been able to locate any letters to Stowe from Post, Cornelia Willis, or Jacobs; or any letters from Stowe to Cornelia Willis. But see W. C. Nell to Post, June 13–July 21, 1854, IAPFP #1028, BAP 08:0870. Stowe later wrote introductions for several books by Afro-Americans, including Nell's history *Colored Patriots* (1855); Frank J. Webb's novel *The Garies and Their Friends* (1857); and Josiah Henson's narrative *Truth Stranger than Fiction* (Boston: John P. Jewett and Co., 1858).

20 Jacobs to Post, [Spring 1853?], IAPFP #80, BAP 16:0707.

21 Jacobs's determination suggests that of Willis's sister Sara Payson Willis Parton (1811–1872), who despite her brother's discouragement, launched a literary career as "Fanny Fern," and whose roman à clef *Ruth Hall* (1855), which dramatized her efforts to establish a home for her children by writing, in many ways parallels *Incidents.*

22 New York *Tribune*, June 21, 1853.

23 Jacobs to Post, June 25 [1853?], IAPFP #1257, BAP 16:0696–97.

24 Another of Jacobs's letters appeared in the *Tribune*, July 25, 1853. I have not located the third. Jacobs to Post, Oct. 9 [1853], IAPFP #85, BAP 16:0713–14 (Letter 7). Also see Jacobs to Post, June 25 [1853?], IAPFP #1257, BAP 16:0696–97.

25 Jacobs to Post, Dec. 21, IAPFP #82, BAP 16:0703–04.

26 Jacobs to Post, Jan. 11, [1854?], IAPFP #786, BAP 16:0674–75.

27 See H. Bruce Franklin on his students' credulity, in *The Victim as*

Criminal and Artist (New York: Oxford University Press, 1978), p. 27. Jacobs to Post, Aug. 7, IAPFP #81, BAP 16:0708–09; George Willets to Isaac and Amy Post, Aug. 18 [185?], IAPFP·#816.

28 Jacobs to Post, June 21 [1857], IAPFP #90, BAP 16:0676–78 (Letter 10). Valerie Smith discusses Jacobs's silences in *Narrative Authority in Modern Afro-American Fiction* (Cambridge, Mass.: Harvard University Press, 1987). Nothing in Jacobs's book is as stylized as her comment to Post: "just now the poor Book is in its Chrysalis state and though I can never make it a butterfly I am satisfied to have it creep meekly among some of the humbler bugs." Jacobs to Post, March [1854], IAPFP #783, BAP 16:0679–80 (Letter 8).

29 Jacobs to Post, Oct. 8 [1860], IAPFP #1259, BAP 16:086–88 (Letter 13).

30 Jacobs to Ann Warren Weston, June 18 [1858 or 1859?], Boston Public Library MS. A9.2.614; BAP 16:0717; 13:0605–06.

31 Jacobs to Post, Oct. 8 [1860], IAPFP #1259, BAP 16:086–88 (Letter 13).

32 Jacobs to Post, [Sept. or Oct.? 1860], IAPFP #1307, BAP 12:0339; Child to Jacobs, Aug. 13, 1860, IAPFP #1330, LMCP 46:1243 (Letter 11); Child to Jacobs, Sept. 27, 1860, IAPFP #1338, LMCP 46:1255 (a detailed explanation of the publisher's contract; Letter 12).

33 Child to Lucy [Searle], Feb. 4, 1861, Cornell University Libraries, Anti-Slavery Collection, LMCP 47:1282. Anonymous review of *Incidents* in the *Anti-Slavery Advocate* (London) 2, no. 53 (May 1, 1861). I am grateful to Henry Louis Gates, Jr., for bringing this review to my attention; it appears in Charles T. Davis and Henry Louis Gates, Jr., eds., *The Slave's Narrative* (New York: Oxford University Press, 1985). The editing of the narratives is discussed in John W. Blassingame, "Using the Testimony of Ex-Slaves: Approaches and Problems," *Journal of Southern History* 60 (Nov. 1975): 473–492; also see William L. Andrews, "The First Fifty Years of the Slave Narrative, 1760–1810," in *The Art of Slave Narrative*, ed. John Sekora and Darwin T. Turner (Macomb: Western Illinois University, 1982), pp. 6–24.

34 Jacobs to Post, Oct. 8 [1860], IAPFP #1259, BAP 16:086–88 (Letter 13). For the importance of the authenticating documents, see Robert B. Stepto, "Narration, Authentication, and Authorial Control in Frederick Douglass's *Narrative* of 1845," in Dexter Fisher and Robert B. Stepto, eds., *Afro-American Literature: The Reconstruction of Instruction* (New York: Modern Language Association of America, 1979), pp. 178–191.

35 Jacobs to Post, Nov. 8, 1860, IAPFP #1354, BAP 13:0879–80. This discussion of the publication of *Incidents* is based on a letter from Child to Jacobs, Sept. 27, 1860, IAPFP #1338, LMCP 46:1255 (Correspondence, Letter

12); and on the following items in the Wendell Phillips Collection, Houghton Library, Harvard University: Child to Wendell Phillips, Dec. 2 and Dec. 6, 1860, LMCP 96:2549, 96:2550; and a receipt from the Hovey Fund signed by Harriet Jacobs, Feb. 1, 1861. For the Hovey Committee, see *Annual Report of the American Anti-Slavery Society for the Year Ending May 1, 1859* (New York, 1860), p. 141.

36 Child to John Greenleaf Whittier, April 4, 1861, Child Papers, Manuscript Division, Library of Congress, LMCP 48:1300. Wendell Phillips (1811–1884), lecturer and reformer, was a champion of Garrisonian abolitionism.

37 This discussion of the marketing of *Incidents* is based on the following items: Jacobs to Rebecca Darby Smith, Jan. 14 [1861], Library Company of Philadelphia; Jacobs's inscription to Smith in a copy of *Incidents,* Library Company of Philadelphia; William C. Nell, "Linda" (advertisement), *The Liberator,* Feb. 8, 1861, ff.; *Anti-Slavery Bugle,* Feb. 9, 1861; *National Anti-Slavery Standard,* Feb. 23, 1861; *Weekly Anglo-African,* April 13, 1861; Child to Henrietta Sargent, Feb. 9, 1861, Child Papers, Anti-Slavery Collection, Cornell University, LMCP 47: 1285; Child to Daniel Ricketson, March 14, 1862, from *Daniel Ricketson: Autobiographic and Miscellaneous,* ed. Anna Ricketson (New Bedford: E. Anthony and Sons, 1910), pp. 137–139, LMCP 47:1295; and Child to John Greenleaf Whittier, March 14, 1861, LMCP 47:1296. The quoted passage is from W. C. Nell, "Linda, the Slave Girl," *The Liberator,* Jan. 25, 1861.

38 The receipt for the Hovey Fund's purchase of *Incidents* is in the Wendell Phillips Collection, Houghton Library, Harvard University (see Illustrations). "Confessions from Boston by an Ordinary Man," *National Anti-Slavery Standard,* Feb. 16, 1861.

39 In 1868 Jacobs and her daughter went to England to raise money for an orphanage and home for the aged in Savannah. Although they succeeded in raising £1,000, they advised that the building not be built because of the "unsettled state of affairs at the South." Jacobs and Louisa established their home in Cambridge, Massachusetts, and then in 1877 moved to Washington, D.C. In 1892 Jacobs sold her grandmother's house and lot in Edenton. She was sick and bedridden when, four years later, Louisa participated in the organizing meetings of the National Association of Colored Women in Washington. Jacobs died on March 7, 1897, and was buried in Mt. Auburn Cemetery in Cambridge, Massachusetts. *The Liberator,* Sept. 5, 1862, and April 10, 1863; *National Anti-Slavery Standard,* April 18, 1863, BAP 15:0310,

and April 16, 1864, BAP 15:0309; Jacobs to Rev. Sella Martin, April 13, [1863], in *Freedman's Aid Society* (London), press copy, Rhodes House, MSS British Empire G88, BAP 14:0799; *Freed-man's Record* (Boston) Feb. 1865, March 1865, Sept. 1865, Dec. 1865, and Jan. 1866. *The Freedman* (New York), April 1865; *The Independent* (New York), April 5, 1866, LMCP 64:1716; *Anti-Slavery Reporter* (London), March 2, 1868; New York Yearly Meeting of Friends, Meeting for Sufferings, *Eighth Report* (1869), p. 4; Cambridge Directory for 1870, p. 182; Diary of Julia A. Wilbur, Nov. 1, 1877; Chowan County Deed Book C-3, p. 189, Office of the Register of Deeds, Chowan County Courthouse, Edenton, N.C.; "Mrs. Jacobs," Francis J. Grimké Papers, Moorland-Spingarn Research Center, Howard University; Death Certificate, District of Columbia.

40 Examining *Incidents* in a discussion of "fictional accounts . . . [in which] the major character may have been a real fugitive, but the narrative of his life is probably false," John Blassingame, in *The Slave Community* (New York: Oxford University Press, 1972), pp. 233–234, judged that "the work is not credible." Others confused *Incidents* with *The Autobiography of a Female Slave* (1857), an antislavery novel by a white southerner, Mattie Griffiths. Jacobs's authorship was authenticated in Yellin, "*Written by Herself*: Harriet Jacobs's Slave Narrative." For a history of the dispute over the authenticity of Jacobs's work, see Jean Fagan Yellin, "Text and Contexts of Harriet Jacobs's *Incidents in the Life of a Slave Girl: Written by Herself* in Davis and Gates, *The Slave's Narrative*, p. 278, n. 2.

41 *Weekly Anglo-African* (New York), April 13, 1861; this review may have been written by George W. Lowther. See Jacobs to Post, Oct. 8 [1860], IAPFP #1259, BAP 16:086–88 (Letter 13).

42 The classic captivity narrative is *A True History of the Captivity and Restoration of Mrs. Mary Rowlandson* (1682); see Annette Kolodny, *The Land Before Her: Fantasy and Experience of the American Frontiers, 1630–1860* (Chapel Hill: University of North Carolina Press, 1984), p. 20.

43 For authorial control of the narratives, see Robert Stepto, *From Behind the Veil: A Study of Afro-American Narrative* (Urbana: University of Illinois Press, 1979).

44 A standard critical comment is that the transformation of the slave narrator from object to subject and his subsequent reversal of the angle of vision of the dominant culture make the revolutionary perspective of the narratives inevitable; see Jean Fagan Yellin, *Intricate Knot* (New York: New York University Press, 1972). The discussion of the narratives here is

informed by Frances Smith Foster, *Witnessing Slavery: The Development of Ante-bellum Slave Narratives* (Westport, Conn.: Greenwood Press, 1979); and by Sekora and Turner, *The Art of Slave Narrative*, and Davis and Gates, *The Slave's Narrative*; all of these contain useful bibliographies.

45 Stepto, *From Behind the Veil*, p. [ix]; also see Henry Louis Gates, Jr., "Preface to Blackness: Text and Pretext," in Fisher and Stepto, *Afro-American Literature*, pp. 44–70.

46 For a discussion of gender-based differences among the narratives, see Frances Foster, "'In Respect to Females': Differences in the Portrayals of Women by Male and Female Narrators," *Black American Literature Forum* 15 (Summer 1981): 66–70.

47 Charles Nichols, "The Slave Narrators and the Picaresque Mode: Archetypes for Modern Black Personae," in Davis and Gates, *The Slave's Narrative*, p. 283. Also see Raymond Hedin, "The American Slave Narrative: The Justification of the Picaro," *American Literature* 53 (Jan. 1982):630–645. In his fiction, Faulkner created and peopled the county of Yoknapatawpha; Theodore Rosengarten published Nate Shaw's oral history as *All God's Dangers* (New York: Knopf, 1974).

48 For attestations of Jacobs's accuracy, see my notes to her text. For the problems involved in analyzing the reliability of the slave narratives, see John Blassingame's "Introduction," in Blassingame, ed., *Slave Testimony: Two Centuries of Letters, Speeches, Interviews and Autobiographies* (Baton Rouge: Louisiana State University Press, 1977), pp. xvii–lxv.

49 Harriet E. Wilson, *Our Nig: or, Sketches from the Life of a Free Black*, ed. Henry Louis Gates, Jr. (New York: Random House, 1983). The literary tradition of Afro-American women is currently producing an exciting body of criticism. See, for example, Mary Helen Washington, "These Self-Invented Women: A Theoretical Framework for a Literary History of Black Women," *Radical Teacher* 17 (1980):3–7; Deborah E. McDowell, "New Directions for Black Feminist Criticism," *Black American Literature Forum* 14 (Winter 1980):153–159; Calvin Hernton, "The Sexual Mountain and Black Women Writers," *Black American Literature Forum* 18 (1984):139–145; Barbara Christian, *Black Women Novelists* (Westport, Conn.: Greenwood Press, 1980), and *Black Feminist Criticism* (New York: Pergamon Press, 1985).

50 Frances Ellen Watkins Harper, "Note," *Iola Leroy; Or, Shadows Uplifted* (1892; New York: AMS Press, 1971), p. 282.

51 Jacobs to Post, quoted by Post in the Appendix. The significance of Jacobs's response to her sale is persuasively argued by Mary Helen Washing-

ton in "Meditations on History: The Slave Narrative of Linda Brent," in Washington, *Invented Lives: Narratives of Black Women, 1860–1960* (New York: Doubleday, 1987).

52 Jacobs to Post, [1852?], IAPFP #84, BAP 16:0700–02 (Letter 4).

53 The seduction novel is discussed briefly in Nina Baym, *Woman's Fiction: A Guide to Novels by and about Women in America, 1820–1870* (Ithaca: Cornell University Press, 1978), p. 51. For classic analyses of the "tragic mulatto," see two articles by Sterling Brown, "Negro Character as Seen by White Authors," *Journal of Negro Education 2* (April 1933): 179–203; and "A Century of Negro Portraiture in American Literature," *Massachusetts Review 7* (1966):73–96.

54 By her choice of tense the narrator indicates that she had distinguished between virginity and integrity even when young: "I wanted to keep myself pure; and, under the most adverse circumstances, I tried hard to preserve my self-respect." Later, however, she writes that she was unable to maintain it consistently: "But now that the truth was out, and my relations should hear of it, I felt wretched . . . My self-respect was gone . . . I had resolved that I would be virtuous . . . And now, how humiliated I felt!"

55 Sojourner Truth, "Ain't I a Woman?" as reported in reminiscences by Frances D. Gage of the Akron, Ohio, Woman's Rights Convention in May 1851, in *History of Woman Suffrage*, ed. Elizabeth C. Stanton et al., 6 vols. (New York, 1881–1922), I, 115–117. For the historic feminism of Afro-American women, see for example Angela Davis, "Reflections on the Black Woman's Role in the Community of Slaves," *The Black Scholar 3* (Dec. 1971):3–15; Paula Giddings, *When and Where I Enter* (New York: Morrow, 1984); Jacqueline Jones, *Labor of Love, Labor of Sorrow* (New York: Basic Books, 1985); and two books by Bell Hooks: *Ain't I a Woman* (Boston: South End Press, 1982), and *Feminist Theory: From Margin to Center* (Boston: South End Press, 1984).

56 Sandra M. Gilbert and Susan Gubar, *The Madwoman in the Attic: The Woman Writer and the Nineteenth-Century Literary Imagination* (New Haven: Yale University Press, 1979).

57 Baym, *Woman's Fiction*, p. 22. For "domestic feminism," see Katherine Kish Sklar, *Catharine Beecher* (New Haven: Yale University Press, 1973). Hazel Carby discusses Jacobs's book as a critique of the ideology of True Womanhood spawned by domestic feminism, in *Reconstructing Womanhood: The Emergence of the Afro-American Woman Novelist* (New York: Oxford University Press, 1987).

58 See Jean Fagan Yellin, *Women and Sisters: The Antislavery Feminists in*

American Culture (New Haven: Yale University Press, 1989). This identification had become standard by the time Elizabeth Cady Stanton wrote in her *History of Woman Suffrage:* "The prolonged slavery of woman is the darkest page in human history."

59 *Appeal in Favor of that Class of Americans Called Africans* (Boston: Allen and Ticknor, 1833) had resulted in Child's ostracism from polite literary circles. Following this, much of her writing was done for the antislavery cause; by 1861, she had touched on various aspects of Jacobs's subject.

60 John S. Jacobs, "A Colored American in England," *The Anti-Slavery Advocate* (London), Sept. 2, 1861.

61 By 1862 John S. had married and made his home in England. After the Civil War he moved to Massachusetts with his family. John S. Jacobs died in Cambridge on December 19, 1873, and was buried in Mt. Auburn Cemetery. Minutes of the London Emancipation Committee, July 8, 1859; Harriet Jacobs to [Amy Kirby Post], Dec. 8, [1862]; Louisa Jacobs to William Lloyd Garrison, Dec. 20, 1873. Thanks to Claire Taylor. William Craft, *Running a Thousand Miles for Freedom; or, The Escape of William and Ellen Craft from Slavery* (London: William Tweedie, 1860).

62 E. B. Long, *The Civil War Day by Day: An Almanac, 1861–1865* (Garden City, N.Y.: Doubleday, 1971).

63 [John S. Jacobs], "A True Tale of Slavery," *The Leisure Hour: A Family Journal of Instruction and Recreation* (London), Feb. 7, 14, 21, and 28, 1861.

64 Louis Billington, "The Religious Periodical and Newspaper Press, 1770–1870," *The Press in English Society from the Seventeenth to Nineteenth Centuries,* ed. Michael Harris and Alan Lee (London: Associated University Presses, 1986), p. 128; Alvar Ellegard, "The Readership of the Periodical Press in Mid-Victorian Britain: II. Directory," *Victorian Periodicals Newsletter* 13 (Sept. 1971), pp. 20–21. "A Word with our Readers," *The Leisure Hour* 1, no. 1 (Jan. 1, 1852), p. 8.

65 R. J. M. Blackett, *Beating Against the Barriers: The Lives of Six Nineteenth-Century Afro-Americans* (Ithaca: Cornell University Press, 1986), pp. 203–204; Diary of Frederick Chesson, Jan.–March, 1862; *The Deeper Wrong; Or, Incidents in the Life of a Slave Girl.* Thanks to Lee Chambers-Schiller.

66 Frederick Douglass, *Narrative of the Life of Frederick Douglass, an American Slave. Written by Himself* (Boston: American Anti-Slavery Society, 1845).

67 Amy Post, Oct. 30, 1859; see Appendix, p. 203. "Editorial Correspon-

dence," *The North Star*, March 9, 1849; "The Walker Meetings," *National Anti-Slavery Standard*, Jan. 6, 1848.

68 "Meeting of Colored Citizens," *National Anti-Slavery Standard*, Oct. 10, 1850.

69 Thomas Wentworth Higginson, "The Romance of History in 1850," Friends of Freedom, *The Liberty Bell* (Boston, 1858), p. 47. Nathaniel Hawthorne, *The Scarlet Letter* (1850). For the authenticity of the narratives—of "the voice of the unwritten self, once it is subjected to the linguistic codes, literary conventions, and audience expectations of a literate population," see Houston Baker, Jr., "Autobiographical Acts and the Voice of the Southern Slave," *The Journey Back* (Chicago: University of Chicago Press, 1980), pp. 27–52. Gender-specific conventions restricting women's discourse in nineteenth-century American letters complicate and intensify this problem.

Preface

1 Harriet Jacobs to Amy Post, March [1854], IAPFP #783, BAP 16:0679–80 (Letters).

2 Bishop Daniel A. Payne (1811–1893) was received as a preacher in the Philadelphia conference of the African Methodist Episcopal church in 1842, the year he met Jacobs. Born of free parents, he established a school in his native Charleston, but went north after South Carolina outlawed the teaching of slaves. Payne later taught and preached throughout the country, including the slave South. He was elected a bishop in 1852 and later became president of Wilberforce University. *Dictionary of American Negro Biography*, ed. Rayford W. Logan and Michael R. Winston (New York: Norton, 1982), pp. 484–485.

3 Jacobs to Post, [1852?], IAPFP #84, BAP 16:0700–02 (Letter 4).

4 "He brought me up also out of an horrible pit, out of the mirey clay, and set my feet upon a rock, and established my goings. And he hath put a new song in my mouth, even praise unto our God: many shall see it, and fear, and shall trust in the Lord." Psalms 40:2–3.

Introduction

1 Lydia Maria Child (1802–1880), author, editor, abolitionist, and reformer, met Harriet Jacobs in 1860. Child was excluded from polite literary circles after she called for the immediate abolition of chattel slavery in her *Appeal in Favor of that Class of Americans Called Africans* (1833). In the years

that followed, she edited numerous antislavery pamphlets and books. Although she continued to produce novels, short stories, and poems, as well as histories and biographies, Child's strongest writings are the polemics and newspaper articles she wrote for the abolitionist movement. Jacobs to Post, Oct. 8 [1860], IAPFP #1259, BAP 16:686–688 (Letter 13); *Lydia Maria Child: Selected Letters, 1817–1880,* ed. Milton Meltzer and Patricia G. Holland (Amherst: University of Massachusetts Press, 1982).

2 Child to Jacobs, Aug. 13, 1860, IAPFP #1330, LMCP 46:1243 (Letter 11); and Sept. 27, 1860, IAPFP #1338, LMCP 46:1255 (Letter 12).

I. Childhood

1 Jacobs's father, Elijah Knox (?–c. 1826), a skilled house carpenter, was the slave of Dr. Andrew Knox. When Knox moved from Edenton, North Carolina, to Nixonton, around 1808, he presumably permitted Elijah to remain in Edenton. After Dr. Knox's death in 1816, Mrs. Knox returned to Edenton and allowed Elijah to work toward his freedom. In 1824, Dr. Knox's daughter Lavinia Matilda married, and Elijah became subject to her husband, James Coffield, who ordered Elijah to his Green Hall plantation. According to Jacobs's brother, Elijah was no longer allowed to hire his time. A man with "an intensely acute feeling of the wrongs of slavery, [he] sank into a state of mental dejection, which, combined with bodily illness, occasioned his death." Will of Dr. Andrew Knox, May 20, 1816, Pasquotank County Original Wills, 1709–1917, NCSA (hereinafter cited as Pasquotank Wills); inventory of the personal estate of Dr. Andrew Knox, 1816, Pasquotank County Estates Records, 1712–1931, NCSA (hereinafter Pasquotank Estates); Edenton *Gazette,* March 23, 1808; *Raleigh Register and North Carolina Gazette,* July 9, 1824 (hereinafter *Raleigh Register);* Estate of Sarah P. Knox, 1833, Chowan County Estates Records, 1728–1951, NCSA (hereinafter Chowan Estates); death certificate of John S. Jacobs, Dec. 19, 1873, Cambridge, Massachusetts; see John S. Jacobs, "A True Tale of Slavery," Chapter I.

2 Jacobs's brother John S. Jacobs (1815?–1873). Louisa Matilda Jacobs to William Lloyd Garrison, Dec. [Nov.] 20, 1873, Anti-Slavery Collection, BPL; Plan of Jacobs plot, Mt. Auburn Cemetery, Cambridge, Mass.

3 Jacobs's grandmother Molly Horniblow (c. 1771–1853). Register entry for Sept. 4, 1853, in Part V, Burials, 1851–1897, Register of St. Paul's Parish, Edenton, N.C., Episcopal Diocese of East Carolina (hereinafter St. Paul's Parish Register).

4 The emancipated family was apparently sailing under British colors

to the British port of St. Augustine; they probably left Charleston between May 1780 and December 1782, while the city was occupied by the English.

5 John Horniblow (1745? 1750?–1799) owned the King's Arms at Edenton, N.C.; after 1776 the inn was called Horniblow's (see Map 2). Horniblow's tax lists record the addition of only one slave among the "negroes under 7 and over 50" between 1779 and 1782; this was probably the child Molly. Chowan County Deed Book 0–1, pp. 132, 145, 294, Office of the Register of Deeds, Chowan County Courthouse, Edenton, N.C. (hereinafter Chowan Deeds); Tax Lists, 1779–1782, in Chowan County Tax Lists, 1717–1909, NCSA (hereinafter Chowan Tax Lists).

6 "Yellow" Molly Horniblow worked as a baker the rest of her life. Dr. James Norcom to Elizabeth [Norcom], June 26, 1846, NFP.

7 John Horniblow's widow was his third wife, Elizabeth Pritchard Horniblow (?–1827). In 1810, at the first division of his property, the evaluators listed "Yellow" Molly at £125, her son Mark [Ramsey] (c. 1800–1858) at £100, and her son Joe (1808–?) at £60. Her daughters, (Becky?), Delilah (1797?–c. 1819), and Betty (1794?–1841), were not mentioned. In 1813, at the second division of John Horniblow's property, the slaves were grouped into four shares of equal value—except for Joe, who was later to be divided between Horniblow's daughters Peggy and Eliza. In 1817, Dr. James Norcom petitioned on behalf of his wife, Mary Horniblow Norcom, and her younger sisters that Joe be sold, and on January 1, 1818, Joe, "aged twelve years or thereabouts," was sold to Josiah Collins the Younger for $675. Receipt for John Metcalf's account with Mrs. Elizabeth Horniblow Dec. 26, 1799, to May 12, 1800, in Cupola House Papers, Edenton Historical Commission, Edenton, N.C. (hereinafter Cupola House Papers); Estate of John Horniblow, 1799, Chowan Estates; Bill of Sale no. 463, Chowan Deeds, Book G-2, p. 375.

8 Jacobs's mother was Molly Horniblow's daughter Delilah. She had been given by Elizabeth Horniblow to her daughter Margaret. Estate of Elizabeth Horniblow, 1827, Chowan Estates; Answer of James Norcom to the bills of complaint in equity of Frederick Hoskins and wife Eliza, 1834, in Estate of Elizabeth Horniblow, 1827, Chowan Estates (hereinafter Answer of James Norcom).

9 Margaret Horniblow (b. 1797) died on July 3, 1825. Elizabeth V. Moore, personal communication to Jean Fagan Yellin, Sept. 5, 1980; will of Margaret Horniblow, 1825, Chowan County Original Wills, 1694–1910, NCSA (hereinafter Chowan Wills).

10 Molly Horniblow had been hired out from March 1824 to November

1825 to Myles Elliot, who was renting the Horniblow tavern, for the sum of $20.00. Estate of Elizabeth Horniblow, 1827, Chowan Estates.

11 Mary Matilda Norcom (1822–?), the daughter of Margaret Horniblow's sister Mary, was not five years old but three at the time of her aunt's death. Will of Margaret Horniblow, 1825, Chowan Wills.

12 Mark 12:31.

13 Matthew 7:12.

14 Margaret Horniblow had owned five of Molly's children and grandchildren: Delilah (now dead), Mark, Betty, Harriet, and John. Three months before her death she bequeathed all four surviving slaves to her mother, Elizabeth Horniblow, then on July 3, 1825, she wrote a deathbed codicil leaving Harriet instead to her niece Mary Matilda Norcom (see Illustrations). Will of Margaret Horniblow, 1825, Chowan Wills.

II. The New Master and Mistress

1 Dr. James Norcom (1778–1850) graduated from the Medical School of the University of Pennsylvania in 1797. After a sensational divorce suit against his first wife, Mary Custis, in 1810 he married Mary (Maria) Horniblow (1794–1868), the sister of Jacobs's first mistress. NFP.

2 John S. Jacobs writes that he was first owned by Penelope Horniblow, but it was Margaret Horniblow who willed him to her mother, Elizabeth Horniblow, who apparently permitted Dr. Norcom to take him from his father's care, move him into the Norcom house, and use him as a shop-boy. Following Elizabeth Horniblow's death, when her property was sold on January 1, 1828, John was bought by Dr. Norcom for $298.50. John S. Jacobs, "A True Tale of Slavery," Chapter I; Will of Elizabeth Horniblow, 1827, Chowan Wills; Estate of Elizabeth Horniblow, 1827, Chowan Estates.

3 John S. Jacobs's comments underscore this incident; see "A True Tale of Slavery," Chapter I.

4 Evidence suggests that Elijah died in the spring of 1826. He was not listed among the slaves Sarah Knox had inherited who survived her. Petition of Andrew Knox and Louisa Matilda Knox, Estate of Sarah P. Knox, 1833, Chowan Estates.

5 Molly Horniblow was sold along with the other property of Elizabeth Horniblow at Edenton on January 1, 1828. Will of Elizabeth Horniblow, 1827, Chowan Wills; Estate of Elizabeth Horniblow, 1827, Chowan Estates; Chowan Deeds, Book G-2, p. 501.

6 Hannah Pritchard (?–1838), a sister of the late Elizabeth Horniblow

who possessed no property of her own, purchased Molly for $52.25 and
Molly's son Mark for $400.00. On April 10, 1828, Pritchard successfully
petitioned the judge of the Superior Court for permission to free Molly. She
signed Molly's emancipation paper with a cross (see Illustrations). John S.
Jacobs presents a different version, suggesting that Congressman Alfred
Moore Gatlin (1790–?) played a crucial role in enabling Molly to become
emancipated, purchase a house, and purchase Mark. St. Paul's Parish
Register; Petition for Emancipation, 1828, Chowan County Miscellaneous
Slave Records, 1730–1836, NCSA (hereinafter Chowan Misc. Slave Records);
"Alfred Moore Gatlin," *Biographical Directory of the American Congress,
1774–1961* (Washington D.C.: U.S. Government Printing Office, 1961),
pp. 900–991; John S. Jacobs, "A True Tale of Slavery," Chapter II.

   7 Molly Horniblow's daughter Betty. Answer of James Norcom.

   8 Evidently Mary Horniblow Norcom's household regime was
antithetical to the flagrant mismanagement of Norcom's first wife. In his
bitter divorce suit, he charged that she drank, was addicted to laudanum,
was promiscuous, and did "suffer the negroes to waste the year's allowance
of provisions . . . by the middle of July." Testimony of Stephen R. Hooker in
"Bill to Divorce James Norcom of Edenton from his Wife Mary," General
Assembly Session Records, Nov.–Dec. 1808, NCSA.

III. The Slaves' New Year's Day

   1 Dr. James Norcom's tax statement for 1827 lists his property as 1,770
acres in Chowan County, 7 town lots (4 improved, 3 unimproved), and 19
Blacks. Chowan Tax Lists.

   2 In Edenton, the annual hiring probably took place at Market House
(see Map 2). See also sketch of hiring day at Wilmington, N.C., Jan. 1, 1840,
in James Sprunt, *Chronicles of The Cape Fear River* (Raleigh: Edwards and
Broughton, 1914), pp. 179–180.

IV. The Slave Who Dared to Feel like a Man

   1 On June 21, 1830, Congressman Gatlin sold Molly Horniblow a house
and lot on King Street "for many good Causes and reasons and also in
Consideration of one Dollar" (see Map 2). The 1830 Census for Chowan
County lists six persons inhabiting the residence of "Marey Horniblow,"
Chowan Deeds, Book I-1, p. 307; Fifth Census of the United States,
1830—North Carolina, Chowan County, p. 335 (hereinafter 1830 Census,
Chowan County).

2 The 12-year-old John S. Jacobs is here described fighting James Norcom, Jr. (1811–?), who was about 17. Family Bible records, NFP.

3 "Thou hypocrite, cast out first the beam of thine own eye, and then shalt thou see clearly to pull out the mote that is in thy brother's eye." Luke 6:42.

4 Jacobs's teenaged uncle Joseph had probably fought his young master, Josiah Collins III (1808–1863). For the Collins house in Edenton, see Map 2. Ultimately one of the three largest slaveholders in North Carolina, Collins by 1860 owned 4,000 acres, which were worked by 328 slaves. *Dictionary of North Carolina Biography*, ed. William S. Powell (Chapel Hill: University of North Carolina Press, 1979).

5 The antebellum criminal code of North Carolina did not address assault and battery, a common law crime. Joseph's public whipping was probably a private punishment ordered by Collins.

6 The 1830 Census of Chowan County (p. 335) includes one female slave aged 10–24 and one free black female aged 24–36 among the inhabitants of Molly Horniblow's house.

7 John S. Jacobs identifies Collins's attorney Joseph B. Skinner (?–c. 1850) as the man who captured Joseph in New York. "A True Tale of Slavery," Chapter II; see also "Joseph B. Skinner," in Richard Benbury Creecy, *Grandfather's Tales of North Carolina History* (Raleigh: Edwards and Broughton, 1901), pp. 132–135.

8 "Mr. [William] Grimes had for a long time held the office of County Jailor and Town Constable, and although in these situations, calculated as they naturally are to produce enmity and ill will, and considered by all as subordinate such has been the line of his conduct, and such the promptness of his action, as to challenge the approbation of every good citizen . . ." Obituary, *Edenton Gazette and Farmer's Palladium*, March 3, 1831. For the location of the county jail, see Map 2.

9 The slave trader was probably Joseph Granier of Norfolk, who began advertising in December 1828 that he had become an agent for the New Orleans slave-trading house of Leon Chambert. *American Beacon and Virginia and North Carolina Gazette* (Norfolk, Va.), Dec. 20, 1828 ff. (hereinafter *American Beacon*).

10 Pennsylvania-born Daniel W. McDowell (c. 1793–1885) apparently moved to Edenton in 1825, and late that year married Mary Cox Norfleet, who had inherited part of a large estate. Collins, Joseph's master, was living at "The Home Place" near the water; it is not clear where in Edenton the McDowells were living when Joseph escaped. Later, in 1838, McDowell

acquired a parcel of land adjoining Molly Horniblow's lot; when she wrote
her will in 1840, he served as one of the witnesses. *Biblical Recorder* (Raleigh,
N.C.), Nov. 11, 1885; Seventh Census of the United States, 1850—North
Carolina, Chowan County, p. 249 (state copy), NCSA (hereinafter 1850
Census, Chowan County); Bond of Daniel McDowell, Dec. 19, 1825, in
Chowan County Marriage Bonds, 1741–1868, NCSA (hereinafter Chowan
Marriage Bonds); will of Molly Horniblow, 1840 (proved 1850), Chowan
Wills.

11 Mark's mistress was his mother, Molly Horniblow (see Chapter II,
note 6), who had apparently hired him out to work on an Edenton-New
York packet. John S. Jacobs recounts the meeting between Joseph and Mark
in "A True Tale of Slavery," Chapter II.

12 On February 9, 1832, Molly Horniblow borrowed $100 from John M.
Roberts and signed a deed of trust for her house and lot to John Cox; she
may have incurred this debt in an attempt to buy Joseph. Chowan Deeds,
K-2, p. 83.

13 The money used in 1827 by Alfred Moore Gatlin to purchase Molly
Horniblow's house ($364.50) plus deed money cited in 1830 ($1.00) plus
Molly's purchase price ($52.25) plus Mark's purchase price ($406.00) comes
to a total of $823.75. It is likely that the money Molly Horniblow had saved
over the years was insufficient to purchase herself, her son Mark Ramsey,
and her house, and that she borrowed the balance necessary from Gatlin,
whom she finally repaid on June 21, 1830. It is possible that the $100 she
borrowed from Roberts was intended not to bargain for her younger son
Joseph but to finish paying for Mark. The "precious document" may well
have evidenced her ownership of Mark. He was probably freed late in 1843.
John S. Jacobs, "A True Tale of Slavery," Chapter II; Josiah Collins to Harriet
Jacobs, July 23, 1859, in Josiah Collins Papers, 1761–1892, NCSA; Petition for
Emancipation, 1828, Chowan Misc. Slave Papers; Will of Molly Horniblow,
1840 (proved 1858), Chowan Wills; Bond of Marcus Ramsey, Nov. 11, 1843,
Chowan Marriage Bonds; Estate of Elizabeth Horniblow, 1827, Chowan
Estates; Chowan Deeds, Book K-2, p. 83, and Book H-2, p. 548.

14 "Poor things, 'they can't take care of themselves,'" was the satirical
caption of a widely reproduced abolitionist cartoon showing leisured whites
watching blacks productively at work. American Anti-Slavery Society,
American Anti-Slavery Almanac for 1840 (New York: S. W. Benedict; Boston:
Isaac Knapp, 1840), p. 29.

·V. The Trials of Girlhood

1 Norcom was actually about thirty-five years older than Jacobs.

2 Complex laws defined the legal status of North Carolina's slaves. They were to be clothed and fed, but they could not bring suit to demand it. The murderer of a slave could be indicted and prosecuted under the common law provision against homicide. Slaves had the right to trial by jury and the right of appeal, yet the prohibition of slave testimony against whites and the inability of a slave to initiate legal actions denied them the courts. The entire system worked against the protection of slave women from sexual assault and violence, as Jacobs asserts. The rape of a slave was not a crime but a trespass upon her master's property. See Acts of the General Assembly of North Carolina, 1753, ch.6, sec. 10, and Acts of 1774, ch. 31, sec. 2, in James Iredell, *Laws of the State of North Carolina* (Edenton: Hodge and Wills, 1791), pp. 153–154, 274; Frederick Nash et al., eds., *Revised Statutes of the State of North Carolina*, 2 vols. (Raleigh, 1837; hereinafter *Revised Statutes)*, ch. III, sec. 50, vol. I, p. 583; Ulrich B. Phillips, *Life and Labor in the Old South* (Boston: Little, Brown, 1930), p. 162.

3 Jacobs refers here to the 1850 Fugitive Slave Law, which was a component part of the 1850 Compromise and the most comprehensive statement since 1793 on the right of slaveholders to reclaim fugitives. Instead of being taken before judicial officers, suspected fugitives were taken before commissioners, and these were paid a higher rate if they found the accused to be slaves. The law also empowered federal officers to demand that all citizens aid in its enforcement; punishment for those who tried to rescue or conceal a fugitive included fines, imprisonment, and civil damages. Lydia Maria Child polemicized against this law in *The Duty of Disobedience to the Fugitive Slave Act: An Appeal to the Legislators of Massachusetts* (Boston, 1860).

4 It may be that Molly Horniblow drew a pistol to defend her daughter in connection with a riot involving Charles H. Leary at Elizabeth Horniblow's tavern on December 10, 1816; Becky (presumably her third daughter) apparently lived at the tavern until given as a wedding present to Elizabeth Horniblow Hoskins in 1820. Grand Jury Presentments, 1816,Chowan County Miscellaneous Records, 1731–1935, NCSA (hereinafter Chowan Misc. Records).

VI. The Jealous Mistress

1 Abolitionists routinely compared the plight of the Irish starving in the potato famine with the plight of Afro-Americans held in slavery. In 1847 John S. Jacobs had publicly joined other antislavery men and women in contributing to Irish relief. This passage echoes a letter Jacobs had written while debating whether to write her narrative. *The Liberator,* Feb. 27, 1847; Jacobs to Amy Post, [1852?], IAPFP #84, BAP 16:0700–02 (Letter 4).

2 Although she early learned to read and spell, Jacobs had not been taught to write. Jacobs to Post, June 25, [1853], IAPFP #1257, BAP 16:0696–97.

3 Elizabeth Hannah Norcom (1826–1849). NFP.

4 Jacobs's aunt Betty had been given by Elizabeth Horniblow to her daughter Mary before Mary's marriage to Norcom. Answer of James Norcom.

5 At this time, c. 1828–29, Norcom apparently had eight or nine living children: John, James Jr., Benjamin Rush, Caspar Wistar, Margaret, Mary Matilda, Elizabeth Hannah, Abner, and Standin. The first Abner (b. 1815) had died; William Augustus was not born until 1836. John married Ann Eunice Walker in 1828. It is possible that their first issue did not survive; their known children were born later. NFP; 1850 Census, Chowan County, p. 261, and Beaufort County, pp. 194–195; *Washington* [N.C.] *Whig,* Nov. 23, 1842; Register entry for Nov. 24, 1842, in Burials, Register of St. Peter's Parish, Washington, N.C., Episcopal Diocese of East Carolina.

6 "Woe unto you, scribes and Pharisees, hypocrites! for ye are like unto whited sepulchres, which indeed appear beautiful outward, but are within full of dead men's bones, and of all uncleanness." Matthew 23:27.

VII. The Lover

1 "O my Father, if it be possible, let this cup pass from me: nevertheless not as I will, but as thou wilt." Matthew 26:39.

2 Lord Byron, "The Lament of Tasso," iv, 7–10.

3 While not forbidden, slave marriage was not sanctioned by civil law. Sexual intercourse between slaves was mere cohabitation or concubinage. Before 1831, marriage between a free black and a slave, which required the consent of the slave's owner, was an informal union; after 1831, such marriages were forbidden. *Revised Statutes,* ch. III, sec. 77, vol. I, p. 590.

4 To be "peeled and pickled" is to be whipped and washed in brine; see Chapter XII.

VIII. What Slaves Are Taught to Think of the North

1 Jacobs echoes other abolitionists, black and white, who argued that black inferiority resulted from slavery, not from race.

2 The Mason-Dixon Line, dividing Pennsylvania from Delaware and Maryland, marked the boundary between slave and free states from the time of the Missouri Compromise in 1820 until 1865. The "peculiar institution" was chattel slavery.

3 "And hath made of one blood all nations of men for to dwell on all the face of the earth . . ." Acts 17:26.

4 While ostensibly ridiculing the woman's belief, this passage ultimately endorses it by transforming the queen into a neoclassical figure. The reference suggests not only Queen Victoria but also African traditions. "In olden times when a chief [of the Ashanti] had to be chosen it was the Queen Mother who had most to say in the choice . . . She alone has the privilege of rebuking him, his spokesman . . . , or his councillors in open court, and of addressing the court and questioning litigants. To her, too, petitions are addressed praying for pardon or mitigation of a sentence . . ." Captain R. S. Ratray, *Ashanti* (Oxford: Clarendon Press, 1923, 1969), pp. 81–84. The armed "Amazons" of the Dahomey are noted in Frederick E. Forbes, *Dahomey and the Dahomans,* 2 vols. (London, 1851), 1, 218.

IX. Sketches of Neighboring Slaveholders

1 This chapter is the result of Lydia Maria Child's editing. The incidents included here have been moved from their original locations in Jacobs's text. Perhaps in consequence of this editing, perhaps because Jacobs was a townswoman generally unacquainted with the countryside, perhaps because it was and is inherently difficult to document atrocities against slaves, this chapter, unlike the rest of the book, does not appear correct in its details. The documentation of the atrocities perpetrated by the Litch brothers, however, suggest that Jacobs's account is substantially accurate.

Mr. Litch was apparently Josiah Coffield (?–1837), owner of extensive land and slaves, who was noted as a young man for his violent behavior. In 1816, the Chowan County Grand jury suggested that "a signal example" be made of him after he had been presented for dangerously beating Mark, a slave, and for two separate violent assaults on white men. He was found guilty of assault and battery with intent to murder, sentenced to sixty days, and fined $400. See Child's Introduction; Child to Lucy [Searle], Feb. 4, 1861, Cornell University Libraries Anti-Slavery Collection, LMCP 47:1282; Chowan County Criminal Action Records, 1820 (State v. Josiah Coffield); Chowan County Criminal Actions Concerning Slaves, 1820 (State v. Josiah Coffield); Chowan County Superior Court Minutes, 1809–1828, pp. 176–179, 182; Chowan County Misc. Records (Inquests); Estate of Josiah Coffield, 1837, Chowan Estates.

2 "Thou shalt not steal." Exodus 20:15.

3 This probably refers to an incident involving Josiah Coffield's older brother, James (?–1843). In 1823, the year before his marriage made him master of Jacobs's father, James Coffield brought charges against two slaves who belonged to his neighbors. He accused them of stealing twenty pounds of bacon, ten pounds of lard, and twenty pounds of pork from his smoke-house, which was evidently at the mill and fishery on the Coffield property at the mouth of Rockahock Creek (see Map 1). Incomplete court records obscure the result of the case. Chowan County Criminal Actions Concerning Slaves 1820, 1823 (State v. James Coffield); Chowan County Superior Court Minute Docket 1809–1828 (incomplete), pp. 162–163; estates of Lavinia Coffield, 1829, Sarah P. Knox, 1833, and James Coffield, 1843, Chowan Estates.

4 William Coffield (1800–1829), the youngest of the three brothers, was also violent. In 1819 he was accused of assaulting a slave by whipping her and cutting her with a knife. Alleging that he could not get a fair trial in Chowan County, he successfully petitioned for a change of venue, and was acquitted. The following year a slave woman was found beaten to death in his house, but a grand jury failed to indict him. He died at age 29, an agonized victim of cholera. The practice of weighting the eyes of the dead with coins to keep them closed, common in the British Isles, remained in use in North Carolina into the present century. Chowan County Criminal Actions Concerning Slaves, 1819 and 1820 (State v. William Coffield); Perquimons County Superior Court Minute Docket, 1807–1847, April Term 1820 (State v. William Coffield); Grand Jury Reports, 1825 and 1827, in Chowan County Misc. Records; Estate of William Coffield, 1829, Chowan Estates; *Edenton North-Carolina Gazette,* Jan. 27, 1829.

5 "Like angel visits, few and far between." Thomas Campbell, "Pleasures of Hope" (1799), ii, 378.

6 I have been unable to identify this quotation.

7 "And he cried mightily with a strong voice, saying Babylon the great is fallen, and is become the habitation of devils, and the hold of every foul spirit, and a cage of every unclean and hateful bird." Revelation 18:2.

X. A Perilous Passage in the Slave Girl's Life

1 Samuel Tredwell Sawyer (c. 1800–1865) lived on King Street on the same block as Molly Horniblow (see Map 2). Educated at the Edenton Academy and the College of William and Mary, Sawyer studied law, was admitted to the bar, and practiced at Edenton. *Biographical Directory of the American Congress, 1774–1961*, p. 1565; Executrix v. Samuel T. Sawyer, Jan. 6, 1844, filed in Estate of James Coffield, 1843, Chowan Estates.

XI. The New Tie to Life

1 "Remember now thy Creator in the days of thy youth, while the evil days come not, nor the years draw nigh, when thou shalt say, I have no pleasure in them." Ecclesiastes 12:1.

2 Joseph Jacobs, born at Edenton (c. 1829–1863?). Writ of venditione exponas against Dr. James Norcom, Oct. 5, 1830, Chowan County Civil Actions Concerning Slaves, 1830, NCSA; Lydia Maria Child to John Fraser, Nov. 20, 1866, LMCP 66:1746.

3 Abolitionists, who characterized slavery as "the national sin," routinely symbolized the institution as a serpent. See, for example, the illustrated broadsides "Declaration of the Anti-Slavery Convention" and "Printers Picture Gallery," New York [1838?], Division of Popular Prints, Library of Congress.

XII. Fear of Insurrection

1 On August 21 and 22, 1831, in Southampton County, Virginia—about forty miles upstream from Edenton—Nat Turner and his followers massacred fifty-five whites in the bloodiest slave insurrection in American history. Turner remained at large for more than nine weeks. Captured, tortured, jailed, interrogated, and tried, he was executed on November 11. In the aftermath of the insurrection, a wave of white terror swept across the entire South. No one knows how many blacks were murdered; historians' estimates range in the hundreds. In Southampton, twenty other blacks were hanged and ten were transported, and elsewhere in Virginia and North Carolina

twenty or thirty more were executed. Thomas Wentworth Higginson, "Nat Turners Insurrection," *Atlantic Monthly* 8 (Aug. 1861): 173–186; Herbert Aptheker, *Nat Turner's Slave Rebellion* (New York: Humanities Press, 1966).

2 Apparently Jacobs wrote this passage in response to a letter from her editor. Child inquired, "What *were* those inflictions? Were any tortured to make them confess? And how? Were any killed? Please write down some of the most striking particulars, and let me have them to insert." Child to Jacobs, Aug. 13, 1860, IAPFP #1330, LMCP 46:1243 (Letter 11).

3 Josiah Coffield; see Chapter IX. Patrol appointments, Dec. Term 1830 and Sept. Term 1831, Chowan County Court Minutes, pp. 102, 123, NCSA.

4 A slave called Small's Jim was examined about the rebellion under oath at Edenton on September 1, 1831; he pictured a conspiracy "to kill the whites" and named more than a dozen names. Seven warrants were issued on that date. Within a week there were five more, and by the end of the month nineteen men belonging to ten slaveholders in the Edenton area had been jailed. In the fall term of court, eight were indicted for conspiring "to rebel and make insurrection." On October 12, "the negro Godfrey," slave of Charles Johnson, was found innocent. All of the other indictments were dropped. On November 10 the Edenton *Gazette* reported that "not the slightest evidence was adduced to warrant the belief of their participation in any plot." Later during fall court term, Brownrigg's Sandy, one of the informers, was indicted for perjury for lying about Godfrey. File marked "Nat Turner's Insurrection" in Chowan County Criminal Actions Concerning Slaves, 1831, NCSA; entry in the minutes of Oct. 12, 1831, Chowan County Superior Court Minutes, Fall Term 1831, NCSA; Robert N. Elliott, "The Nat Turner Insurrection as Reported in the North Carolina Press," *North Carolina Historical Review* 38 (Jan. 1961):17.

5 In 1830, slaves were cut off from Bible reading when it was made a crime punishable by thirty-nine lashes to teach "slaves to read and write, the use of figures excepted." The following year, it became a crime for "any slave or free person of color to preach, exhort, or teach 'in any prayer-meeting or other association of worship where slaves of different families are collected together.'" *Acts Passed by the General Assembly of the State of North Carolina . . . 1830–31* (Raleigh: Lawrence and Lemay, 1831), ch. 6, p. 11; *Revised Statutes,* ch. III, sec. 27, vol. I, p. 578; John S. Bassett, *Slavery in the State of North Carolina,* series 17, no. 7–8 (Baltimore: Johns Hopkins University Press, 1899), pp. 48–49.

6 "For one is your master, even Christ; and all ye are brethren." Matthew 23:8.

XIII. The Church and Slavery

1 Massachusetts-born John Avery, D. D. (?–1837), educated at Williams College and Yale, went to Edenton as a teacher in the Edenton Academy, became a candidate for holy orders, and served as rector of St. Paul's Episcopal Church. Records of the Proceedings of the Vestry of St. Paul's Church, Edenton, N.C., 1701–1841, Vestry Book, vol. II, NCSA; Joseph B. Cheshire, ed., *Sketches of Church History in North Carolina* (Wilmington, N.C., 1892), pp. 256–258; *Raleigh Register,* Feb. 14, 1837.

2 Ephesians 6:5.

3 "Mr. Pike" is preaching against established Afro-American cultural practices. The use of coffee for divination and cards for conjuring was common, as was the making of balls filled with roots. The African origins of the latter practice are spelled out by Robert F. Thompson: "Kongo civilization and art were not obliterated in the New World: they resurfaced in the coming together, here and there, of numerous slaves from Kongo and Angola." "According to Kongo mythology, the first *nkisi* given to man by God was Funza . . . himself incarnate in unusual twisted-root formations." *Flash of the Spirit: African and Afro-American Art and Philosophy* (New York: Random House, 1983), pp. 104–105, 130–131; also see Newbell Puckett, *Folk Beliefs of the Southern Negro* (Chapel Hill: University of North Carolina Press, 1966), pp. 296, 355.

4 The reference is to the good Samaritan; Luke 10:33.

5 Sterling Stuckey discusses the significance of Afro-American folklore in "Through the Prism of Folklore: The Black Ethos in Slavery," *Massachusetts Review* 9, no. 3 (Summer 1968). Jacobs's text is similar to the "specimen" reproduced in the first notice of slave songs in an American musical journal:

> Oh, Satan he came by my heart,
> Throw brickbats in de door,
> But *Master Jesus* come wid brush,
> Make cleaner dan before.

A second parallel appears in a nineteenth-century novel by James S. Peacocke

> Old Satan is like a howling dog,

He throwed blocks in my way;
Jesus was my bosom friend,
And he cast dem all away.

The reference is apparently to Isaiah 47:14, "And shall say, Cast ye up, cast ye up, prepare the way, take up the stumbling block out of the way of my people" and to Romans 14:13, "Let us not therefore judge one another any more; but judge this rather, that no man put a stumbling block or an occasion to fall in his brothers way." "Stam'ring tongue" suggests a line from William Cowper:

When this poor lisping, stammering tongue
Lies silent in the grave,
Then in a nobler, sweeter song
I'll sing thy power to save.

Dena Epstein spelled out this concordance in a personal communication to Jean Fagan Yellin, Oct. 9, 1985; *Musical Gazette of Boston,* 1 (July 6, 1846): 91; James S. Peacocke, *The Creole Orphans; or, Lights and Shadows of Southern Life* (New York, 1856), p. 74. This discussion of origins is based on personal communications to Jean Fagan Yellin from Wayne D. Shirley, Oct. 16, 1985, and from George Stevenson, Jan. 31, 1986; Cowper, "There is a fountain filled with blood."

6 Wayne D. Shirley comments that although "the unrhymed verse of this example is unusual . . . the variance between rhythm (and poetic diction) of verse and refrain is quite common in Southern hymnody." Lawrence W. Levine cites Jacobs's verse to illustrate the assertion that although the trickster is rarely present in religious songs of the slaves, this figure "is sometimes felt in the slave's many allusions to his narrow escapes from the devil." Personal communication from Wayne D. Shirley to Jean Fagan Yellin, Oct. 16, 1985; Levine, "Slave Songs and Slave Consciousness," in Alan Weinstein and Frank Gatell, eds., *American Negro Slavery,* 2nd ed. (New York: Oxford University Press, 1973), p. 153.

7 Dr. Avery resigned on October 5, 1835, to become rector of St. John's in the Prairies, Greensboro, Alabama. Records of the Proceedings of the Vestry, 1701–1841, vol. 2, pp. 33–34, St. Paul's Church, Edenton, N.C. (hereinafter St. Paul's Vestry Minutes).

8 Rev. William D. Cairnes (c. 1803–1850) of the Missionary Society began his ministry in March 1836. St. Paul's Vestry Minutes, Vol. 2, p. 40.

9 Jacobs evidently conflates two separate but related events: the

death of Cairnes's wife on September 11, 1836, and the death two months later of a wealthy parishioner, the widow Mary Bissell. Cairnes wrote and witnessed the will in which Mrs. Bissell bequeathed her slaves to the American Colonization Society and provided the funds necessary to send them to Africa. This will was bitterly contested. Although nine years after her death the North Carolina Supreme Court finally ruled Mrs. Bissell's bequest legal, there is no record that her slaves ever left the state.

Cairnes's dispute with the vestrymen, among whom was Dr. Norcom, came to a head almost immediately. It seems clear that they were aware of the minister's grave doubts about the spiritual authority for slavery and that they accused him of improperly influencing Mrs. Bissell. On March 14, 1837, Cairnes offered his resignation, saying that he would remain at St. Paul's only if the vestrymen unanimously asked him. Instead, on March 24, they unanimously voted to accept his resignation.

Three days later Dr. Norcom was appointed Senior Warden for the next year, and it was "Ordered, that the North side of the Gallery of the Church be given up to the use of the colored people." This did not, however, solve the problem of ministering to the black members of the congregation without offending their white coreligionists. On July 22, 1841, the vestrymen voted to close to blacks the pews of those communicants who were "opposed to their occupancy by negroes." In order to "provide means and opportunities of affording to the colored population religious worship," they resolved to attempt to raise money for "a building for the colored population to worship in." Will of Mary Bissell, 1836, Chowan Wills; Memory F. Mitchell, "Off to Africa—With Judicial Blessing," *North Carolina Historical Review* 53 (July 1976):269–271; St. Paul's Vestry Minutes, vol. 2, pp. 40–41, 44, 46–49, 50, 52, 72.

10 "And whosoever will, let him take the water of life freely." Revelation 22:17.

11 "For with thee is the fountain of life: in thy light shall we see light." Psalms 36:9.

12 "And another angel came out of the temple, crying with a loud voice to him that sat on the cloud, Thrust in thy sickle, and reap; for the time is come to reap; for the harvest of the earth is ripe." Revelation 14:15. "Behold, I say unto you, lift up your eyes, and look on the fields; for they are white already to harvest." John 4:35.

13 The Reverend Nehemiah Adams (1806–1878), pastor of Essex Street Church, Boston, returned from a trip to the South an apologist for slavery

and wrote *A South-Side View of Slavery; or, Three Months in the South in 1854* (Boston: Ticknor and Fields, 1854).

14 For a contemporary discussion of the debate over slavery that was splitting American churches, see, for example, Harriet Beecher Stowe, *A Key to Uncle Tom's Cabin* . . . (Boston, 1853). Stowe suggested that she incorporate Jacobs's story into this volume. Jacobs to Amy Post, April 4 [1853], IAPFP #788, BAP 16:3681–82 (Letter 6); Jacobs to Post, Oct. 9 [1853], IAPFP #85, BAP 16:0713–14 (Letter 7).

15 The date when Norcom became a communicant of St. Paul's is not recorded. Fragmentary records show that he subscribed to repaint and furnish the church in 1805, and list him among the vestrymen on February 14, 1828. Resolution to restore the church and list of subscriptions (n.d., but before June 13, 1805), in file marked "Restoration of 1806–1809," records of St. Paul's Church, Edenton, in custody of the rector; St. Paul's Vestry Minutes, vol. 2, p. 15.

XIV. Another Link to Life

1 "Wherefore I abhor myself, and repent in dust and ashes." Job 42:6.

2 The widespread practice of shaving the head of a whore is grounded in Scripture; see Isaiah 4:24.

3 According to her gravestone at Mt. Auburn Cemetery, Cambridge, Mass. (which was erected by Edith Willis Grinnell), Louisa Matilda was born on October 11, 1836, and died on April 5, 1917. According to Chapter XVII of *Incidents*, however, Jacobs's daughter was two years old when Jacobs went into hiding in June 1835; the year of Louisa Matilda's birth must have been 1833. Burial record, Mt. Auburn Cemetery.

4 Samuel Tredwell Sawyer's mother, Margaret Blair Hasmer Sawyer, died on November 16, 1826. *Raleigh Register* (semi-weekly), Dec. 15, 1826.

5 Harriet Jacobs named her son after her uncle Joseph.

6 Molly Horniblow doubtless attended services at St. Paul's Episcopal Church in Edenton (see Map 2) for years before she was officially listed as a communicant in 1842. Personal communication to Jean Fagan Yellin from the Reverend R. W. Stone, Rector, St. Paul's Church, Edenton, N.C., Aug. 24, 1981.

7 The baby was named for Louisa Matilda, Dr. Knox's younger daughter.

8 A search for papers establishing that Dr. Knox purchased the

carpenter slave Elijah has been unsuccessful. If her father Elijah was born on the Knox plantation, it is likely that Harriet Jacobs's paternal grandfather was Henry Jacobs, an illiterate white small farmer who owned no slaves and from 1781 to 1789 lived with his wife and children within a mile of the Knox plantation on the Yeopim Raver across the county line in Perquimans (see Map 1). Yeopim bridge provided easy access between the Jacobs farm and the Knox plantation. This man apparently fathered Elijah sometime during the 1780s, while the widow Christian Knox was mistress of the plantation and young Andrew Knox was completing his education; he is the only Jacobs whose actions appear in Chowan County records between 1776 and 1892. Chowan Deeds S-I, p. 139–140; Tax List for 1781, Chowan Tax Lists; State Census of North Carolina, 1786–1787, Chowan County, NCSA; Will of Andrew Knox, 1775, Perquimans County Original Wills, 1711–1909, NCSA; Estate of Andrew Knox, 1775, Perquimans County Estates Records, 1740–1930, NCSA; Sales from the Estate of Andrew Knox, 1787, Secretary of State Records—Inventories and Sales of Estates, 1712–1798, NCSA.

9 "The iron entered into his soul." Book of Common Prayer, Psalm 105:18.

XV. Continued Persecutions

1 "Wash you, make you clean; put away the evil of your doings from before mine eyes; cease to do evil." Isaiah 1:16.

2 Norcom was a loving and dominating husband and father. In his serious and sophisticated interest in medicine, his commitment as a physician, and his educated discourse, he appears unlike the villain Jacobs portrays. But his humorlessness, his egoism, his insistently controlling relationships with his wife and children, and particularly with his daughters—for example his obdurate response to the disobedience of his beloved daughter Mary Matilda, mentioned in Chapter XLI—suggest the portrait Jacobs draws. This impression is supported by his quarrelsomeness with his neighbors and his unforgiving fury against those he viewed as enemies. It is underscored by his admitted passionate responses to women. Norcom to Mary Horniblow Norcom, c. 1809 and Sept. 6, 1846; to Mary Matilda Norcom, Aug. 2, 1836, Aug. 26, 1836, and Feb. 18, 1837 ff.; to Elizabeth Norcom, Aug. 15, 1844, and Sept. 30, 1844 ff.; to granddaughter Emily, March 29, 1848; to [Mr. Skinner], March 14, 1848; to Miss Haworth, May 22, 184?; to

"Dear Sir," April 27, 1850; to [Mr. Cox], n.d.; Mary Matilda Norcom Messmore to Mary Horniblow Norcom, July 4, 1848; Norcom's unsigned, undated fragment "The character of my fortunes," NFP.

3 James Norcom, Jr., received Auburn, a 435-acre plantation near Albemarle Sound that produced cotton and corn (see Map 1), from his father on September 26, 1834, as his patrimony in anticipation of his impending marriage to Penelope Hoskins (1812–1843). Chowan Deeds, Book K-2, pp. 497–498; James Norcom to [Dr. John Norcom], Dec. 26, 1849, NFP.

XVI. Scenes at the Plantation

1 A system of patrols—often connected with the militia and usually composed of a captain and three others appointed for only a few months— monitored the roads and periodically checked the slave quarters. Slaves leaving the plantation were required to have a certificate signed by a master or overseer; if caught without passes, they were summarily punished by the patrol. Franklin, *From Slavery to Freedom,* pp. 188–189; "An Act Concerning Servants and Slaves," 1741, sec. 38, reported in Henry Potter, *Laws of the State of North-Carolina . . .* (Raleigh, 1821), 2 vols., 1, 165; *Revised Statutes,* ch. III, sec. 24, p. 578; ch. 86, sec. 3, p. 458.

2 Hannah Pritchard.

3 "There the wicked cease from troubling; and there the weary be at rest. There the prisoners rest together; they hear not the voice of the oppressor. The small and great are there; and the servant is free from his master." Job 3:17–19.

4 James Norcom, Jr., was married on Wednesday, May 27, 1835. NFP.

XVII. The Flight

1 In addition to posted broadsides, Norcom ran ads in eight issues (June 30–July 13, 1835) of the daily *American Beacon* (Norfolk, Va.). He offered $100 for Jacobs, asserting that she had left "without any known cause," and commenting on her person, her manners, and her wardrobe (see Illustrations). Such newspaper advertisements customarily reduced the reward money offered after quickly printed, locally circulated broadsides proved ineffective.

XVIII. Months of Peril

1 Discussing Afro-American folk medicine, Newbell Puckett cites an African remedy for swelling that involves steeping rusty nails in cream of

tartar and vinegar. As early as her *American Frugal Housewife* (1829), Child had suggested the use of salt for snakebite. Puckett, *Folk Beliefs of the Southern Negro*, p. 388; *American Frugal Housewife*, 20th ed. (Boston, 1836), p. 30. For the significance of black folk medicine, see Eugene Genovese, *Roll, Jordan, Roll: The World the Slaves Made* (New York: Random House, 1972), p. 228.

2 Patrick Henry, speech to the Virginia Convention, March 1775.

3 It is likely that Jacobs's protectress was Martha Hoskins Rombough Blount (1777–1858), eulogized as a woman who "studied the welfare of her whole household both black and white." The kind and philanthropic daughter of Richard Hoskins and his wife Winifred, she had known Horniblow's slave Molly all her life; her first husband was William Rombough, whose sister was John Horniblow's wife. Widowed, she married William Blount, who died in 1819. Blount's will left her the owner of five slaves; three others were lent to her until Blount's son came of age. In 1835, Martha Hoskins Rombough Blount was living in her house in Queen Street (see Map 2) with three slaves of taxable age. If she was Jacobs's protectress, her extraction of a solemn promise never to connect her with Jacobs's concealment, and her statement that it would ruin her and her family, reflect realistic fears. Punishment in North Carolina for harboring a runaway slave included fines and imprisonment, and she must have worried about inviting hostility against her brother Edmund Hoskins, a leading merchant and Baptist deacon who was Clerk of the County Court. J. R. B. Hathaway, ed., *North Carolina Historical and Genealogical Register* (Edenton: 1900–1903), 3 vols., 1, 460–461; obituary of Martha Blount, *Biblical Recorder*, Dec. 23, 1858; Tax Lists, 1819–1837, Chowan County Tax Lists, NCSA; Bassett, *Slavery in North Carolina*, p. 15.

4 John S. Jacobs discusses this imprisonment in "A True Tale of Slavery," Chapter II.

XIX. The Children Sold

1 Dr. Norcom's correspondence testifies to his absence from Edenton in July 1835. According to John S. Jacobs, "T" (James Iredell Tredwell), a former North Carolinian living in New York, had reported to Norcom that Jacobs was in jail. "This called the old man from home. He had got to prove property and pay expenses." James Norcom to "My dear Son," July 9, 1835, NFP; John S. Jacobs, "A True Tale of Slavery," Chapter II.

2 Two years later Norcom repaid his daughter by substituting two other

slaves for Joseph and Louisa (see Illustrations). Chowan Deeds, Book L-2, p. 256.

3 John S. Jacobs writes that his chains were removed outside J. B. S[kinner]'s house; "A True Tale of Slavery," Chapter III.

4 "Home, Sweet Home," a song from *Clari, the Maid of Milan,* by J. Howard Payne (1792–1852).

5 John S. Jacobs writes that although he had been bought to be a body servant, Sawyer had sent him out to the plantation for three months to keep him away from Norcom. "A True Tale of Slavery," Chapter III.

XX. New Perils

1 The traitorous Jenny is the only Edenton person Jacobs names in her book—if indeed Mrs. Blount was Jacobs's protectress and if the woman Jenny she had inherited in 1819 was still alive in the summer of 1835. Will of William Blount, 1819, Chowan Wills.

2 Mrs. Blount's brother Baker Hoskins died on May 19, 1835, while Jacobs was at the Norcom plantation. If Mrs. Blount was Jacobs's protectress, she was visiting her late brother's family at Clement Hall, which still stands about a mile north of Edenton. Obituary of Baker Hoskins, *Biblical Recorder* (Raleigh), June 17, 1835.

3 According to John S. Jacobs, Stephen, the seaman husband of Jacobs's aunt Betty, "had intended to take [Jacobs] to New York, but the doctor's threats frightened him so much, that he did not dare make the attempt." Norcom even forbade Stephen to see Betty, to whom he had been married for twenty years. "A True Tale of Slavery," Chapters II and III.

4 Cabarrus Pocosin, "Snaky Swamp," lies southwest of Edenton (see Map 1); it is visible from the shipping channel in Albemarle Sound used by east-by-northeast traffic headed out to sea. This wild growth of bamboos and briars—which hid maroons (encampments of fugitive slaves) that sheltered legendary outlaws who raided nearby plantations and even Edenton—was repeatedly invaded by armed patrols searching for escaped slaves. *Edenton Gazette,* March 22, 1811; March 2, 1819; May 11, 1819.

XXI. The Loophole of Retreat

1 A reference to William Cowper's "The Task," IV.88–90:
'Tis pleasant, through the loopholes of retreat,
To peep at such a world, to see the stir

Of the great Babel, and not feel the crowd.

Jacobs was not the first Afro-American to use Cowper's phrase. In 1838 the phrase "From the loop-holes of Retreat" appeared as an epigraph to "The Curtain," a column in *Freedom's Journal* (New York).

2 John S. Jacobs describes the hiding place in "A True Tale of Slavery," Chapter IV. For a reconstruction of the plan of Molly Horniblow's house, see Illustrations.

3 Jacobs had bored the "loophole" on the south side of the house, facing West King Street. Norcom's office was across Broad on East King Street, less than a block away; his home on Eden Alley was a block north of Molly Horniblow's house (see Map 2).

4 Correspondence indicates that Norcom was traveling in August 1835. John Norcom to B. R. Norcom, M.D., NFP.

5 Meteorological data are not available for 1835–1842. From 1896–1913, the average mean temperature of Edenton was 60.65°F. Winters usually began after Christmas and were over by March 20. During the winter of 1896–97, the average mean temperature in January, the coldest month of the year, was 39.9°F. W. Scott Boyce, *Economic and Social History of Chowan County, North Carolina*, 1880–1915, Studies in History, Economics and Public Law, 76, no. I (New York: Columbia University Press, 1917), pp. 19–21; monthly reports from the Edenton Weather Station, 1896–1897, NCSA.

XXII. Christmas Festivities

1 Writing to his daughter in 1838, Norcom noted, "Had it not been for the John Koonahs that paraded through the town in several successive gangs Christmas day would have pass'd without the least manifestation of mirth cheerful joy or hilarity." James Norcom to Mary Matilda Norcom Jan. 13, 1838, NFP.

The festival has been extensively studied. In the words of John W. Nunley: "Jonkonnu (John Conner, etc.) is a creolized masquerade tradition that has incorporated African and English traditions of masking. Along the coast of West Africa and particularly in Freetown, two opposite manners of dressing frame the African masquerades. One consists of fancy paper and cloth stripes and beautiful headdresses; the other is made of animal parts, plain dark gunney sack material, and skin-covered horn headpieces. The same stylistic and aesthetic parameters are found in Jonkonnu of the West Indies, New Orleans, and the Carolinas. On both sides of this Atlantic tradition, the musical ensemble includes a metal-type gong (triangle), skin-headed drum, and wind instrument. The penchant for rum and the collecting of money by the maskers is also a shared trans-Atlantic tradition." Personal communication to Jean Fagan Yellin, Nov. 4, 1985. For African observances, see two articles by Nunley: "The Fancy and the Fierce: Yoruba Masking Traditions of Sierra Leone," *African Arts* 14 (Feb. 1981):52–58; and "Images and Printed Words in Freetown Masquerades," *African Arts* 15 (Aug. 1982): 42–46.

Frederick G. Cassidy, who points out that Jacobs's description is the sole citation in both the *Dictionary of American English* and in the *Dictionary of Americanisms,* stresses the Gold Coast origins of the celebration and its broad observance in the New World. "'Hipsaw' and 'John Canoe,'" *American Speech* 41 (1966): 145–51. For North Carolina observances, see Richard Walser, "His Worship the John Kuner," *North Carolina Folklore* 19 (1971):160–172; and Nancy Ping, "Black Musical Activities in Antebellum Wilmington, North Carolina," *The Black Perspective in Music* 8 (1980):139–160.

2 Dena Epstein reproduces this verse while discussing the John Canoe festival and comments that "the parallel with African songs of derision is evident." *Sinful Tunes and Spirituals* (Urbana: University of Illinois Press, 1977), p. 131. Lawrence Levine quotes an eighteenth-century English visitor to the United States who asserted that the slaves sang about their treatment by their masters and cites this verse with the comment, "Harriet Brent Jacobs recorded that during the Christmas season the slaves would ridicule stingy whites by singing [it]." *Black Culture and Black Consciousness: Afro-American Folk Thought from Slavery to Freedom* (New York: Oxford University Press, 1977), p. 12.

XXIII. Still in Prison

1 Albert Gallatin Brown (1813–1880) of Mississippi said on February 24, 1854, during congressional debate on the Kansas-Nebraska Bill, "I believe that slavery is of divine origin, and that it is a great moral, social, and political blessing—a blessing to the slave, and a blessing to the master." *Speeches, Messages and Other Writings of the Hon. Albert G. Brown,* ed. M. W. McLuskey (Philadelphia, 1859), p. 335.

2 Thomsonian medicine, originated by Samuel Thomson (1763–1843), treated illness by raising the internal temperature of the body.

3 The scriptural language and spiritual content of this passage testify to Jacobs's Bible reading while in hiding. See, for example, Job 8:3, 1 Corinthians 2:7, 13:12.

XXIV. The Candidate for Congress

1 On August 10, 1837, by a vote of 317–172 in the district and 191–15 in Edenton, Samuel Tredwell Sawyer was elected to the Twenty-Fifth Congress as a Whig, defeating Dr. G. C. Moore. Fourteen years earlier, before the clear emergence of two-party competition in North Carolina, Norcom had supported the successful Democratic congressional candidate Alfred M. Gatlin against Sawyer's uncle, the incumbent. Jacobs's description of Norcom's electioneering tactics in 1837 recalls his recital of this triumphant earlier effort: "I made Chowan give [Gatlin] 400 out of 480 votes . . . On the day of the election I fed & refreshed 290 persons in my own house & thereby secured to our friend the decisive . . . vote . . ." Election Returns for Member of Congress, 1837, Chowan County Records, 1772–1864, NCSA; Dr. James Norcom to John Norcom, Aug. 9, 1823; for Norcom's politics, also see his letters of July 9, 1827, June 14, 1841, Aug. 7, 1847, Nov. 25, 1847, Dec. 12, 1847, Nov. 15, 1848, and Aug. 3, 1850, NFP.

2 The first session of Congress began on September 4, 1837.

XXV. Competition in Cunning

1 By this time—probably late 1839—Stephen, the sailor husband of Jacobs's aunt Betty, had escaped. John S. Jacobs, "A True Tale of Slavery," Chapter III.

2 In denunciations of the *Tribune*'s Horace Greeley and his "nigger worshippers," the sensational New York *Herald,* founded in 1835 by James Gordon Bennett (1795–1872), openly expressed its antiblack, antiabolitionist bias. The *Herald* consistently opposed emancipation. Frank L. Mott, *American Journalism,* 3rd ed. (New York: Macmillan, 1962), p. 350; Don C. Seitz, *The James Gordon Bennetts, Father and Son* (Indianapolis: Bobbs-Merrill, 1928), p. 134.

3 Following the publication in Boston in 1829 of the incendiary pamphlet *An Appeal . . . to the Colored Citizens of the World* by North Carolina-born David Walker, and the establishment of William Lloyd Garrison's weekly newspaper *The Liberator* in 1831, Boston became known as the center of antislavery activity. In 1832, blacks and whites organizing the

New England Anti-Slavery Society formed a committee to defend kidnapped blacks, and Society counsel Samuel Sewell sued for the freedom of a
man called Francisco; in 1836, the judgment in the case of the slave child
Med (Commonwealth v. Aves) established that slaves brought into Massachusetts by their owners were free; in 1838, the Massachusetts legislature
voted that runaway slaves in Massachusetts had a right to trial by jury. The
state was antislavery in sentiment, and the abolitionists, although a minor-
ity, were indeed able to "get up a row" in Boston by 1839–1840. *William Lloyd
Garrison, The Story of his Life Told by his Children,* ed. Wendell Phillips
Garrison and Francis Jackson Garrison, 4 vols. (1885–1889, New York: Negro
Universities Press, 1969; hereinafter Garrison, *Life),* I, 159–161, 281–282; II, 79,
127–128; *The Letters of William Lloyd Garrison,* ed. Walter M. Merrill and
Louis Ruchames, 6 vols. (Cambridge, Mass.: Harvard University Press,
1971–1981; hereinafter Garrison, *Letters),* II, 195; 35 Mass. 193 (1836).

4 "There the wicked cease from troubling; and the weary be at rest." Job
3:17.

5 John S. Jacobs describes her cell in "A True Tale of Slavery" Chapter
IV.

XXVI. Important Era in My Brother's Life

1 Samuel Tredwell Sawyer was expected in Edenton in the late autumn
of 1838, after serving in Congress and getting married. John S. Jacobs
accompanied Sawyer and his bride-to-be, Lavinia Peyton (c. 1818–?), on
their wedding journey to Chicago, where they were married on August 11,
1838. Sawyer and his party then went to Canada before spending a few days
in New York en route to Edenton. John L. Cheney, Jr., *North Carolina Government,* 1585–1974 (Raleigh: North Carolina Department of the Secretary of
State, 1974), p. 680; Rev. Horace Edwin Hayden, *Virginia Genealogies*
(Washington, D.C.: The Rare Book Shop, 1931), p. 500; marriages and deaths
published in the *National Intelligencer, 1805–1850;* 1850 Census, Norfolk, Va.,
p. 103; John S. Jacobs, "A True Tale of Slavery," Chapter V.

2 John S. Jacobs identifies this neighbor as Aunt Sue Bent. She is
perhaps the slave woman Sue who, with two of her children and the other
property of the late James R. Bent, had been sold on January 2, 1826. She and
her son David were bought by Thomas M. Blount for $275.00; a boy called
Joseph Bent was bought by A. W. Mabine for $175.50. John S. Jacobs, "A True
Tale of Slavery," Chapter VI; Estate of James R. Bent, 1825, Chowan Estates.

3 John S. Jacobs writes of his leaving in "A True Tale of Slavery," Chapter V.

XXVII. New Destination for the Children

1 Mrs. Sawyer's sister Cornelia (c. 1810–?) and her husband B. F. Russell (c. 1800–1861) lived in Chicago; they later had a child, Peyton (born c. 1849). Hayden, *Virginia Genealogies*, p. 500; Chicago City Directory, 1839; 1850 Census, Chicago, Cook County, Illinois, p. 839.

2 Louisa Matilda was to be sent to James Iredell Tredwell (1799–1846), a Brooklyn merchant. Tredwell and Sawyer were first cousins, the sons of Helen Blair and Margaret Blair, respectively. Hathaway, *Register*, II, 458–463; Brooklyn City Directory, 1839; 1840 Census, Kings County, p. 680; New York *Evening Post*, July 25, 1846.

3 Laura, the Sawyers' oldest daughter, was born in Washington, D.C., and baptized at St. Paul's, Edenton, in January 1840. Entry for Jan. 1840, baptisms, St. Paul's Parish Register; 1850 Census, Norfolk, Va., p. 103.

4 Both of Lavinia Peyton Sawyer's sisters visited Edenton; this could refer either to Cornelia Peyton Russell or to Laura Peyton, later Laura Peyton Richards (c. 1813–?), who was baptized at St. Paul's along with Lavinia and baby Laura. 1850 Census, Alexandria, Va., p. 394; entry for Jan. 1840, baptisms, St. Paul's Parish Register.

5 Actually, Mary Matilda Norcom turned 18 on April 9, 1840. NFP.

6 The Brooklyn Tredwells had four daughters; Margaret, the oldest, was born in 1828. Hathaway, *Register*, II, 459–461.

XXVIII. Aunt Nancy

1 This infant probably was born at about the same time as Jacobs's son, Joseph. Writ of venditione exponas against Dr. James Norcom, Oct. 5, 1830, Chowan County Civil Actions Concerning Slaves, 1830, NCSA.

2 The assertion that Linda Brent's mother and aunt were twins is an exception to the generally striking accuracy in *Incidents* about Jacobs's family. It is not consistent with the statements in Chapter I that her mother was born three months before Margaret Horniblow and in Chapter XXVIII that her aunt was the "foster-sister" of Mary Matilda Horniblow Norcom, or, alternatively, was born c. 1790–91. Elsewhere Jacobs routinely refers to Betty (Aunt Nancy) as her mother's sister (although in the first sentence of this

chapter she calls her "my great-aunt"). Twins are nowhere mentioned in records referring to Molly Horniblow and her children.

3 Norcom's youngest son in 1842 was William Augustus (b. 1836). NFP.

4 Molly Horniblow's total of nine doubtless includes miscarriages and children dead in infancy; Mark Ramsey was now her only living child. Administrator's account, 1808, Estate of John Horniblow, 1799, Chowan Estates; Estate of Elizabeth Horniblow, 1827, Chowan Estates; Chowan County Record of Hiring of Slaves Belonging to Estates, 1808–1817, NCSA.

XXIX. Preparations for Escape

1 Jacobs apparently left the "den" in the middle of June 1842; she had entered it in August 1835. John S. Jacobs counted six years and eleven months. "A True Tale of Slavery," Chapter VI.

2 The North Star, which pointed the fugitives' way to freedom, was a subject of Afro-American culture. Slaves traced the shape of the Little Dipper, singing "Follow the drinking gourd," and in 1847 Frederick Douglass (c. 1817–1855), the most famous American fugitive slave, adopted *The North Star* as the name of his newspaper.

3 "Then one of the twelve, called Judas Iscariot, went unto the chief priests, And said unto them, What will ye give me, and I will deliver him unto you? And they covenanted with him for thirty pieces of silver." Matthew 26:14–15.

4 In fact, Jacobs visited Edenton after the Civil War and wrote a letter "sitting under the old roof." See Letter 15 in this volume, Jacobs to Ednah D. Cheney, April 25 (1867).

XXX. Northward Bound

1 Dismal Swamp, ten miles wide and thirty miles broad, begins in Virginia and extends into North Carolina to a point thirty miles north of Cabarrus Pocosin.

XXXI. Incidents in Philadelphia

1 Jacobs apparently arrived in Philadelphia during the third week in June 1842. Joshua Coffin to Lydia Maria Child, June 25, 1842, Anti-Slavery Collection, BPL, LMCP 14:389 (Letter 1).

2 Money of account (not a coin) used in Alexandria as well as in Philadelphia, a levy was worth eleven cents. Mary G. Powell, *The History of Old Alexandria, Virginia* . . . (Richmond: William Byrd Press, 1928), p. 345.

3 The Reverend Jeremiah Durham of the African Methodist Episcopal church was elected as a delegate to the General Conferences of 1836 and 1840, but records are not clear about his relationship to Bethel Church. Jeremiah Durham appears in the Philadelphia Directory as a carter living at 6 Barley Street in 1842; in 1846 Rev. J. Durham is reported as Pastor of Shiloh Church. The support of Bethel Church for the Philadelphia Vigilant Committee is documented by Committee records of September 2, 1841, which acknowledge a donation of $13.00 collected at Bethel. Daniel A. Payne, *History of the African Methodist Episcopal Church*, ed. Rev. C. S. Smith (Nashville, 1891), pp. 106, 111, 124; *McElroy's Philadelphia Directory for 1842*, p. 73; *Philadelphia Directory for 1846*, pp. 97, 453; Joseph A. Borome, "The Vigilant Committee of Philadelphia," *Pennsylvania Magazine of History and Biography* 92 (July 1968):320–351.

4 According to its records, the Philadelphia Vigilant Committee, an independent group with ties to the Anti-Slavery Society, aided 117 individuals between June 9 and September 8, 1842. Organized in 1837 under the leadership of black abolitionist Robert Purvis (1810–1898), the Committee was functionally a black organization after 1839. Among its members was Daniel Payne (see Preface by the Author, note 2). The group was reorganized in 1852 and led by black abolitionist William Still (1821–1902). Borome, "Vigilant Committee of Philadelphia"; Benjamin Quarles, *Black Abolitionists* (New York: Oxford University Press, 1969), pp. 154–155; William Still, *Still's Underground Rail Road Records*, 3rd ed. (Philadelphia, 1883), pp. 611–612.

5 "Fire—An alarm fire which prevailed about two o'clock yesterday morning, proved to be without foundation." Philadelphia *Public Ledger*, June 22, 1842, p. 2.

6 Robert M. J. Douglass, Jr. (1809–1887), a black Philadelphia portrait painter and lithographer who had studied in England with American artist Thomas Sulley, was in 1842 listed as a signpainter at 54 Mulberry in Philadelphia. In July of that year, however, he advertised his Gallery of Paintings at 202 William Street, New York City, where he offered to give instruction. *McElroy's Philadelphia Directory for 1842*, p. 70; *The Liberator*, July 8, 1842, p. 107.

7 Lymis Johnson, a member of the Philadelphia Vigilant Committee, was probably Jacobs's escort. The Philadelphia group worked in concert with the New York Committee of Vigilance. Stressing the importance of publicizing the resistance of fugitive slaves, abolitionist Joshua Coffin described Jacobs's escape—although he did not mention her name—to Child, then editor of the *National Anti-Slavery Standard*. Coffin to Child,

June 25, 1842, BPL Anti-Slavery Collection, LMCP 14:389 (Letter 1); Borome, "Vigilant Committee of Philadelphia."

8 The improvement was the result of struggle. For years, black and white abolitionists protested—in the words of Stephen S. Foster—against "the 'negro pew' ... wherever it may be found, whether in a gentile synagogue, a railroad car, a steamboat, or a stage coach." Quoted in Garrison, *Life*, III, 28. Nevertheless, as the system of railroads grew, black passengers were restricted to a segregated car even when they bought first-class tickets; black servants were permitted to travel with their employers. After Massachusetts antislavery advocates distributed petitions for equal accommodations in public transportation, the Massachusetts railroads voluntarily abolished segregation in 1843.

While working on *Incidents*, Jacobs wrote to Amy Post about her own experiences with segregated transportation: "I was in New York the week before Louisa and myself I stoped ten days to do the Winter shoping for Mrs Willis having a young baby she could not go herself and I had the little Girl portrait painted while there and I had a long distance to go to the Artist and they refused one day to take me in the Cars." Black New Yorkers, organizing themselves into a Legal Rights Association, repeatedly protested segregated streetcars. After a series of legal actions, this discrimination ended in 1861, although one line persisted in posting signs telling blacks that riding was not a right but a privilege. Jacobs to Post, Jan. 11 [1854?], IAPFP #786, BAP 16:0674–75; *The Liberator*, 11:132, 11:139, 11:175, 180, 182; Louis Ruchames, "Jim Crow Railroads in Massachusetts," *American Quarterly* 8 (1956):61–75; Leon F. Litwack, *North of Slavery* (Chicago: University of Chicago Press, 1961), pp. 111–112; *Anglo-African* (New York), Oct. 19, 1861, and July 16, 1864.

XXXII. The Meeting of Mother and Daughter

1 In 1842 James Iredell Tredwell, with whose family Louisa Matilda was living, resided on Lafayette near Jackson; his optical business was on Schermerhorn near Hoyt. *Brooklyn Alphabetical and Street Directory and Yearly Advertiser for 1842 and 1843.*

2 At that time, Myrtle Avenue ran from Fulton Street to Washington Park.

3 Mary Bonner Blount (1808–1869) had married Tredwell at Edenton in 1827; by 1842 they had five children. Hathaway, *Register*, II, 459–461.

4 Louisa Matilda had been away from her mother for two years, but

lived with the Tredwells only a part of that time; for five months she had lived in Washington with her father.

Louisa Matilda's Brooklyn years were an important time for black education in the city. In 1827, after being cast out of the segregated district school they had attended since 1816, black Brooklynites had built an African Free School on Nassau Street. In 1841—when Louisa Matilda might have attended the school its principal was William J. Wilson, "one of early Brooklyn's most respected Black intellectual leaders." A second African Free School had been opened at Carrville in Brooklyn's ninth ward in 1839. The following year, a committee including the mayor of Brooklyn met to discuss improvements in black education; subsequently, three blacks were appointed as district trustees of the African Free Schools. These schools were later incorporated into the Board of Education and renamed Colored Schools. Robert J. Swan, "Synoptic History of Black Public Schools in Brooklyn," in Charlene Claye Van Derzee, curator, *The Black Contribution to the Development of Brooklyn* (New York: New Muse Community, 1977), pp. 63–71.

5 James I. Tredwell is listed at "Custom House. Lafayette n. Carll," in the Brooklyn Directory for 1844. The 1846 entry reads, "James Tredwell. Clerk U.S.N. Willoughby near Gold." *Brooklyn Alphabetical and Street Directory . . . for 1844 and 1845; Brooklyn Directory . . . for 1846 and 1847.*

6 After his escape from slavery, John S. Jacobs had judged himself in need of education. Finding it difficult to work by day and attend school in the evening in New Bedford, he "thought the better plan would be to get such books as I should want, and go a voyage to sea." He shipped out on the whaler *Frances Henrietta* on August 4, 1839. "A True Tale of Slavery," Chapter VI; Alexander Starbuck, *History of the American Whale Fishery from its Earliest Inception to the Year 1876* (1878; New York: Argosy-Antiquarian, 1964), 2 vols., I, 354–355.

XXXIII. A Home Found

1 Mary Stace Willis (c. 1816–1845), daughter of General William Stace of Woolwich, England, and wife of American litterateur Nathaniel Parker Willis (1806–1867), had given birth to a daughter, Imogen, in the spring of 1842. The Willis family had moved to New York City a few months later, taking rooms at the Astor Hotel. Beers, *Willis,* pp. 170, 177, 264.

2 Samuel M. Elliott, M.D., was listed as an oculist and professor of the

diseases of the human eye at 261 Broadway, corner of Warren, upstairs, in *Longworth's American Almanac, New York Register, and City Directory* (New York, 1842), p. 25.

3 After a voyage of three and a half years, John S. Jacobs's ship returned to port on February 16, 1843. He writes that he "hurried on shore, drew some money of the owners, and made my way to New York. I found my sister living with a family as nurse at the Astor House. At first she did not look natural to me; but how should she look natural, after having been shut out from the light of heaven for six years and eleven months!" Starbuck, *American Whale Fishery,* I, 354–355; "A True Tale of Slavery," Chapter VI.

XXXIV. The Old Enemy Again

1 "It taught me the way to live / It taught me how to die." George Pope Morris (1802–1864), "My Mother's Bible."

2 Mary Matilda Norcom had several younger brothers: Abner (B. C. 1828), Standin (b. 1829), and William Augustus (b. 1836). John S. Jacobs presents a somewhat different account of this letter, naming Caspar Wistar (b. 1818), an older brother, as its signator, and dating it earlier as part of the correspondence between Jacobs and the Norcoms before her escape from the South. NFP; "A True Tale of Slavery," Chapter VI.

XXXV. Prejudice against Color

1 The *Knickerbocker,* run by the Troy Line, was built in 1843. Personal communication to Jean Fagan Yellin from Mrs. Michael Sweeney, City Historian, Saratoga Springs, N.Y., Oct. 23, 1985.

2 The United States Hotel at Saratoga Springs was one of America's most popular luxury hotels, and a favorite of Southerners, "the rich merchants from New Orleans, and the wealthy planter from Arkansas, Alabama, and Tennessee, with the more haughty and more polished landowner from Georgia, the Carolinas and Virginia." James Silk Buckingham, *America, Historical, Statistic, and Descriptive* (London, 1841), 3 vols., II, 435, quoted in John Hope Franklin, *A Southern Odyssey: Travelers in the Antebellum North* (Baton Rouge: Louisiana State University Press, 1976), p. 26.

3 In 1838 the car to which blacks were restricted was referred to as "the dirt car." In 1841 it was widely spoken of as the "Jim Crow" car, a reference to

the blackface song and dance routine of white performer Thomas D. Rice, who impersonated a black man called "Jim Crow." Ruchames, "Jim Crow Railroads in Massachusetts," p. 62; Robert C. Toll, *Blacking Up: The Minstrel Show in Nineteenth-Century America* (New York: Oxford University Press, 1974), p. 28.

4 The "large and splendid" Marine Pavilion at Rockaway, Queens, was built in 1833; before it burned three decades later, it hosted American writers such as Henry Wadsworth Longfellow and Washington Irving. "Resort Spot of the East," *South Shore Record* (Long Island), Sept. 16, 1971.

XXXVI. The Hairbreadth Escape

1 This was doubtless Joseph Blount, Mary Bonner Blount Tredwell's next-oldest brother, who was a bachelor. Hathaway, *Register,* 1, 34–35, 522–523.

2 Jacobs evidently revealed to Mary Stace Willis that she was a fugitive slave; she apparently did not, however, divulge her sexual history. Jacobs to Post [1852?], IAPFP #84, BAP 16:0700–02 (Letter 4).

3 Arent Van der Poel (1799–1870), twice elected to the New York State Legislature and twice to Congress, was judge of the Superior Court from 1843 to 1850. John Hopper (1815–1864), lawyer and agent for the New England Life Insurance Company, was the son of Quaker abolitionist reformer Isaac T. Hopper, who in 1847 founded the New York State Vigilance Committee. *National Cyclopedia of American Biography* XI:396; Child, *Letters,* p. 140; Quarles, *Black Abolitionists,* p. 154.

4 In the late 1830s a railroad was built from Providence, R.I. (already linked to Boston), to Stonington, Conn., where it connected with the Sound steamers from New York. Robert G. Albion, *The Rise of New York Port, 1845–1860* (New York: Scribner's, 1939, 1970), p. 155.

5 The *Rhode Island,* completed in 1836, was part of the fleet of the Rhode Island Steamboat Company, which maintained a regular schedule from New York to Providence. Henry Whittemore, *Fulfillment of Three Remarkable Prophecies in the History of the Great Empire State, Relating to the Development of Steamboat Navigation and Railroad Transportation, 1808– 1908* (1909), p. 91.

6 In Boston in 1844—while Jacobs and her children were there—the black community organized to press for integrated public schools, which

had been established elsewhere in the state. Particularly objectionable was Boston's inadequate Smith School. The struggle, led by Jacobs's friend the black abolitionist William C. Nell (1816–1874) and supported by white abolitionists, took various forms, including the creation of an interracial Negro School Abolition Society, a petition campaign, the organization of an alternative school, and a boycott. Louis Rucharies, "Race and Education in Massachusetts," *Negro History Bulletin* 13 (Dec. 1949):53–58, 71; Litwack, *North of Slavery,* pp. 143–150; James Oliver Horton and Lois E. Horton, *Black Bostonians: Family Life and Community Struggle in the Antebellum North* (New York: Holmes and Meier, 1979), pp. 70–76.

XXXVII. A Visit to England

1 Mary Stace Willis died giving birth to a stillborn child on March 25, 1845. Beers, *Willis,* p. 276.

2 Jacobs apparently apprenticed her son Joseph to a printer, for in a letter dated September 7, 1845, her brother refers to Joseph Jacobs as being in the *Rambler's* office. The owners were listed as printers in the 1846 Boston Directory, and the first number of the weekly newspaper *The Saturday Rambler* (Boston) appeared on May 2, 1846. John S. Jacobs to Sydney Howard Gay, Sept. 7, 1845, Gay Collection, Manuscript Division, Columbia University Libraries; Winifred Gregory, *American Newspapers, 1821–1936: A Union List* (1937; New York: Kraus, 1967), p. 280; *Stimpson's Boston Directory 1846,* p. 489; *Adams's New Directory of the City of Boston, 1846–47,* p. 31.

3 Jacobs sailed with Nathaniel Parker Willis and his daughter Imogen on the *Britannic.* Beers, *Willis,* p. 276.

4 Jacobs and Imogen Willis stayed at the Steventon Vicarage with Anne Stace Vincent and Rev. William Vincent, sister and brother-in-law of the late Mary Stace Willis. Ibid., p. 283.

5 In *Letters from the United States, Cuba and Canada* (1856), the English visitor Hon. Amelia Matilda Murray (1795–1884) presented a highly favorable view of slavery in America.

6 Initially, Willis planned to leave Imogen to be educated for a year in England. His language in a letter seems to suggest that Jacobs may have considered staying there: "Harriett, ... [Imogen's] maid, is still here, & will return with me probably." Willis to Mrs. Stetson, Nov. 25 [1845], N. P. Willis Collection, University of Iowa Libraries.

XXXVIII. Renewed Invitations to Go South

1 The printing trades in Boston were generally closed to blacks, although Garrison's *Liberator* and some other abolitionist presses hired blacks and in 1838 a black printer established a small shop for their training and employment. Martin R. Delany, *The Condition, Elevation, and Destiny of the Colored People of the United States* (1852; New York: Arno and The New York Times, 1968), pp. 27–28; Horton and Horton, *Black Bostonians*, p. 76.

2 Joseph Jacobs evidently did not return until early May 1849. Isaac Post to Amy Post, May 7, 1849, IAPFP #729.

3 Mary Matilda Norcom married Daniel Messmore in 1846. NFP.

4 John S. Jacobs, writing from Chelsea, Mass., reported to abolitionist Sydney Howard Gay that Jacobs "received a very affectionate letter lass week from her young mistress Mrs Mesmore." He mentioned in addition letters to Jacobs from other members of the Norcom family, and a letter from Norcom to the New York City police offering a reward of $100 for Jacobs. See Letter 2 in this volume, John S. Jacobs to Sydney Howard Gay, June 4, 1846, Sydney Howard Gay Collection, Columbia University (Letter 2).

5 "'Will you walk into my parlour?' said a spider to a fly; / 'Tis the prettiest little parlour that ever you did spy.'" Mary Howitt, "The Spider and the Fly."

6 Many believed that the Massachusetts personal liberty laws—and similar laws passed by other Northern states—virtually annulled the Fugitive Slave Law of 1850. Further, in 1851 black Bostonians rescued the escaped slave Shadrach from the courthouse, an act that suggested that public opinion would defy the new law. But shortly thereafter, when Thomas Sims was seized and jailed in the courthouse—inside the jury room reserved for federal cases, hence technically in a federal cell—authorities placed chains around the building to prevent a rescue effort and succeeded in returning Sims to slavery. Abolitionists made much of the symbolism of justices stooping under the chain. Three years later, chains were again placed around the courthouse and under the guns of the city police, the militia, the marines, and some regular troops. Anthony Burns was remanded from Boston to Virginia. Garrison, *Life*, III, 59, 92, 409–411, 416–417; Leonard W. Levy, "Sims' Case: The Fugitive Slave Law in Boston in 1851," *Journal of Negro History* 35 (1950):39–74; Samuel Shapiro, "The Rendition of Anthony Bums," *Journal of Negro History* 44 (1954):34–51.

XXXIX. The Confession

1 The Boston Directory for 1849–50 lists "Jacobs, Harriet N. dress maker, house 87 Charter."

2 Louisa Matilda Jacobs was evidently enrolled in the Young Ladies Domestic Seminary at Clinton, N.Y. Founded and administered by abolitionist Hiram H. Kellogg (1803–1881), this innovative institution combined the theoretical and the practical; from 1848 to 1850 it was coeducational. Louisa Matilda Jacobs to [John S. Jacobs], Nov. 5, 1849, IAPFP #765; "Class of 1822," *Hamilton Literary Monthly,* Jan. 1881, p. 204; Helen R. Rudd, *A Century of Schools in Clinton* (Clinton: Clinton Historical Society, 1964), pp. 18–20; A. D. Gridley, *History of the Town of Kirkland, New York* (New York, 1874), pp. 141–143.

3 Jacobs joined her brother in March 1849 and remained in Rochester until September 1850. He was lecturing and organizing for the Massachusetts Anti-Slavery Society and the New England Anti-Slavery Society, and from March to July 1849 was manager of the Anti-Slavery Office and Reading Room. She is listed in the Rochester City Directory for 1849–50 as "Jacobs, Harriet A., Mrs., Agent Anti-Slavery Reading Rooms, over 25 Buffalo." John S. Jacobs to Sydney Howard Gay, Sept. 7, 1845, Gay Papers, Columbia University Libraries; *The Liberator,* June 5, 1846, June 1, 1849, and Feb. 8, 1850; *North Star,* Dec. 29, 1848, and March 23–July 29, 1849, BAP 05:1067; *Daily American Directory of the City of Rochester for 1849–1850,* p. 155.

4 For about half of her Rochester stay, Jacobs lived in the home of abolitionist Quakers Isaac (1798–1872) and Amy Post (1802–1889), a local center of radical reform. Jacobs's correspondence with Amy Post begins during this period. In the first letter, written while Post was away on vacation, Jacobs reports on home matters. Jacobs to Post, Aug. 9 [1857? 1858?], IAPFP #1258, BAP 16:089; Nancy A. Hewitt, "Amy Kirby Post," *University of Rochester Library Bulletin* 37 (1984):5–22; Nancy A. Hewitt, *Women's Activism and Social Change, Rochester, New York, 1822–1871* (Ithaca: Cornell University Press, 1984); Jacobs to Post [May 1849], IAPFP #787, BAP 16:0678–79 (Letter 3).

XL. The Fugitive Slave Law

1 The reduction of Louisa Matilda's expenses was in accord with a practice whereby Hiram H. Kellogg, the founder of the school she attended, offered needy students reduced rates, underwriting half the expense himself and receiving the other half from abolitionist philanthropist Gerrit Smith (1797–1874); as early as 1839, this arrangement aided the education of at least four black women. Kellogg to Smith, April 30, 1839, Gerrit Smith Papers, Syracuse University.

2 In October 1846 Nathaniel P. Willis married Cornelia Grinnell (1825–1904), daughter of Cornelius Grinnell, Jr., and Mary Russell Grinnell and adopted daughter of her uncle Joseph Grinnell (1788–1885) and Sarah Russell Grinnell of New Bedford, Mass. Cornelia Willis's first child, Grinnell, was born on April 28, 1848. The following autumn the Willis family had bought a house at 198 Fourth Street. E. W. Grinnell, *Charts and Chronicles of Matthew Grenelle's Descendants, Sponsored by the Grinnell Family Association* (New Bedford Free Public Library, n.d.); Beers, *Willis*, pp. 287, 294.

3 "Nor grandeur hear with a disdainful smile / The short and simple annals of the poor." Thomas Gray, "Elegy in a Country Churchyard."

4 Metropolitan Hall, the popular name for Tripler Hall, was erected in 1850 on the west side of Broadway opposite Bond Street specifically for the American debut of Swedish singer Jenny Lind (1820–1887). Although not ready for her first performances in September, it was the site of her seventh New York appearance and of many of her later concerts. New York *Daily Tribune*, Sept. 22 and Oct. 24, 1850; Mary Henderson, *The City and the Theatre* (Clifton, N.J.: James T. White, 1973), pp. 107, 109.

5 At Zion Chapel Street Church on October 1, 1850, more than 1,500 people—most of them black—met to protest the arrest of James Hamlet, the first New York victim of the new fugitive slave law. John S. Jacobs was among those who spoke. He proposed that they organize a registry to enable quick gathering and dispensing of information about slavecatchers, then urged armed defiance of the law: "My colored brethren, if you have not swords, I say to you, sell your garments and buy one . . . They [earlier speakers] said that they [slavecatchers] cannot take us back to the South but I say, under the present law they can; and now I say unto you, let them only take your dead bodies . . . I, and my friends, advise you to show a front to our tyrants, and arm yourselves; aye, and I would advise the women to have knives too." This meeting raised $800 to buy Hamlet's freedom, and on

October 5 "several thousand" participated in a victory celebration welcoming him back to the city. Marion Gleason McDougall, *Fugitive Slaves, 1619–1865* (1891; New York: Bergman, 1969), pp. 43–44; Leo Hirsch, Jr., "The Negro and New York, 1783 to 1865," *Journal of Negro History* 16 (1931):408; *National Anti-Slavery Standard, Oct.* 10, 1850.

6 The black population of Manhattan grew from 10,886 in 1820 to 16,358 (5.5 percent) in 1840. Then it dropped to 13,815 (2.7 percent) in 1850 and to 12,574 (1.6 percent) in 1860. Mary White Ovington, *Half a Man: The Status of the Negro in New York* (1911; New York: Hill and Wang, 1969), p. 6; also see Hirsch, "The Negro and New York."

7 "I have not heard from the South in a great while I never go out in the day light accept I ride insite." Jacobs to Post [winter 1850–51?], IAPFP #788A, BAP 16:0683R.

8 "Many shall run to and fro, and knowledge shall be increased." Daniel 12:4. Jacobs evidently was involved in an organized effort to gather and pool information, such as her brother had proposed. Vigilance committees had operated in Manhattan since the black New York Committee of Vigilance was founded in 1835 under the leadership of abolitionist David Ruggles (c. 1811–1849). Quarles, *Black Abolitionists,* pp. 150–154.

9 Lilian, Cornelia Grinnell Willis's second child, had been born on April 27, 1850. Beers, *Willis,* p. 294.

10 Apparently Jacobs took little Lilian to the home of the baby's grandparents in New Bedford, Mass. Joseph Grinnell was not a Senator; he served in the House of Representatives as a Whig from 1843–1851. Grinnell absented himself from voting on the slave bill, as did many Northerners, to ensure the Compromise would be effected. *Biographical Directory of the American Congress,* 1774–1961, p. 977; *Congressional Globe* (Washington, D.C.), Sept. 12, 1850, pp. 1806–1807; Harriet Beecher Stowe, *Uncle Tom's Cabin,* ch. IX.

XLI. Free at Last

1 "Oh, free at last, free at last, / I thank God, I'm free at last." Anonymous spiritual. John W. Work, *Folk Song of the American Negro* (Nashville: Fisk University Press, 1915), pp. 45–46.

2 "And God shall wipe away all tears from their eyes; and there shall be no more death, neither sorrow, nor crying, neither shall there be any more pain; for the former things are passed away." Revelation 21:4.

3 "Remember now thy Creator in the days of thy youth, while the evil days come not, nor the years draw nigh, when thou shalt say, I have no pleasure in them." Ecclesiastes 12:1.

4 Dr. James Norcom died in Edenton on November 9, 1850. NFP.

5 The item "D. Missmore & I. Edenton" appeared under "Taylor's Hotel" (at 28 Courtland) in the column "Arrivals at City Hotels," New York *Evening Express*, Saturday, Feb. 28, 1852. *New York Business Directory, 1851–1852.*

6 Norcom excoriated Daniel Messmore as "a man whose origin & history nobody knows, who has no character amongst us; who is alike destitute of manners, morals & education, who in fact, is nothing less than an impersonation of impudence lewdness & obscenity! a reckless desperado, one of a set of wild & unprincipled adventurers who have been trying for more than a year now to establish a trading house here, without capital, credit, or character of any kind; & with any sort of recommendation." Messmore married Norcom's beloved daughter Mary Matilda in 1846 without obtaining Norcom's consent, following a series of violent episodes that split the Norcom family and the Edenton community: On January 7, 1845, Messmore assaulted Norcom's son Caspar Wistar with a stick and cowhide. Two days later, when Messmore was released from jail, young Norcom shot and wounded him and Messmore shot back. On March 1, a group of thirteen young men, including Dr. Norcom's son James, mobbed Messmore. In consequence, Messmore was indicted for perjury and Caspar Norcom was imprisoned. Daniel and Mary Matilda Norcom Messmore left Edenton, and in 1848 moved from Cincinnati, apparently to Norfolk; they eventually settled in New York. Norcom never forgave his disobedient daughter. Dr. James Norcom to [John Norcom], April 28, 1845, NFP; State v. Daniel Messmore, 1845, and State v. John Cox & Others, 1845, Chowan County Criminal Action Papers, 1844–1845, NCSA; Mary Matilda Norcom Messmore to Maria Norcom, July 4, 1848, NFP.

7 "The spirit of the Lord God is upon me; because the Lord hath anointed one to preach good tidings unto the meek; he hath sent me to bind up the brokenhearted, to proclaim liberty to the captives, and the opening of the prison to them that are bound." Isaiah 61:1. "Therefore all things whatsoever ye would that men should do to you, do ye even so to them: for this is the law and the prophets." Matthew 7:12.

8 In 1854 John Mitchel (1815–1875), Irish nationalist founder of the proslavery newspaper *The Citizen* (New York), wrote: "We, for our part, wish

we had a good plantation, well-stocked with healthy negroes, in Alabama." This provided considerable discussion in *The Liberator,* Jan. 27 and Feb. 10, 1854; William Dillon, *Life of John Mitchel* (London, 1888), 2 vols., II, 44.

9 "Surely oppression maketh a wise man mad; and a gift destroyeth the heart." Ecclesiastes 7:17.

10 Messmore apparently assumed—correctly—that Jacobs did not · know that Norcom, acting as his daughter's natural guardian, had in 1837 legalized his sale of the children with a bill of substitution that assigned two other slave children of equal value to his daughter's estate (see Illustrations). Chowan Deeds, Book L-2, p. 256.

11 "He hath stripped me of my glory, and taken the crown from my head." Job 19:9.

12 This transaction, effected with the aid of Rev. John B. Pinney of the New York Colonization Society, is explained in a letter from Cornelia Grinnell Willis to Elizabeth Davis-Bliss Bancroft [May 3, 1852], Bancroft-Bliss Family Papers, Library of Congress.

13 "There the wicked cease from troubling; and there the weary be at rest." Job 3:17. Molly Horniblow was buried at Edenton on September 4, 1853. Personal communication to Jean Fagan Yellin from Rev. R. W. Storie, Rector, St. Paul's Parish, Edenton, Aug. 24, 1981.

14 Mark Ramsey (also known as Mark Horniblow?) died in the fall of 1858. Josiah Collins to Jacobs, July 23, 1859, Josiah Collins Papers, 1761–1892, NCSA.

15 This eulogy has not been found. For other instances of black men being eulogized in the North Carolina press of the period, see *Abstracts of Vital Records from Raleigh, North Carolina Newspapers, 1799–1819,* comp. Lois Smathers Neal (Spartanburg, S.C.: The Reprint Company, 1979), 1, 259, 270.

16 In 1844 the North Carolina Supreme Court declared that "free persons of color in this State are not to be considered as citizens . . ." State v. Elijah Newsome, Dec. Term 1844, 27 *N.C. Reports* 250, quoted in Bassett, *Slavery in North Carolina, p. 37.*

Appendix

1 Post's endorsement was written in response to Jacobs's request and follows the outline Jacobs proposed. Jacobs to Post, June 21 [1857], IAPFP #90, BAP 16:0676–678 (Letter 10).

2 The story of Jacob serving for Rachel is in Genesis 29:20–28. "He hath stripped me of my glory; and taken the crown from my head." Job 19:9.

3 George W. Lowther (1822–1898) was the son of Polly Lowther (?–1864), a free black neighbor and contemporary of Jacobs's grandmother who was, like her, a baker in Edenton. Lowther was privately educated in Edenton. He moved to Boston in 1838, and during the 1850s renewed his friendship with Jacobs. A member of W. C. Nell's circle, Lowther earned his living as a hairdresser. After the Civil War, he became active in the Republican Party, and in 1878 and 1879 was elected to the Massachusetts House of Representatives. 1840 Census—North Carolina, Chowan County, p. 208; 1850 Census—North Carolina, Chowan County, p. 251; Eighth Census of the United States—North Carolina, Chowan County, p. 276; Estate of Polly Lowther, 1864, Chowan Estates; W. C. Nell to Amy Post, Sept. 11–13, IAPFP #112, and July 31, 1854, IAPFP #1031; Massachusetts State Library Legislative Biographical File; Boston *Journal,* Oct. 7, 1898, p. 5.

A True Tale of Slavery

1 John's first owner was Margaret Horniblow (1797–July 3, 1825), the invalid daughter of the tavern owner John Horniblow (1745? 1750?–1799) and Elizabeth Pritchard Horniblow (1771?–1827); why he here calls her "Penelope" is a mystery. (Perhaps he is thinking of his father's mistress, Sarah Penelope Knox.) In her will, dated April 8, 1825, Margaret Horniblow bequeathed to her mother Elizabeth Horniblow "one negro boy named John," as well as his uncle Mark Ramsey, his aunt Nancy, and his sister Harriet. Then, in a deathbed codicil, she gave Harriet to her niece Mary Matilda Norcom. *Raleigh Register* (weekly issue), July 22, 1825; Will of Margaret Horniblow, 1825, Chowan Wills. See Illustrations.

2 John S. Jacobs's father, Elijah (?–c. 1826), was the slave of Dr. Andrew Knox, and after 1816, of the doctor's widow, Sarah Penelope Knox. John S.'s mother, Delilah (?–c. 1819), was the daughter of Molly Horniblow (c. 1771–1853) the slave of Elizabeth Pritchard Horniblow, who gave Delilah to her daughter Margaret. Will of Dr. Andrew Knox, May 20, 1816, Pasquotank Wills; inventory of the personal estate of Dr. Andrew Knox, 1816, Pasquotank Estates. Estate of Elizabeth Horniblow, 1827, Chowan Estates; Answer of James Norcom.

3 Slaves could own no real property and could not receive legacies. A 1741 act prohibited their ownership of livestock, but they were allowed to

own poultry and dogs. This act also forbade slaves to leave their master's plantation without a written pass. It was apparently common for masters to permit slaves to raise small amounts of crops such as cotton, corn, and potatoes, which the masters then sold, paying the proceeds to the slaves. The North Carolina Supreme Court refused to hear arguments of self-defense or accidental homicide in an 1857 appeal from a slave husband condemned to die for the attempted rescue of his wife, which resulted in the death of the overseer who was beating her. See Thomas Cunningham's Heirs v. Thomas Cunningham's Executors, 1 N.C. 519 (1801); "An Act Concerning Servants and Slaves," 1741, sec. 43, 44; Robert McNamara v. John Kerns et al., 24 N.C. 66 (1841); Thomas Waddill v. Charlotte D. Martin, 38 N.C. 562 (1845); see State v. David, a Slave, 49 N.C. 353 (1857).

4 Dr. James Norcom (1778–1850) was the husband of Mary Horniblow Norcom (1794–1808), sister of John's first owner, Margaret Horniblow, who had already taught John's sister Harriet how to read. See *Incidents,* p. 9; NFP.

5 John's recollection of the sequence of events appears faulty. In 1824 Elijah's young mistress Lavinia Matilda Knox married James Coffield, and it was probably shortly after this time that Elijah came under Coffield's rule. Elijah apparently died in the spring of 1826. Lavinia Matilda Knox Coffield died in 1828; Elijah's old mistress Sarah Penelope Knox lived on until 1833. *Raleigh Register,* July 9, 1824; Estate of Sarah P. Knox, 1833, Chowan Estates.

6 Elizabeth Horniblow died in 1827, and on January 1, 1828, her executors, Dr. James Norcom and William R. Norcom, auctioned off her property. John's uncle Mark at $406.00 and his grandmother Molly at $52.25 were bought by Hannah Pritchard, sister of the dead Elizabeth Horniblow. Pritchard owned no property, and John S. here perhaps suggests that it was to Congressman Alfred Moore Gatlin (1790–?), Pritchard's attorney, that Molly entrusted her savings. Molly's younger son Joseph had earlier been bought by Josiah Collins the younger, and her daughter Betty was the property of Mary Horniblow Norcom. John does not here mention Molly's other daughter, Becky, the property of Elizabeth Horniblow Hoskins, who had left Edenton. Will of Elizabeth Horniblow, 1827, Chowan Wills; Estate of Elizabeth Horniblow, 1827, Chowan Estates; Chowan Deeds G-2, p. 395 (1817); Answer of James Norcom; "Alfred Moore Gatlin," *Biographical Directory of the American Congress, 1774–1961* (Washington, D.C.: U.S. Government Printing Office, 1961), pp. 990–991.

7 Records indicate that a slave named Bridget brought the lowest price;

she was bought by Dr. James Norcom for $17.50. Charles was sold to Joseph H. Skinner for $630.00, the highest price of the day. Norcom bought John for $298.50. Tom, Esther, and Mourning brought $279.00, $80.00, and $150.00. Estate of Elizabeth Horniblow, 1827, Chowan Estates; also see *Incidents*, p. 13.

8 Less than four months after Molly's sale, the Superior Court granted Hannah Pritchard's petition to free her. In giving Molly her freedom, the Court bound Hannah Pritchard, John W. Littlejohn, James Moffatt, and Alfred Moore Gatlin—who had written Pritchard's original petition—as guarantors that Molly would not become a dependent of the county. John S. here suggests that although both Molly and Mark were sold to Miss Pritchard, Molly herself was their actual purchaser, and that Gatlin was instrumental in this transaction, as well as in effecting Molly's freedom. Petition for Emancipation, 1828, Chowan Miscellaneous Slave Records.

9 Joseph ran from Josiah Collins the younger; in New York he was spotted by Collins's attorney, Joseph B. Skinner. Harriet Jacobs describes Joseph's return to Edenton in chains, his half-year in the jail, his sale to New Orleans, and his escape to New York; *Incidents*, pp. 26–29.

10 Harriet Jacobs describes their meeting; *Incidents*, p. 31.

11 Harriet Jacobs describes the events discussed in this paragraph in *Incidents*, Chapters XI, XIV, XVI, and XVII.

12 John is quoting Patrick Henry's speech to the Virginia Convention, March 1775. Deciding to attempt her escape, Harriet Jacobs uses this same quotation; *Incidents*, p. 127.

13 Harriet Jacobs quotes from a broadside in which Dr. Norcom offered a reward of $150.00 if she was captured in North Carolina and $300.00 if she was taken outside the state; *Incidents*, p. 125. Norcom also advertised for her capture in the daily *American Beacon* (Norfolk, Va.) from June 30 to July 13, 1835, offering a reward of $100.00 (see Illustrations).

14 In 1834 James Iredell Tredwell (1799–1846)—first cousin to Samuel Tredwell Sawyer, the father of Harriet Jacobs's children—was living at 81 Chambers Street in New York; by 1836 he had moved to 371 Broadway. Dr. Norcom's absence from Edenton in July 1835 is documented; see James Norcom to "My dear Son," dated Philadelphia, July 9, 1835, NFP; and John Norcom to "Dear Rush," Washington [N.C.], Aug. 10, 1835, noting that Norcom visited on his way back to Edenton, NFP. Harriet Jacobs discusses Norcom's trip; *Incidents*, pp. 134–135. J. P. B. Hathaway, ed. *The North*

Carolina Historical and Genealogical Register II (Baltimore: Genealogical Publishing Co., 1970), pp. 459, 463; *Longworth's American Almanac, New-York Register, and City Directory* for 1834, p. 681; for 1836, p. 664.

15 George Lamb, an immigrant from London, England, became a U.S. citizen in 1825 and, following William Grimes's death in 1831, succeeded Grimes as jailor. Evidently he had taken tea with John at the home of Gustavus Adolphus Johnson (1790–1842), the son of an unknown slave woman and Congressman Charles Johnson of Bandon Plantation. Gustavus A. Johnson occupied an unusual position in Edenton: manumitted in early childhood by private act, under the guardianship of Samuel Tredwell, he was educated by private tutors and taught cabinetmaking by James Borritz, a master craftsman. In 1814 he purchased and married Elizabeth. Johnson lived with his wife and their six children (emancipated by him or born free), at the northeast corner of Broad and Albemarle, where he established his home and cabinetmaker's shop. Order to deliver jailed slaves, April 4, 1831, in Hayes Collection, 1694–1928, Southern Historical Collection, University of North Carolina Library, Chapel Hill; Sketch of Charles Johnson in William S. Powell, ed., *Dictionary of North Carolina Biography;* "Bill to Emancipate a mulatto boy by the name of Gustavus Adolphus Johnston in the County of Chowan" in N.C. General Assembly Session Records, Nov.–Dec. 1795—Senate Bills, Dec. 1, 1795, NCSA; 55 letters and notes, 1815–1828, from G. A. Johnson to Samuel Tredwell, and memorandum of "vouchers omitted in annexed account of G. A. Johnson" [1826], in Charles E. Johnson Collection, NCSA; Bill of Sale, Dec. 30, 1813, James R. Bent to Gustavus A. Johnson, for "a certain yellow girl named Betty," in Chowan Deeds F-2, p. 389; Petition for Emancipation of Elizabeth, Mary, Ann, and Charles, and attendant papers, 1822, Chowan Misc. Slave Papers; order of manumission, Sept. Term 1822, Minutes of the Chowan County Court, 1812–1827, P. 321, NCSA; Apprentice bonds of Thomas J., William, and Elizabeth G. Johnson, Feb. 6, 1843, in Chowan County Apprentice Bonds, 1830–1843, NCSA; 1830 Census of Chowan Co., N.C., p. 337, and 1840 Census of Chowan Co., N.C. p. 207; will of Gustavus A. Johnson, 1842, in Chowan Wills.

16 Gustavus A. Johnson had three daughters: Mary, b. 1816; Ann, b. 1818; and Elizabeth, b. 1828. In 1843 Ann would marry John's uncle Mark Ramsey. Bond of Marcus Ramsey for his marriage to Ann Johnson, Nov. 22, 1843, in Chowan County Marriage Bonds, 1741–1868, NCSA; will of Ann Ramsey Mayo, 1890, in Chowan Wills.

17 Starting in 1828, Joseph Granier of Norfolk advertised that he had

become an agent for the slave-trading house of Leon Chambert in New Orleans. *American Beacon and Virginia and North-Carolina Gazette* (Norfolk, Va.), Dec. 20, 1828 ff. Harriet Jacobs reports that, through a speculator, Samuel Tredwell Sawyer offered $900 for John and $800 for Joseph and Louisa; *Incidents,* p. 136.

18 Uncle-in-law Stephen and his owner have not been identified. "What therefore God hath joined together, let not man put asunder." Mark 10:9.

19 Samuel Tredwell Sawyer, the father of Harriet Jacobs's children.

20 Harriet Jacobs describes these events in *Incidents,* pp. 136–137. Later Norcom, "in consideration of the sum of five hundred dollars received from the sale of two mulatto Slaves named Joe & Luisa, the Children of woman Harriet who was bequeathed to my daughter Mary Matilda Norcom," substituted two other slaves, "the Children of Melah named Penelope & John," to repay his daughter. Chowan Deeds, Book L-2, p. 256. See Illustrations.

21 Before Nat Turner's insurrection, free persons of color who could not pay their fines, court costs, and jail fees were permitted relief under the insolvent debtors act. But the 1831–32 "Act to Provide for the Collection of Fines Upon Free Negroes or Free Persons of Colour" stipulated that the sheriff hire out any free person of color unable to pay; if the person hired out were to run off, "he or she shall be liable and bound to make up such time so elapsed by serving double the time thereof." This act does not mention selling the bondservant into slavery. *Acts Passed by the General Assembly of the State of North Carolina . . . 1831–32* (Raleigh: Lawrence and Lemay, 1832), ch. 13, p. 10.

22 John's chains were removed at the home of J. B. Skinner, who at retirement had moved to a farm one mile from Edenton. Richard Benbury Creecy, "Joseph B. Skinner," *Grandfather's Tales of North Carolina History* (Raleigh: Edwards and Broughton, 1901), pp. 132–135.

23 Sawyer sent John out to the plantation on the Hertford Road, a little more than a mile from downtown Edenton; Deposition of James I. Tredwell in response to interrogatories submitted to him on Jan. 5, 1831, in the suit, M. E. Sawyer versus James C. Johnston, Chowan County Road Records, 1830–1839, NCSA. Harriet Jacobs discusses learning that Sawyer had bought her brother and the children, whom he sent to her grandmother; she also discusses Norcom's threats against John and the arrest of Mark Ramsey; *Incidents,* pp. 139–142.

24 Samuel Tredwell Sawyer's house was near the western end of the

block where Molly Horniblow's house stood on King Street between
Granville and Broad (see Map 2). In his will, Sawyer's father left his estate to
Samuel Tredwell Sawyer with instructions to care for his brother and sister.
Sawyers sick sister, Helen, died July 6, 1836; his sick brother, Dr. Matthias E.
Sawyer, died in 1837. Estate of James Coffield, 1843, Chowan Estates; Will of
Matthias E. Sawyer, 1835, Chowan Wills; Entry for Helen Sawyer in Part I,
Communicants, St. Paul's Parish Register; *Raleigh Register,* Dec. 18, 1837.

25 Frederick Douglass, condemning the medical care afforded the slaves,
recalled the prescriptions of "Uncle" Isaac Cooper: "For diseases of the body,
epsom salts and castor oil. . ." *Life and Times* (1892) (New York: Collier,
1962), p. 42.

26 Some of the 27 adult and 23 children Samuel Tredwell Sawyer listed in
his 1835 inventory of slaves served the family in town. The rest worked on
Sawyer's 250-acre plantation producing crops of clover, oats, corn, and
cotton. Estate of Matthias E. Sawyer, 1835, Chowan Estates.

27 For Harriet Jacobs's description of "the loophole of retreat," see
Incidents, pp. 146–147. For a reconstruction of the plan of Molly Horniblow's
home, see Illustrations.

28 Samuel Tredwell Sawyer was elected to the 25th Congress as a Whig
on August 10, 1837, defeating Dr. G. C. Moore by a vote of 191–15 in Edenton
and 317–172 in the district. See *Incidents,* p. 159. Election Returns for Member
of Congress, 1837, Chowan County Records, 1772–1864, NCSA.

29 During the first session, September 4–October 16, 1837, Sawyer lived
at Mrs. Lindenberger's on Capitol Hill and boarded at Mrs. Ann Eliza
Peyton's Congress Boarding House, where Peyton's nieces Laura (c. 1813–?)
and Lavinia (c. 1818–?) were staying. During the second session, December 4,
1837–July 9, 1838, he lived at Gadsby's National Hotel. Rev. Horace Edwin
Hayden, *Virginia Genealogies* (Washington, D.C.: The Rare Book Shop, rpt.
1931), p. 500; P. M. Goldman and J. S. Young, eds., *U.S. Congressional
Directories 1789–1843* (New York: Columbia University Press, 1973), pp. 278,
318–319; *Washington Directory* (Washington, D.C.: S. A. Elliot, 1830), p. 61;
Full Directory for Washington City, Georgetown, and Alexandria (Washington, D.C.: Wm. Greer, 1834), pp. 21, 43.

30 Sawyer's fiancée, Lavinia Peyton, had a sister, Cornelia Peyton Russell,
who was married to Col. Ira B. F. Russell, U.S.A. The Russells lived in
Chicago. Hayden, *Virginia Genealogies,* p. 500; Chicago City Directory, 1839.

31 Sawyer and Lavinia Peyton were married in Chicago on August 11,

1838, by Rev. Dr. Johnson. Marriages and deaths published in the *National Intelligencer, 1800–1850.*

32 The slaves' "grapevine" was still functioning five years later when, on first arriving in New York, Harriet Jacobs got in touch with "an old friend from my part of the country"; *Incidents*, p. 211. In 1835, when the Astor House Hotel was under construction on Broadway between Vesey and Barclay Streets, the *Mirror* commented that already a number of suites had been booked by "the most fashionable and wealthy people." In *Wilson's Business Directory*, Johnson Jeremiah & Co. is listed under "Trunkmakers" at three locations: 40 Fulton, 263 Pearl, and 102 Maiden Lane; the Fulton Street shop would have been visible from the Astor. John A. Kouwenhoven, *The Columbia Historical Portrait of New York* (Garden City, N.Y.: Doubleday, 1953), p. 176; *Wilson's Business Directory of New-York City* (New York: H. Wilson, 1848), p. 234.

33 Connecting New York City to Providence, Rhode Island, was the Rhode Island Steamboat Company, which had launched the modern steamers the *Massachusetts* and the *Rhode Island* in 1836. John S. probably took the Boston and Providence railroad to Taunton, Massachusetts, and the New Bedford and Taunton railroad on to New Bedford. Henry Whittemore, *Fulfillment of Three Remarkable Prophecies in the History of the Great Empire State, Relating to the Development of Steamboat Navigation . . . and Railroad Transportation, 1808–1908* (1909), p. 91; Kenneth T. Jackson and James Truslow Adams, eds., *Atlas of American History*, rev. ed. (New York: Charles Scribner's Sons, 1978), p. 127.

34 Dr. James Norcom died in Edenton on November 9, 1850. NFP. Writing that he would be pleased to meet Sawyer "as a countryman and a brother," John S. Jacobs is signifying on both the abolitionist slogan "Am I Not a Man and a Brother?" and the fact that Sawyer, who had fathered Harriet Jacobs's children, was functionally his brother-in-law.

35 Virginia-born William Piper (1786–1870), a hostler who in 1841 lived at 46 Bedford Street in New Bedford, was a community leader and an activist, as was Amelia J. Piper, his wife. James de T. Abajian, comp., *Blacks in Selected Newspapers, Censuses and Other Sources . . .* , III (Boston: G. K. Hall, 1977), p. 70; cemetery card, Oak Grove Cemetery, New Bedford, Mass.; New Bedford *Evening Standard,* June 13, 1870, p. 3; "Index of Blacks of New Bedford as Surveyed from the New Bedford City Directories, 1838–1845," comp. Judith Downey, New Bedford Whaling Museum; Marilyn Baily,

"Index of Activist Black Women" (manuscript); *Frederick Douglass' Paper,*
Sept. 30, 1853; *Liberator,* May 26, June 5, 1840, and July 15, 1859. Thanks to the
late Marilyn Baily, to Judith Downey of the New Bedford Whaling Museum,
and to Joan E. Barney of the Free Public Library of the City of New Bedford.

36 The whaler *Frances Henrietta* weighed anchor at New Bedford on
August 4, 1839, and returned on February 16, 1843. Alexander Starbuck,
*History of the American Whale Fishery from its Earliest Inception to the Year
1876* (1878; New York: Argosy-Antiquarian, 1964), 2 vols. I, 354–355.

37 Robert H. Piper (1814–1875), son of William and Amelia Piper, in 1841
worked aboard the ship *Jefferson.* Jacobs describes her visit to New Bedford
in search of her brother; *Incidents,* p. 214. Abajian, *Blacks in Selected
Newspapers, Census and Other Sources . . .* , III, p. 70; "Deaths Registered in
the City of New Bedford," *Vital Records,* vol. 4, p. 35, Free Public Library of
the City of New Bedford; New Bedford *Evening Standard,* Sept. 23, 1875.
Thanks to Joan E. Barney.

38 John S.'s timing tallies with his sister's: she had escaped from
Norcom's plantation in June of 1835, and after her years in hiding, sailed
north to Philadelphia, where she stayed briefly until traveling to New York
on June 24, 1842. Advertisement for the capture of Harriet Jacobs, Illustrations, p. 215; Joshua Coffin to Lydia Maria Child, Philadelphia, 25 June 1842
(Letter 1). Harriet Jacobs describes their meeting; *Incidents,* p. 218.

39 It was Samuel Tredwell Sawyer who had written ahead to prepare his
house, and it was Molly Horniblow's neighbor Dr. Edward C. Warren
(1828–1893)—later chosen by her to act as a co-executor of her will—who
queried Sawyer. "Aunt" Sue Bent may have been the woman who, along with
two of her sons, was among the twenty slaves belonging to the late James R.
Bent who were sold on January 2, 1826. With her son David, Sue was bought
for $275.00 by Thomas M. Blount; A. W. Mabine bought a boy called Joseph
Bent for $175.50. Will of Molly Horniblow, 1853, Chowan Wills; Estate of
James R. Bent, 1825, Chowan Estates. In Harriet Jacobs's description of this
scene she calls the neighbor "Aggie" and renders her speech in dialect;
Incidents, pp. 171–172.

40 Harriet Jacobs writes that this letter from Norcom's son was written
after her escape north in 1842 in response to her request that Norcom and
his daughter consent to her sale. See *Incidents,* p. 213; Jacobs includes a
lengthier version of the letter on pp. 219–221.

41 For Jacobs's discussion of her passage north, see *Incidents,* pp. 189–
203.

42 This paragraph collapses two events that Jacobs reports as years apart. John S. Jacobs writes that Mary Bonner Blount Tredwell (1808–1869), the wife of Sawyer's cousin James Iredell Tredwell, warned Jacobs that she had been betrayed to Dr. Norcom; for Harriet Jacobs's account, see *Incidents*, p. 230. Back in New York several years later, Harriet Jacobs received a letter from her young mistress Mary Matilda Norcom Messmore, who in 1846 had left Edenton after marrying Daniel Messmore; *Incidents*, pp. 238–240. Hathaway, ed., *North Carolina Historical and Genealogical Register*, II, no. 3, July 1901, p. 459. Also see Dr. James Norcom to [John Norcom], April 28, 1845, NFP; State v. Daniel Messmore, 1845, and State v. John Cox & Others, 1845, Chowan County Criminal Action Papers, 1844–45, NCSA; Dr. James Norcom to Miss Haworth, 22 May, 1846, NFP. For John S. Jacobs's immediate comment on Mary Matilda Norcom Messmore's letter, see John S. Jacobs to Sydney Howard Gay, June 4, 1846, Sydney Howard Gay Collection, Columbia University (Letter 2).

43 The reference is to the Fugitive Slave Law, passed by Congress as part of the Compromise of 1850, which commanded "all good citizens to aid and assist" in the apprehension and return of fugitive slaves. The penalty for harboring a fugitive or hindering an arrest was set at $1000 and imprisonment of not more than six months. *United States Statutes at Large*, 9:1850, c. 60. For Harriet Jacobs's account of her escape to Boston, see *Incidents*, pp. 231–233.

44 According to Harriet Jacobs, the chronology is this: in 1844, threatened with capture by Norcom, she fled from New York to Boston with the aid of her brother. In 1846—when she returned from her trip to England with Nathaniel Parker Willis and his daughter Imogen—she received a letter from Mary Matilda Norcom Messmore urging her to return south. In 1848, after her daughter left for boarding school, she joined her brother in Rochester, where he was lecturing for the antislavery movement. Then in 1850, when John S. Jacobs decided to join the California gold rush, he conferred with Cornelia Grinnell Willis, his sister's New York employer. See *Incidents*, pp. 231–233, 238–340, 242–243, 245–246.

45 For Harriet Jacobs's account, see *Incidents*, pp. 253–258.

46 Stephen Cabarrus of Bayonne, France, arrived in North Carolina in 1776 and acquired by marriage the estate of Pembroke, one mile west of Edenton on Pembroke Creek, which empties into Edenton Bay on Albemarle Sound. At his death, his brother Auguste Cabarrus was bequeathed a life estate in the personal property, and in 1820, after the death of Auguste,

the slaves were sold. In his will, Stephen Cabarrus mentions George, one of the children of "Mariann the washing woman." This appears to be the young man bought by John Popelston at the Cabarrus estate sale. On June 20, 1829, hurt by the bank closings, Popelston sold thirty-five-year-old George Cabarrus to Jonathan B. Haughton. Haughton probably sold George to the trader in 1832 or 1833. Will of Stephen Cabarrus, 1808, Chowan Wills; Chowan County Deed Book 1–2, p. 247, NCSA.

47 On Sunday, September 16, 1833, Thomas V. Hathaway, Chowan County Coroner, testified that an inquest was held at Haughton and Booth's wharf over "the body of a negro Man (name unknown) . . . found in a canoe up the creek, in a coave, near Pembroke, lying dead . . . The Body burried under the direction of the coroner . . ." Chowan County Miscellaneous Records—Inquests (various dates, 1803–1834), NCSA.

Harriet Jacobs had reported this atrocity in her pseudonymous letter to the New York *Tribune* of July 25, 1853: "It was a slave that been a runaway from his master twelvemonths. After that time a white man is justified in shooting a slave, he is considered an outlaw. This slave man was brought to the wharf, placed in a small boat, by two white men, early in the morning, with his head severed from his body, and remained there in an August sun until noon, before an inquest was held. Then he was buried, and not a word of murder or of arrest was heard." Writing to Amy Post concerning this letter, she commented, "I was at home when the poor outlawed was brung in town with his head severed from his body." Harriet [Jacobs] to My Dear Friend, Oct. 9, [1853] (Letter 7).

48 Tom Hoskins was owned by Dr. Norcom's son James Jr., from whom Harriet Jacobs escaped. In June 1836, a year after she fled, Tom Hoskins ran away from Auburn. Three days later he was shot and killed near Edenton. Abigail, a slave woman owned by Martha Blount (who may have been Jacobs's protectress) told the coroner that on Thursday, June 16, near the Chinquapin Chapel on the outskirts of Edenton, "she saw Mr Wm Rea Shoot a gun off . . . [and] she heard the groans of what she thought to be some human being." Chowan County Miscellaneous Records—Inquests (1836), NCSA.

49 The initial "N" appears to be a printer's error. It was the three Coffield brothers who were named William, James, and Josiah. Dr. Matthias E. Sawyer's shop was located in East King Street to the west of Dr. Norcom's shop where John S. served as shop boy (see Map 2). Deed from Samuel T. Sawyer to Sarah M. Webb, 1837, Chowan Deeds, Book M-2, p. 453.

Information about the Coffields' runaway slaves is hard to find, and 1820s copies of the *Edenton Gazette* are rare: for 1822, only January and February issues exist; there are none for 1823–1826, only four for 1827, and seven for 1828. The paper ceased publication on December 28, 1831. The issues that have survived record that between August 21, 1820, and July 18, 1829, James Coffield advertised on six different occasions for runaway slaves. Outlawry—a legal status assigned by three justices to individuals involved in felonious activity—is mentioned in one of these: in the *Edenton Gazette* of Sept. 17, 1821, Dick, belonging to Coffield, and Bob, belonging to Willis Elliott, "runaways lurking about Chowan County and committing depreciations on property or threatening the lives of citizens," were given five days to surrender or be declared outlaws.

50 Agnes (1800–?), a slave belonging to Augustus Moore, was whipped by the man who hired her sometime between 1830 and 1835, while the teenaged John S. Jacobs was working in Dr. Norcom's shop. Personal communications from Miss Elizabeth Vann Moore to Jean Fagan Yellin, Nov. 10, 1986, and Nov. 6, 1999.

Reading John S. Jacobs's account of Agnes's whipping, Judge Moore's great-granddaughter Elizabeth Vann Moore recalled that in the 1930s she and her father spoke with an old man who identified himself as Agnes's grandson. He was living in a house his father had built before the Civil War on one of Augustus Moore's former farms near Albemarle Sound, and he said he remembered his grandmother as a skillful seamstress and a "high-tempered" woman. He recalled that when only a lad, he had saved the farm from the Yankees. The federal gunboats came up the sound after the fall of Roanoke Island, he explained, and a landing party told him to take them to Moore's plantation house, but he instead led them through swamps until they abandoned their mission. Asked why he had protected the family, he answered that earlier, after his grandmother was severely whipped by a man to whom she had been hired, Augustus Moore had set her free—thus ensuring the freedom of the child she was carrying, of her subsequent children, and of all of their children, including himself.

Miss Moore comments that she never expected that story to be confirmed in "A True Tale." But she judges John S. Jacobs's version of Agnes's whipping inaccurate and worse, false, because partial. She writes: "Every person in Chowan County knew that Aggy was emancipated at once, and knew why. And John Jacobs suppressed that fact. Presenting himself as a witness to the truth, he deliberately did not tell the whole truth. The omission of half the story in order to make the other half a more damning indictment falsifies the whole thing . . . The fact that John Jacobs omitted what was for Aggy the most important part of her story invalidates his testimony, as far as I can see." Personal communication from Miss Elizabeth Vann Moore to Jean Fagan Yellin, Nov. 19, 1986.

A careful search through Chowan County Superior Court records—which are very incomplete for this period—has yielded no record of Agnes's emancipation. Nor does an examination of the censuses of 1850 and 1860 identify a free black family living in the area of the Moore farm that fits the description given by Miss Moore's narrator—a grandmother, a father, a mother, and their children. It is certainly possible that, without formally emancipating Agnes, Moore could have given her a place to live and manumitted her from further labor, and that her entire family could have lived as a *de facto* free family while still legally enslaved.

A parallel to Agnes's whipping is reported in the narrative of Allen Parker, another Chowan County slave who escaped to freedom. When a child, Parker saw the man who had hired his mother knock her down and pound her face bloody. When his mother's owner learned of this, she recalled his mother and her children to her plantation. Allen Parker, *Recollections of Slavery Times* (Worcester, Mass.: Charles W. Burbank and Co., 1895), pp. 34–35.

John S. Jacobs is incorrect when he writes that the death of a slave subsequent to a severe whipping would not be considered a murder; it was murder if a person died within a year and a day of being wounded. Had Agnes died a week after the whipping, Moore could have brought a criminal prosecution against John E———. But the law was on the side of John B———when as Agnes's master he whipped her, although he was not her owner. In 1829 the state Supreme Court, overturning the verdict of a Chowan County jury that had found a temporary master guilty of battery committed on a hired female slave, ruled that temporary masters had the same authority over their slaves as did the owners. State v. John Mann, 13 N.C. 263 (1829).

51 "The land of the free and the home of the brave!" Francis S. Key, "The Star-Spangled Banner." "We hold these truths to be self-evident,—that all men are created equal; that they are endowed by their Creator with certain unalienable rights; that among these are life, liberty, and the pursuit of happiness." Thomas Jefferson, Declaration of Independence.

52 "These are the times that try men's souls." Thomas Paine, *The*

American Crisis. "They shall beat their swords into ploughshares, and their spears into pruning-hooks . . ." Isaiah 2:4; Micah 4:3. The first to fall in the Boston Massacre was Crispus Attucks (1750?–1770), a man of African and Natick Indian descent. *Dictionary of American Negro Biography,* ed. Rayford W. Logan and Michael R. Winston (New York: Norton, 1982), pp. 18–19. In 1846 John S. Jacobs, "hoping to secure freedom to his brother," attempted to rescue an escaped New Orleans slave who had reached Boston. The effort failed. W[illiam] C. N[ell], "Jonathan Walker and John S. Jacobs" *North Star,* March 31, 1848; also see *Address of the Committee Appointed by a Public Meeting Held in Faneuil Hall, September 24, 1846, for the Purpose of Considering the Recent Case of Kidnapping from our Soil and of Taking Measures to Prevent the Recurrence of Similar Outrages* (Boston, 1846), cited in Quarles, *Black Abolitionists,* p. 280, n. 26. Thanks to Dorothy Sterling.

53 "That *is* property which the law declares *to be* property," Henry Clay, "Petitions for the Abolition of Slavery in the Senate of the United States, February 7, 1839," *Life and Speeches of the Hon. Henry Clay,* comp. Daniel Mallory (New York: Van Amringe and Bixby, 1844), II, p. 368. "Organic sin is no sin at all": In 1845 the *Boston Recorder* published a series of articles by Henry Ward Beecher on organic sins. In the second of these he wrote that slavery is "an organic sin of unequaled enormity and guilt . . . the community who make and sustain the system are guilty . . ." "Dr. Beecher on Organic Sins.—No. II," *Boston Recorder,* Oct. 23, 1845, p. 170. Thanks to Steve Babich.

54 Here John S. Jacobs refers to the popular abolitionist slogan "Am I Not a Man and a Brother?" first adopted in England in 1787 by the Committee to Abolish the Slave Trade and popularized throughout the world. Thomas Clarkson, *History of the Rise, Progress, and Accomplishment of the Abolition of the African Slave Trade by the British Parliament,* 2 vols. (London: R. Taylor, 1808), 1, 450–451.

Selected Bibliography

Accomando, Christina. "'The Laws Were Laid Down to Me Anew': Harriet Jacobs and the Reframing of Legal Fictions." *African American Review* 32, 2 (1998): 229–244.

Andrews, William L. "Culmination of a Century: The Autobiographies of J. D. Green, Frederick Douglass, and Harriet Jacobs." In *To Tell a Free Story: The First Century of Afro-American Autobiography, 1760–1865*, ed. William L. Andrews, 239–275. Urbana: University of Illinois Press, 1986.

————. "Free at Last: Front Disclosure to Dialogue in the Novelized Autobiography." In *To Tell a Free Story: The First Century of Afro-American Autobiography, 1760–1865*, ed. William L. Andrews, 320–331. Urbana: University of Illinois Press, 1986.

————. "The Changing Moral Discourse of Nineteenth-Century African American Women's Autobiography: Harriet Jacobs and Elizabeth Keckley." In *De/Colonizing the Subject: The Politics of Gender in Women's Autobiography*, ed. Sidonie Smith and Julia Watson, 225–241. Minneapolis: University of Minnesota Press, 1992.

————. "The Changing Rhetoric of the Nineteenth-Century Slave Narrative of the United States." In *Slavery in the Americas,* ed. Wolfgang Binder, 471–486. Würzburg, Germany: Honighausen and Neumann, 1993.

Baker, Houston A., Jr. *The Journey Back: Issues in Black Literature and Criticism.* Chicago: University of Chicago Press, 1980.

Bartholomaus, Craig. "'What Would You Be?' Racial Myths and Cultural Sameness in *Incidents in the Life of a Slave Girl.*" *College Language Association Journal* 39, 2 (December 1995): 179–194.

Becker, Elizabeth C. "Harriet Jacobs's Search for Home." *College Language Association Journal* 35, 4 (June 1992): 411–421.

Berlin, Ira. *Generations of Captivity: A History of African-American Slaves.* Cambridge, Mass.: Harvard University Press, 2003.

Blassingame, John W. *The Slave Community: Plantation Life in the Antebellum South.* New York: Oxford University Press, 1979.

Braxton, Joanne. *Black Women Writing Autobiography: A Tradition within a Tradition.* Philadelphia: Temple University Press, 1989.

Braxton, Joanne M., and Sharon Zuber. "Silences in Harriet 'Linda Brent' Jacobs's *Incidents in the Life of a Slave Girl.*" In *Listening to Silences: New Essays in Feminist Criticism,* ed. Elaine Hedges and Shelley Fisher Fishkin, 146–155. New York: Oxford University Press, 1994.

Burnham, Michelle. "Loopholes of Resistance: Harriet Jacobs' Slave Narrative and the Critique of Agency in Foucault." *Arizona Quarterly* 49, 2 (Summer 1993): 53–73.

Carby, Hazel V. "Hear My Voice: Ye Careless Daughters." In *Reconstructing Womanhood: The Emergence of the Afro-American Woman Novelist,* ed. Hazel V. Carby, 45–61, 183–185. New York: Oxford University Press, 1987.

Cope, V. "'I Verily Believed Myself to Be a Free Woman': Harriet Jacobs's Journey into Capitalism." *African American Review* 38, 1 (2004): 5–20.

Couser, G. Thomas. *American Autobiography: The Prophetic Mode.* Amherst: University of Massachusetts Press, 1979.

Cutter, Martha J. "Dismantling 'The Master's House': Critical Literacy in Harriet Jacobs's *Incidents in the Life of a Slave Girl.*" *Callalo* 19, 1 (1996): 209–225.

Dalton, Anne B. "The Devil and the Virgin: Writing Sexual Abuse in *Incidents in the Life of a Slave Girl.*" In *Violence, Silence, and Anger: Women's Writing as Transgression,* ed. Deirdre Lashgari, 38–61. Charlottesville: University of Virginia Press, 1995.

Daniel, Janice B. "A New Kind of Hero: Harriet Jacobs's 'Incidents.'" *Southern Quarterly: A Journal of the Arts in the South* 35, 3 (Spring 1997): 7–12.

Davie, Sharon. "'Reader, My Story Ends with Freedom': Harriet Jacobs's *Incidents in the Life of a Slave Girl*." In *Famous Last Words: Changes in Gender and Narrative Closure,* ed. Alison Booth, 86–109. Charlottesville: University of Virginia Press, 1993.

Davis, Angela Y. "The Legacy of Slavery: Standards for a New Womanhood." In *Women, Race, and Class,* ed. Angela Y. Davis, 3–29. New York: Random House, 1981.

Davis, Charles T., and Henry Louis Gates, Jr., eds. *The Slave's Narrative.* New York: Oxford University Press, 1985.

Doriani, Beth Maclay. "Black Womanhood in Nineteenth Century America: Subversion and Self-Construction in Two Women's Autobiographies." *American Quarterly* 43, 2 (June 1991): 199–222.

duCille, Ann. *The Coupling Convention: Sex, Text, and Tradition in Black Women's Fiction.* New York: Oxford University Press, 1993.

Eyerman, Ron. *Cultural Trauma: Slavery and the Formation of African-American Identity.* New York: Cambridge University Press, 2001.

Ferguson, Sally Ann H. "Christian Violence and the Slave Narrative." *American Literature* 68, 2 (June 1996): 297–320.

Fisch, Audrey, ed. *The Cambridge Companion to the African American Slave Narrative.* New York: Cambridge University Press, 2007.

Foreman, P. Gabrielle. "The Spoken and the Silenced in *Incidents in the Life of a Slave Girl* and *Our Nig*." *Callaloo* 13, 1 (Spring 1990): 313–324.

Foster, Frances Smith. *Written by Herself: Literary Production by African American Women, 1746–1892.* Bloomington: Indiana University Press, 1993.

Franklin, John Hope, and Loren Schweninger. *Runaway Slaves: Rebels on the Plantation.* New York: Oxford University Press, 1999.

Garfield, Deborah M. "Speech, Listening, and Female Sexuality in *Incidents in the Life of a Slave Girl*." *Arizona Quarterly* 50, 2 (Summer 1994): 19–49.

Garfield, Deborah M., and Rafia Zafar, eds. *Harriet Jacobs and "Incidents in the Life of a Slave Girl": New Critical Essays.* New York: Cambridge University Press, 1996.

Gates, Henry L., Jr., and K. A. Appiah, eds. *Harriet Jacobs: Critical Perspectives Past and Present.* New York: Amistad, 1997.

Genovese, Eugene D. *Roll, Jordan, Roll: The World the Slaves Made.* New York: Pantheon Books, 1974.

Gould, Philip. *Barbaric Traffic: Commerce and Antislavery in the Eighteenth-*

Century Atlantic World. Cambridge, Mass.: Harvard University Press, 2003.

Greeson, J. R. "The 'Mysteries and Miseries' of North Carolina: New York City, Urban Gothic Fiction, and 'Incidents in the Life of a Slave Girl.'" *American Literature* 73, 2 (June 2001): 277–309.

Gutman, Herbert. *The Black Family in Slavery and Freedom, 1750–1925*. New York: Pantheon Books, 1976.

Hanrahan, H. M. "Harriet Jacobs's *Incidents in the Life of a Slave Girl*: A Retelling of Lydia Maria Child's 'The Quadroons.'" *New England Quarterly—A Historical Review of New England Life and Letters* 78, 4 (December 2005): 599–616.

Humphreys, Debra. "Power and Resistance in Harriet Jacobs' *Incidents in the Life of a Slave Girl*." In *Anxious Power: Reading, Writing and Ambivalence in Narratives by Women*, ed. Carol J. Singley and Susan Elizabeth Sweeney, 143–155. Albany: State University of New York Press, 1993.

Johnson, Walter. *Soul by Soul: Life inside the Antebellum Slave Market*. Cambridge, Mass.: Harvard University Press, 2000.

Jones, Anne Goodwyn. "Engendered in the South: Blood and Irony in Douglass and Jacobs." In *Haunted Bodies: Gender and Southern Text*, ed. Anne Goodwyn Jones and Susan V. Donaldson, 201–219. Charlottesville: University of Virginia Press, 1997.

Kaplan, Carla. "Recuperating Agents: Narrative Contracts, Emancipatory Readers, and *Incidents in the Life of a Slave Girl*." In *Provoking Agents: Gender and Agency in Theory and Practice*, ed. Judith Kegan Gardiner, 280–301. Urbana: University of Illinois Press, 1995.

Kolchin, Peter. *American Slavery: 1619–1877*. London and New York: Penguin, 1995.

Ligon, Glenn. "Narratives." *Yale Journal of Criticism* 7, 1 (1994): 31–40.

Marshall, Elaine. "Irruptions of the Grotesque in Harriet Jacobs' *Incidents in the Life of a Slave Girl*." *JAISA: The Journal of the Association for the Interdisciplinary Study of the Arts* 2, 2 (Spring 1997): 17–34.

McKay, Nellie Y. "The Girls Who Became the Women: Childhood Memories in the Autobiographies of Harriet Jacobs, Mary Church Terrell, and Anne Moody." In *Tradition and the Talents of Women*, ed. Florence Howe, 106–124. Urbana: University of Illinois Press, 1991.

Mills, Bruce. "Lydia Maria Child and the Endings to Harriet Jacobs's *Incidents in the Life of a Slave Girl*." *American Literature* 64, 2 (June 1992): 255–272.

Mullen, Harryette. "Runaway Tongue: Resistant Orality in *Uncle Tom's Cabin, Our Nig, Incidents in the Life of a Slave Girl,* and *Beloved.*" In *The Culture of Sentiment,* ed. Shirley Samuels, 244–264, 332–335. New York: Oxford University Press, 1992.

Nudelman, Franny. "Harriet Jacobs and the Sentimental Politics of Female Suffering." *English Literary History* 59 (Winter 1992): 939–964.

Painter, Nell Irvin. "Three Southern Women and Freud: A Non-Exceptionalist Approach to Race, Class, and Gender in the Slave South." In *Feminist Revision History,* ed. Ann Louise Shapiro, 195–216. New Brunswick, N.J.: Rutgers University Press, 1994.

Peterson, Carla. *Doers of the Word: African-American Women Speakers and Writers in the North (1830–1880).* New York: Oxford University Press, 1995.

Pryse, Marjorie, and Hortense J. Spillers, eds. *Conjuring: Black Women, Fiction, and Literary Tradition.* Bloomington: Indiana University Press, 1985.

Rifkin, Mark. "'A Home Made Sacred by Protecting Laws': Black Activist Homemaking and Geographies of Citizenship in *Incidents in the Life of a Slave Girl.*" *Differences: A Journal of Feminist Cultural Studies* 18, 2 (Summer 2007): 72–102.

Sale, Maggie. "Critiques from Within: Antebellum Projects of Resistance." *American Literature* 64, 4 (December 1992): 695–718.

Sánchez-Eppler, Karen. "Righting Slavery and Writing Sex: The Erotics of Narration in Harriet Jacobs's *Incidents.*" In *Touching Liberty: Abolition, Feminism, and the Politics of the Body,* ed. Karen Sánchez-Eppler, 83–104. Berkeley: University of California Press, 1993.

Sekora, John. "Briton Hammon, the Indian Captivity Narrative, and the African American Slave Narrative." In *When Brer Rabbit Meets Coyote: African-Native American Literature,* ed. Jonathan Brennan, 141–157. Urbana: University of Illinois Press, 2003.

Sekora, John, and Darwin D. Turner, eds. *The Art of Slave Narrative: Original Essays in Criticism and Theory.* Moline: Western Illinois University Press, 1982.

Smith, Valerie. "Form and Ideology in Three Slave Narratives." In *Self-Discovery and Authority in Afro-American Narrative,* ed. Valerie Smith, 9–43. Cambridge, Mass.: Harvard University Press, 1987.

———. "'Loopholes of Retreat': Architecture and Ideology in Harriet Jacobs's *Incidents in the Life of a Slave Girl.*" In *Reading Black, Reading*

Feminist: A Critical Anthology, ed. Henry Louis Gates, Jr., 212–226. New York: Meridian, 1990.

Spillers, Hortense J. "Mama's Baby, Papa's Maybe: An American Grammar Book." In *Black, White, and in Color: Essays on American Literature and Culture,* ed. Hortense J. Spillers. Chicago: University of Chicago Press, 2003.

Stampp, Kenneth M. *The Peculiar Institution: Slavery in the Ante-Bellum South.* New York: Knopf, 1956.

Stauffer, John. *The Black Hearts of Men: Radical Abolitionists and the Transformation of Race.* Cambridge, Mass.: Harvard University Press, 2002.

Stepto, Robert B. *From Behind the Veil: A Study of Afro-American Narrative.* Urbana: University of Illinois Press, 1979.

Stover, Johnnie M. "Nineteenth-Century African American Women's Autobiography as Social Discourse: The Example of Harriet Ann Jacobs." *College English* 66, 2 (2003): 133–154.

Stuckey, Sterling. *Slave Culture.* New York: Oxford University Press, 1987.

Sundquist, Eric J. *To Wake the Nations: Race in the Making of American Literature.* Cambridge, Mass.: Harvard University Press, 1993.

Tate, Claudia. *Domestic Allegories of Political Desire: The Black Heroine's Text at the Turn of the Century.* New York: Oxford University Press, 1992.

Taves, Ann. "Spiritual Purity and Sexual Shame: Religious Themes in the Writings of Harriet Jacobs." *Church History* (March 1987): 59–72.

Tricomi, A. "Dialect and Identity in Harriet Jacobs's Autobiography and Other Slave Narratives." *Callaloo* 29, 2 (Spring 2006): 619–633.

Walker, Peter F. *Moral Choices: Memory, Desire, and Imagination in Nineteenth-Century American Abolition.* Baton Rouge: Louisiana State University Press, 1978.

Walter, Krista. "Surviving in the Garret: Harriet Jacobs and the Critique of Sentiment." *American Transcendental Quarterly* 8, 3 (September 1994): 189–210.

Wardrop, Daneen. "'I Stuck the Gimlet in and Waited for Evening': Writing and *Incidents in the Life of a Slave Girl.*" *Texas Studies in Literature and Language* 49, 3 (Fall 2007): 209–229.

Warhol, Robyn R. "Reader, Can You Imagine? No, You Cannot: The Narratee as Other in Harriet Jacobs's Text." *Narrative* 3, 1 (1995): 57–72.

Warner, Anne Bradford. "Harriet Jacobs's Modest Proposals: Revising Southern Hospitality." *Southern Quarterly: A Journal of the Arts in the South* 30, 2–3 (Winter–Spring 1992): 22–28.

————. "Santa Claus Ain't a Real Man: Incidents and Gender." In *Haunted Bodies: Gender and Southern Text*, ed. Anne Goodwyn Jones and Susan V. Donaldson, 185–200. Charlottesville: University of Virginia Press, 1997.

White, Deborah Gray. *Ar'n't I a Woman: Female Slaves in the Plantation South*. New York: W. W. Norton, 1985.

White, Shane, and Graham White. *The Sounds of Slavery: Discovering African American History through Songs, Sermons, and Speech*. Boston: Beacon, 2005.

Yellin, Jean Fagan. *The Intricate Knot: Black Figures in American Literature, 1776–1863*. New York: New York University Press, 1972.

————. "Written by Herself: Harriet Jacobs' Slave Narrative." *American Literature* 53, 3 (November 1981): 379–486.

————. "Texts and Contexts of Harriet Jacobs' *Incidents in the Life of Slave Girl*." In *The Slave's Narrative*, ed. Charles T. Davis and Henry Louis Gates, Jr., 262–282. New York: Oxford University Press, 1983.

————. *Women and Sisters: The Anti-Slavery Feminists in American Culture*. New Haven: Yale University Press, 1989.

————. "Harriet Jacobs's Family History." *American Literature* 66, 4 (December 1994): 765–767.

————. "*Incidents* in the Life of Harriet Jacobs." In *The Seductions of Biography*, ed. Mary Rhiel and David Suchoff, 137–147. New York: Routledge, 1996.

————. *Harriet Jacobs: A Life*. New York: Basic Books, 2004.

————. "*Incidents* Abroad: Harriet Jacobs and the Transatlantic Movement." In *Monuments of the Black Atlantic: Slavery and Memory*, ed. Joanne Braxton and Maria Diedrich. Brunswick, N.J.: Transaction Publishers, 2004.

————, ed. *The Harriet Jacobs Family Papers*. 2 vols. plus CD-ROM. Chapel Hill: University of North Carolina Press, 2008.

Zafar, Rafia. *We Wear the Mask: African Americans Write Literature, 1760–1870*. New York: Columbia University Press, 1997.

Acknowledgments

This edition of *Incidents* represents the collective effort of a diverse group of people. I am grateful to them all, and especially to my black feminist colleagues who welcomed this project. Years ago, Sherman Paul urged me to explore beyond the traditional literary canon, and Jean B. Hutson and Dorothy B. Porter introduced me to the study of Afro-American literature and culture. The late Charles T. Davis encouraged my early work on Harriet Jacobs. Dorothy Sterling, who originally planned to be my coeditor, provided consistent encouragement and countless citations. Elizabeth Vann Moore made the initial identification of the black and white Horniblows, despite serious misgivings, out of her life-long commitment to scholarship. It would have been impossible to document John S. Jacobs's "A True Tale of Slavery" or Harriet Jacobs's life in North Carolina without the impressive detective work of George Stevenson. Most of the historical notes to the first twenty-nine chapters are based on his work, as well as on that of Bruce S. Cheesman, Jesse R. Lankford, Keith Strawn, and other members of the staff at the North Carolina State Archives. Documentation of Jacobs's Rochester connections is largely the result of the efforts of Karl Kabelac, Mary Huth, and their colleagues at the University of Rochester Library, and of Nancy Hewitt, who graciously provided unpublished research on the Rochester women. Hazel Carby, Valerie Smith, and Mary Helen Washington generously allowed me to read their rich unpublished manuscripts on Jacobs. The owners of Jacobs's portrait enthusiastically offered memories and memorabilia. Carl R. Lounsbury of Colonial Williamsburg created the scale drawing of Jacobs's hiding place in Molly Horniblows house. Kathleen B. Wyche of the North Carolina State Archives drew the maps of Jacobs's Edenton and its environs. Frances Smith Foster, Nellie McKay, and the late Frederick C. Stem provided much needed readings of an early draft of the Introduction. Delano R. Copprue provided timely help annotating John S. Jacobs's text. At Harvard University Press, Aida Donald tamed rough versions of the Introduction and the notes, and Camille Smith rescued the Correspondence from confusion and sympathetically and expertly edited the entire manuscript.

An equally large and heterogeneous group responded to specific pleas for help: Louise Bindman, John W. Blassingame, Carolyn Davis, Lois R. Densky, Ralph W. Donnelly, Dena J. Epstein, Sue Gillies, Catherine M. Hanchett, Kenneth Hawkins, Leo Hershkovitz, Carolyn Karcher, Frank K. Lorenz, Carleton Mabee, Jay Meisner, Elizabeth H. Moger, Philip Munson, Daniel McFarland, William S. McFeeley, John W. Nunley, Thomas C. Parramore, Gerald E. Parsons, Daniel W. Patterson, Carlin P. Peyton, Labelle Prussin, Bernice Reagon, Wayne D. Shirley, Joel Silby, Rev. R. W. Storie, Robert J. Swan, Beatrice Sweeney, Howard Temperley, Joan M. Warren, Susan F. Watkins, Henry L. Watson, and Anita Wright.

Permission to quote from and to reproduce letters is by courtesy of the Trustees of the Boston Public Library; the Sydney Howard Gay Papers, Rare Book and Manuscript Library, Columbia University; Cornell University Library; Isaac and Amy Post Family Papers, Department of Rare Books and Special Collections, Rush Rhees Library, University of Rochester; and the Sophia Smith Collection (Women's History Archive), Smith College, Northampton, Massachusetts (New England Hospital Papers).

I am also grateful to the staffs of the Berkshire Record Office of the Royal County of Berkshire, the Brooklyn Historical Society, and the Brooklyn Public Library; Laura V. Monti and her colleagues in the Division of Rare Books and Manuscripts at the Boston Public Library; Kenneth A. Lohf, Rudolph Ellenbogen, and the staff of the Butler Library of Columbia University; Anne-Marie T. Schaaf, Glenys Waldman, and their colleagues at the Historical Society of Pennsylvania; Phil Lapsansky and his colleagues at the Library Company of Philadelphia; Leslie A. Pasch of the Little Falls Public Library; James H. Hutson and the staff of the Manuscript Division of the Library of Congress; Allan W. Robbins and his colleagues at Lloyd House; librarians at the Massachusetts Historical Society and at the Moorland-Spingarn Research Center at Howard University; Byron Rushing and the staff of the Museum of Afro-American History/African Meeting House at Boston; Mrs. William S. Portlock and the staff of the Norfolk Public Library System; the staff of the New Bedford Free Public Library; Jean Ashton and her colleagues at the New-York Historical Society; the staff of the Queensborough Public Library and that of Alexander Library at Rutgers University; the librarians at Sarah Lawrence College; Robert C. Morris, Ernest Kaiser, Betty Gubert and their colleagues at the Schomburg Center for Research in Black Culture of the New York Public Library; Mary-Elizabeth Murdock and the staff of the Sophia Smith Collection at Smith College; and the staff of the North Carolina Collection at the University of North Carolina at Chapel Hill.

At Pace University, I am indebted to Chancellor Edward J. Mortola; Executive Vice President Joseph M. Pastore; Joseph E. Houle, Dean of Dyson College; and Sherman Raskin, Chair, Department of English, for granting me the time needed to complete this project; to Bruce Bergman and the staff of the University library for responding pleasantly to my insistent questions; and to Marilyn T. Williams for judging this edition so important that she assumed my administrative tasks to enable me to prepare it.

At home, Ed tinkered with the word processor and once more listened, believed, and did what was needful.

Index